THE
LATINO
ENCYCLOPEDIA

THE
LATINO
ENCYCLOPEDIA

Volume 2

Chicano Park – Flores Salinas, Juan

Editors

RICHARD CHABRÁN AND RAFAEL CHABRÁN

Marshall Cavendish
New York • London • Toronto

Published By
Marshall Cavendish Corporation
99 White Plains Road
Tarrytown, New York 10591-9001
United States of America

∞ The paper in these volumes conforms to the American National Standard for Permanence of Paper for Printed Library Materials, Z39.48-1984.

Library of Congress Cataloging-in-Publication Data

The Latino encyclopedia / editors, Richard Chabrán, and Rafael Chabrán,
    p. cm.
   Includes bibliographical references and index.
   1. Hispanic Americans—Encyclopedias. I. Chabrán, Richard II. Chabrán, Rafael
E184.S75L357 1995
973′ .0468′003—dc20   95-13144
ISBN 0-7614-0125-3 (set).   CIP
ISBN 0-7614-0127-X (vol. 2).

First Printing

Contents

THE
LATINO
ENCYCLOPEDIA

Chicano Park (San Diego, Calif.): Museum site. Chicano Park holds one of the world's largest collections of murals celebrating Chicano history and culture. In the 1950's and 1960's, the Logan Heights barrio of San Diego was twice disrupted, first by the construction of California Interstate 5 and then by the creation of the San Diego-Coronado Bay Bridge. In April, 1970, the city began construction of a new California Highway Patrol station under the bridge. Protesters converged on the site, insisting it be made into a park. Two weeks later, the city capitulated.

In the 1970's and 1980's, the park was a focal point of Chicano consciousness in Southern California. The murals painted on the highway and bridge abutments depict Chicano history from pre-Columbian times to the late twentieth century.

Chicano Research Collection (Tempe, Ariz.): This major Latino collection, founded in 1970 as the Chicano Studies Collection, is located in the Hayden Library at Arizona State University. The collection at first was a circulating library that reflected and represented the ideology and philosophy of the Chicano movement. The collection became a growing ethnic collection of books, periodicals, magazines, microfilms, and other materials, with an emphasis on the areas of Chicano literature, contemporary Chicano history, bilingual education, immigration, civil rights, and Chicana feminism. In 1985, the collection became part of the Department of Archives and Manuscripts. The Chicano Studies Collection continued to support the libraries and campus community as a depository of primary and secondary documents. Under its new name, the Chicano Research Collection, it seeks to expand and reinforce its primary sources on Arizona in particular and on the Southwest more generally.

Chicano Studies Library (Berkeley, Calif.): This major Latino collection was founded by students in 1969. First known as La Raza Library, this collection is part of the Chicano Studies Program at the University of California, Berkeley. The library collects primary and secondary materials on the Chicano experience, with particular strength in serial publications. These serial collections are the base of the National Clearinghouse of Chicano Serials. The library also has an archival program highlighted by the Antonio Hernandez Collection and the Richard and Gloria Santillan Collection. Subject strengths of this collection include Chicano literature, administration of justice, bilingual/bicultural education, and immigration. The library's

publishing unit is recognized as a leader in Latino reference publishing. It has produced bibliographies, indexes, guides, and occasional monographs within the field of Chicano studies. Its two most important bibliographic products are *The Chicano Index* (previously the *Chicano Periodical Index*) and the *Chicano Database. The Chicano Database*, the most comprehensive bibliographic resource on people of Mexican descent living in the United States, has been available in CD-ROM format since 1990.

Chicano studies programs: Chicano studies programs are designed to enhance students' understanding of the influence of the Mexican American community on life in the United States. They also provide students with an appreciation of the dynamics of the increasingly multicultural U.S. society. The programs foster a sociohistorical knowledge of the political and cultural roots of Chicanos as well as increasing critical understanding of the construction and institutionalization of knowledge. A foundation in Chicano studies enables students to comprehend better the racial and ethnic tensions that are a part of life in the United States.

History. Chicano studies programs can be considered to be a direct result of intense activism during the 1960's among minority populations in the United States to develop academic programs that would address their needs. The first Mexican American studies program was established in the fall of 1968 at Los Angeles State College by political scientists Ralph C. GUZMÁN and Carlos MUÑOZ, Jr.

Toward the end of the 1960's, there was increased interest in the recruitment and retention of Chicano students throughout the Southwest and California. Chicanos also perceived a need for vindication of their cultural heritage at an institutional level. Chicano activists believed that institutional resources should be used for the benefit of the community and that courses should be established that would be of interest to Mexican American students. These components were later formally outlined in *El PLAN DE SANTA BÁRBARA: A CHICANO PLAN FOR HIGHER EDUCATION*, a declaration calling for the formation of Chicano studies programs in California. It was drawn up during a Chicano conference held in Santa Barbara in April of 1969. The plan called on California colleges and universities to admit and actively recruit Chicano students, faculty administrators, and staff; develop a curriculum program and an academic major relevant to the Chicano cultural and historical experience; provide academic support and tutorial programs; establish research and publication

Carlos Muñoz, Jr., helped establish a Mexican American studies program at Los Angeles State College and later taught in the Chicano studies program at the University of California, Berkeley. (David Bacon)

programs; and create community and social action centers.

The Rise of Chicano Studies Programs. The creation of Chicano studies programs in California, the Southwest, and Texas was considered by many activists as fundamental in the liberation of the Chicano community. Chicano activists were quick to acknowledge the importance of HIGHER EDUCATION to the progress and development of the community as a whole. Creation of Chicano studies programs at major institutions was seen as a first step toward accomplishment of their goals.

From 1968 to 1973, enrollment of Chicano students at universities and colleges increased, more so than at any other time in history. Following this influx of undergraduate students, from 1973 to 1977 more Chicanos than ever entered graduate and professional schools. Between 1968 and 1973, more than fifty Chicano studies programs were established throughout California. In 1971, the National Association for Chicano Studies (NACS) was established. The NACS is an organization of university professors, researchers, and students dedicated to promoting Chicano studies across the country and to building Chicano political, cultural, and educational awareness through publications.

The National Chicano Council on Higher Education (NCCHE) was established in the early 1970's, at about the same time that the National Chicano Research Network, or La Red, was founded. La Red was dedicated to becoming a clearinghouse for Chicano research. Both organizations received extensive funding through the Ford Foundation and other national foundations during the late 1970's. La Red and NCCHE joined forces and moved to Southern California's, Claremont colleges, where the Tomás Rivera Center was established in 1985. The center carries out studies that directly affect the quality of life and education for both Mexican Americans and members of the larger Hispanic community.

Obstacles to Development. One of the overriding concerns of Chicano activists was advocacy of research in support of the community and in defense of the interests of the poor. This stance was seen as too militant and too controversial by some Chicano scholars. This division between some scholars and the professed ideals of the movement caused weakening in Chicano studies programs during the late 1970's.

The idealism and militancy of the 1960's began to diminish as self-interest became prominent in national consciousness. During the 1970's and 1980's, student activism declined with respect to social issues in general. Following this national trend, many Hispanic students became more interested in acquiring marketable skills than in serving the needs of the Mexican American community. As a result, some of the community-oriented Chicano studies programs suffered. Programs were also weakened in response to economic considerations.

During the 1970's, many universities and colleges suffered severe funding shortages. These financial difficulties frequently manifested themselves in reduction of ethnic studies programs, which were often considered unnecessary in meeting the overall educational goals of the institution. Some programs had to contend with forces that regarded them as a trend that had outlived its time.

The decline in Chicano studies programs does not diminish the tremendous impact they have had in the United States as a progressive force in keeping the Chicano cause alive. The many surviving programs have contributed substantially to the articulation of the Chicano experience and created new generations of academic professionals who are studying myriad topics related to Mexican Americans.

May and June of 1992 saw the first burst of Chicano activism in many years, on the part of students at the University of California, Los Angeles (*see* UCLA STUDENT DEMONSTRATION FOR A CHICANO STUDIES DEPARTMENT). When the university declined to grant the Chicano studies program the status of a department, students protested. Nearly one hundred protesters were arrested, and a faculty center was damaged. Later, nine activists went on a hunger strike for fourteen days to protest the decision. They were led by Jorge Mancillas, a professor from the UCLA medical center. A compromise was finally reached in which the program received many of the powers of an independent department but did not gain departmental status.

The Rise of Chicana Studies. One of the most important outgrowths of Chicano studies and women's studies programs was the development of CHICANA studies. Many Chicanas perceived themselves to be oppressed on three fronts, as a consequence of their race, class, and gender. They saw neither the traditionally male-dominated frameworks of Chicano studies programs nor the platform of evolving women's studies programs as appropriate for addressing their needs.

Chicana activists maintained that the Chicano studies paradigms typically analyzed race, ethnic, and class domination but avoided a serious critique of gender issues. Chicana scholars objected to the Chicano movement's concentration on Chicano males and its use of primarily male cultural symbols.

UCLA students protested against budget cuts and the decision not to create a department of Chicano studies. (Bob Myers)

In the late 1970's, several female graduate students and one assistant professor from Chicano studies at the University of California, Berkeley, organized Mujeres en Marcha to protest male domination within Chicano studies programs as well as in the National Association for Chicano Studies (NACS). Further activism was demonstrated at a 1982 conference of the NACS held at Arizona State University, where Chicana academic professionals presented a panel on sexual politics. The Chicana Caucus was formed in 1983 at the annual NACS conference. The 1980's thus saw the emergence of Chicana studies, formalized with the creation of MUJERES ACTIVAS EN LETRAS Y CAMBIO SOCIAL in 1983. The group dedicated itself to the documentation, analysis, and interpretation of the Chicana/Latina experience in the United States.

Most U.S. colleges and universities with Chicano studies programs began offering courses on the CHICANA experience by the early 1990's. UCLA's program was renamed the Chicana and Chicano Program in recognition of the shift in emphasis.

Status of Chicano Studies. As of the early 1990's, nearly twenty major U.S. institutions offered degrees in Chicano studies. Most were in California. One of the most important and innovative programs was established at the University of California, Santa Barbara (UCSB).

UCSB had the distinction of being the only school in the nine-campus University of California system to have a department of Chicano studies. The degree offered was interdisciplinary, offering students the opportunity to explore dimensions of the Chicano experience within such disciplines as history, dance, sociology, political science, music, art, and anthropology. Faculty members were primarily from the arts, humanities, and social sciences.

Courses offered at UCSB were by far the most wide-ranging and comprehensive in the country regarding the Chicano experience. Among them could be found courses on race and ethnicity in American history, psychological issues and the Chicano child, Chicana history, barrio popular culture, Chicano art, and Chicana artists. Many of the courses crossed topical fields to discuss race, gender, and political issues.

Loyola Marymount University in Los Angeles, California, also offered an extensive array of courses to complete the bachelor of arts degree requirements in Chicano studies. The program revolved around the concept that a liberal studies education should expose students to as many cultures and perspectives as possible. Courses at Loyola Marymount included "The Latino Experience in the U.S. Church," "Sociolinguistics in a Multicultural Setting," "Chicano Psychology," "Chicano Politics," and "Chicanas and Latinas in the United States." A number of cross-listed courses incorporated Chicano dimensions, such as "History of Los Angeles," "Twentieth Century Latin American Women Novelists," and "Race and Ethnic Relations."

Strong programs existed at many other institutions, including UCLA, the Claremont colleges, the University of Minnesota, and the University of Texas, El Paso. Programs remained concentrated in California and the Southwest. Many institutions permitted courses to be used as an emphasis or minor to complement degree programs. Even at universities and colleges that do not specifically grant a degree, emphasis, or minor in Chicano studies, there are usually at least a few courses related to the history of Hispanic Americans. This demonstrates the significant and continuing impact that the Chicano studies movement, as first articulated in *El* Plan de Santa Bárbara, has had on higher education in the United States.

—*Melissa A. Lockhart*

Suggested Readings:

• Acuña, Rodolfo. *Occupied America: A History of Chicanos.* 3d ed. New York: Harper & Row, 1988. One of the most important and comprehensive books dealing with Chicano history, including the establishment and rise of Chicano studies programs.

• Burrola, Luis Ramón, and José A. Rivera. *Chicano Studies Programs at the Crossroads: Alternative Futures for the 1980's.* Albuquerque: Southwest Hispanic Research Institute, University of New Mexico, 1983. Part of a series of working papers from the Hispanic Research Institute. Includes substantial bibliographic references.

• De la Torre, Adela, and Beatríz M. Pesquera, eds. *Building with Our Hands: New Directions in Chicana Studies.* Berkeley: University of California Press, 1993. Invaluable source for exploring some of the research on the Chicana experience. Offers a series of studies done by Chicana scholars throughout the country on the Chicana experience. Some are historical, others are sociological, and others involve cultural manifestations of Chicana artists and writers.

• Duran, Livie Isauro, and H. Russell Bernard, eds. *Introduction to Chicano Studies.* New York: Macmillan, 1973. Important for its detailed description of the inception of Chicano studies programs. Reprints *El*

Plan de Santa Bárbara, which established a framework for such programs around the country.

• Rojas, Guillermo. "Social Amnesia and Epistemology in Chicano Studies." In *Estudios Chicanos and the Politics of Community: Selected Proceedings.* Cheney, Wash.: National Association for Chicano Studies, 1989. A response to the autobiography by Richard Rodriguez, *Hunger of Memory: The Education of Richard Rodriguez* (1981).

Chicano Studies Research Library (Los Angeles, Calif.): This library was the first Chicano library established in an institution of higher education. It is part of the Chicano Studies Research Center at the University of California, Los Angeles. It was founded in 1969 as the Mexican American Cultural Center Library. In its formative years, it sought not only to develop a research-level collection but also to develop reference works such as *La Chicana: A Comprehensive Bibliographic Guide.* This library was among the first Latino collections to make its materials available through an online catalog. Subject strengths of the collection include Chicano history, immigration, labor, education, and literature. The library collections include a large serial set, with the bulk of the retrospective titles on microfilm, and a major collection of documentary films and videos. The library has also developed a major collection of dissertations on Latinos.

Chicano Youth Liberation Conference (March, 1969): Political organizational meeting. In March, 1969, more than fifteen hundred delegates from around the United States gathered in a church in a barrio of Denver, Colorado, to organize a Latino political party. Rodolfo "Corky" Gonzáles, a Denver activist, presented a platform calling for the creation of a Latino homeland in the Southwest. This new state would re-create the Aztec Aztlán, the legendary birthplace of Aztec civilization said to be in southern Arizona and New Mexico. The Aztecs left that homeland in the mid-1300's and moved to Mexico.

The Denver meeting produced a document titled *El* Plan Espiritual de Aztlán and led to the creation of the Colorado La Raza Unida Party, which issued a series of goals, "Demandas de la Raza," promoting better education, improved public housing, more emphasis on Latino history and culture in schools serving the Hispanic population, and land reform based on the Aztec principle of community-owned lands. Gonzáles brought some of the group to Washington, D.C., later in 1969 to join in a "poor people's march" on the

Chicano leaders such as United Farm Workers president Arturo Rodriguez work with practical workplace issues as well as the larger issues of cultural identity. (David Bacon)

White House. In the 1970's, participants in the Chicano Youth Liberation Conference helped organize the CRUSADE FOR JUSTICE, headed by Gonzáles.

Chicanos: People of Mexican ancestry. The term "Chicano" refers particularly to those in the United States who affiliate themselves with the ideology of CHICANISMO and the Chicano movement. The word may derive from the Aztec language, although some scholars trace it only to the late nineteenth century, when it was used to refer to poor Mexican immigrants in the American Southwest. It may be an adulterated version of *mejicano* or MEXICANO. Chicano leaders of the 1960's gave the term new meaning, using it to identify themselves culturally and ethnically as a unique group of individuals, those with a mixture of Indian and Spanish roots and living in the United States. The term "Chicano" carries a political meaning of self-determination and ethnic pride.

Chicharrones: Fried pork rinds. When a fresh pork rind is deep-fat fried, it becomes a light, porous, crisp, golden sheet. These *chicharrones* are a common snack in Mexico, and they also can be crushed in bean dishes for flavor or used with sauce as a taco filling. Although preparing *chicharrones* is not particularly difficult, most Mexicans purchase theirs from the many stalls specializing in them. In the American Southwest and Southern California, they are available commercially in markets. Puerto Rican *chicharrones* are like their Mexican counterparts. In most of Central America, *chicharrones* are a foodstuff much like Mexican CARNITAS.

Chilam Balam, Books of: Religious narratives of the Mayan civilization. Written in Yucatec Maya, the Books of Chilam Balam contain information on Mayan civilization, history, religion, customs, and prophecies. They were transcribed into Spanish characters during the seventeenth and eighteenth centuries. The books record dates of events that occurred after the Spanish Conquest, such as the foundation of the city of Mérida. Because scholars know when these events occurred according to the modern calendar, the books have helped to provide an understanding of the Mayan calendar. They have become an invaluable source of information for specialists on Mayan culture.

Child labor: The FAIR LABOR STANDARDS ACT of 1938 outlawed the use in the United States of children under sixteen for industrial labor. Because of the power of the farm bloc in Congress and the demand for cheap labor, agricultural labor was not included in this ban until 1966. Mechanization reduced the number of farmworkers to about 350,000 by 1990, but many states, including California, Texas, Ohio, and New Jersey, still allowed children as young as twelve years old to work when school was not in session. More than 80,000 children worked in agricultural jobs because of this provision. Mexican and Mexican American families formed the backbone of this labor force.

Many children supplement family incomes by picking crops of apples, tomatoes, oranges, celery, lettuce, or any of the other vegetables and fruits grown across the United States. Many work eight-hour days, tugging baskets weighing up to forty pounds. Farm labor is the most dangerous job category in America, and thousands of farmworkers are injured every year in accidents and from pesticide poisoning.

More than 100,000 Mexican American families living in the Rio Grande Valley of Texas travel north in the spring and summer, following the crops. Since 1966, farmworkers have been covered by the minimum wage law, but Department of Labor studies have indicated that more than half of all farmworker employers violated this law. In addition, workers sometimes had to give part of their pay to labor contractors. Illegal workers were not covered by the minimum wage. Thousands of such workers, including children, annually head north from central Mexico to the United States, where they could make four times as much money or more, working fewer days.

Conditions in farm labor camps are usually dismal. Not only are children and others exposed to dangerous working conditions and pesticides, but they live in substandard housing, attend poor schools, and have little medical care. The children grow up uneducated, hardened, and scarred for life. One Texas study showed that almost all children in a migrant labor camp had some physical abnormality. Children were undersized, underweight, and apathetic. More than 90 percent were below grade level in school.

New machines, such as mechanized cotton and tomato pickers, have severely reduced the need for farm laborers. Mechanized cotton pickers reduced demand for workers by more than 90 percent. Machines did not solve the problem of poverty, however, and in many cases made economic survival more difficult.

Education remains a major problem for migrant children. Many attend school in two or more states every year. Head Start programs had some impact, but most programs had long waiting lists and inadequate funding. With the reduction of child labor on farms,

This migrant farmworker in Florida takes time out from picking to feed breakfast to her children; older children typically work with their parents. (Impact Visuals, Lonny Shavelson)

other problems have arisen, including the employment of very young children in sweatshops, factories, and fast-food restaurants at subminimum wages.

Children: The conditions of children's lives have deteriorated in recent years. Statistics on poverty, homelessness, violence, substance abuse, and sexual abuse show that American children are experiencing historically unprecedented levels of risk. Children also face heightened ethnic tensions that affect their learning, economic potential, and mental health. Latino children carry many of the burdens associated with these issues, particularly as their numbers increase at a high rate and as their access to education, health care, and other human services remains inadequate.

The Latino population grew by 61 percent between 1970 and 1980, and by 53 percent between 1980 and 1990, to comprise 9 percent of the U.S. population. About half of this growth came from immigration.

With 29 percent of Latinos living in POVERTY in 1990, including 38 percent of children under the age of eighteen, it is clear that the needs of this burgeoning population are not being met.

Demographic and Socioeconomic Characteristics. Latinos are the youngest racial/ethnic group in the United States, with children making up a larger proportion of the whole than in other groups. School-age children constituted 24 percent of all Latinos but only 18 percent of whites and 23 percent of African Americans in 1988; 11 percent of Latinos were under five years old compared to 7 percent of whites and 9 percent of African Americans. These large proportions of children can be traced to Latinas having the nation's highest fertility rate, ninety-three births per thousand women in 1992. The high proportion of children in the population puts greater pressure on Latino adults to provide for their needs, a situation made more difficult by the relatively low socioeconomic status of Latino adults.

The increasing pressure of children among the poor has been frequently noted by social scientists and commentators in the late twentieth century. Children made up the single largest segment (40 percent) of all poor Americans in the early 1990's. In 1990, 20 percent of all children and 38 percent of Latino children under the age of eighteen lived in poverty. The figures were worse for Puerto Rican children on the mainland (49 percent), somewhat better for Central and South American children (28 percent), and best for Cuban American children (18 percent). Among Latino families living in poverty, including an increasing number of single-parent families, 86 percent had children under the age of eighteen. The effects of poverty on Latino children are many, ranging from limited educational opportunity to greater potential exposure to crime and gangs in inner-city areas.

Most Latino children under the age of fourteen (68 percent) in 1990 were born in the United States, although many of them were the offspring of immigrants. Of the approximately one-third of foreign-born Latinos under fourteen years of age, 92 percent, or some 685,600 children, immigrated between 1980 and 1990. Like other immigrant children, they had to grow up with a new language and culture and make special efforts to acclimate themselves to American society.

Among Latinos between five and seventeen years old in 1990, about one-quarter did not speak English well, and 19 percent lived in what the U.S. Bureau of the Census termed "linguistically isolated households," in which Spanish was spoken primarily and little English was understood. Most Latino immigrant children, however, learn English quickly and become accustomed to serving as translators and mediators for their Spanish-speaking elders in contact with the broader English-speaking society.

Young Latinos face a number of unique challenges in education. First, 75 percent come to kindergarten with no preschool experience, compared to 50 percent of white children. More than five million Latinos are enrolled in public (93 percent) and private (7 percent) elementary and secondary schools. In many areas, they form a substantial part of the public school population, yet they are often poorly served by the system. For example, young Latino children may be mistakenly placed in special education programs or held back

Latino children enter kindergarten with less likelihood than others of having preschool experience. (Impact Visuals, Mark Ludak)

PERCENTAGE OF CHILDREN LIVING IN POVERTY, 1973-1990

Source: Data are from Bureau of the Census, *Statistical Abstract of the United States: 1992* (Washington, D.C.: Bureau of the Census, 1992), Table 718.

Note: Percentages include children under the age of eighteen and include only children living in family groups to which they are related. In 1983 and 1987, definitions and procedures for compiling data were changed, so percentages are not directly comparable to those of previous years.

because of their language difficulties; some are kept for years in overcrowded bilingual classrooms where they learn neither Spanish nor English well.

Latino Children and Their Families. Latino children generally live in larger families than non-Latino children, with 38 percent of Latino families having four or more members compared to 30 percent of non-Latino white families (*see* FAMILY LIFE). Mexican American families tend to be the largest among Latino subgroups and Cuban American families the smallest, a fact that correlates with differences in family and per capita income for these subgroups. Latino families are also more likely to have children under the age of eighteen (65 percent in 1990 compared to 48 percent of all American families). As in other groups, the percent of children living with both parents has shrunk, from 78 percent in 1970 to 67 percent in 1989. Mexican Americans were less likely and Puerto Rican children more likely to be living in households headed by women, which made up 23 percent of Latino families.

Figures from a 1989 census study of Latino children paint a revealing portrait of children's living arrangements. Nearly all children (91 percent) lived in urban areas, and a majority lived in rental housing. More than half had two or more siblings. Most lived with both parents, and about half of them had a parent who was a high school graduate. About 73 percent of them

had working parents, but fewer of them had both parents working (29 percent) than did other American children (41 percent). One-quarter of them had relatives besides parents and siblings living in the household, a sign of the continuing hold of the extended family in Latino culture.

Latino families are generally close-knit and a source of strength in the lives of Latino children, despite economic and educational disadvantages. Members of the extended family play important roles in children's lives, whether they live in the same household, across town, or across international borders, which might be frequently crossed. Latino schoolchildren are more likely than others to come home to a house where an adult is present rather than be "latchkey children." Catholic children have *compadres* (godparents) who sponsor important ritual events in their lives such as baptism, confirmation, and marriage. *Compadres* may act as guardians. Children traditionally are expected to show respect to their elders, but this norm is loosening as Latino children become more assimilated into American society and its more independent youth culture.

Challenges for the Future. Both the bleak socioeconomic conditions and the discrimination that many Latino families face have potentially harmful effects for children. For example, in the early 1990's, one-third of Latino children in California had no health insurance, and many did not receive vaccinations. Some immigrant children from Central America have been traumatized by war, and others have been separated from their parents through deportation. Many children from migrant farmworker families live in substandard housing and receive only minimal education, despite government programs set up to help them. Each of these situations represents issues that are of particular importance to Latino children.

Research has shown consistent differences between the parenting styles of low-income, less-educated parents and those with more education and higher incomes. Middle-class mothers are more likely to reinforce children's behavior and less likely to physically punish their children. More research is needed on child development among the diverse Latino communities in the United States. This research must be sensitive to the history, migration patterns, and cultural values that influence family life and child rearing.

—Gloria Gonzalez Kruger and
Francisco A. Villarruel

SUGGESTED READINGS:
• Fisher, Celia B., and Richard M. Lerner. *Applied Developmental Psychology*. New York: McGraw-Hill, 1994. • Garcia, Eugene E. "'Hispanic' Children: Theoretical, Empirical, and Related Policy Issues." *Educational Psychology Review* 4 (March, 1992): 69-93. • Gibson, Margaret, and John Ogbu, eds. *Minority Status and Schooling: A Comparative Study of Immigrant and Involuntary Minorities*. New York: Garland Press, 1991. • Hernandez, Donald J. *America's Children: Resources from Family, Government, and the Economy*. New York: Russel Sage Foundation, 1993. • Lerner, Richard M., and Nancy A. Busch-Rossnagel, eds. *Individuals as Producers of Their Development: A Life-Span Perspective*. New York: Academic Press, 1981.

Chile relleno: Stuffed, battered, and fried chile, prominent in Mexican cooking. Although *chiles rellenos* are made in other Latin American countries, notably Chile and Peru, the Mexican *chile relleno* is by far the best known. Mexican *chiles rellenos* take many regional forms, but the most common variant uses *poblano* chiles. These are skinned, seeded, slit down one side, stuffed with a savory filling, battered, fried, and sauced. Typical fillings include simple cheese, shredded meat, shrimp, crab, and mixtures. Sauces usually are based on tomatoes or TOMATILLOS. In northern Mexico, *chiles verdes* are the most common chile for *chiles rellenos*, while JALAPEÑOS are typically used in Veracruz.

Chiles: Hot peppers, widely used in the cuisine of Mexico. Chiles were one of the earliest domesticated plants in the Americas, used regularly in Mexico by 4000 B.C.E. and throughout Latin America shortly thereafter. The traditional distinction between hot and sweet peppers is not sustained by botany, and there is a gradation of spiciness. Chiles can be used fresh, dried, or pickled, each method imparting a different taste to food. Chiles are heavily used in Mexico and parts of Central America; they are used more sparingly elsewhere in Latin America. They can be eaten ripe (red or yellow) or underripe (green). There are several dozen

PERCENTAGES OF RELATED CHILDREN UNDER 18 YEARS OF AGE LIVING WITH TWO PARENTS, 1970-1990

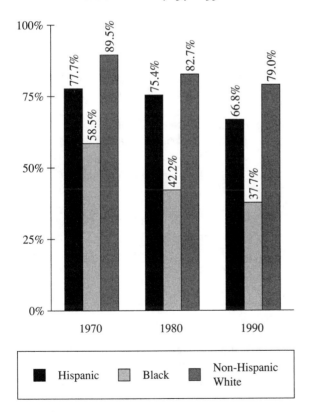

Source: Data are from Carol Foster et al., eds., *Minorities: A Changing Role in American Society* (Wylie, Tex.: Information Plus, 1992), p. 117, Table 9.6.

Note: Persons of Hispanic origin may be of any race. Numbers exclude persons under eighteen years of age who maintained households or family groups.

recognized varieties of chiles, a few of the more common of which are (in approximate order of increasing hotness): bell peppers, *amarillo*, *poblana*, *pasilla*, *cascabel*, *ancho*, *guajillo*, *mulato*, jalapeño, cayenne, *tabasco*, *japonés*, *de árbol*, *serrano*, *piquín*, *chiltepin*, and *habañero*. Generally speaking, smaller and pointier chiles are hotter. *Chipotle* is a Mexican smoked jalapeño chile, available dried and in cans. The chile is called *ají* in some parts of Latin America.

Chimichanga: Filling wrapped with a wheat flour tortilla, then fried. A chimichanga is simply a fried BURRITO. A filling is wrapped in a large wheat flour TORTILLA, and the whole thing is deep-fat fried. Fillings usually are beans and cheese or shredded meat, usually with added SALSA. Chimichangas originated in northern Mexico, but are common in adjacent parts of the United States, especially in take-out restaurants.

China poblana: Mexican costume used in traditional dances. The *china poblana* costume is used in certain traditional Mexican dances. The costume includes worked shifts, a light open jacket, a richly embroidered skirt, satin shoes, a gold-laced *reboso* or brightly colored crepe shawl, a lace-trimmed chemise, long earrings, and numerous chains and medals. *China poblana* was the name given a mestizo woman who lived with relative economic independence as a result of her own work or the generosity of a lover. These women were easily identifiable by their dress and tidiness. After disappearing from the rest of Mexico, the type survived for some time in Puebla.

Cholo: Pejorative term for a Mexican immigrant or lower-class Mexican American or Mexican. During the nineteenth century, *cholo* originated as a derogatory name for Mexican immigrants to the United States. Most were poor and uneducated. The term also referred to Mexican soldiers of the 1840's—many of them felons—who were sent to California. Within the Mexican-heritage community, the term came to be a derogatory reference to Mexicans from the lower socioeconomic classes. In particular, *cholo* can signify a youth, possibly a gang member, who engages in hoodlum behavior. Some people see such youths as more modern versions of the PACHUCO.

Chorizo: Sausage. Sausages are made in almost all places, and each Latin American country has its own. The *chorizo* most commonly used in Mexican cooking is a fresh pork sausage, cured with chile, vinegar, garlic, and other seasonings. It usually is crumbled and cooked to season a dish or cooked as part of a filling for a taco or similar snack. When Puerto Rican cooking requires *chorizo*, the sun-dried Spanish sausage available in cans usually is intended. These Spanish *chorizos* usually are sliced into thin rounds and included in soups, casseroles, and other dishes.

Cíbola: Myth of seven golden cities in the southwestern United States. Cíbola was the name given to seven mythical rich and populous cities in the American Southwest. The origin of this myth lies in two unrelated sources. First, during the Middle Ages in Europe, a legend evolved concerning seven cities called Antilia. When Arab Muslims attacked southern Europe, the legend stated, Portuguese bishops fled west into the sea and founded these cities in some unknown islands. The other source of the Cíbola legend is Nuño Beltrán de Guzmán, a Spanish conquistador. While governor of Pánuco, in 1527, he met an Indian who told him about fabulous cities to the north. These two pieces of information combined into the legend of Cíbola, which fueled several expeditions to the north. Although the Pueblo Indians did live in the north in organized settlements, their cities contained none of the supposed riches ascribed to Cíbola.

Cid, Armando: Artist and Chicano activist. Cid's individual paintings and public murals incorporate pre-Columbian motifs with representations of the daily life and mannerisms of Latinos, and his art has been credited with affirming common Latino goals and experiences.

Cid is best known as one of the most active members in the poster and mural programs of the Royal Chicano Air Force (RCAF), an organization founded in 1970 to promote Chicano culture and make art accessible to ordinary people. He cofounded the group with José MONTOYA, Esteban Villa, and Juanishi Orozco.

As a member of the RCAF, Cid worked closely with Latinos living in urban areas of Sacramento to make meaningful outdoor murals in their neighborhoods. In addition to nurturing a cooperative spirit and offering guidance on the kinds of ethnic symbols and everyday images incorporated into the murals, Cid encouraged barrio residents to take part in other positive activities to safeguard and maintain their Latino culture.

Cigar manufacturing: Cuba has been noted for centuries for its fine cigar tobacco. Tobacco is produced

Cuban tobacco, noted for its quality, was controlled by Spain until the nineteenth century. (Library of Congress)

at thousands of locations in more than one hundred countries, but Cuban cigar tobacco is regarded as the finest.

History of the Cuban Industry. The Cuban cigar industry can be traced to the pre-Columbian era. On his first voyage to the New World in 1492, Christopher Columbus and his companions found the Native American residents of Cuba smoking cigars.

Adoption of the use of tobacco by Europeans was slow. Nearly a century passed before Spaniards began the cultivation of tobacco in Cuba. By the 1580's, a number of tobacco farms had been established in close proximity to Havana.

From 1630 until 1817, tobacco was controlled by the Spanish Crown. During these years, a succession of government institutions controlled this important industry. These institutions included the Real Factoría (1717), Real Compañía de Comercio de la Habana (1739), and Nueva Factoría (1761), all of which prohibited the manufacture of tobacco products in Cuba. These institutions purchased all Cuban tobacco, exporting most of it to Spain, where it was manufactured into various tobacco products. During this early colonial era, production of cigars by individuals in Cuba was illegal. Cuban cigars were discreetly manufactured, however, throughout the island.

The Cuban cigar industry expanded through the nineteenth century, aided by abolition of the old royal tobacco monopoly in 1817. In 1827, there were only about 3,500 tobacco farms on the island. Two decades later, the number of tobacco farms had increased to 9,000, and by 1860 there were 11,500 farms.

Much of Cuba's tobacco continued to be exported in the early nineteenth century, although elimination of the royal tobacco monopoly led to establishment of cigar manufacturing enterprises on the island. The first cigar-rolling shop of importance was established in Havana in 1810, before the collapse of the Spanish tobacco monopoly. The industry grew rapidly, and by the 1820's Havana had more than four hundred rolling shops. Because of its huge output of fine cigars, Havana was soon known as "tobacco city."

The major export market for Cuban cigars in the 1830's was England. By 1846, about one thousand Cuban factories and workshops were engaged in the production of cigars and other tobacco products, employing nearly ten thousand workers. A few large firms employed most of the workers.

Production peaked in the mid-1850's, when about 360 million cigars were exported annually. Exports were aided by expanding markets in Germany, Denmark, France, and the United States. Of the 1,217 cigar rolling shops found on the island in 1861, 516 were located in Havana. Many of the other factories were located in the province of Pinar del Río.

In the 1860's, the industry entered a long period of decline. Development of cigar industries in several of Cuba's traditional markets, particularly France and Germany, resulted in a decreased demand for Cuban cigars. Efforts of foreign countries to protect their home industries with high tariffs also resulted in a loss of traditional markets. The McKinley Tariff Law, passed in the United States in 1890, was devastating to the Cuban cigar industry, cutting exports to the United States by about two-thirds between 1889 and 1897.

As the export of Cuban cigars declined in the second half of the nineteenth century, exports of tobacco leaf increased. In 1859, the value of Cuban cigar exports was twice that of tobacco leaf exports. Less than two decades later, the value of Cuban leaf tobacco exports was twice that of cigar exports. This shift resulted from the fact that tariffs generally applied to tobacco products but not tobacco itself.

The Twentieth Century. The trend of the Cuban cigar industry in the first half of the twentieth century was toward decline. Labor problems created by militant labor unions contributed to this decline, as did the prolonged worldwide depression that began in 1929. Cigar exports for 1936-1940 were only 15 percent of the 1906-1910 level.

The decline of the Cuban cigar industry accelerated following the 1959 Cuban Revolution, largely because of a loss of foreign markets. Prior to the 1959 Cuban Revolution, about 60 percent of Cuban tobacco exports were sold to the United States. Cuban tobacco exports declined sharply, however, with the imposition of a U.S. embargo in early 1962.

Since its decline in the early 1960's, the Cuban cigar industry has been stagnant. Periodic shortages of tobacco leaf have forced the closure of factories. In 1979, a fungus known as the blue mold spread through Cuban tobacco fields. Virtually the entire crop was lost. Consequently, in January, 1980, cigar factories were closed and Cuba withdrew temporarily from the

Florida early became the center for the Cuban American cigar industry. (Impact Visuals, Anita Bartsch)

Skilled tobacco workers sort tobacco for quality and must work with leaves with different characteristics. (Impact Visuals, Jack Kurtz)

export market. Cuba had to import tobacco in order to meet export commitments.

History of the Cuban American Industry. As early as the 1830's, a few immigrants from Cuba had established small cigar manufacturing enterprises in Key West and Tampa, Florida. More cigar manufacturers arrived in Florida from Cuba in the 1860's following a large increase in U.S. tobacco tariffs in the late 1850's. The most dramatic growth in the U.S.-based Cuban cigar industry occurred in the late nineteenth century, especially after passage of the McKinley Tariff Law.

Many successful Cuban cigar manufacturers immigrated to the United States to take advantage of a U.S. market that was protected by high tariffs. Cuban immigrants established cigar manufacturing operations in New York, New York, and New Orleans, Louisiana, after 1890, but the focus of the Cuban American cigar industry remained in Florida.

One of the most prominent of these immigrants was Vicente MARTÍNEZ YBOR, a Spaniard who had moved to Cuba in 1832 and established a successful cigar manufacturing firm in Havana. In 1869, Ybor moved his factory to Key West; in 1878, he relocated to New York City. Because of persistent labor problems in New York, Ybor relocated his factor to a swampy wasteland two miles west of Tampa, Florida, in 1885. Soon a number of other cigar manufacturers from Cuba joined Ybor. These entrepreneurs were followed by hundreds of skilled Cuban cigarworkers. Within a decade, YBOR CITY had been established. By the turn of the century, Ybor City was recognized as the center of quality cigar production in the United States.

Union Activity. Soon after the emergence of the cigar manufacturing industry in Florida, workers organized a labor union, La Sociedad de Torcedores de Tabaco de Tampa. The union was strongly opposed not only by factory owners but also by Tampa's government officials and the local business community. Union members received virtually no support from state and government officials or even from the larger American labor movement.

Union demands for higher wages and better working conditions met strong opposition. Union leaders and workers were harassed, and vigilante groups went as far as kidnapping and beating workers. In addition, local authorities often arrested and jailed workers on vagrancy charges. Union members were frequently threatened with deportation, and workers were deported periodically.

Cigar Workers. Cigar manufacturing is labor intensive. Tobacco workers (TABAQUEROS) usually received relatively high wages until the early twentieth century. The highest wages went to the *escogedores*, who separated the tobacco by its color and quality. Although the *torcedores* (cigar rollers) received less money for their work, their wages were still higher than those of most other industrial workers in Havana.

Cigar rolling required substantial skill because the finished product had to meet rigid standards. One problem was that the raw materials were not standard. Cigars were formed from filler, which consisted of tobacco in a multitude of sizes and shapes, enclosed in a wrapper of one piece. No two tobacco leaves possess precisely the same form, size, thickness, strength, pliability, texture, and other attributes important to the manufacture of cigars. Consequently, the cigar industry was not easily mechanized.

Mechanization. Only since the beginning of the twentieth century has mechanization been widely utilized. Machine production poses inherent difficulties, and Cuban workers strongly opposed use of machines because they believed that machines could replace workers.

The failure of the Cuban cigar industry to mechanize resulted in high production costs, which in turn resulted in diminished foreign sales and ultimately a loss of domestic jobs. This is reflected in the decline in the number of cigar rollers employed in Cuba in the early twentieth century. Between 1899 and 1945, the number of Cuban cigar rollers declined from about twenty thousand to twelve thousand. As late as 1953, less than 20 percent of Cuban cigars were machine-made.

In contrast, the U.S. cigar industry began to mechanize early in the twentieth century. By 1930, more than half of U.S. cigars were machine-made. Introduction of machines in the U.S. cigar industry caused shops and factories to increase in size but fall in number. Of more than twenty-two thousand producers of cigars in 1910, less than six thousand were operating in 1936.

—*Robert R. McKay*

SUGGESTED READINGS:
• Baer, Willis N. *The Economic Development of the Cigar Industry in the United States*. Lancaster, Pa.: Art Printing Company, 1933. A brief study of the early development of the cigar industry. Particularly useful

in understanding the rapid growth of the industry in the late nineteenth century.
• Cooper, Patricia A. *Once a Cigar Maker: Men, Women, and Work Culture in American Cigar Factories, 1900-1919*. Urbana: University of Illinois Press, 1987. The most comprehensive study of the U.S. cigar industry in the twentieth century. A major strength is use of oral history sources.
• Duarte Hurtado, Martin. *La maquina torcedora de tabaco y las luchas en torno a su implantacion en Cuba*. Havana: Instituto Cubano del Libro, 1973. This brief study focuses on developments in the Cuban cigar industry following the 1959 revolution.
• Ortiz, Fernando. *Cuban Counterpoint: Tobacco and Sugar*. Translated by Harriet de Onís. New York: Alfred A. Knopf, 1947. This classic volume examines differences between the Cuban sugar and tobacco industries.
• Stubbs, Jean. *Tobacco on the Periphery: A Case Study in Cuban Labor History, 1860-1958*. Cambridge, England: Cambridge University Press, 1985. One of the best studies of Cuba's cigar industry in the nineteenth and early twentieth centuries. Particularly useful for its corrections of misconceptions regarding the Cuban cigar industry.
• Werner, Carl. *A Textbook on Tobacco*. New York: Tobacco Leaf, 1914. Provides basic information on the emergence of the tobacco industry in the United States and perceptions of it in the early twentieth century.

Cilantro: Herb introduced by the Spanish to the Americas. The leaves of the plant that produces coriander seeds are known as cilantro in most of Latin America, *culantro* in Puerto Rico, and *cilantrillo* in the Dominican Republic. Probably native to India, the plant was carried to the Americas by the Spanish. Its leaves are used by most Latino and Latin American groups, both as an ingredient in cooking and as a garnish. In Mexico, it most often is used with tomatoes or TOMATILLOS in salsas, and in the Caribbean it is often used with fish.

Cimarrones: Runaway slaves. The term refers to *genizaros* (detribalized Indians) who escaped from conditions of SLAVERY in the northern Spanish frontier. Theoretically, Indian slavery had been outlawed in all of Spain's possessions with the 1542 publication of the New Laws; however, on the remote margins of the Spanish empire, in places such as New Mexico, slavery was tolerated. Slaves were a form of compensation to men who colonized these regions. Indians who refused to submit to Spanish rule and who resisted the word of God could be captured as slaves (and recaptured as *cimarrones*) and kept in bondage for ten to twenty years.

Cinco de Mayo: Holiday. On May 5, 1862, French troops were driven out of Puebla, Mexico, by Mexican troops under the command of General Ignacio Zaragoza. May 5 is often mistaken for the Mexican Independence Day, which falls on September 16 (Dieciséis de Septiembre).

The Battle of Puebla took place during a time in Mexico's history when conservatives, who wanted Mexico to have a rule by monarchy, and liberals, who preferred a republican form of government, were disputing reform of the Mexican government. Benito Juárez, the liberal president of Mexico, had both economic and political problems. He called for a two-year moratorium on all foreign debts. The French wanted payment of debts owed to France and to take over parts of Mexico, such as Sonora, known to have silver.

Mexican conservatives assisted French troops, led by Napoleon Bonaparte's nephew, Leon Bonaparte, to occupy Veracruz, Mexico, in January of 1862. The troops began their march to Mexico City, but when they reached the city of Puebla they were taken by surprise by gunshots from General Zaragoza's troops and an additional battalion of three thousand Zacapuaxtlas Indians.

The battle was a major victory for the republicans, but France sent reinforcements to Mexico. Eventually Archduke Maximilian of France came to rule Mexico. Maximilian was executed in 1867. Juárez resolved never to allow foreigners to control Mexico again.

Cinco de Mayo is a celebration that affirms Mexican nationalism. The anniversary of the battle of Puebla is celebrated throughout Mexico and in many cities in the United States, particularly in the West.

Cinco de Mayo celebrations in any city may be marked with brightly colored costumes, folkloric dancers, Mexican craft and food booths, MARIACHI bands, banquets, and PIÑATAS, but celebrations in Mexico and the United States differ. To the people of Puebla, Mexico, who are proud of their ancestors' part in evicting the French from the city, it is an especially patriotic celebration. All schools hold parades during

A Cinco de Mayo celebration in the Mission District of San Francisco, California. (Robert Fried)

the day, and in the evening teenagers participate in a ritual called "el combate de las flores," in which they exchange flowers with people they like.

In Texas, Cinco de Mayo has a special meaning because General Zaragoza was born in Texas when it was still a Mexican territory. In Arizona, which has a large Mexican American population, the holiday is often tied to advertising campaigns. At least seven Arizona cities, including Phoenix, Tucson, and Flagstaff, have Cinco de Mayo celebrations. Denver, Colorado, has honored the holiday with contests and displays by CHARROS (Mexican horsemen). Los Angeles has held voter registration campaigns, registering thousands of Mexican American voters, in honor of the occasion. The Comité Cívico Patriótico Mexicano (Mexican Civil and Patriotic Committee) in San Francisco sponsors a celebration in which only Spanish is spoken and both the Mexican and American national anthems are sung. The festival is a grand expression of Mexican ethnic identity.

Circular migration: Frequent movement of people back and forth between two countries. Many Latinos, especially Mexican Americans, Puerto Ricans, and Dominican Americans, shuttle between the mainland United States and their countries of origin. Circular migrants are typically married men who leave their families behind and support them by sending money earned in the United States. Most work in temporary occupations such as seasonal agriculture and return home after the job is done. The proximity of Mexico, the Dominican Republic, and Puerto Rico facilitates circular migration to the United States. Access to cheap transportation and communications also increases contact across national borders.

As U.S. citizens, Puerto Ricans have had free access to the mainland United States since 1917. Just as the search for jobs motivates Puerto Ricans to move to the mainland, the loss of mainland jobs sends many back home. Many Puerto Ricans on the U.S. mainland view themselves as temporary residents and hope to return to the island once they achieve financial security. Consequently, Puerto Rican migration to the United States is often not a one-way phenomenon but instead a series of tentative moves in both directions. The magnitude of circular migration distinguishes Puerto Ricans from other Latinos, such as Cuban Americans, who rarely return to live in their home countries. Mexican Americans, however, particularly those who live in border states, often cross back into Mexico to maintain ties with family (*see* BORDER REGION AND CULTURE).

Most Latino communities are not temporary settlements but permanent abodes with strong neighborhood institutions. Relatively few immigrants are engaged in a restless circulation between the sending and receiving societies. According to a 1993 study by Clara Rodriguez, less than 14 percent of all Puerto Ricans migrate back and forth between the island and the mainland. Still, many Latinos maintain close ties to their home societies through personal visits, remittances, letters, and phone calls. The diaspora communities established by Latinos in New York, Los Angeles, Miami, San Antonio, and elsewhere are the result of the constant exchange of people, capital, commodities, ideas, and practices between the United States and Latin America. The Latino experience has been a continual crossover across geopolitical and cultural boundaries.

Circular migration may contribute to Latino poverty by limiting opportunities for upward mobility in local labor markets or disrupting access to education. Circular migration can also have positive cultural and economic effects. First, it reinforces cultural values and social institutions crucial to family and neighborhood stability. Thus, Latinos maintain networks of mutual aid widely distributed across space. Second, circular migration serves as a survival strategy for low-income families seeking better employment opportunities in other places. Third, circular migration nurtures the bicultural and bilingual character of Latino communities. Spanish and English language skills are essential for people who may have to live in different cultural environments throughout their life cycles. Finally, circular migration fosters the growth of transnational communities whose members live across a political border yet remain closely linked with their countries of origin. Under such conditions, immigrants develop multiple identities and loyalties, especially in the second generation. The terms Chicano, Neo-Rican, and Dominican-York reflect the trend to create hybrid identities among Latinos.

Cisneros, Evelyn (b. 1955, Long Beach, Calif.): Ballet dancer. Reared in Huntington Beach, California, Cisneros began dancing at the age of eight. She studied as a teenager at the San Francisco Ballet School and the School of American Ballet in New York. In 1971, she apprenticed at the San Francisco Ballet, and six years later she was asked to join the company. Known for a dramatic, theatrical style filled with softness and subtlety, she gave numerous leading performances in such ballets as *Scherzo*, *Romeo and Juliet*, and *Cinder-*

These Puerto Rican women were trained by the Puerto Rican government as domestic workers; many would return to their home country from jobs in the state of New York. (AP/Wide World Photos)

Henry Cisneros addresses the 1984 Democratic National Convention. (AP/Wide World Photos)

ella. In 1984, Cisneros gained instant celebrity when she appeared on national television in *A Song for Dead Warriors* and *The Tempest*, dancing roles that had been choreographed specifically for her.

Her other important ballet credits include *Pas de Trois*, *Confidencias*, *Valses Poeticos*, *The Comfort Zone*, *Don Carlos*, and *Swan Lake* (her name, appropriately, means "keepers of the swans"). She and her regular partner Anthony Randazzo have become well known for the wonderful sense of amorous play that they bring to their duets. In 1989, Cisneros was named spokesperson of the Chicano/Latino Youth Leadership Conference.

Cisneros, Henry Gabriel (b. June 11, 1947, San Antonio, Tex.): Public official. Cisneros was born in a Mexican American barrio in San Antonio, Texas. Educated in parochial schools, he completed both his undergraduate and graduate studies at Texas A&M University. In 1970, he moved to Washington, D.C., where he enrolled in the graduate degree program at George Washington University. Cisneros worked at the National League of Cities while completing his graduate work.

In 1971, Cisneros became the youngest person in history to be accepted as a White House Fellow. He later completed a master's program at Harvard University as well as doctoral studies at George Washington University.

Returning to San Antonio, Cisneros began his political career as a city councilman in 1975. He served as mayor of San Antonio from 1981 to 1988. President Bill Clinton appointed Cisneros as U.S. Secretary of Housing and Urban Development in 1993.

Cisneros, Sandra (b. Dec. 20, 1954, Chicago, Ill.): Writer. Cisneros is a highly acclaimed writer. She received her master of fine arts degree in 1978 from the prestigious University of Iowa Writers' Workshop. Poet Gary Soto helped publish her first collection, a chapbook titled *Bad Boys* (1980). She later published portions of that chapbook, along with her master's thesis, as *My Wicked Wicked Ways* (1987). She did not, however, receive national recognition until she began writing prose.

Cisneros used her childhood experiences of growing up in a Puerto Rican neighborhood on Chicago's north side as the backdrop for her first prose publication, *The House on Mango Street* (1984), which won the Before Columbus Foundation's American Book Award for 1985. The forty-four vignettes that make up young

Esperanza's voyage through puberty and her dreams of transcending life in an urban ghetto are rare depictions in Mexican and Mexican American literature, which is dominated by male coming-of-age stories.

Cisneros' second prose collection, *Woman Hollering Creek and Other Stories* (1991), created no less a sensation in the literary world. Published by a mainstream press, Cisneros' short-story collection won the Lannan Literary Award for 1991 and a listing as a noteworthy book of 1991 by *The New York Times*.

Cisneros v. Corpus Christi Independent School District (Aug. 2, 1972): Segregation case. This Fifth Circuit Court of Appeals case is numbered 71-2397. Circuit Judge Dyer ordered the school district to employ BUSING and clustered school attendance zones to end the segregation of Mexican American pupils, even though the district had never employed de jure segregation of Mexican Americans.

This case was filed as a class action suit by Mexican American pupils against the school district. They sought an end to de facto segregation of Mexican American pupils and teachers. The plaintiffs were successful in their suit in the United States District Court for the Southern District of Texas, and the school district appealed without success.

Finding racial segregation against black and Mexican American students, the district court found the school district in violation of *Brown v. Board of Education* (1954). After two district court cases considered racial patterns in the school district, the district court devised a school assignment plan aimed at eliminating segregation in Corpus Christi schools and creating a unitary school system.

Although the appellate court modified the remedy decreed by the district court, it accepted the district court's conclusion that de facto segregation of Mexican Americans in Corpus Christi was constitutionally unacceptable. Both courts held that Mexican Americans were a racially identifiable class in the Corpus Christi school district.

In its argument, the school district claimed that unlawful segregation in the constitutional sense could not exist without proof of intent to discriminate. Although the Fifth Circuit was unwilling to use the terms de facto and de jure segregation, it found violations of the FOURTEENTH AMENDMENT and *Brown v. Board of Education*, based on the district's use of school attendance zones that isolated Mexican American students.

When the appellate court attempted to devise a remedy for the discriminatory patterns of student and teacher assignment in the Corpus Christi public schools, it placed less emphasis on busing as the route to a unitary school district than had the district court. In remanding the case to the district court, the Fifth Circuit Court made several conditions. The Corpus Christi School District should retain control of school assignments. The school district had a duty to remedy school assignment plans found discriminatory, and the district court could make school assignments if the school district refused to act. Neighborhood-based school assignments should be used where this was possible. Pairing or clustering of schools and portable classrooms should be used where necessary to create a unitary school system. Noncontiguous schools should be paired if necessary. Finally, necessary busing should not discriminate against minorities.

This case provided important protection to Mexican American students, who were the victims of de facto school segregation based on segregated housing patterns. The court extended the reach of *Brown v. Board of Education* by stressing that proof of discriminatory intent was not needed to document unconstitutional segregation. Like Mexican American students, Mexican American teachers received protection against discriminatory assignments in this case.

Citizenship, paths toward: The United States and Canada have various paths that people can take to become citizens. These paths vary between the two countries and will be discussed separately. Both involve first being admitted to the country, then being naturalized as a citizen.

United States. Before naturalization can take place, a person has to be admitted to permanent residence in the United States. Immigration law (as of the early 1990's) is founded primarily on the McCarran-Walter Immigration and Nationality Act of 1952 with amendments, the Immigration Reform and Control Act of 1986, and the Immigration Act of 1990, which extensively revised immigrant categories.

Foreign nationals wishing to come to the United States are divided into two major classifications: those who wish to remain and those who come as visitors. The first step for both is to obtain a valid home-country passport, which must then be taken to the United States embassy or a consulate in the home country, where an application for admission is completed.

In addition to the passport, the consular officer reviewing the request must be given the applicant's birth certificate and, if married, marriage certificate, as well as birth certificates of the applicant's spouse and any children under the age of twenty-one who are also immigrating. Consular officers must also receive the applicant's police certificate, indicating absence or presence of a criminal record; record of any marriage or divorce; military record; affidavit of ability to support oneself; certificate of an offer of employment, if any; medical records; and personal photographs. The consular officer may also request other records. Birth certificates of unmarried children under the age of twenty-one who will not be immigrating may not be required.

Except as otherwise provided by law, immigrants within any of the following classes are not eligible to receive an immigrant visa. The first class consists of various groups. One group consists of people who are mentally retarded, are insane, or have suffered one or more attacks of insanity; those afflicted with psychopathic personality, sexual deviation, a mental defect, narcotic drug addiction, chronic alcoholism, or any dangerous contagious disease; and those who have a physical defect, disease, or disability affecting their ability to earn a living. Also ineligible are those who are paupers, professional beggars, or vagrants; those convicted of a crime involving moral turpitude, or who admit committing the essential elements of such a crime, or who have been sentenced to confinement for at least five years in total for conviction of two or more crimes; those who are polygamists or who practice or advocate polygamy; and those who are prostitutes or who have engaged in, benefited financially from, procured, or imported persons for the purpose of prostitution, or who seek entry into the United States to engage in prostitution, other commercialized vice, or any immoral sexual act. Ineligible on economic grounds are those who seek entry to perform skilled or unskilled labor and who have not been certified by the secretary of labor, along with those likely to become public charges in the United States.

A second class of people ineligible for admission includes those who seek re-entry within one year of their exclusion from the United States or who, within the past five years, have been arrested and deported from the United States, or removed at government expense in lieu of deportation, or removed as an alien in distress or as an alien enemy. Also in this class are those who procure or attempt to procure a visa or other documentation by fraud or willful misrepresentation, those who would not be eligible to acquire United States citizenship, those who have departed from or remained outside the United States to avoid United

Volunteers from Medgar Evers College in New York assist applicants for amnesty under an Immigration and Naturalization Service program. (Impact Visuals, H. L. Delgado)

States military service in time of war or national emergency, and those who have been convicted for violating or for conspiring to violate certain laws or regulations related to various regulated drugs. Another group excluded within this class consists of aliens seeking entry from foreign contiguous territory or adjacent islands within two years of their arrival there on a nonsignatory carrier, those unable to read and understand some language or dialect, those who knowingly and for gain have encouraged or assisted any other alien to enter, or attempt to enter, the United States in violation of law, and former exchange visitors who have not fulfilled the two-year foreign residence requirement. Those who are graduates of foreign medical schools and intend to offer medical services are ineligible for a visa unless they have passed parts 1 and 2 of the National Board of Medical Examiners Exam or an equivalent exam as determined by the Department of Health and Human Services.

Politically Undesirable Aliens. A third class of ineligible persons includes such persons as the United States deems to be politically undesirable. These include aliens who are, or at any time have been, anarchists or members of (or affiliated with) any communist or other totalitarian party, including any subdivision or affiliate. This provision applies broadly to anyone who has advocated or taught, either personally or by means of any written or printed matter, opposition to organized government, the overthrow of government by force and violence, the assaulting or killing of government officials because of their official character, the unlawful destruction of property, sabotage, or the doctrines of world communism or the establishment of totalitarian dictatorship in the United States. Similarly ineligible are aliens who seek to enter the United States to engage in prejudicial activities or unlawful activities of a subversive nature.

A fourth class of ineligibility comprises aliens who, under the indirect or direct control of the Nazi government of Germany or of the government of any area occupied by, or allied with, the Nazi government of Germany, ordered, incited, assisted, or otherwise participated in the persecution of any person because of race, religion, national origin, or political opinion, during the period beginning on March 23, 1933, and ending on May 8, 1945.

The United States accepted thousands of Cuban refugees during the Mariel boat lift in 1980. (AP/Wide World Photos)

Applicants for admission to the United States must indicate whether any of the foregoing classifications apply. If any apply, an explanation must be given. Any willfully false or misleading statement or willful concealment of a material fact may subject the applicant to permanent exclusion from the United States and, if such person is allowed to enter, to criminal prosecution and/or deportation.

Classifications of Immigrants. Immigrants enter the United States in the following categories, which are given different preferences and are described below: immediate relatives, those who are family sponsored, those with an employment petition, special immigrants, transition immigrants, refugees, those seeking political asylum, and those under special programs.

Immediate Relatives. An immediate relative is the spouse, child, parent, or widow or widower of a United States citizen. A widow or widower must petition for admittance within two years of the death of the spouse. A citizen must be at least twenty-one years of age to petition for his or her parents. The word "child" means legitimate or legitimated, including stepchildren and adopted children, under certain conditions.

Family Sponsorship. There are four preference categories within family sponsorship. The first preference includes unmarried sons and daughters of a U.S. citizen. The second preference includes the spouse, children, and unmarried sons and daughters of a lawful permanent resident who is not a U.S. citizen. The third preference includes married sons and daughters of U.S. citizens and their children under the age of twenty-one. The fourth preference includes brothers or sisters of a U.S. citizen.

The United States has set targets for the number of family-sponsored admittances. For each fiscal year, with certain exceptions, the limit is approximately 480,000 persons, except that the number was 465,000 for each of the fiscal years 1992, 1993, and 1994. In no case is the number to be less than 226,000.

Employment Petitions. Employment petitions are divided into several classes: priority workers with extraordinary ability in arts, sciences, education, business, or athletics; outstanding professors and researchers; members of professions holding advanced higher education degrees or, in lieu of such degrees, persons who have indicated exceptional abilities or skills; skilled workers; certain special immigrants; and those employed in creative work.

Special Immigrants. This category refers to various cases such as someone lawfully admitted for permanent residence who is returning from a temporary visit abroad, a person who was a citizen who desires reacquisition of citizenship, someone who wishes to enter the United States solely to act as a minister of a religious denomination, an employee of the United States who performed faithful service abroad for a total of fifteen years or more, or an employee of the Panama Canal Company or Canal Zone Government prior to October 1, 1979, the date on which the Panama Canal Treaty of 1977 entered into force. The category also includes Panamanian nationals and, if married, their spouses and children, who were retired from employment by the United States government prior to October 1, 1979. Also in this category are immigrants who served honorably on active duty in the armed forces of the United States after October 15, 1978, and after original lawful enlistment outside the United States (under a treaty or agreement in effect on October 1, 1991) for a certain number of years.

A special category of "employment creation" refers to aliens who seek to enter the United States so that they can participate in their own new business. It also applies to aliens who participate in a company in which they invested after November 29, 1990, or in which they are currently investing. These companies must be judged to benefit the U.S. economy and to have created full-time employment for no fewer than ten authorized residents of the United States. No less than three thousand visas are to be made available in this category each fiscal year.

Transition Immigrants. This category primarily includes qualified applicants for a visa under the IMMIGRATION REFORM AND CONTROL ACT OF 1986 who were notified of their eligibility before May 1, 1990, but who did not receive visas. It also includes certain other persons who could be admitted during the fiscal years 1992 and 1994.

Refugees. Refugees are defined for immigration purposes as persons outside their country of nationality or, in the case of a person having no nationality, outside the country in which he or she last habitually resided (*see* REFUGEES AND REFUGEE STATUS). A refugee must be either unwilling or unable to return to his or her home country or country of last habitual residence because of his or her race, religion, nationality, political views, or membership in a particular social group. The president of the United States also has the power to designate persons as refugees.

The category of refugees became particularly applicable to Latinos during the 1980's, when various countries including Nicaragua and El Salvador underwent civil war. The term "refugee" does not include any

A Nicaraguan refugee is processed in Florida. (UNHCR/L. Solmssen)

person who ordered, incited, assisted, or otherwise participated in the persecution of any other person because of that other person's race, religion, nationality, membership in a particular social group, or political views.

Political Asylum. The attorney general of the United States may grant ASYLUM to any alien physically present in the United States or at a land border or point of entry, irrespective of the alien's status, if the attorney general determines that such an alien is a refugee within the meaning of the law. Such asylum may be terminated if the attorney general determines that the alien is no longer a refugee owing to a change in circumstances in the alien's home country or, in the case of a person having no nationality, in the country in which the person last habitually resided. The spouse or child of such a person granted asylum may not necessarily be granted the same status as the alien. Furthermore, no alien who has been convicted of an aggravated felony may apply for or be granted asylum. The problem with this last provision is that any person who has worked against a brutal dictatorship in his or her home country would most likely have been convicted of a felony by the courts of that country.

In addition to these categories, aliens can be admitted under a variety of special programs. These programs include diversity, special agricultural workers, entrepreneurs, and those under recorded admission.

Diversity. Diversity admittances refer to persons from countries and regions that in recent years have been less represented in admissions. Such persons must have a high school education or two years of work experience in an occupation requiring two years of training or experience.

Special Agricultural Workers. Special agricultural workers are granted temporary resident status to allow performance of seasonal agricultural work. The attorney general of the United States may adjust the status of any alien thus provided lawful temporary resident status to that of an alien lawfully admitted for permanent residence. This change in status can be made if such a worker performed seasonal agricultural services in the United States for at least ninety working days during each of the twelve-month periods ending on May 1 of 1984, 1985, and 1986, in addition to other requirements. These provisions shall not apply to more than 350,000 aliens. The secretaries of the departments of labor and agriculture also have the joint right to decide the number of additional aliens who can be admitted to the United States or acquire the status of being lawfully admitted for temporary residence. This right is invoked to meet shortages of workers.

Entrepreneurs. The term "entrepreneur" in immigration law refers to someone who, in addition to creating employment, establishes a new commercial enterprise and invests approximately $500,000 to $3,000,000 in that enterprise.

Recorded Admission. In the discretion of the attorney general, an alien residing in the United States may be given permanent residency if he or she can show that he or she entered the United States prior to January 1, 1972, has had his or her residency continuously since such entry, is a person of good moral character, and is not ineligible for citizenship.

Naturalization. After being legally admitted, a person who wants to become a U.S. citizen undergoes the process of naturalization. A successful applicant for naturalization must meet the following requirements. He or she must be at least eighteen years of age; have been a lawful permanent resident in the United States for at least five years immediately prior to filing the petition for naturalization, or for three years if the applicant has been married to a U.S. citizen for those three years and continues to be married to that citizen; have residence in the IMMIGRATION AND NATURALIZATION SERVICE district of the region where the petition is filed; and have no convictions for murder or an aggravated felony at any time, good moral character, and belief in the principles of the Constitution. An additional requirement is that the applicant not be a member of the Communist Party or a similar party within or outside the United States within ten years prior to filing a petition for naturalization. This includes membership or connection with any group that teaches the overthrow of the U.S. government by force or violence, injuring or killing officers of the United States, or sabotage.

Successful applicants for naturalization must also be able to speak, understand, read, and write simple English. A person above the age of fifty on the date of the examination who has been living in the United States for at least twenty years as a lawful permanent resident, or who is above fifty-five years of age and has been living in the United States for at least fifteen years as a lawful permanent resident, may become a citizen even though he or she cannot speak, read, or write English. Applicants must also pass an examination on the history of the United States and its form of government. There are no exceptions to this require-

ment. Finally, applicants must take an oath of allegiance, in which they surrender any foreign allegiance and any foreign title and in which they promise to obey the Constitution and the laws of the United States and to bear arms or fight for the United States. If fighting or bearing arms for the United States is against the applicant's religion, then that person must promise to perform other types of service.

These requirements apply to every applicant unless he or she belongs to a special class that exempts the applicant from one or more requirements. Such special classes include service persons, veterans, spouses and children of United States citizens, surviving spouses of United States service persons, seamen, and employees of organizations promoting United States interests abroad. Children under the age of eighteen may automatically become citizens when their parents naturalize. These children may obtain certificates of citizenship in their own names by filing the Application for Certificate of Citizenship (form N-600).

The naturalization process is begun by filing form N-400, An Application to File Petition for Naturalization, along with providing a fingerprint card (FD 258) except for children under the age of fourteen and per-

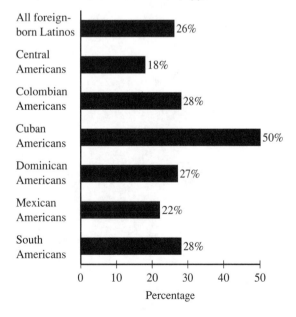

FOREIGN-BORN LATINOS WITH U.S. CITIZENSHIP, 1990

Source: Data are from Bureau of the Census, *1990 Census of Population: Persons of Hispanic Origin in the United States* (Washington, D.C.: Bureau of the Census, 1993), Table 1.

sons over the age of seventy-five. The applicant must also provide two color photographs taken within thirty days of the application and pay the application fee. The applicant must appear before a naturalization examiner for examination on literacy and knowledge of history and government. If denied naturalization, the applicant may request a hearing by filing form N-336 and paying the applicable fee.

Successful applicants attend an oath ceremony before either an Immigration and Naturalization Service officer or a judge. The applicant has his or her choice of ceremony.

Canada. The Immigration Act of April 10, 1978, as amended February 1, 1993, is based on such basic principles as nondiscrimination, family reunion, concern for refugees, and the promotion of Canada's economic health. The act requires the minister of employment and immigration to state annually the number of immi-

grants and refugees Canada plans to admit each year. Starting in the 1991-1995 period, immigration plans were to be developed for five-year periods. The federal government is required to consult the provinces regarding distribution and settlement of immigrants. The 1990 Canada-Quebec Accord required the division of responsibilities for immigration to Quebec to be divided between Quebec and the federal government.

Canada uses three major classes for immigrants desiring permanent residence in Canada: family class, refugees, and independent immigrants. Family class consists of close relatives sponsored by Canadian citizens or permanent residents who are aged nineteen and above and are living in Canada. Such relatives include a spouse, fiancé, or fiancée; a dependent son or daughter; parents; grandparents; siblings; nephews and nieces; and grandchildren who are orphans, unmarried, and under the age of nineteen.

Carlos Romero-Gaitan, 101 years old, in 1988 was the oldest applicant for legalization under reformed U.S. immigration laws. (AP/Wide World Photos)

Demonstrators in a New York City Labor Day parade protest the U.S. government's policy of treating many Salvadoran refugees as illegal aliens. (Impact Visuals, Les Stone)

Refugees are persons sponsored by at least five Canadian citizens or permanent residents aged nineteen or older. Under certain conditions, sponsors can be legally incorporated organizations.

Independent immigrants consist of assisted relatives, entrepreneurs, and investors. Assisted relatives are persons who do not qualify for the family class but who have a relative in Canada able and willing to help them become established there. Entrepreneurs intend to and have the ability to establish, purchase, or make a substantial investment in a business in Canada. This business must create or maintain one or more jobs in Canada for Canadian residents other than the entrepreneur and his or her dependents. Investors are persons with personal net worth of $500,000 or more. An investor has the option of subscribing in any one of three tiers, which vary in the amount of investment required, the amount of time the investment must be held, and the province in which the immigrant chooses to settle.

Independent immigrants, including those desiring to reside permanently in Canada through the assisted relative program, must also meet the requirements of a point system. The system awards points based on various factors such as age, education, employment, occupation, specific vocational preparation, work experience, language ability, demographics, and personal suitability. Bonus points are given for having a relative in Canada.

Inadmissible classes include persons who pose a threat to public health, safety, order, or national security; persons who fail to have, when required, visas, visible means of support, and valid travel documents; and persons who have been identified as participants in organized crime, terrorists, hijackers, or war criminals. Inadmissibility on criminal grounds is determined in accordance with the sentence that could have been given for equivalent offenses under Canadian law, but the prospect of rehabilitation might vary this.

Naturalization. Successful applicants for Canadian naturalization must be at least eighteen years of age and be permanent residents of Canada for three of the four years immediately preceding application for citizenship (each day of permanent status is counted as one day, while each day of residency prior to permanent status is counted as one-half day). They must make application to the Office of the Citizenship Court with such documents as a birth certificate, passport, evidence of lawful admission to Canada, two documents for proof of identity, two photographs, and an attested affidavit to the truth of statements. Other documents may be required. Applicants must also exhibit literacy in either French or English (for Quebec, French) and must undergo an interview with a citizenship judge.

Other methods of obtaining citizenship also exist. For example, anyone born in Canada, or, after February 15, 1977, any person born abroad of a Canadian mother or father holding citizenship, is automatically a citizen of Canada. —*Robert M. Spector*

SUGGESTED READINGS:

• Canadian Government. *Citizenship and Immigration Canada: The Immigrant Investor Program*. Hull, Quebec, Canada: Minister of Supply and Services, 1994. This pamphlet deals with the investor in Canada. The 1993 amendment to the immigration law details stricter enforcement methods with regard to investors.

• Canadian Government. *Immigration Act and Regulations*. Hull, Quebec, Canada: Supply and Services Canada, 1993. Gives the full legal requirements and procedure for immigration into Canada, permanent residence, and naturalization.

• Canadian Government. *Immigration Canada: Applying for Permanent Residence in Canada. A Self-Assessment Guide for Independent Applicants*. Hull, Quebec, Canada: Public Affairs and International Service Group, Citizenship and Immigration Canada, 1993. A brief pamphlet that deals with the class of independent applicants for immigration. No information on naturalization.

• Canadian Government. *Immigration Canada: Canada's Immigration Law*. Hull, Quebec, Canada: Supply and Services Canada, 1992. A pamphlet intended to give the prospective immigrant a thumbnail sketch of Canada's immigration law. Provides no information on naturalization.

• Canadian Government. *Immigration Canada: Immigration and Doing Business in Canada*. Hull, Quebec, Canada: Minister of Supply and Services, 1993. This pamphlet deals with the entrepreneur in Canada.

• Deutsch, Howard D. *Immigration the Easy Way*. Hauppauge, N.Y.: Barron's, 1992. Covers U.S. immigration. Part 1 deals with preparing the way for entry, and part 2 discusses achieving permanent residence.

• Fragomen, Austin J., et al. *1993 Immigration Procedures Handbook*. Deerfield, Ill.: Clark, Boardman, Callaghan, 1992. An extensive paperback with a 1993 supplement that gives a full presentation of the different visa types, acquisition of permanent status in the United States, and forms. Extremely useful.

• Rovner, Gerald, et al. *Immigration Law for the Non-Specialist*. Boston: Massachusetts Continuing Legal Education, 1994. Excellent digest of U.S. immigration law. The beginning section deals with how to get into the country, U.S. taxation of foreign nationals, employment of foreign nationals, and criminal law issues. Concludes with an elaborate series of exhibits, including the 1952 Immigration and Nationality Act.

• U.S. Department of Justice. *Naturalization Requirements and General Information*. Washington, D.C.: Author, 1992. A good summary of naturalization procedures in the United States.

• U.S. Immigration and Naturalization Service. *Guide to the Immigration and Naturalization Service*. South Burlington, Vt.: Author, 1994. A brief pamphlet that deals with the mission and structure of the Immigration and Naturalization Service, U.S. immigration law, naturalization procedures, the Immigration Reform and Control Act of 1986, and various programs.

Civil rights: Latinos have had a long struggle for civil rights, but it was not until the middle of the twentieth century that this struggle became a significant factor in mainstream life in the United States and Canada. Since that time, Latinos have made notable gains in politics, economics, and social areas, through both direct action and legal battles.

The Hispanic influence in North America predates the founding of English colonies on the eastern seaboard by more than a century. The dominant culture of North America nevertheless was based on the Anglo-American and Anglo-Canadian experience, and Latinos have frequently found their civil rights ignored or even denied. A history of western expansion by the United States and its citizens, the series of wars and border clashes between the United States and Mexico, and the economic domination of the continent by the northern nations have reinforced this tendency. The continued struggle of Latinos to exercise their civil rights is an important part of the development of both the United States and Canada.

Denial of Rights. For practical purposes, Latino involvement in civil rights issues was largely nonexistent until the twentieth century, for a number of rea-

Farmworkers with little political power were long denied basic rights. (Impact Visuals, Allan Hoeltje)

sons. First, Latinos generally were in the lowest economic levels of their communities and thus had limited political and economic power. Second, Latinos were concentrated in a few geographic areas, primarily Florida, Texas, New Mexico, California, and New York City. Within those areas, they were further compressed into smaller communities known as BARRIOS. Latinos and their concerns thus did not receive widespread notice or attention. Third, the Hispanic culture, including its distinctive adherence to Roman Catholicism, was significantly different from that of the dominant Anglo society. Fourth, Latinos as a group were noticeably different from non-Hispanics in their physical characteristics, and this was used as a means to identify them and as an excuse for relegating them to second-class treatment.

The weak economic status of Latinos was most detrimental to their civil rights. There were Hispanics in the Southwest long before the United States was established, but once the region had been incorporated into the United States following the MEXICAN AMERICAN War (1846-1848) and the GADSDEN PURCHASE (1853), residents of Hispanic descent suffered from prejudice, discrimination, and exploitation, especially in economic matters. Agriculture depended heavily upon migrant laborers, many of them citizens of Mexico, who tended fields and harvested crops under extremely difficult conditions for low wages. Often, the judicial system and law enforcement officers cooperated openly with landowners to restrict even the most fundamental rights of Latinos.

Government's Restriction of Rights. Immigration law was written to favor employers. During World War I, for example, the United States government allowed fifty thousand "temporary" workers a year to enter from Mexico to assist with harvesting and processing the larger crops demanded by the war. Most of them remained in the United States in badly paid jobs,

These two youths were attacked in the zoot-suit riots of 1943; one was beaten and the other was stripped of his zoot-suit apparel. (AP/Wide World Photos)

and with no guarantee of their civil rights, until the Great Depression, when they were summarily returned to Mexico.

Governments on all levels have abetted discrimination against Latinos. In 1931, the WICKERSHAM COMMISSION REPORT analyzed the extent of criminal involvement by foreign-born Americans and the perceptions of law enforcement officials. In general, the report found that law officers tended to view Mexican Americans as "lawless and criminal," a view that made POLICE BRUTALITY against Latinos much more common and pervasive, and less likely to be corrected by court action.

The Sleepy Lagoon Case. The pervasiveness of discrimination against Latinos, both overt and covert, was made evident during World War II, particularly through the Sleepy Lagoon case. In August of 1942, seventeen Latino youths, fifteen of them born in the United States, were arrested for the murder of Jose Diaz following a party at the Sleepy Lagoon ranch near Los Angeles. Twelve of them were convicted the following January and received sentences that ranged from a few months to life imprisonment.

During the course of the trial, intense anti-Hispanic attacks had been published in Los Angeles newspapers and made by the legal and judicial establishments. Police officers had automatically labeled all Mexican American youths as potential killers and systematically harassed them. This harassment included attaching razor blades to sticks and using these tools to rip the characteristic baggy trousers and wide-shouldered jackets worn by many Latino youths as part of their "zoot suit" apparel. Beatings and assaults were also reported. The Sleepy Lagoon case aroused national and even international interest and concern. It was one of the first to focus attention on the systematic discrimination against Latinos. The Latino response began to gather in force.

Latino Response. The significant movement for Latino civil rights came after World War II, when Dr. Héctor Pérez GARCÍA organized the AMERICAN G.I. FORUM in 1948. The impetus behind the forum was the refusal by cemeteries and mortuaries in a Texas community to handle the body of Félix Longoria, a Mexican American soldier. The organization soon expanded its activities to include investigations of alleged discrimination in education, public facilities, health care, and voting.

Organizations that followed in the footsteps of the American G.I. Forum included the MEXICAN AMERICAN POLITICAL ASSOCIATION (formed in 1960) and La Huelga, formed by César CHÁVEZ in 1965. Collectively, these social action and political groups revealed

incontrovertible evidence that Latinos were being systematically discriminated against in education, health care, and other aspects of community life.

These issues came before the federal courts in 1954. In *HERNÁNDEZ V. TEXAS*, the United States Supreme Court recognized Hispanics as a separate class of people who suffered from discrimination. This landmark decision provided Latinos with the legal and constitutional basis to attack discriminatory attitudes and activities.

Following the assassination of President John F. Kennedy in 1963, the United States Congress overcame a lengthy filibuster to enact the CIVIL RIGHTS ACT OF 1964. This sweeping legislation addressed discrimination in employment, education, and public fa-

The American G.I. Forum was formed to address issues involving Latino soldiers and veterans but expanded into other areas. (AP/Wide World Photos)

cilities. It established the Equal Employment Opportunity Commission, a key federal agency in handling claims of discrimination in the workplace.

Latino political power had been increasing throughout the 1950's and 1960's. In the close presidential race between Kennedy and Richard Nixon in 1960, for example, the overwhelming Latino vote for the Democratic candidate helped Kennedy carry Texas.

Once the political power of Latinos became evident, it was reflected in an increased number of Latinos in elected and appointed positions. In the fall of 1966, for example, a number of prominent Mexican Americans, many of them political leaders, protested to President Lyndon B. Johnson that Hispanics were being ignored in important federal programs. In response, Johnson appointed Vicente Treviño XIMENES to the Equal Employment Opportunity Commission and in 1967 created the INTER-AGENCY COMMITTEE ON MEXICAN AMERICAN AFFAIRS to coordinate federal activities. In 1969, Congress transformed the committee into the CABINET COMMITTEE ON OPPORTUNITIES FOR SPANISH SPEAKING PEOPLE.

Judicial Decisions. Despite such increased political influence, the court system remained an important route for Latinos seeking to secure their civil rights, particularly regarding education. In 1974, in *LAU V. NICHOLS*, the United States Supreme Court ruled that a California school system had denied meaningful opportunity for students to participate in public education programs by failing to provide English-language instruction to non-English-speaking students. Specifically, the Court found that the school system had violated Title VI of the 1964 Civil Rights Act.

Although Congress subsequently enacted provisions of the 1974 EQUAL EDUCATIONAL OPPORTUNITY ACT designed to make bilingual education available to

The U.S. Supreme Court and various laws have recognized children's right to education. (James Shaffer)

Latinos, the issue remained controversial. In 1974, a New Mexico Court ruled in SERNA V. PORTALES that bilingual education was constitutional. Substantial opposition to BILINGUAL EDUCATION remained, as did opposition to other forms of MULTICULTURALISM, such as bilingual ballots for elections.

The courts also have been called on to determine the extent to which school systems must serve children whose parents are not United States citizens and may be in the country illegally. A significant ruling was made by the United States Supreme Court in PLYLER V. DOE (1982). The decision struck down a Texas law allowing only citizens of the United States and legally admitted aliens to receive tuition-free education through public schools. In its ruling, the Supreme Court declared that the Texas statute violated the "equal protection" clause of the United States Constitution by discriminating against a class of children "not accountable for their disabling status." In other words, the fact that children had parents who were not documented legal residents of the United States was not relevant to the state's responsibility to afford equal educational opportunities to all children. This decision also aroused considerable opposition and prompted attempts at legislative changes.

Conclusion. In education, employment, VOTING RIGHTS, access to public facilities, and other areas of community life, Latinos have made significant gains in civil rights, particularly since the 1960's. Many of these gains have been achieved as part of a larger political and social effort to increase participation of and opportunity for members of minority groups. Many changes, especially in areas of the United States where Latinos compose a significant portion of the population, have been the result of concerted, organized, and often courageous efforts by Latinos themselves, who have used the legal system, the political process, and individual initiative to assert their full civil and human rights.   —*Michael Witkoski*
SUGGESTED READINGS:

- Abalos, David. *Latinos in the United States: The Sacred and the Political.* Notre Dame, Ind.: University of Notre Dame Press, 1985. A study of how the unique religious and moral culture of Latinos has played a significant role in shaping social and political beliefs and activities.
- Cafferty, Pastora San Juan, and William C. McCready, eds. *Hispanics in the United States: A New Social Agenda.* New Brunswick, N.J.: Transaction Books, 1985. A collection of essays that collectively survey the status of Latinos in the areas of culture,

religion, education, employment, health care, criminal justice, and politics.

- Cortes, Carlos, ed. *The Mexican American and the Law.* New York: Arno Press, 1974. A collection of reprints covering significant events and legal cases involving Mexican Americans and the United States criminal justice and civil rights systems. The entries, which date as far back as the 1930's, provide an overview of legal developments involving this Latino population.
- Graham, Hugh Davis. *The Civil Rights Era: Origins and Development of National Policy, 1960-1972.* New York: Oxford University Press, 1990. A scholarly but readable examination of the approach the United States took toward civil rights during this pivotal era.
- Kanellos, Nicolás, ed. *The Hispanic-American Almanac.* Detroit: Gale Research, 1993. A wide-ranging and extremely useful overview of the subject, with brief but informative articles on a variety of topics, including notable civil rights issues and decisions.
- Moore, Joan, and Harry Pachon. *Hispanics in the United States.* Englewood Cliffs, N.J.: Prentice Hall, 1985. An overview of the rapidly expanding Hispanic populations (specifically Mexican, Puerto Rican, and Cuban) and their impact on social, cultural, and political life in the United States.
- Moore, Joan, and Raquel Pinderhuges, eds. *In the Barrios: Latinos and the Underclass Debate.* New York: Russell Sage Foundation, 1993. A collection of essays by various authors on the impact of poverty and economic deprivation among Latinos and the various responses shaped by communities and governments.
- Shorris, Earl. *Latinos: A Biography of the People.* New York: W. W. Norton, 1992. A highly personal and personalized study of the various Hispanic populations throughout the United States. Largely anecdotal.
- Weyr, Thomas. *Hispanic USA: Breaking the Melting Pot.* New York: Harper & Row, 1988. An overview of the roles played by Hispanics in local, regional, and national life in the United States, with particular emphasis on Hispanic influence in politics and economics.

Civil Rights Act of 1964: Outlawed discrimination in public facilities, public accommodations, employment, and institutions on federal contracts. The bill that became the Civil Rights Act of 1964 was introduced into Congress in the summer of 1963 by then-president John F. Kennedy. It outlawed discrimination based on race and gender in virtually every sector of public life. After the assassination of Kennedy on November 22, 1963, President Lyndon Johnson continued the fight for the bill's passage in Congress. Johnson spoke to a joint session of Congress and urged African American leaders to lobby on behalf of the bill.

On February 10, 1964, the bill passed the House by a vote of 290 to 130. It then went to the Senate, where its primary opposition was aided by Senator Richard B. Russell (Democrat of Georgia) and a group called the Coordinating Committee for Fundamental American Freedoms, headed by William Loeb of New Hampshire. After much discussion and a lengthy filibuster, the Senate voted to end debate on June 10, 1964. On June 19, 1964, the Senate passed the bill with a vote of 73 to 27. Because amendments had been added by the Senate, the bill had to be returned to the House for final approval. The House passed the bill on July 2, 1964, and President Johnson signed it into law the same day.

The Civil Rights Act of 1964 is the most massive piece of legislation on one subject since the Civil War. Its provisions specify nondiscrimination in rights to vote and register, to use public accommodations such as businesses, to use public facilities such as parks, to public education, and to participation in federally assisted programs. Other parts of the bill strengthened the authority of the Commission on Civil Rights, called for equal opportunities in employment, allowed intervention by federal courts in discrimination cases, established the Community Relations Service to deal with prejudice, and mandated jury trials in certain civil rights cases. The bill represents a high point of cooperation among Americans of diverse backgrounds working for a common goal.

The act created the Equal Employment Opportunity Commission (EEOC) and renewed and expanded the FAIR EMPLOYMENT PRACTICES COMMITTEE. It also served as the basis for school desegregation (*see* SEGREGATION, DESEGREGATION, AND INTEGRATION). Historically, Latinos have suffered from the types of discrimination that the act sought to end. For this reason, it has been perhaps the most important law on which Latinos have relied in pursuing civil rights litigation.

Civil rights movements: No social movement of the twentieth century has affected American society as much as the Civil Rights movement of the 1950's, 1960's, and 1970's. Black Americans, the country's largest racial minority, were suffering under an invidious racism most notable in the South. They initiated a crusade that raised national consciousness concerning their plight. The results of their activism were sweep-

ing federal and state statutes that effectively eliminated their second-class citizenship under the law and brought them into the American mainstream.

The activism that spawned changes for African Americans also affected other groups in American society that were subjected to systemic discrimination and prejudice. Women, the elderly, homosexuals, Native Americans, Asian Americans, and Latinos were among the many groups energized to seek improvements of their own status, often adopting similar methods and slogans. Like the broader Civil Rights movements, the Chicano civil rights movement sought to challenge the dominance of white RACISM. Although it was less well-known outside the Southwest and smaller in scale, the CHICANO MOVEMENT won advances that continued to affect the lives of Latinos in the late twentieth century.

Historical Background. In numerous ways, the historical condition of Latinos in the twentieth century paralleled that of African Americans. They were politically powerless in their own communities and often segregated in or denied use of public facilities. Discriminated against in housing, education, employment, and basic social services, many Latinos found their opportunity to realize the American Dream limited (*see* DISCRIMINATION, BIGOTRY, AND PREJUDICE AGAINST LATINOS). Prejudice against their skin color, language, and ethnicity effectively blocked their advancement. This has been especially true of Mexican Americans, who have always composed the largest segment of the Latino population.

Until 1900, Mexican Americans had been largely invisible, constituting a small percentage of the U.S. population and confined primarily to California and the border areas of the Southwest. After 1910, however, their numbers increased significantly. Revolution in Mexico sparked the initial wave of immigration, but the search for better economic conditions escalated legal and illegal movement across the U.S.-Mexico border during and immediately after World War I. Although some immigrants found employment in midwestern war and industrial plants, or as household and unskilled service workers, the vast majority toiled as poorly paid farm and ranch hands working in the states extending from Texas to California. By 1930, the total population of Mexican descent in the United States had reached nearly 1.5 million persons.

The Mexican Americans' increased presence evoked considerable concern among Anglos, especially when the two groups competed for jobs. During the Great DEPRESSION of the 1930's, waves of homeless and

Revolution in Mexico sent many Mexicans north to the United States; refugee camps such as the one at Fort Bliss in El Paso, Texas, accommodated them. (Institute of Texan Cultures)

jobless Arkies and Okies from Arkansas and Oklahoma migrated to Arizona and California, exacerbating already poor employment conditions. Willing to accept even the traditional stoop labor associated with Mexican American farmworkers, these recent arrivals intensified the mounting pressure on the California and U.S. governments to stop or even reverse the Mexican immigration flow. The Mexican American population declined by nearly 500,000 persons during the 1930's. Many immigrants, including families with American-born children, were forcibly deported, or "repatriated," by the federal government (*see* DEPORTATIONS, EXPATRIATIONS, AND REPATRIATIONS).

Most of those who remained in the United States faced hard times. Western produce growers paid the workers less than a subsistence wage, and the Great Plains "Dust Bowlers" added competition for even this miserable pay. Living conditions remained squalid in the barrios of cities. Already poorly educated and overcrowded in segregated schools, Chicanos faced increasing discrimination in education. The demands of World War II made conditions both better and worse.

World War II. War exigencies and federal antidiscriminatory policies in the defense-related industries opened new job opportunities for Chicanos in the West. Previously a largely rural population, they joined other Americans in a national trend of migration to the cities, where jobs existed. Southern California urban centers, with their shipyards and aircraft factories, soon swelled with both documented and UNAUTHORIZED WORKERS. The need for seasonal farmworkers inspired the BRACERO PROGRAM, sponsored by the U.S. and Mexican governments. The program recruited and employed tens of thousands of temporary Mexican laborers during and following the war. Meanwhile, large numbers of Chicanos from southwestern and western barrios and rural towns donned American military uniforms, in primarily segregated units, to fight the Axis Powers.

Despite this entry into the mainstream, frustrations continued. Labor unions and company officials found ways to effectively block Latinos from industrial training programs and job advancement. The bracero program failed to deliver on its promise of fair wages, a minimum number of working days, and decent housing. De facto segregated public schools in highly concentrated Chicano areas limited real educational opportunity for children. Mexican American soldiers fought valiantly and often heroically on the European and Pacific battlefields but realized that the United States was not always the land of opportunity to minorities at home.

These railroad workers are returning home to Mexico in 1946 after filling U.S. jobs left vacant during World War II. (AP/Wide World Photos)

Black-white racial violence flared, and bloody riots erupted in cities such as Detroit, Michigan. Chicanos were also victims of violent white outbursts. The most notable incident occurred in 1943, when white servicemen from a nearby military installation terrorized Latinos in Los Angeles in the so-called zoot-suit riots after hearing about an alleged Mexican American attack on a white sailor (*see* SLEEPY LAGOON CASE). These self-styled "federal vigilantes," soon joined by civilian ruffians, targeted PACHUCOS, young male Latinos who wore the popular "zoot suit," for brutal beatings. Chicanos retaliated, subjecting themselves, rather than the white instigators, to harsh police treatment and arrests. Similar disturbances against zoot suiters erupted in other cities. Such incidents fueled black and brown resentment of police and government during the 1940's and helped to shape postwar African American and Chicano civil rights activism.

Early Organizing Efforts. For many Latinos of the twentieth century, confronting discrimination and prejudice constituted almost a daily ordeal. Although not subjected to the pervasive Jim Crow laws and racist policies that oppressed southern blacks, Chicanos chafed under a system that forced them to occupy the same low political, social, and economic status. They began organizing to eliminate the proscriptions long before the crucial decades identified with the modern Civil Rights movement.

Efforts to organize Mexican American workers to secure higher pay, better working conditions, and equal treatment, for example, date back to the late nineteenth century. Numerous regional organizations such as Arizona's ALIANZA HISPANO-AMERICANA sought secondarily to advance Chicano civil rights, especially in education, during the World War I era. At the same time that Mississippi-born Ida B. Wells heroically criticized the southern practice of lynching blacks, a Laredo, Texas, newspaper editor named Clemente Idar was equally strident in his crusade to end this ugly crime against Mexican Americans.

In 1929, the LEAGUE OF UNITED LATIN AMERICAN CITIZENS began its pioneering work to win justice and advancement for Chicanos in all aspects of social, political, and economic life. In the late 1940's, California's Unity Leagues and the COMMUNITY SERVICE ORGANIZATION mobilized Latinos to encourage their participation in the political process.

These early organizations and leaders achieved varying degrees of success. Their work helped pave the way for more substantial progress after World War II. In the forefront of the activism were war veterans such as Héctor Pérez GARCÍA, who refused to return from fighting Nazi racism in Europe only to accept it at home. Through various organizations including the AMERICAN G.I. FORUM, the Council of Mexican American Affairs, the Association of Mexican American Educators, the League of United Latin American Citizens, the MEXICAN AMERICAN POLITICAL ASSOCIATION, and the POLITICAL ASSOCIATION OF SPANISH SPEAKING ORGANIZATIONS, a new generation of leaders pushed an agenda of Chicano rights and cultural unity that mobilized their communities and promoted a greater awareness of discrimination against Mexican Americans.

Rise of the Chicano Movement. Chicano leaders supported many of the campaigns of the larger Civil Rights movement that led to major legislative victories. Although measures such as the CIVIL RIGHTS ACT OF 1964 outlawed overt de jure discrimination against racial and ethnic minority groups, young activists became frustrated over the lack of substantive changes in their communities. Militants challenged the traditional civil rights leadership and its nonviolent philosophy, believing that a more aggressive approach would produce quicker and better results. In the black community, this militancy manifested itself in the slogan "Black Power" and the formation of organizations such as the gun-wielding Black Panther Party.

Young Chicano activists, especially students, experienced similar disillusionment and organization. They saw little value in the slow process of court litigation, such as the work of the MEXICAN AMERICAN LEGAL DEFENSE AND EDUCATION FUND aimed at eliminating barriers to political participation.

"Brown Power" became the rallying cry among Chicano militants who sought greater political and economic control over their neighborhoods. They re-

jected the label "Mexican American" as an expression of their identity, preferring instead "Chicano," which soon became popular. Rodolfo "Corky" GONZÁLES, a Denver activist who founded the Cruzada Para La Justicia (CRUSADE FOR JUSTICE), left little doubt about the emerging consciousness movement in his program of community economic and political power tied to cultural and ethnic nationalism. The BROWN BERETS, a paramilitary group resembling the Black Panther Party, appeared in 1967 under the leadership of David Sánchez, Carlos Montez, and Ralph Ramirez. It enjoyed immense popularity in the barrios for its attempts to defend Chicano youth against police harassment and brutality.

Beginning in California in 1968 and then spreading to Chicano communities elsewhere, high school and college students began the push for equal, quality education. They demanded bilingual and bicultural curricula, better facilities, more Hispanic educators, and the adoption of CHICANO STUDIES PROGRAMS. Unmet demands were successfully challenged with walkouts, sometimes called "BLOWOUTS," as well as boycotts, sit-ins, and other demonstration tactics borrowed from the Civil Rights movement. In 1969, student leaders formally organized their various college and university group into the MOVIMIENTO ESTUDIANTIL CHICANO DE AZTLÁN (MECHA) to more effectively air Chicano demands.

César Chávez. Much of this Chicano awakening manifested itself in the urban centers where approximately 85 percent of the population lived. It was the rural organizing efforts of César CHÁVEZ with migrant laborers beginning in the mid-1960's that garnered the greatest national attention for the Chicanos' quest for justice. As a youth, Chávez had himself toiled as a farmworker and experienced the degradation and poverty of migrant work. He became an activist in the 1950's working as a COMMUNITY SERVICE ORGANIZATION agent in California. In 1962, he founded the UNITED FARM WORKERS Association to address the exploitation of rural laborers.

A charismatic figure who espoused Martin Luther King, Jr.'s philosophy of nonviolence, Chávez sought to present the migrants' problems in the context of the national civil rights effort. Like King, Chávez led marches to dramatize the migrant workers' plight and demands. He was more effective, however, in mobilizing national sentiment in their favor by organizing consumer boycotts. In 1965, he launched direct action against California grape, lettuce, and other growers in La Huelga (the strike) against producers who refused

César Chávez focused attention on farmworkers' rights. (AP/Wide World Photos)

union demands for better wages and working conditions.

Chávez won recognition of his union and major concessions from some California growers and obtained state laws stipulating collective bargaining rights for organized field hands. Like King, Chávez was revered as a hero; he is the best-known symbol of the CHICANO MOVEMENT.

Impact. The Civil Rights movement provoked a domestic crisis as disadvantaged and oppressed groups forced Americans to face the issues of RACISM and discrimination (*see* DISCRIMINATION, BIGOTRY, AND PREJUDICE AGAINST LATINOS). Chicanos were one of several minority groups who helped to sensitize the nation and demand that the liberties of the Declaration of Independence be extended to all people. Change often came slowly and grudgingly, but it did come. Enhanced voting rights, increases in the number of Chicano and Latino elected and appointed officials, better jobs, a stronger economic status, the establishment of Chicano studies programs, more equitable educational opportunities, and a stronger sense of ethnic identity all attest the success of the Chicano movement. Problems persist, but however short the organized movement fell in realizing its goals, it ultimately made life better for Chicanos, as well as the broader Latino population. —*Robert L. Jenkins*

SUGGESTED READINGS:

• Acuña, Rodolfo. *Occupied America: A History of Chicanos.* 3d ed. New York: Harper & Row, 1988. One of the best accounts available. Particularly useful for understanding the modern period.

• Daniels, Cletus. "César Chávez and the Unionization of California Farm Workers." In *Labor Leaders in America*, edited by Melvyn Dubofsky and Warren Van Tine. Urbana: University of Illinois Press, 1987. A scholarly portrait of Chávez emphasizing his role in the larger labor movement.

• Mazon, Mauricio. *The Zoot-Suit Riots: The Psychology of Symbolic Annihilation.* Austin: University of Texas Press, 1984. A comprehensive study of one of the important wartime outbursts of racism and violence.

• Meier, Matt S., and Feliciano Rivera. *Mexican Americans, American Mexicans.* Rev. ed. New York: Hill and Wang, 1993. An easily read, competently organized survey discussing the major personalities, issues, and events of Chicano history.

• Moquin, Wayne, and Charles Van Doren, eds. *A Documentary History of the Mexican Americans.* New York: Praeger, 1971. An excellent collection of documents that gives a good understanding of Chicano history to 1970.

• Servín, Manuel P., ed. *The Mexican Americans: An Awakening Minority.* Beverly Hills, Calif.: Glencoe Press, 1970. An anthology of Mexican American history with emphasis on twentieth century Chicano consciousness.

Clemente, Roberto (Aug. 18, 1934, Carolina, Puerto Rico—Dec. 31, 1972, near Carolina, Puerto Rico): Baseball player. Clemente was among the best players in baseball history. He spoke up boldly for fair treatment of Latin American players and attempted to improve life for the youth of Puerto Rico throughout his career. He died in an airplane that crashed on its way to deliver food and supplies to earthquake victims in Nicaragua.

As a boy, Clemente and his friends played baseball with balls they made from golf balls, string, and tape. Before he was graduated from high school, he was playing for the Santurce, Puerto Rico, baseball team. In 1954, at nineteen years of age, he signed a contract to play with the Brooklyn Dodgers. Perhaps because of unwritten restrictions on the number of black players on a team, Clemente spent the season with a Dodger farm team in Montreal. The Pittsburgh Pirates drafted him at the end of the year, and for the rest of his career he was a Pirate.

Clemente's first five years with Pittsburgh were good, but from 1960 through 1972 he was exceptional. He hit for excellent averages with good power, ran the bases well, and intimidated opposing runners with his spectacular throws from right field. His lifetime batting average with the Pirates was .317, and he had exactly three thousand career base hits, even though he was still near the peak of his career when he died. He won the Gold Glove Award, given each year to the best defensive player at each position, every year from 1961 to 1972. He was a National League all-star twelve times, won four batting championships, and won the National League Most Valuable Player Award in 1966. He played on two world championship teams and was chosen as the most valuable player of the 1971 World Series.

Clemente came into the National League shortly after Jackie Robinson became the first black man to play major league baseball. Prejudice against black players was still intense. As a black Spanish-speaking player, Clemente had both color and language problems. As a result of his experience, he became an outspoken critic of the treatment of Latin American

Roberto Clemente. (AP/Wide World Photos)

ballplayers. His voice was instrumental in the gradual and continuing struggle to correct inequities and prejudice.

Clemente returned to Puerto Rico between baseball seasons and worked to improve conditions for young people there. In the winter of 1972, his humanitarian instincts were touched by the tragedy of an earthquake in Nicaragua. He participated in gathering food for distribution to the earthquake victims and boarded the airplane scheduled to deliver it. The plane crashed off the coast of Puerto Rico, and everyone aboard was killed.

The National Baseball Hall of Fame mandates that five years pass after a player's retirement before he can be considered for membership. In 1973, the Hall of Fame committee voted to forgo that requirement and to enshrine Clemente as one of baseball's greatest players. Clemente set an example for Puerto Rican and other Latin American youth as a ballplayer determined to be the best and as a person determined to do his best for others.

Clifton-Morenci strikes (June 1-11, 1903; Sept. 11, 1915-Jan. 25, 1916; July 1, 1983-late 1986): Labor disturbances. The Clifton-Morenci district of Arizona is an important copper-mining area. Workers in the district, many of them Mexican Americans, have often called strikes. The most important occurred in 1903, 1915-1916, and 1983-1986.

On March 13, 1903, Arizona territorial governor Alexander Brodie signed a law reducing the workday for miners to eight hours. Mine operators in Clifton and Morenci responded by cutting pay. Although they had no union, the miners walked out on June 1. Troops were sent to Morenci at the request of the copper companies. Anglo workers did not cooperate with the strike, and a flash flood on June 9 dampened the spirits of the striking workers. A court order forced the miners to return to work on June 11.

In 1915, the Western Federation of Miners (WFM) attempted to organize miners in the district. Workers were displeased with the disparity in pay and working conditions between Mexican and Anglo workers. In addition, wages for all workers had remained low even as company profits were rising. On September 11, 1915, workers called a strike.

Governor George W. P. Hunt ordered the state militia to keep strikebreakers out of Morenci. Greenlee County Sheriff James G. Cash deputized striking workers to guard the mines. Federal officials met with representatives of both sides in El Paso, Texas, but

Dodge hired permanent replacement workers and began firing strikers. Governor Bruce Babbitt provided heavily armed troops and police to protect strikebreakers and guard the mines. Phelps Dodge, which owned most of the housing in Morenci, evicted strikers. At the strike's end in late 1986, the unions were defeated.

Mexicans and Mexican Americans have been central in the history of labor movements in the Clifton-Morenci district, both as workers and as leaders. The quick end to the 1903 strike showed that laws supporting workers were not effective as long as corporations had influence in the courts. Some consider the 1915-1916 strike to have been a success because no strikers were seriously injured or killed, because the governor and local sheriff supported the strike, and because it ended wage discrimination against Mexican workers. Others argue that the final agreement was no better than what the companies had offered at the beginning of the strike.

Because of the relative strength shown by labor in the 1915-1916 strike, the copper companies became more united in their opposition to labor, leading to the BISBEE DEPORTATIONS of 1917. The 1983-1986 strike was weakened by government support for management. The failure of the strike effectively ended union representation in the district. Many miners lost their jobs and their homes.

Clothing: Traditional Latino clothing is a mixture of colonial Spanish and native Indian styles worn as national costume in the countries of Latin America. The Spanish colonial costume is virtually identical in each Latin American country, but Indian folk dress varies.

Spanish Colonial Dress. Spanish colonial clothing from the eighteenth and nineteenth centuries has become traditional fiesta wear for Latin Americans and North American Latinos. Men wear a linen or cotton shirt and *calzoneras* (long pants) or knee breeches.

A couple wearing variations on fiesta clothing. (Security Pacific Bank Collection, Los Angeles Public Library)

Performers in clothes from various periods. (Security Pacific Bank Collection, Los Angeles Public Library)

Over the shirt is worn a short jacket; a brocade, velvet, or satin waistcoat (vest); and a brightly colored sash with beaded or fringed ends. The outfit is completed by shoes or boots, a wide-brimmed hat, and a *SARAPE* or poncho (blanketlike overwrap worn instead of a coat). A man dressing in the *VAQUERO* (cowboy) tradition adds protective leather leggings, spurs, and a brightly colored neck scarf.

The *calzoneras* and jacket are often decorated with intricate designs made of gold or silver braid. Sometimes the outer seam of the *calzoneras* is not stitched shut but instead is fastened by silver, gold, or ribbon lacing or by small metal buttons. The edges of the outer seams are often lined in a contrasting color.

Women wear a form-fitting bodice with short or long sleeves and a ruffled or flounced skirt, often made of satin or lace. Layers of petticoats or a single hooped petticoat hold the skirt away from the body. The skirt usually covers the ankles, but it may be worn shorter

for dancing. Accessories include silk neck scarves, lavishly embroidered shawls with long, silky fringe, and flowers worn in the hair or pinned to the dress. The entire costume is vividly colored.

Unmarried women wear their hair down or in two braids, while those who are married wear their hair up, often with ringlets framing the face. Their hair is covered by a *REBOZO* (a cotton, lace, or silk veil). Black *rebozos* are traditional for married women, and white or colored *rebozos* for unmarried women. For dance costumes, a *mantilla* (an ornate lace veil) replaces the *rebozo*. Generally, the *mantilla* covers a high, carved comb that is worn on top of the head, toward the back. The *mantilla* is arranged so that most of it falls behind the head, with a small flounce in front. *Rebozos* and *mantillas* are removed indoors, except in church, where head coverings for women are traditional. Other accessories include strings of pearls or glass beads and a lace or silk folding fan. Shoes are either pumps with

A Guatemalan woman weaving cloth. (Cleo Photography)

a low-to-medium heel or flat slippers held on by criss-crossing ribbons.

Indian Clothing-Making Techniques. The native peoples of Latin America share many clothing-making techniques. Garments are cut in simple shapes and rely on embroidery, hand-weaving, appliqué, and dyeing for their decoration. Because men from Indian villages often travel far to find work and come in contact with other cultural groups, their clothing tends to be more Westernized and less distinctive than that of Indian women, who usually stay in their home villages.

Plants that provide fibers to weave into cloth include the palm tree, agave plant, and yucca bush. Thread can also be spun from wild silk, rabbit hair, and feathers. Bark is stripped from wild fig trees, is soaked in water, and is then beaten to make barkcloth. For the most part, however, ready-made cotton, wool, and synthetic fabrics have replaced homemade cloth.

Natural dyes are made from flowers, fruits, bark, roots, and leaves. Red and red-orange dyes come from ACHIOTE seeds, red-violet and lavender dyes from the fuchsia plant, and blue-black dyes from the indigo plant. Another shade of orange is made from the ground shells of the cochineal beetle. Vivid synthetic dyes in pinks, reds, greens, purples, yellows, and blues are also used.

Ombré dyeing and overdyeing are popular techniques. *Ombré* refers to yarn or cloth that has been repeatedly dipped in dye in such a way that the color is darker at one end than at the other. Fabrics that have been purchased already dyed are often overdyed (redyed) in a different color to give them a more appealing hue or to make a collection of different fabrics coordinate with one another.

Hand-woven fabric is made on a loom. Backstrap looms are popular because they are so portable. The backstrap loom is attached to a pole, a tree, or even the weaver's big toe and can be moved at any time; floor looms are too large to be moved easily. Weaving is often considered women's work, but men do the weaving in some villages.

Embroidery is used to personalize store-bought cloth and to hide seams. Birds, flowers, and geometric motifs are the most traditional designs. *Randas*, wide bands of satin-stitch embroidery, are used to hide seams. Skirts and pants are not as highly decorated as blouses and shirts.

Appliqué (the use of fabric designs stitched to an underlying piece of cloth) is also traditional. The appliqué technique called *mola* is especially favored by Guatemalan and Panamanian Indians. *Mola* is created by layering different colors of fabric together, stitching elaborate patterns, and cutting away the layers in places to make a multi-colored design.

Mexican Folkwear. Spanish colonial dress and native Indian costumes are commonly worn in Mexico. Indian women wear a wraparound skirt called an *enredo*, a sash to hold the skirt in place, and a *huipil*, a short tunic worn like a blouse or dress. In some areas, the skirt is bunched together in back to form a fabric shelf (*rollo*) used for carrying a child or bulky items. Women's sashes are believed to have health-related benefits (especially during pregnancy) because they support the stomach. *Rebozos* are very common because they can be used as shawls or veils. For festivals, women coax their hair into horn-like rolls worn on the sides of the head, crowns of braids woven with ribbons, or simple buns. Flowers, silky cords, pom-poms, and beads are all used to ornament the festival hair-styles.

The traditional costume of Mexican Indian men has almost been lost as a result of contact with other cultures. It most commonly consists of *calzoncillo* (long pajamalike pants) or mid-calf-length trousers, an embroidered shirt, a sash, a straw sombrero (wide-brimmed hat), and sandals made from leather or woven plant fibers. Often the trousers and shirt are white, and the sash is red. For warmth, a *sarape*, *gabán*, or *jorongo*—blanketlike overwrap—is worn draped around the body. The *gabán* and the *jorongo* each have an opening for the wearer's head.

Central American Folkwear. In Costa Rica, El Salvador, Guatemala, Honduras, Nicaragua, and Panama, the two styles of folk dress are Spanish colonial and Indian. In Belize, Indian- and African-influenced styles are more common than Spanish. The greatest variety of styles, however, can be found in Guatemala and Panama.

Guatemalan Folkwear. Guatemala is famous for its many distinctive Indian costumes. Guatemalan folkwear is highly esteemed by textile collectors for its bold colors, expert weaving techniques, and highly skilled use of appliqué stitching.

The women typically wear a *huipil* (a cross between a blouse and a poncho), a *refajo* or *corte* (a skirt without a waistband), a *faja* (sash) that holds up the skirt, a *tzute* (shawl), and a woolen headdress or woolen cords woven into their hair. The headdresses have several names—*tocoyal*, *tupui*, and *cinta*. If the skirt is made from a single piece of fabric wrapped around the body, it is called an *envuelton*; if it is made from a single piece of pleated fabric, it is called a *plegado*. The *tzute* is worn tied in front with a square knot.

This Guatemalan American girl is wearing folk clothing at New York City's Hispanic Day Parade. (Frances M. Roberts)

The men wear *pantelones* or *calzones* (simple pants), a *camisa* (shirt), and a belt or *banda* (sash). White cotton fabric striped with blue is favored for making the *pantelones* or *calzones*. Sometimes men sew red ribbons horizontally across their striped pants, giving a plaid effect. The *camisa* usually is made with a collar, often of the same fabric as the pants. Bandannas are worn under straw hats. Sturdy leather thong sandals (*caites*) complete the outfit.

Some garments are worn by both men and women; these include the *tzute*, the poncho, the *ponchito*, the *manga*, and the *rodillero*. All these are overwraps or shawls that are also used for carrying. Large burdens are carried in a *bolsa* (bag), often worn so that the strap crosses the wearer's forehead; the pouch hangs down the back, leaving the hands and arms free. *Bolsas* are important because Indian garments often have no pockets. Protective goatskins are also common and are worn in back when carrying heavy loads and in front when gardening. Lightweight raincoats are made out of layers of palm fronds woven together into a shaggy fringe.

The garments are decorated with elaborate embroidery that varies by region. Individual villages can often be identified by a distinctive stitchery style. Clothing seams are often covered by a *randa*, a wide band of embroidery. Traditionally, men weave woolen cloth and women weave cotton cloth.

Panamanian Folkwear. Panamanian women have their own version of Spanish colonial dress, the *pollera*, which consists of two pieces: a long, full, flounced skirt and a blouse made of tiers of ruffles or lace. A pom-pom with ribbons hanging from it decorates the center of the neckline. The costume is usually white, with colorful designs appliquéd onto the skirt. When wearing the *pollera*, women braid their hair into a glossy crown festooned with flowers and ribbons.

Panamanian Indian women wear a costume consisting of a skirt, blouse, and sash, brightly decorated with embroidery and trim such as colored braid or *ric-rac* (a zig-zagging braid). Intricate *mola* panels are displayed on blouses made of two panels seamed together or on extra-wide sashes that come up high on the chest. Women wrap strings of beads around their arms and legs to form vivid striped patterns; the bands of beads are called *winis*. Layers of beaded necklaces are worn, as are earrings and, sometimes, nose ornaments. Shawl-like veils are worn to cover the hair.

Dominican participants in New York City's Hispanic Day Parade display native costumes. (Odette Lupis)

Latino Caribbean Folkwear. In Cuba, the Dominican Republic, and Puerto Rico, the Spanish colonial style is worn with some African elements, such as turbans and hip wraps. The Indian costumes common in Central America and Mexico are not usually seen.

In Cuba, there are traditional Cuban dance costumes as well as Spanish colonial dress. Men wear a shirt with long sleeves covered in rows of ruffles. Pants are long and often are decorated with contrasting braid or other trim on the outer seams. The other distinguishing features are a straw hat, with a low crown and a broad brim, and a neck scarf and sash made from cotton or silk. The women's dance costume consists of a full, ruffled skirt, often longer in back than in the front; a bodice with large puffed sleeves; a colorful neck scarf or a beaded necklace; a cotton or silk hip sash; and a cotton head scarf wrapped as a turban.

—Kelly Fuller

SUGGESTED READINGS:
- Cobb, Charles E. "Panama: Ever at the Crossroads." *National Geographic* 169 (April, 1986): 466-493. An overview article that has beautiful color photographs of Panamanian Indians in traditional dress.
- De La Haba, Louis. "Guatemala, Maya, and Modern." *National Geographic* 146 (November, 1974): 660-689. An overview article with many beautiful color photos of traditional Indian dress and Indian costumes associated with religious holidays.
- Dieterich, Mary, Jon T. Erickson, and Erin Younger. *Guatemalan Costumes*. Phoenix, Ariz.: The Heard Museum, 1979. The catalog from a major exhibition of Guatemalan costumes. Included are beautiful color photos, diagrams that can be used to re-create the costumes, and a glossary.
- Mackey, Margaret Gilbert, and Louise Pinkney Sooy. *Early California Costumes*. Stanford, Calif.: Stanford University Press, 1932. An early text that illustrates the strong Spanish influence on Mexican and Mexican American folk dress.
- Oakes, Maud van Cortlandt. *The Two Crosses of Todos Santos*. New York: Pantheon Books, 1951. The history of an anthropologist's two-year stay among Guatemalan Indians. Includes useful black-and-white photographs and detailed costume descriptions.
- Sayer, Chloë. *Costumes of Mexico*. Austin: University of Texas Press, 1985. An excellent book that covers Mexican costume history in depth. Includes color photos, maps, glossary, index, and detailed descriptions of weaving and embroidery techniques.
- Spicer, Dorothy Gladys. *Latin American Costumes*. New York: Hyperion Press, 1941. Virtually the only commonly available book that adequately covers Central America and the Latino Caribbean. Still useful, despite a lack of racial sensitivity.

Coahuila: Spanish colony. Coahuila is located north of Nueva Vizcaya and southwest of Texas. It was one of the last Spanish colonies to be occupied in what later became Mexico. Attempts to settle Coahuila in the 1500's failed, mostly because of the hostility of the natives. In 1674, religious and civil authorities arrived in the area. Farmers and cattlemen soon followed. Coahuila served as the base for the occupation of Texas, and Texas belonged to the governmental jurisdiction of Coahuila until 1722.

Coalition for Humane Immigrant Rights of Los Angeles (CHIRLA): Organization promoting immigrant and refugee rights. CHIRLA was established in 1986 in response to the passage of the IMMIGRATION REFORM AND CONTROL ACT OF 1986. It comprises leaders from the immigration, government, labor, religious, legal, and other fields and works for the fair treatment and advancement of immigrants and refugees. CHIRLA has become an authority on California immigration issues and, through its creation of an immigrant organization network, has developed an exceptional information and referral service. It coordinates community education for both immigrants and the general public through various programs. CHIRLA also serves as a coordinator in bringing together organizations and community members to advance the civil rights of immigrants and refugees through committees specializing in workers' rights, citizenship, legal services, and community and human relations.

Cocoa: Ground beans of the cacao tree, used widely in Mexican cooking. The cacao plant is a native of Central America, and most modern words for its products come from the Mayan word *kakau*. Native Mexican mythology describes cocoa as a gift of the god Quetzalcóatl, and its pre-Columbian culinary use was restricted to the nobles, who were considered Quetzalcóatl's descendants. It was used in ritual drinks and foods, and only after the Spanish conquest was it available to all. Cocoa is simply ground beans (actually seeds) of the cacao tree. Although bitter in its natural state, it becomes edible when sweetened or mixed with strong seasonings. Mexican cooking uses cocoa in many distinctive ways, especially in MOLE poblano (a turkey dish with chile and cocoa sauce) and CHAMPURRADO (a thick, hot chocolate drink).

Code switching: Code switching refers to the alternate use of two languages by one speaker in the same conversation. The phenomenon of code switching is common among individuals who are fluent to some degree in both English and another language. Code switching is difficult to define linguistically and sociologically because researchers define and categorize it differently. For example, one researcher may examine code switching in terms of the speaker's characteristics, such as language proficiency, language preference, and social identity. Another researcher may examine code switching in terms of the functions or purposes achieved by switching from one language to another.

Switching may be done for emphasis, to focus on a topic, to clarify, to elaborate, to attract or retain the attention of an audience, or to introduce a new topic. Code switching can also take place when a new participant who enters the conversation has certain characteristics that are markedly different from those of the person addressed before. Still other researchers examine the elements involved in the code-switching

Code switching is relatively common among Latinos who cross cultures frequently such as these students in a San Antonio, Texas, high school. (James Shaffer)

process, such as the setting, situation, conversational topic, and sex, age, and education of participants, along with their degree of BILINGUALISM.

Code switching can take place on the word, phrase, clause, or sentence level. For example, a person speaking in English may include the Spanish word *puerta* in an utterance rather than the English term "door." A switch occurs when one word or phrase from the second language is used in an utterance of the first language. If, after switching and then speaking in the second language for a period of time, the speaker then switches back to the first language, a "switch-back" is said to have occurred.

Code switching may occur at different points in an utterance, but the speaker unconsciously follows certain syntactical rules. Switching can occur in the middle of the sentence; after markers (which are speech particles, such as English "mmm" or Spanish *pues*); in utterances where pauses occur; when the topic being discussed is more relevant to one language than to the other; at the word level, where the speaker does not have equal or near-equal proficiency in both English and the other language; and between and within turns of speaking.

Researchers agree that code switching carries meaning and that there are many types of code switches. Code switching occurs in the speech of children as well as in that of adults. Research on code switching has focused not only on how bilingual speakers code switch but also on why they do this and on who code switches. Furthermore, sociolinguists have studied speakers' attitudes toward code switching. Some have discovered that code switching is considered by some speakers as a sign of linguistic decay. In other words, some people consider speakers who code switch to lack proficiency in either language. For other speakers, code switching has become yet another way to communicate. Researchers continue to examine bilingual communities, trying to establish reasons for and patterns of code switching.

Cofer, Judith Ortiz. *See* **Ortiz Cofer, Judith**

Coffee: Berry (bean) of an Ethiopian shrub and the beverage made from it. Coffee was domesticated by Ethiopians millennia ago, but Europeans did not easily acquire a taste for it. Only in the seventeenth century did they begin drinking it much, and it was not introduced to the Americas until 1723, when the French planted it on the island of Martinique. From there it spread, and Latin Americans gradually began drinking the infusion made from its slightly fermented beans. Coffee is widely grown in Latin America at higher elevations. Coffee in Mexico is most often drunk with sugar and cream, reflecting the French influence there. Elsewhere in Latin America, coffee usually is drunk black with sugar.

Colección Tloque Nahuaque (Santa Barbara, Calif.): The Latino collection located in the university library at the University of California, Santa Barbara, specializes in twentieth century literature and the arts. Its origins lie in student requests for a Chicano collection.

In 1968, members of UNITED MEXICAN AMERICAN STUDENTS met with the library director to develop a separate collection. In 1969, when Chicanos at the University of California, Santa Barbara, developed a proposal for a Chicano Center, they included their desire to establish a Chicano research library as part of their center. The outcome was a plan to develop two collections: one in the Chicano Center and one in the university library. The former would be oriented toward research, and the latter would be a reading room. The name of the Center-operated library was the Centro Library. The Colección Tloque Nahuaque, founded in 1971, developed into a research collection while the Centro Library remained a reading room. In 1977, the Centro Library merged into the Colección. In the early 1980's, the Colección acquired many archival collections. These collections are now part of the California Ethnic Materials Archive. Its biannual acquisitions publication, *Chicanos: A Checklist of Current Materials*, is widely used by other libraries as a collection development tool.

Collazo, Oscar (1914, Puerto Rico—Feb. 20, 1994, Vega Baja, Puerto Rico): Puerto Rican nationalist. On November 1, 1950, Collazo and Griselio Torresola opened fire on Blair House in Washington, D.C., in an armed assault on President Harry S Truman. The president had been staying at Blair House while renovations were being made at the White House.

The attack by the Puerto Rican nationalists was motivated by a desire to gain support for the independence of their homeland. The governor's mansion in San Juan had been attacked by a nationalist several days earlier. The attacks on Blair House and in San Juan were followed by uprisings that resulted in the deaths of thirty-two people.

Although President Truman was not injured in the attack, Torresola and a White House guard were killed. Collazo was sentenced to death for his role, but his

Oscar Collazo (center, in handcuffs) was sentenced to death for his attempted assassination of President Harry S Truman but was freed by President Jimmy Carter. (AP/Wide World Photos)

sentence was commuted to life imprisonment in 1952. Collazo was freed in 1979 by President Jimmy Carter.

Colón, Jesús (1901, Cayey, Puerto Rico—1974, New York, N.Y.): Writer. Colón published only one work in his lifetime, a widely read collection of autobiographical essays titled *A Puerto Rican in New York and Other Sketches* (1961). Colón left Puerto Rico for the United States at the age of sixteen. Once in New York, he worked at one hazardous job after another. *A Puerto Rican in New York and Other Sketches* consists of essays chronicling his experiences as an immigrant working in New York City and depicts the harsh living and working conditions that most Puerto Ricans in New York City endured.

Unlike his Puerto Rican contemporaries, Colón wrote his essays in English, hoping to reach a wide audience. Colón took an active interest in bettering not only the lives of his compatriots but also those of other working-class people. As a member of the Communist Party, he wrote a column for the *Daily Worker*, a party publication that also published some of the essays that later appeared in his book. He also was president of Editorial Hispánica, a Spanish-language press. Another collection of essays, titled *The Way It Was and Other Writings: Historical Vignettes About the New York Puerto Rican Community* (1993) was published posthumously.

Colón, Miriam (b. 1945, Ponce, Puerto Rico): Director and actress. Colón was reared in her native Ponce and in New York City. She attended the University of Puerto Rico; in New York, she studied at the Erwin Piscator Dramatic Workshop and the Actors' Studio. Her film career began with the 1951 Spanish-language feature *Los peloteros*. In 1967, Colón founded the PUERTO RICAN TRAVELING THEATER, which began as a small company performing on the streets and in community centers in New York's Puerto Rican neighborhoods. The group produced plays by local Puerto Rican writers and offered performances in both English and Spanish. In 1974, the company moved into an old converted firehouse near New York's Broadway theatrical district.

Through her work at the helm of the Puerto Rican Traveling Theater, Colón became known as the first lady of Hispanic theater in New York. Her many stage credits include *The Innkeepers* (1956), *Me, Cándido!* (1965), *The Oxcart* (1966), *Winterset* (1968), *The Passion of Antígone Pérez* (1972), *Julius Caesar* (1979), *Orinoco* (1985), and *Simpson St.* (1985). Colón was

named an honorary doctor of letters by New Jersey's Montclair State University in 1989; the following year, she received the White House Hispanic Heritage Award.

Colón, William Anthony "Willie" (b. Apr. 28, 1950, New York, N.Y.): Bandleader and trombonist. Colón was born to Puerto Rican parents. In 1964, he began his musical studies and formed his first band. He signed a recording contract in 1967 with Fania Records. Colón's first album, *El malo*, was released that same year. His band included two trombone players and singer Hector Lavoe.

Colón employed the *bugalú* style on the popular *El malo* album. He believed in experimenting with various Latin rhythms, and by the 1970's, he had begun using some innovative South American rhythms. In 1972, he released *Cosa nuestra*, which became his first gold-selling album. It included the hit "Che che colé." The song was based on a West African children's song, but Colón added a mixture of many Latin rhythms to enhance the song.

By 1974, Colón had become dissatisfied with the two-trombone sound. Leadership of the band was turned over to Lavoe. In 1975, Colón invited Rubén BLADES to sing with the band, along with Lavoe. The result of this collaboration was the album *The Good, the Bad, the Ugly* (1975). This album is a classic example of what can be done with the New York salsa sound. Colón expanded his horizons in the late 1970's by singing and working with other musicians. He produced and recorded with Celia CRUZ and Blades as well as other important recording artists. His 1982 album with Blades, *Canciones del Solar de los Aburridos*, won a Grammy Award. In Latin America, Colón is considered a cultural hero.

Colonia: Neighborhood of a particular Latino group. A *colonia*, also called a barrio (*see* BARRIOS AND BARRIO LIFE), is a neighborhood inhabited primarily by a particular group of Latinos. The term originated from the immigration experience. Immigrants from a particular country or region tended to settle together, in colonies, within an area of a city. New immigrants often move into low-rent areas of big cities, as was the case of Puerto Ricans in New York City's Spanish Harlem. *Colonias* are often segregated from surrounding society. Businesspeople within the neighborhoods provide vital services, and virtually all ordinary daily needs can be met within the *colonia*. This segregation works to maintain social and cultural institutions such

Willie Colón. (AP/Wide World Photos)

as family structures and ethnic ties. In less urban areas, *colonias* began around agricultural regions, railroads, and other places of work. Many towns of the American Southwest were settled by Mexicans, who developed these towns in the colonial style with marketplaces, churches, and plazas. Some *colonias* are not formally incorporated into cities (though this is becoming less common); they therefore have no formal government and can lack such basic amenities as police and fire protection, electricity, sewers, and plumbing.

Colonial period: The period in the seventeenth and eighteenth centuries during which Spain established a colonial administration. This period saw continued expansion into North America and the introduction of enduring patterns of life in the American Southwest.

Colonial Organization. The Viceroyalty of NEW SPAIN included Central America, Mexico, what is now the southwestern United States, Florida, and the islands of the Caribbean. The institutions established by the Spanish in America reflected the need for the Crown to organize a government, control and religiously convert native populations, exploit the resources of the land, and defend against claims made by other European countries. Success in these enterprises depended on the ability to resolve differences arising from relations with the church and with the colonists.

Both Ferdinand and Charles V exerted great efforts to balance these sometimes conflicting needs during the sixteenth century. The New Laws (1542) attempted to improve the lives of native peoples and to reduce the power of *encomenderos*, Spanish conquistadores who held grants (*encomiendas*) that entitled them to land and Indian labor (*see* ENCOMIENDA SYSTEM). Faced with open opposition from colonists who needed Indian labor, viceroys in both Mexico City and Lima never implemented the laws fully. During the seventeenth century, however, the rights of colonists to bequeath their *encomiendas* were restricted, and the Crown established an elaborate administrative system that separated Spanish colonists from Indian communities.

The *República de los Españoles* included all Spanish communities. It was administered through town councils (*cabildos* or *ayuntamientos*) locally, by governors (*gobernadores*) districtwide, and by a panel of administrative judges (*audencias*) regionally. Although *gobernadores* and members of the *audencias* served under the jurisdiction of a viceroy, all were

This engraving, The First Mass in the Temples of Yucatán, *depicts a scene during Hernán Cortés' conquest in 1519.* (Institute of Texan Cultures)

SPANISH VICEROYALTIES AND CAPTAINCIES GENERAL IN THE COLONIAL PERIOD

NEW SPAIN

Mexico City

Havana

CUBA

SANTO DOMINGO

GUATEMALA

Caracas

VENEZUELA

Bogotá

GUYANAS

NEW GRANADA

Quito

Lima

PERU

BRAZIL (Portuguese)

Rio de Janeiro

LA PLATA

Santiago

Montevideo

Buenos Aires

CHILE

VICEROYALTIES
New Spain
Peru
New Granada
La Plata

CAPTAINCIES GENERAL
Santo Domingo
Guatemala
Cuba
Venezuela
Chile

Source: Information taken from Edmund Stephen Urbanski, *Hispanic America and Its Civilizations* (Norman: University of Oklahoma Press, 1978), p. 97.

appointed directly by the Crown through the Council of the Indies in Spain. This ensured that each level of administration was directly controlled by the Spanish king. It also created conflicts and opportunities for corrupt officials to act without close supervision.

The *República de los Indios*, which encompassed Indian communities, was administered by Indian leaders (*caciques*) subservient to Spanish authority. The CACIQUES were supposed to represent their community, but many found opportunities for graft. By the seventeenth century, Indian communities had been decimated by disease and overwork; the Indian population of central Mexico had shrunk from approximately twenty-five million before the conquest to one million by 1650. Many Indians remained in distinct Indian communities, but others began to migrate to the Spanish cities, haciendas, and mines, where work was available.

The church was an important part of colonial society. In theory, these two peoples—Spanish and Indian—were governed fairly by the Crown, served and protected by the church, and given opportunities for employment. Some of the greatest buildings in New Spain were churches. The cathedral of Mexico City was an architecturally imposing structure that took more than two hundred years to complete. Most charities in New Spain were operated by the church. The two thousand priests and fifteen hundred nuns of the capital ran schools, hospitals, and a women's shelter. The church was also an important economic institution, acting as banker to miners and merchants.

One of the greatest conflicts between the church and the colonial government was the *Tumulto* of 1624, which involved the archbishop of Mexico, Juan Pérez de la Serna, and the viceroy, the marques de Gelves. When the marques de Gelves arrived in Mexico in 1621, he attempted to solve a problem that had produced suffering among the people of Mexico. Corrupt government officials would buy up grain and hoard it until periods of famine, when prices were much higher. Their enormous profits resulted from, and in part caused, the misery of the population.

In his campaign to control food distribution, Gelves closed a slaughterhouse run illegally by the church in the archbishop's palace. When the archbishop objected, Gelves fined him. This led to Gelves' excommunication by the archbishop and an escalating conflict. By the time the conflict had ended, both the archbishop and the viceroy had left. The government thus discovered how serious an opponent the church could be.

Dominican and Franciscan missionaries and priests labored to instruct their Indian charges in religious faith. Many were successful, teaching Indians to be assistants in religious services and training them in ceramics, masonry, and carpentry. Many Indians were employed on church lands or in the building of churches. The priests and missionaries organized each Indian parish into brotherhoods (*cofradías*) to arrange religious celebrations that helped ease Indian villages into Christianity. The very success of the church led to criticism from Spanish colonists, who complained that the church monopolized Indian labor. These colonists urged the Crown to impose taxes or work requirements that would provide them with the labor they needed for their lands and their mines. The REPARTIMIENTO SYSTEM decreed that every adult Indian male had to perform about forty-five days of service each year, usually a week at a time.

The Colonial Economy. Mining was key to the economy of New Spain. Silver was found in Zacatecas, north of Mexico City, and silver mining soon became one of the principal economic activities of New Spain. Soon nearly two-thirds of all silver produced in the world came from Mexican mines and was shipped to Spain. Many mine owners became rich; some used their newfound wealth to obtain titles of nobility. Antonio Obregón, for example, earned two hundred million pesos from his mine at La Valencia. For several thousand pesos, he purchased the title "Count of Valencia."

Estates, called haciendas, sprung up around the mines to provide the food and materials needed. Draft animals were bred and sold to the mines. Cattle produced meat and leather. Maize and foodstuffs were grown and sold to mine owners. Even the king depended on MINING for his 20 percent, or "Royal Fifth," in taxes. So dependent was the colonial economy on mining that serious economic consequences resulted during the seventeenth century, when silver output declined. Some historians refer to the period as the "century of depression."

Indians and MESTIZOS (those of mixed parentage) provided labor for both the mines and the haciendas, although working conditions and treatment were different (*see* HACIENDA SYSTEM). In the mines, Indians and mestizos received wages that were high by local standards. Much of their income, however, was taken by the mine owners for commodities purchased at company stores, and debt peonage was common. On the haciendas, conditions reflected a form of patronage, as landowners would establish close ties with

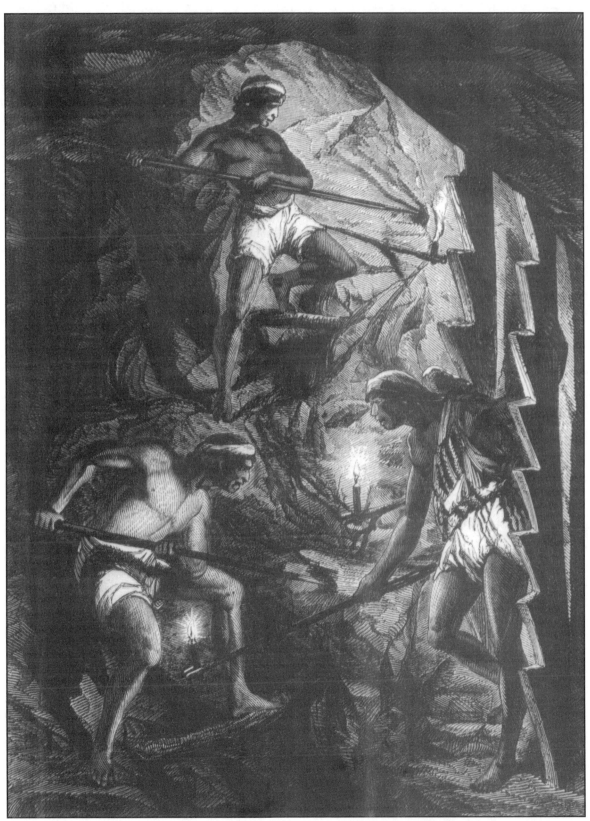

Indians provided much of the labor in Mexican mines. (Institute of Texan Cultures)

their workers, sometimes acting as godfathers of workers' children or loaning money to pay for religious ceremonies. Laborers on haciendas also were often indebted to the owners and not free to leave their service.

Colonial Society. Colonists in New Spain were very conscious of racial purity. Spaniards were the highest social class and looked down on whites born in the Americas. These Creoles were inferior to those born in Spain because of suspicion that their blood was tainted with that of the native Indians. In truth, there were many unions between Spanish conquistadores and Indians, especially in the first decades after conquest. Marriages were eventually discouraged, but many mestizo children were born of Spanish fathers and Indian mothers. Mestizos would become the largest single group in Spanish America. Those mestizos who were part of Spanish society, spoke Spanish, and lived in the city were often skilled artisans who crafted jewelry and built furniture or were peddlers who sold items in the markets. Others, who were more Indian in their appearance and culture, usually became peons on haciendas or in mines. Still others plagued the cities as beggars, called *léperos,* or thieves.

The Spanish of New Spain imported slaves from Africa to perform household duties and to act as overseers of Indian labor. By 1650, there were 150,000 Africans and mulattoes (individuals of mixed, partly African, descent). Africans were an important part of colonial society. Some were treated well by their owners; others were mistreated. Many tried to obtain their freedom, through either purchase or a variety of other legal means or, more rarely, through escape.

One slave, Diego, hoped to use the power of the Inquisition, which had the authority to investigate individuals for unorthodox religious beliefs and punish them for heresy. Overworked by his owner, a priest, the slave blasphemed loudly enough to be taken before the Inquisition, where he pleaded his case. Claiming that he was badly mistreated, he asked for freedom to save his soul. Not all slaves were as enterprising, but most sought their freedom. Those who had skills were often hired out. On their days off, they could work for payment. Many would save their wages and contract with their owners to pay for their own freedom.

Mexico City was the viceregal capital of New Spain and was its largest and most important city, with a population of approximately one hundred thousand. Mexico City contained the palace of the viceroy and fashionable homes of the wealthy, and it was the center of colonial society. Elegantly dressed ladies rode through the city in fine coaches. One observer estimated in 1625 that the city had fifteen thousand coaches, some trimmed with gold and silver.

Ladies traveled to the balls and dances celebrated among the wealthy, or to the theater. The center of social life, however, was the viceregal court. Juana Inés de Asbaje was brought there as a child in the 1650's to serve the wife of the viceroy. A child prodigy, this young woman captivated the court and seemed destined for an excellent marriage. At the age of eighteen she chose instead to take vows as a nun and became Sor (Sister) Juana Inés de la Cruz. She later wrote some of the finest poetry in the history of the Spanish language, corresponded with the greatest minds of Europe and America, and challenged a male-dominated society with her biting and brilliant poetry. Even if chastised on occasion by her superiors for her worldly concerns, Sor Juana served her order faithfully until her death in 1695.

Colonial Expansion and Defense. Although Mexico City was the center of New Spain's government and society and controlled much of its wealth, the viceroyalty stretched south to Panama and north to California. The Crown needed to populate these lands and defend its claims against other nations. Although exploration continued throughout the sixteenth century, it was not until much later that Spain would effectively settle these areas.

In addition to the administrative centers in Mexico City and Santo Domingo, there were *audencias* in Guatemala City, covering Central America, and in Guadalajara (New Galicia), encompassing northern Mexico and California. These fringe areas were difficult to control. Panama was separated from the rest of Central America and would be attached permanently to the viceroyalty of Lima in 1567. The church in Central America was also subordinate to Mexico City until 1743, when an archbishop was appointed in Guatemala.

The Spanish population of Central America remained small and largely confined to the highlands. Spanish society was provincial, although the Dominican college of Santo Tomás in Guatemala was made a royal and pontifical university in 1676. It became well known for its theological studies. Large Indian populations were reduced in Guatemala through overwork, and most natives were subject to Spanish control. Central America experienced numerous Indian revolts as working conditions deteriorated.

In Nicaragua, highland Indians all but disappeared, but the coastal regions, especially in the east, where few Spaniards ventured, was a haven for the Misquito and other tribes. Further south, in Costa Rica, few Indians survived, so Spanish settlers took control of the land, creating small farms. Such smallholdings set Costa Rica apart from other regions because it had no large dominated work force and therefore lacked the strong distinction between rich and poor present in other parts of Central America.

During the seventeenth century, cacao was the major export crop. In northern Nicaragua and Honduras, cattle ranching was a major activity. During the eighteenth century, indigo became the most important crop. A few large landowners controlled much of the crop, leading to solidification of social and economic patterns. The lack of opportunities for immigrants, Indian uprisings, attacks by pirates, famine between 1680 and 1690, and earthquakes made the region uninviting, and it remained a marginal part of Spain's empire.

Economic and political reforms by the Bourbon monarchy in Spain during the eighteenth century brought some important changes. The Crown was determined to improve the colonial administration in Guatemala City. It attempted to reinvigorate the economy by stimulating trade and to halt English encroachments on the coast.

For more than a century, Spain was troubled by English colonies in Central America and along the Atlantic seaboard. English loggers had established permanent camps in Belize in the 1600's. The English took Providence Island, off the coast of Nicaragua, in 1631 and held it for ten years before the Spanish dislodged them. In the 1630's, the English began to exert a presence along the coast of the mainland and developed strong ties with the Misquito Indians.

The northern reaches of Spain's empire were never as important as Mexico City and the wealth that Mexico produced. The periphery had been explored in the

A Mexican family of the eighteenth century. (Institute of Texan Cultures)

sixteenth century and found to be devoid of great native empires or precious metals. Spain's control over much of this area had been tenuous and was strengthened only in the face of encroachment by other European powers.

The Seven Years' War (1756-1763) resulted in several significant changes in the Caribbean and in Spain's North American colonies. When the war ended with the Treaty of Paris, England's presence in Belize was recognized. In return for giving up Havana, the English received Florida; Spain got Florida back for a short time after the American War of Independence. The region was sparsely inhabited and undeveloped throughout the period of Spain's empire.

The French also worried Spain, especially in Florida and along the Gulf of Mexico. The French fort at Pensacola was captured by the Spanish and, in 1763, Spain received the Louisiana Territory from France. José de Gálvez, a royal official, came to America to build up the army of New Spain. He strengthened Spain's forces in New Orleans under General Alejandro O'Reilly. Even though the port and the Mississippi River were controlled by Spain, the territory was not heavily populated. Finally, in 1803, the territory was ceded back to France, which sold it to the United States the same year.

Fray Antonio Olivares, a missionary, was important in the settlement of Texas. (Institute of Texan Cultures)

New Spain in the Southwestern United States. Texas, New Mexico, and California formed the northwestern territories of the Viceroyalty of New Spain. The three interlocking institutions of empire in these areas were the mission, the presidio (fort), and the colonial settlement, in the form first of large haciendas and later, smaller ranchos.

Many of the northern regions were first explored and settled by missionaries. Fray Antonio Olivares began the settlement of Texas. There were few settlers, and those few were concentrated in the northeast, close to French territory. The Indians of Texas were unwilling to submit to Spanish domination, so the territory remained a backwater. Northern Mexico and Arizona were explored by Jesuit missionaries Eusebio Francisco KINO and Juan María Salvatierra. Other missionaries focused on converting as many Indians as possible.

The Pueblo Indians of New Mexico were converted and lived under Spanish protection. The Apache and the Navajo were not subdued. Neither were the Comanches, who tamed the wild horses left by the Spanish. They became excellent horsemen and raided Pueblo communities, which in turn believed that the Spanish were not providing adequate protection to their new subjects. The Pueblo rebelled against the Spanish in 1680, in what is called POPÉ'S REVOLT, and maintained their independence for ten years.

Mission settlements anchored the Spanish empire in North America for many years (*see* MISSION SYSTEM). Many missions were at least partially successful in converting the Indians and establishing stable communities. In these communities, the missionaries taught Indians to perform skilled labor while they attempted to destroy some of the native religious practices they found most objectionable, especially the Snake Dances. Other missionaries faced strong opposition, and many were martyred.

The Spanish found little of interest in California until fear of Russian claims in the eighteenth century led to a string of mission settlements. In 1769, Father Junípero SERRA led Franciscan missionaries into California. They built a string of twenty-one missions between San Diego and San Francisco. These missions, joined by a royal road, the CAMINO REAL, effectively stopped Russia's advance. Nevertheless, California attracted few settlers.

The need for protection as well as fear of foreign encroachments led to reforms in the 1700's that created a line of presidios (*see* PRESIDIO SYSTEM) to guard the frontier. The Royal Regulation of 1772 created new provinces including Newer and Older California,

This cross commemorates the founding of Los Angeles in 1781. (Security Pacific Bank Collection, Los Angeles Public Library)

New Mexico, New Vizcaya, and the Province of Sonora and Sinaloa in the west. In the east, new provinces were established in Texas, Coahuila, New León, and New Santander. These provinces were placed under the authority of a commandant-general, Hugo O'Conor, an Irish mercenary who served long and successfully in Spanish service. O'Conor was ordered to build a string of presidios at about forty-mile intervals as a cordon to guard the northern boundary of Spain's empire. These forts were to be square adobe structures with towers at their corners.

Lacking sufficient funds, the Spanish built too few forts, then undermanned and undersupplied them. The effectiveness of these forts was questionable. Soldiers were usually mestizo recruits from Mexico. Some brought their families and settled them on land nearby. Most of the soldiers were ill-equipped and poorly trained. They were assigned duties outside the presidio in an attempt to make up for the lack of guards at missions and the lack of postal carriers. They could defend themselves against poorly equipped Indians but could not subdue roving tribes or completely pacify their region. They did act as a symbol of Spain's determination to control these vast reaches in the north.

Perhaps the most enduring institution of the Spanish colonists was the cattle ranch. Ranches required large tracts of land and were formed similarly to the haciendas in Mexico that provided food to the mining communities. Cattle ranching on the open plains of the American Southwest relied on VAQUEROS (cowboys) to control vast herds. The roundups and cattle drives of the seventeenth and eighteenth centuries remained largely unchanged by American cowboys until the end of the nineteenth century.

Ranches were generally successful but brought few colonists to the area, and Spanish settlements remained relatively small and scattered. Many farmers found that their lands and crops were destroyed by roaming cattle, a problem that continued for many years. Settlements on the periphery were not well integrated into NEW SPAIN and remained a tenuous part of the Spanish empire.

Smaller properties, called RANCHOS, became common in New Mexico after the Pueblo revolt drove out many of the previous Spanish HACENDADOS. These settlers returned to the Rio Grande Valley, establishing small communities. Most people lived on scattered small clusters of ranchos adjacent to fields or orchards that they tended.

The first civilian settlements in California were SAN JOSE (1777) and LOS ANGELES (1781). These settle-ments were opposed by the missionaries because they represented a threat to missionaries' control over the Indians. Early Spanish settlers required Indian labor and often found the church unwilling to supply a reliable work force. When Spanish colonists could not be induced to settle in these regions, Spain had to rely on a variety of people.

One indication of the difficulties Spanish authorities had in bringing settlers to California is illustrated by the composition of Los Angeles' first group of twelve settlers. Only two were Spanish, and they had Indian wives and mestizo children. Four men were Indian; there were two mestizos, two mulattoes, and two persons listed as "Negros."

Colonial Legacy. Three hundred years of Spanish rule had its impact on Mexico and what is now the American Southwest. Eventually losing its lands in Florida and around the Mississippi River, Spain maintained control over the region from Texas to California. Along with missionaries and soldiers, Spain sent several important scientific expeditions along the West Coast. The first, under Francisco Hernández, traveled through New Spain between 1570 and 1576, studying the flora and fauna of the region.

In 1791-1792, another expedition sailed north along the Pacific Coast. Searching for a passageway connecting the Atlantic and Pacific oceans, Alejandro Malaspina reached the Strait of Juan de Fucha and Vancouver Island. In addition to illustrations of the area and maps, the expedition provided research on native Indian languages along the coast southward to Monterey, leaving an anthropological record otherwise unavailable.

Spain's method of settlement through missions and ranchos had a profound impact on the land and the people. The mission settlements converted many Indians, and the Roman Catholic church is still an important institution in the region. Most of the California missions are now museums and serve as reminders of the importance of missionaries in claiming the West Coast for Spain. The old royal road, the CAMINO REAL, still runs through many modern towns in California. The ranchos established a pattern of cattle raising that North Americans would adopt, and many of the customs, equipment, and words were passed down from Spanish settlers. *Vaquero*, for example, became "buckaroo," and *la reata* became "lariat."

Spanish laws identified the rights of married women, influencing the concept of community property in modern laws, and Spain's empire built towns that served as administrative centers. (*See* LEGAL SYS-

Missions such as this one in Carmel, California, are legacies of the colonial period. (Library of Congress)

TEM, SPANISH/MEXICAN COLONIAL.) San Antonio, Santa Fe, and Los Angeles remain important cities in the American Southwest and contain large numbers of Spanish-speaking citizens. Although most of these people are recent arrivals, others are descendants of the first settlers. Finally, the people—Spaniards, Creoles, mestizos, mulattoes, and Africans—who settled this region became the foundation for the Southwest's Spanish-speaking society, which has contributed much to the development of the region and the country.

—James A. Baer

SUGGESTED READINGS:

• Haring, Clarence H. *The Spanish Empire in America*. New York: Harcourt, Brace & World, 1963. A relatively old but authoritative institutional history of Spanish America, with detailed accounts of offices and duties of imperial institutions.

• Humbolt, Alexander von. *Political Essay on the Kingdom of New Spain*. Edited by Mary Maples Dunn. New York: Alfred A. Knopf, 1972. A classic work by the Prussian scientist, who comments on the society, industry, and organization of New Spain at the end of the colonial period.

• Kandell, Jonathan. *La Capital: The Biography of Mexico City*. New York: Random House, 1988. A thorough but not scholarly book on Mexico that focuses on the capital city. Kandell describes much about life during the colonial period.

• Meyer, Michael C., and William L. Sherman. *The Course of Mexican History*. 2d ed. New York: Oxford University Press, 1983. One of the best textbooks on Mexican history. Covers the era from prehistory, through the Mexican Revolution, until the 1980's. Good chapters on settlement and colonial life.

• Perez-Brignoli, Hector. *A Brief History of Central America*. Berkeley: University of California Press, 1989. This translation of a short but succinct work by a Central American historian covers most of the major themes, from settlement and colonial society to the conflicts of the present.

• Simpson, Lesley Byrd. *Many Mexicos*. 4th ed. Berkeley: University of California Press, 1966. A charming history of Mexico with colorful details. Pages 143-147 present an edited version of the diary of Don Gregorio Martin de Guijo between 1648 and 1664. This excerpt describes floods, hangings, assaults, and processions in Mexico City.

• Weber, David J., ed. *New Spain's Far Northern Frontier: Essays on Spain in the American West, 1540-1821*. Dallas: Southern Methodist University Press, 1979. These essays cover a variety of topics, including settlement, scientific explorations, institutions, and society. Some of the essays are reprints from classic works of the early twentieth century; others reflect up-to-date research.

Columbian exchange: Transfer of plants, animals, and diseases between the Old World and the Americas following Christopher Columbus' voyage to America. The Americas and the Old World were effectively separated between the time of the peopling of the Americas and Columbus' voyage of 1492. During this time, the American Indians developed immunities to local American diseases and domesticated wild American plants. When people from the Old World entered the Americas following Columbus, they brought with them diseases that the Indians were immunologically unable to combat, and the death toll was staggering. Purely by chance, the Americas had few diseases to transmit to the Europeans and Africans who first appeared there, and no comparable epidemic raged in the Old World (*see* EPIDEMICS AND INDIGENOUS POPULATIONS).

In contrast, the exchange of plants and animals for food was favorable to both parties. The Americas provided corn, potatoes, TOMATOES, CHILES, AVOCADOS, SQUASHES, most types of BEANS, COCOA, CHAYOTE, MANIOC, PEANUTS, PINEAPPLES, sweet potatoes, CILANTRO, guinea pigs, and turkeys to the Old World. They received in return wheat, oats, rice, yams, bananas, plantains, garbanzos, peas, COFFEE, grapes, breadfruit, almonds, olives, cinnamon, chickens, cows, pigs, sheep, and goats. Some of these plants and animals revolutionized local cuisine, as evidenced by the importance of potatoes in Ireland and northern Europe and of chickens in Mexico. The impact of some of these new foodstuffs, particularly in Europe and Africa, permitted major population growth following the advent of the Columbian exchange.

Columbus Day: Celebration of Christopher Columbus' landing in the Americas. As of 1994, the holiday was celebrated officially in forty-two U.S. states, in Washington, D.C., and in several United States territories. It is traditionally observed on October 12. Beginning in 1971, many states observed it on the second Monday in October.

The first known celebration of the "discovery" of the Americas was on October 12, 1792. It was held by the Tammany Society in New York, New York. On the same day, in Baltimore, Maryland, a monument to Columbus was dedicated.

The Spanish Columbus Day parade in New York City celebrates Spanish and Latino contributions to American life. (Impact Visuals, T. L. Litt)

Throughout the nineteenth century, numerous statues, buildings, and monuments were erected in honor of Columbus. In the 1860's, Italian communities in New York, Philadelphia, St. Louis, Boston, Cincinnati, San Francisco, and New Orleans began celebrations of Columbus Day. On the four hundredth anniversary, three major events took place: Chicago held the Columbian Exposition; President Benjamin Harrison declared Friday, October 12, 1892, a holiday for the United States; and Francis J. Bellamy, the editor of *The Youth's Companion*, wrote and distributed the pledge of allegiance in order to teach children to celebrate Columbus' achievements. In 1907, Colorado became the first state to declare Columbus Day a holiday. In 1937, President Franklin Roosevelt made it a national holiday.

Many Hispanic people in the United States and throughout Latin America now celebrate DÍA DE LA RAZA (day of the race) rather than Columbus Day. This is a recognition of the MESTIZO race (the race created by the mixing of European and Indian blood) originated during the conquest of the Americas. Many Hispanics as well as native people in North and Central America see Columbus Day as an offensive celebration of a cruel man who brought wealth and power to the Europeans at the expense of the indigenous people, through enslavement, murder, rape, and the elimination of native culture and religions.

The concept of Columbus' "discovery" of America has been rejected by many in favor of the idea of an encounter or meeting of two worlds. This notion has been viewed by some, however, as a request by the victims of the conquest to express solidarity with those who victimized them.

Twenty-two U.S. states, Spain, and several Latin American countries planned celebrations of the five hundredth anniversary of Columbus' arrival in the Americas. The Latin American Catholic Bishop's Conference and other Catholic organizations backed by the Vatican and Pope John Paul II also planned celebrations. These organizations commemorated five hundred years of "evangelization" while calling for a "new evangelization" in Latin America. Many organizations, including the Latin American Justice and Peace Commission, the Mexican-American Catholic Center, the United Nations, and the National Council

Comales have been used for more than 2,500 years. (Ruben G. Mendoza)

of Churches condemned the celebrations. Opposition from Hispanics at the grassroots level came in the form of various convocations, symposia, and declarations.

Comadre: Godmother. The term also indicates a deep friendship between one woman and another. When a Latino child is born, the parents choose a set of godparents for the child. The parents and godparents call each other *compadre* and *comadre* (co-parent). This relationship is one of mutual respect and responsibility, both among the adults and to the child. Being chosen as a *comadre* is an honor. The *comadre* becomes like a second mother to the godchild as well as becoming an accepted member of the godchild's family. A Latino woman may call a close friend a *comadre* even if she is not actually a godmother to that woman's child; the designation indicates a close, trusting level of friendship. Latino women sometimes form groups of *comadres* to discuss personal or social issues with one another.

Comal: Flat cooking griddle in the Mexican and Central American tradition. The *comal* can be traced back to pre-Columbian Mexico and adjacent Central America, where it was a flat, disk-shaped ceramic dish. Modern *comales* are occasionally made of hard-fired pottery, but most are made of cast iron. Many poor people use barrel lids or other scrap metal for *comales*. *Comales* are used primarily to cook corn and wheat TORTILLAS, but they are also used to cook certain kinds of *ANTOJITOS*.

Comancheros: Mexicans who traded with Comanche tribes during the nineteenth century. *Comancheros* was the name given to Mexicans from the Texas and New Mexico region who traveled out to the Great Plains to trade with Comanche tribes. Much of the trade involved the sale of weapons to Comanches. Such trade was made illegal in the 1830's because it affected the ability of the Mexican government to control what it called "barbarous Indians," or *indios bárbaros*:

Apaches, Comanches, and other tribes from the areas surrounding El Paso, Texas, and Santa Fe and Taos, New Mexico.

Comedia: Type of Spanish dramatic genre. Originally, the term *comedia* designated a generic dramatic genre, much like the words "play" in English and *Schauspiel* in German. In sixteenth century Spain, *comedias* were classified as *comedias de noticias* (based on actual events) and *comedias de fantasía* (based on fictitious events). More recently, the term *comedia* has become associated with comic or satirical representations of everyday life, some with purposes such as correction of vices. This style of *comedia* developed into two trends, the vaudeville, with exaggerated comedic aspects, and the *comedia dramática*, centered on social problems.

Comisión Femenil Mexicana Nacional: Women's rights organization. This group was founded in 1970. By the early 1990's, it had more than five thousand members, a staff of three, and more than twenty regional, twenty state, and ten local groups. Its main objectives include advancing the cause of Hispanic women from a feminist perspective. It focuses on all aspects of women's rights, encompassing the political, social, economic, and educational arenas.

The commission maintains the Chicana Service Action Center, which provides job skills training. It also supports and maintains the Centro de Niños (a center for bilingual child development programs) and Casa Victoria (a home for teens). The agency also conducts research and compiles statistical information. Another service the agency offers is a database of women's and Hispanic organizations and national Latina leaders.

Committees specialize in development, education, health/welfare, legislation, reproductive rights, and teen pregnancy. Agency publications include a periodic newsletter, the semiannual *La Mujer*, and an annual report, all of which include statistical and other types of information relevant to the issues with which the agency works.

Committee in Solidarity with the People of El Salvador (CISPES): Founded in 1980. CISPES is a grassroots organization supporting self-determination for Salvadorans and opposing United States intervention in Central America.

CISPES was founded in October of 1980 by Farid Handal, Heidi Tarver, Sandy Pollack, and Suzanne Ross. Gross human rights violations occurred in El Salvador in 1980, including the murder in March of

Archbishop of San Salvador Oscar Romero as well as the rape and murder of four United States churchworkers in December by rightist military forces supported by the United States. These violations of human rights aroused indignation on the part of many American citizens. CISPES was born out of the belief that American tax money should not be used to support an unpopular and violent government and that the United States should maintain a policy of nonintervention in the Salvadoran civil war.

CISPES is devoted to the dissemination of information regarding human rights abuses committed by the military in El Salvador, with a goal of pressuring the U.S. government to end military aid to the region. It has organized demonstrations in cities around the United States and sponsored tours by Salvadoran labor, religious, and human rights activists.

CISPES sought to influence Congress through letter-writing campaigns and demonstrations as well as through the promotion of local government resolutions concerning El Salvador. CISPES actively campaigned in the presidential elections of 1984, 1988, and 1992, succeeding in making noninterventionist politics one of the central issues debated. In November of 1989, the murder of six Jesuit priests and their two housekeepers by the military once again brought Salvadoran human rights violations to the forefront. These violations undermined congressional support for the government of El Salvador.

Although CISPES did not succeed in ending U.S. aid to El Salvador during the course of that country's civil war, the group was the primary force fueling public sentiment against such aid. It succeeded in ensuring that military aid be contingent upon improvements in human rights in the region and direct negotiations between the two sides in the conflict. Many congressional leaders supported the movement. Their efforts, as well as the regular protests and demonstrations, letter-writing campaigns, and teach-ins, were able to shape public opinion.

A tremendous influx of refugees from Central America into urban areas of the United States occurred during the 1980's. Groups such as CISPES have had a large effect on treatment of these refugees, with resulting effects on Hispanic communities. CISPES members campaigned to allow Salvadoran and other Central American political REFUGEES to remain in the United States rather than risk their lives by returning to their home countries. With the end of the Salvadoran civil war in 1992, CISPES turned its attention to obtaining material aid for the war-ravaged country.

CISPES was instrumental in bringing attention to conditions in El Salvador. (James Shaffer)

CISPES has its national headquarters in Washington, D.C. In the early 1990's, more than one hundred local groups existed around the country. In addition to its advocacy and educational programs, CISPES publishes pamphlets and holds conventions twice yearly.

Communal property: Ownership of land or other property by a large group. The European concept of private property was foreign to most Native American tribes. Although personal effects such as weapons, works of art, and clothing were owned by individuals and in some cases inherited by the next generation, ownership of land and food was either communal or entirely absent.

Many Indian tribes were nomadic; to them, the ownership of land was a meaningless concept. Among those tribes with permanent homes and long-lasting buildings, individual housing units were often owned by family units; even among these, however, there were exceptions. Many northeastern tribes, for example, lived in communal longhouses. In virtually all cases, the land itself was either considered to "belong to itself" or to be owned by a tribal unit. Hunting and farming were communal tasks, and food was stored in common areas, used as needed by all tribal members.

Early Contacts. When the conquistadores arrived in the Americas, they brought with them a long tradition of private ownership. Typically the first symbolic gesture of Europeans landing on American shores was to claim the land in the name of their king or queen.

Gradually, as the explorers became settlers, they established European traditions in the new lands. The difference in concepts of land ownership was a significant factor in the relative ease of early conquest: Many Indian tribes were willing to sell their land for trivial amounts of real goods, as they did not believe that they owned the land in the first place.

Some modern Latinos, many of them descended from Indians, have retained elements of this concept of communal property. That largest single group of Latinos in North America is of Mexican descent. Many are migrant workers who have adopted an attitude toward the land that is very close to that of the original natives. They build temporary shelters or live in shelters built for them by farm owners and they move on with the harvest.

Among both rural and urban Latinos, the extended family and associated living arrangements are common. Adult siblings and their families may share a house or apartment, and more than two generations might live together.

Another interesting parallel is the "rotating credit" system used by many Latino communities, most notably Puerto Ricans in New York. Every family periodically contributes a certain amount of money to a fund with periodic withdrawals by the members on a rotating basis. The money is owned by all members.

Communities Organized for Public Service (COPS): Community activist group. COPS was organized in San Antonio, Texas, in 1974. Its founders included Bishop Patricio Fernández FLORES, a religious activist, and Ernie CORTÉS. Their goal was to establish a group of parishioners to work for social change in Mexican American communities. COPS trained its leaders at Saul Alinsky's Industrial Areas Foundation in Chicago, which advocated confrontation as a means of social change. COPS differed from other activist groups of the 1960's in its heavy use of electoral politics to achieve goals. It lobbied for more state funds for local schools, worked toward electing progressive candidates to the city council, and lobbied the city council to provide better infrastructure in Latino neighborhoods. COPS served as a model for its sister organization in Los Angeles, UNITED NEIGHBORHOODS ORGANIZATION.

Community Service Organization: Mexican American self-help association. The Community Service Organization, founded in the late 1940's in Los Angeles, California, was instrumental in the 1948 election of Edward ROYBAL as the first Hispanic member of the Los Angeles City Council in the twentieth century. The organization spread throughout California and the Southwest.

The organization's main agenda includes political activism, including voter registration drives, organiz-

COPS focused on working within the political system. (Institute of Texan Cultures)

ing citizen classes, and lobbying to various community, state, and national power brokers. It has been responsible for getting governments to approve infrastructural improvements in many Hispanic barrios and for legislative gains. In the California state legislature, the Community Service Organization won many legislative battles, including that for old-age pensions for noncitizens.

Some leaders of the primarily urban group have moved to farm-oriented organizations. Among them are César CHÁVEZ and Dolores HUERTA. During the 1960's, the organization suffered from withdrawal of funding by the Industrial Areas Foundation. In addition, other organizations competed with the Community Service Organization for members. When community attitudes moderated in the 1970's, the organization won back members from some of its more radical and activist rivals.

Commuters and guestworkers: Primarily residents of Mexico who regularly cross the border to work in the United States. Other Latinos also commute between the United States and their home countries, notably Puerto Rico and the Dominican Republic.

The classic example of Latino guestworkers is the BRACERO PROGRAM, which operated between 1942 and 1964 as a result of formal agreements between the U.S. and Mexican governments. The program recruited Mexicans for farm labor in the United States on six-month contracts, particularly in the agricultural regions of California and Texas. Migrants were employed during the harvest but were expected to return home when it ended. Many braceros stayed and became undocumented residents. Other Mexicans not in the Bracero Program entered the United States illegally because temporary visas were in short supply. Although the Bracero Program aimed to curb illegal migration, it unwittingly stepped up the influx by creating a seasonal pool of labor from across the border.

Puerto Ricans were also recruited as farmworkers, especially in the American Northeast. The history of Puerto Rican contract workers dates to 1900-1901, when thousands were shipped to the sugar plantations of Hawaii. Even more Puerto Rican farmers went to the U.S. mainland after World War II under contracts negotiated by the Puerto Rican government and American agricultural employers. Most were young married men experienced in seasonal agriculture who

Thousands of workers cross the U.S.-Mexico border on a regular basis to commute to jobs; these braceros returned to Mexico in 1949. (AP/Wide World Photos)

commuted to New Jersey, Connecticut, Massachusetts, and other states. The number of Puerto Rican contract farmworkers declined in the 1970's when most migrants flocked to urban rather than rural areas. Still, hundreds of farm laborers move from the island to the mainland every year.

Many Latinos with permanent residence status have become commuters. Those with legal documents such as a green card have virtually unrestricted access to the United States, whereas UNAUTHORIZED WORKERS rarely become commuters because they may be caught and deported. Some Mexicans return to their communities of origin several times a year, various times each month, or even daily, as is the case in cities along the U.S.-Mexico border such as TIJUANA and Ciudad Juárez. Most come to the United States for a few months to several years and then return home. Caribbean migrants such as Dominicans and Haitians usually stay longer in the United States because of the higher cost of the journey home.

Commuters face distinct disadvantages in the receiving labor market in the United States. They lack protection of their basic rights as workers, such as overtime pay and grievance procedures. Labor laws governing employer relations with commuter employees are often nonexistent or unenforced. Commuters tend to cluster in low-wage manual labor, such as crop picking, restaurant work, and domestic service. They displace native workers in seasonal and temporary jobs that are held in low esteem by the local population. This, in turn, provokes antagonism from the host society, even though it benefits employers by maintaining low wages and a docile labor force. Finally, because commuters are hard to organize into labor unions, they weaken existing unions by offering an alternative to employers. Because commuters lack control over the terms under which they labor, they constitute one of the most vulnerable segments of the working class.

Compadrazgo: Godparenthood. Godparenthood is an important element of Latino family structure, sometimes extending beyond blood relatives, bringing them into the closeness of the family. A child's parents choose *padrinos* (godparents) from relatives or close friends. The godparents have special duties to the parents and to the *ahijado* (godchild), such as sponsoring the godchild's baptism and confirmation and serving as best man and bridesmaid at the child's wedding. If the godchild's parents die, the *padrinos* are expected to act as parents to the child. Similarly, the godchild takes

responsibility for the godparents when they become elderly or need help. Equally important is the relationship between the parents and godparents, who call each other *compadre* and *comadre* (co-parent). *Compadres* and *comadres* have close, lifelong friendships. In times of immigration, *compadres* often supply or help one another find food, access to resources, employment, and other support. *Compadrazgo* serves also to bind communities and neighborhoods together and helps maintain cultural, social, and religious values. Over time, godparenthood has become less important to some Latinos, particularly in large urban areas, but it is still an important relationship.

Company E, 141st Regiment of 36th Division: Infantry division. World War II presented Mexican Americans as well as other Latinos with a rare opportunity to compile a distinguished war record. For many, the risks involved appeared worth the potential benefits in terms of economic opportunity and status in the community.

Latinos fought with great distinction during World War II. Seventeen Hispanic infantrymen were awarded the Congressional Medal of Honor, and many others won the Distinguished Silver Cross, the Silver Star, and the Bronze Star for bravery under fire. Company E, 141st Regiment of the 36th Division, contained an infantry company composed entirely of Spanish speakers, primarily from El Paso, Texas, and the surrounding area.

Comprehensive Employment and Training Administration (CETA): Federal agency created in 1973. CETA was responsible for overseeing all government-funded training and employment programs. Under CETA, the government provided many block grants to state and local governments, allowing them to make more decisions about what kinds of programs would be funded. Because the agency initially did not have to meet affirmative action guidelines, few Latinos or other minorities were consulted about how the funds would be spent. Nevertheless, the agency improved its record for serving the Latino community. This was particularly true during the Jimmy Carter Administration, when CETA programs helped train more than 140,000 Latino youths in 1978 alone.

Despite its successes, CETA was replaced when Congress passed the Job Training Partnership Act (JTPA) of 1983. This act encouraged private employers to provide training services to disadvantaged young people. Some critics complained that the JTPA

CETA and JTPA programs trained hundreds of thousands of Latino youths. (AP/Wide World Photos)

had income-based eligibility guidelines that discriminated against many potential Latino participants. These Latinos did not qualify for the program because they tended to pool their family economic resources and avoided accepting food stamps, thus failing to meet key requirements of the JTPA.

Con safos: Expression used in GRAFFITI. Meaning "same to you" or "forbidden to touch," this expression has PACHUCO origins. Writing *con safos* or "C.S." next to a slogan or insult is meant to reverse its meaning. A signature of *con safos* on a poem, mural, or other work of art is a warning that the work should be respected and is not to be defaced. *Con safos* is also the name of a literary magazine published between 1968 and 1973. The magazine reflected barrio life and served as a major outlet for Chicano literature.

Concepción, Dave (David Ismael Concepción y Benitez; b. June 17, 1948, Aragua, Venezuela): Baseball player. Shortstop Concepción was synonymous with the Cincinnati Reds organization for nearly two decades. He was a key part of the "Big Red Machine" that won consecutive World Series titles in 1975 and 1976; in 1977, he was named team captain.

A superb infielder, Concepción retired with a .972 career fielding percentage and five Gold Glove Awards. He popularized the technique of bouncing long throws to first base on artificial turf in order to reduce arm strain. His stable batting also made Concepción a threat. In 1978, he became the first Cincinnati shortstop to top .300 since 1913, and he also broke the .300 mark in two other seasons. He was also an excellent hitter in postseason play, batting .351 in five National League playoff series and hitting above .300 in three of four World Series.

Dave Concepción stretches to reach a grounder. (AP/Wide World Photos)

Selected to nine National League All-Star teams (1973, 1975-1982), he was honored as the All-Star Game Most Valuable Player in 1982. He also received the 1977 Roberto Clemente Award as the top Latin American major league player. When he retired in 1988 after nineteen seasons with the Reds, he ranked among the club's all-time leaders in runs, doubles, games, hits, and stolen bases.

Concepción de Gracia, Gilberto (July 9, 1909, Vega Alta, Puerto Rico—Mar. 15, 1968, Santurce, Puerto Rico): Political leader. Concepción de Gracia studied business administration and law at the University of Puerto Rico. He earned his law degree at George Washington University in Washington, D.C., and returned home to join the struggle for Puerto Rican independence.

He became active in political organizations with ideologies embracing the concept of a free Puerto Rico. Concepción de Gracia held the concept of independence so strongly that he soon came into conflict with the leadership of the Popular Democratic Party, the organization with which he was most strongly affiliated. In 1946, he led others who shared his vision in organizing the Popular Independence Party. Concep-

ción de Gracia often traveled to New York City, where hundreds would gather to hear him speak of independence for Puerto Rico. His death in 1968 was widely mourned.

Conchas: Yeasty Mexican sweet rolls. A *concha* is a round, slightly spongy bun with a thin sugar topping and a pattern of curved lines radiating from one edge, much like a scallop shell. It is from this pattern that *conchas* derive their name, which means "shells." *Conchas* with a cross-hatched pattern are often known as *chicharrones*, not to be confused with the fried pork rinds of the same name. *Conchas* rise a long time and are yeasty, and they are topped with a mixture of sugar, cocoa, and cinnamon before baking. Available at most Mexican *panaderías*, *conchas* are one of Mexico's best-known *panes dulces*.

Confederación de Uniones de Campesinos y Obreros Mexicanos (CUCOM): Labor union. The CUCOM was established in El Monte, California, in 1933 during the EL MONTE BERRY STRIKE. At the end of the strike, the union negotiated a wage increase for farmworkers. Membership reached five thousand, and the CUCOM was one of the largest California agricultural unions in the 1930's. The union joined the UNITED CANNERY, AGRICULTURAL, PACKING AND ALLIED WORKERS OF AMERICA in 1937. At the end of the 1930's, the union lost membership and force as a result of a glut of farmworkers and aggression on the part of growers.

Confederación de Uniones Obreras Mexicanas (CUOM): Labor union. The CUOM was established in 1928 in Los Angeles, California, as one of the first Mexican American labor organizations. It was organized to protect Mexican Americans from losing their jobs to workers being imported from Mexico by growers. At its peak, the CUOM represented three thousand workers in twenty-two unions. The union quickly declined as a result of the Great Depression. The CUOM is noted for the training it provided to leaders who would later establish other Mexican American labor unions such as the CONFEDERACIÓN DE UNIONES DE CAMPESINOS Y OBREROS MEXICANOS.

Confederación Regional Obrera Mexicana (CROM): Labor union. The CROM was established in Mexico in 1918. It encouraged Mexican laborers in the United States to organize during World War I.

Confianza: Trust between Latinos in interpersonal relationships. *Confianza* means "trust" and is an important underlying factor in Latino relationships, whether personal or business-related. *Confianza* between two parties is a relationship of respect, intimacy, and care. Relationships such as *parentesco* and COMPADRAZGO are based on *confianza*. People who are not kin can act as close family members if they have acquired a deep trust of one another. *Confianza* is particularly important in communities of immigrants, where support systems must be built among individuals who are not necessarily blood relatives.

Conga: Afro-Cuban music/dance genre and instrument. Conga music is in duple time with a syncopation anticipating the second beat. It is danced by couples executing three steps followed by a syncopated forward leap. It is an essential element in *comparsas* (Latin American carnival celebrations), where it is most commonly danced in a line, with the syncopation expressed with a kick or a flick of the foot. It was introduced into Europe and North America in the 1930's and remained popular until the 1970's. Conga drums are long, tapered, single-headed percus-

Students experiment with a conga drum. (Hazel Hankin)

sion instruments played with fingers and the palm of the hand.

Congressional Hispanic Caucus: Legislative service organization founded in 1976 to support the work of Hispanic members of Congress. Members of Congress often work together to advance common causes. Geographical, economic, and partisan concerns often prompt members to band together in legislative service organizations to promote a common interest. The five congressional members of Latino descent came together in 1976 to form the Congressional Hispanic Caucus (CHC), a legislative entity designed to pool their strengths and talents to advance legislation aimed at the nation's Latino community. Edward Roybal (D-California), elected in 1962, advocated the notion that strength comes with numbers. He convinced his Latino colleagues—Herman BADILLO (D-New York, elected 1970), Eligio "Kika" DE LA GARZA (D-Texas, elected 1964), Henry B. GONZÁLEZ (D-Texas, elected 1961), and Baltasar Corrada (D-Puerto Rico, elected 1976)—to join him in the establishing the CHC. Because so few Latinos served in Congress in the 1970's, the CHC set about initially to educate other members of Congress and their staffs about the needs of the Latino community.

Following the 1980 census and subsequent redistricting, the 1982 congressional elections enlarged the CHC to nine members. The 1980's brought the election of the first Hispanic Republican member of Congress, Manuel LUJÁN (R-New Mexico), who later served as Secretary of the Interior in the George Bush Administration, and the first Latina, Ileana Ros-Lehtinen (R-Florida). The CHC participated in a host of legislative initiatives: policies dedicated to eliminating banks' redlining (policies of not lending in certain geographic areas), voting and civil rights initiatives, inclusion in minority contracting for the government, and an elevated status within the Congress during the debate on the IMMIGRATION REFORM AND CONTROL ACT OF 1986.

The Voting Rights Act required that, where possible, states create districts in which the minority population constituted a majority. This would, theoretically, make it possible for more members of minority groups to reach elected office. The 1992 redistricting, based on population shifts indicated in the 1990 census, saw the creation of eight Latino-majority districts, and the 1992 elections pushed the total number of Latinos in Congress to seventeen voting members. The three elected delegates from Guam, Puerto Rico, and the

Virgin Islands could not vote on legislation before the House.

The CHC in the 1990's attained the subethnic, gender, and geographical diversity to make it a legitimate forum for national Latino leadership. The CHC was regularly consulted by the Bill Clinton Administration on a variety of subjects that related to the Latino community. Having educated public officials about the needs and concerns of Latinos, the CHC was able to focus on legislative initiatives and had become

Herman Badillo, shown in 1971 shortly before beginning his first term in Congress, was a founding member of the Congressional Hispanic Caucus. (AP/Wide World Photos)

LATINO CONGRESSIONAL MEDAL OF HONOR RECIPIENTS

Civil War
Philip Bazaar, U.S. Navy
John Ortega

Boxer Rebellion
France Silva, U.S. Army

World War I
David Barkley, U.S. Army

World War II
Lucian Adams, U.S. Army
Macario García, U.S. Army
Harold Gonsalves, U.S. Marines
David González, U.S. Army
Silvestre Herrera, U.S. Army
José López, U.S. Army
Manuel Pérez, Jr., U.S. Army
Cleto Rodríguez, U.S. Army
Alejandro Ruíz, U.S. Army
José Valdez, U.S. Army
Ysmael Villegas, U.S. Army

Korean War
Reginald Desiderio, U.S. Army
Fernando Luis García, U.S. Marines
Edward Gómez, U.S. Marines
Ambosio Guillén, U.S. Marines
Rodolfo Hernández, U.S. Army
Baldomero López, U.S. Marines
Benito Martínez, U.S. Army
Eugene Obregón, U.S. Marines
Joseph Rodríguez, U.S. Army

Vietnam War
Roy Benavidez, U.S. Army
Emilio de la Garza, U.S. Marines
Ralph Dias, U.S. Marines
Daniel Fernández, U.S. Army
Alfredo Gonzáles, U.S. Marines
José Jiménez, U.S. Marines
Miguel Keith, U.S. Marines
Carlos Lozada, U.S. Army
Louis Rocco, U.S. Army
Eurípides Rubio, U.S. Army
Héctor Santiago-Colón, U.S. Army
M. Sando Vargas, Jr., U.S. Marines
Máximo Yabes, U.S. Army

the congressional political power Roybal originally envisioned.

Congressional Medal of Honor recipients: The highest and most prestigious U.S. military award given for valor is the Medal of Honor awarded by Congress. The medal is presented to soldiers, sailors, or air personnel who distinguish themselves by gallantry, at risk of life, above and beyond the call of duty.

The Medal of Honor was created by an act of Congress signed by President Abraham Lincoln on December 21, 1861. This was the first decoration formally authorized by the American government to be worn as a badge of honor. By the 1990's, more than thirty-three hundred members of the U.S. armed forces had been judged to have performed outstanding individual feats of bravery that set them apart from their comrades.

After several alterations since its date of institution, the medal now consists of a bronze five-pointed star resting upon a laurel wreath enameled green. On each ray of the star is a green oak leaf. The center has the head of Minerva in a circle bearing the words "United States of America." It hangs from a bar bearing the word "valor" surmounted by an eagle.

The ribbon is light blue with thirteen white stars. To show its presence over and above all other awards, it is now ordered to be worn around the neck. The complete medal is suspended by a plain blue ribbon fastened to the back of the bar above the shorter ribbon with the thirteen stars.

Latinos did not play a large role in U.S. military forces prior to the twentieth century. They were called on extensively in World War II, and eleven Latinos were awarded the Medal of Honor for their valiant deeds. Nine Latinos won the award in the Korean War, and thirteen received it for service in the Vietnam War.

Conjunto: Band of musicians, or *cumparza* bands. *Cumparza* bands are typical of western Cuba, where during Carnival season they parade the streets dressed in elaborate and colorful costumes, followed by the celebrating crowd. Their musicians play a variety of percussion instruments, including conga drums, MARACAS, and claves. *Conjuntos* later added iron triangles and the jawbone of an ass to their percussion ensemble, providing variety against the background of regular and accented drum beats. From their onset, *conjuntos* have used the human voice as their exclusive melody source. *Conjuntos* gave birth to the CONGA and

In 1948, Conjunto Felix Borrayo, consisting of Felix Borrayo on accordion, Frank Corrales on guitar, and Luis Martinez on bass, performs its daily live show on station KCOR in San Antonio, Texas. (Institute of Texan Cultures)

developed it into what later became a frenzy in the twentieth century.

Constitutional Convention of Puerto Rico: Political meeting. A select group of Puerto Rican citizens met to draft a constitution in February of 1952. The Puerto Rican Constitution and its Bill of Rights contained language that closely followed the original wording of the U.S. Constitution. The provisions of the Puerto Rican Constitution were to take effect within sixty days of its ratification by Puerto Rican voters. Elections of government officials were to be held within six months of its ratification, and a second general election was scheduled to be held in November of 1956. Several resolutions were also passed estab-

lishing the official name of the Commonwealth of Puerto Rico in Spanish and in English. This constitution established a level of autonomy and political accountability in Puerto Rican government and affirmed the country's commonwealth status.

Contradanza: European court dance brought to the Caribbean region through Spain. The original *contradanza* was characterized by two lines of dancers facing each other; they performed intricate figures on the dance floor. With its numerous step variations and figures, the *contradanza* lacked the spontaneity of folk dance of the colonies. Although it retained the floor patterns from Europe, it gained a new identity in the colonies through the interpretations and style given to

Ángel Cordero, Jr., photographed in 1968. (AP/Wide World Photos)

it by the natives of the tropics. The *contradanza* gave rise to the *DANZA*; both coexisted in many regions.

Contratista: Labor contractor. Synonyms for *contratista* include *enganchador*, *enganchista*, and COYOTE. *Contratista* derives from the Spanish word *contratar*, to contract for. Mexican and Mexican American labor contractors played a significant role in bringing unskilled Mexican workers to serve in United States agriculture and industry. Operating as freelance agents or working for railroads, growers' associations, or other U.S. employers, contractors could be found in almost every U.S. border town. Among workers, the labor contractor often had a reputation for sharp deals and cheating. Today the activities of labor contractors are more closely regulated, although some still operate covertly.

COPS. *See* **Communities Organized for Public Service**

Cordero, Ángel Tomás, Jr. (b. Nov. 8, 1942, Santurce, Puerto Rico): Jockey. Cordero, a member of a famous Puerto Rican racing family, became one of the top jockeys in his homeland by the age of twenty. After two failed attempts to break into the U.S. racing circuit, he succeeded in 1965. Under the direction of agent Vince DeGregory, he became one of the sport's leading jockeys by 1968.

Cordero's first Triple Crown win came on Cannonade in the 1974 Kentucky Derby. He followed with a second Derby win and a Belmont Stakes victory in 1976 on Bold Forbes, helping him to become the top money-winning rider for that year (a feat he repeated in 1982 and 1983). He added his name to the record books with a third Derby win in 1985 on Spend a Buck. His Triple Crown record also includes wins in the 1980 and 1984 Preakness Stakes.

Known for powerful finishes, Cordero had a strong desire to win that brought him more than two hundred suspensions for rough riding. He amassed a remarkable career record of more than seven thousand wins (behind only Bill Shoemaker and Laffit PINCAY, Jr.) and more than $160 million in prize money. After a serious riding accident, he retired in 1992.

Córdova, Arturo de (Arturo García; May 8, 1908, Mérida, Yucatán, Mexico—1973, Mexico City, Mexico): Actor. Córdova, a leading Mexican film actor and sex symbol known for his striking good looks and devilish grin, came from a family that went into exile during the Mexican Revolution. He was educated in New York City and Lausanne, Switzerland, and he worked as a radio announcer in Mérida and Mexico City. With the encouragement of film director Arcady Boytler, he began acting in film in 1935. He rose to fame in his native land in such films as *Cielito lindo* (1936), *La Zandunga* (1937), *Que viene mi marido* (1939), *El* (1951), and *Fruto prohibido* (1952).

In 1938, Córdova began working in Hollywood, where he appeared as a leading man in *For Whom the Bell Tolls* (1943), *Hostages* (1943), *Frenchman's Creek* (1944), *A Medal for Benny* (1945), *Masquerade in Mexico* (1945), *The Flame* (1947), *New Orleans* (1947), *The Adventures of Casanova* (1948), and *Kill Him for Me* (1953). His pairing with Betty Hutton in the 1945 feature *Incendiary Blonde* sparked protests by women's groups and an outright boycott of the film in Salt Lake City. Ultimately feeling underused by the U.S. film community, Córdova returned to resume his career in Mexico, South America, and Spain.

Corona, Bert N. (b. May 29, 1918, El Paso, Tex.): Labor leader. Using his skills as an organizer and a sense of how politics and bargaining work, Corona devoted some sixty years to improving the situation of Mexican American workers. In the 1930's and 1940's, he worked to organize Mexican Americans in low-paying cannery and warehouse jobs in Southern California. Later, he helped found the COMMUNITY SERVICE ORGANIZATION and the MEXICAN AMERICAN POLITICAL ASSOCIATION.

In the 1940's and 1950's, Corona was accused by the government of supporting communism, and he found it difficult to get paying jobs. As regional organizer for the National Association of Mexican Americans, he helped fight McCarthyism and the McCarran-Walter Immigration Act. In the 1960's, he served as an adviser to President Lyndon Johnson and campaigned vigorously against the Vietnam War. He had a long tenure as president of the Association of California School Administrators. Although he supported the cause of migrant farmworkers, he differed from César CHÁVEZ by promoting the unionization of undocumented workers.

Coronado, Francisco Vázquez de (c. 1510, Salamanca, Spain—Sept. 22, 1554, Mexico): Explorer. Coronado came to the New World in 1535 to work under Antonio de Mendoza, the viceroy of NEW SPAIN. He rose through the ranks of colonial society quickly, and Mendoza named him governor of the neighboring colony of New Galicia in 1538.

Frederic Remington's drawing of the Coronado expedition to Cíbola and Quivira. (Library of Congress)

When Fray Marcos de Niza returned from a trip to unknown lands in the north, he brought news of a wealthy city, which he called CÍBOLA, that he had seen from a distance. Coronado soon organized a new expedition to these lands.

Coronado's expedition north began in 1540. In July, he reached Hawikuh, a Zuni pueblo in modern New Mexico. His forces attacked the village, and Coronado was almost killed before the Indians were driven away. Although the pueblos were sophisticated settlements, they contained nothing of the fortunes that Fray Marcos had reported.

In 1541, Coronado heard of another land, Quivira, where gold and silver were plentiful. He journeyed to the northeast and, after many hard days of travel through deserts, reached Quivira. The area, in modern Kansas, was beautiful but did not hold the desired gold and silver. The Wichita Indians of Quivira lived in simple settlements of thatch houses. Frustrated and ill, Coronado returned to Mexico, where he met with Mendoza's disappointment for not having stayed to settle the region. Coronado remained in Mexico for the rest of his life, occupying several important civil posts.

Coronel, Antonio (Oct. 21, 1817, Mexico City, Mexico—Apr. 17, 1894, California): Educator and politician. Coronel, a Mexican schoolteacher, made a modest fortune in the California gold fields during the late 1840's. His wealth allowed him to finance his activities as a CALIFORNIO community leader and politician.

Coronel became Los Angeles' first superintendent of schools in 1852, then the city's mayor in 1853. He also chaired the Los Angeles County Democratic Committee. As a member of the Los Angeles School Board in 1854, Coronel unsuccessfully tried to promote bilingual schooling. Coronel also served four terms on the Los Angeles Common Council during the Civil War and became state treasurer in 1867.

Coronel participated in innumerable civic causes before retiring from local politics in the 1880's. He served as a railroad booster, as director of the Spanish-American Mutual Benefit Society, and as adviser to the Los Angeles Centennial Committee. He bought into the weekly newspaper *La Crónica* in 1873 and remained active in its affairs for four years.

Coronel's career illustrates the racial tensions that afflicted California politics in the mid-1800's. For example, local Anglos met his campaign for mayor in

1856 with open slander. The same attitude prevented his appointment as subagent for Indian affairs in southern California in 1853.

Corpi, Lucha (b. Apr. 13, 1945, Jáltipan, Mexico): Poet. Corpi immigrated to the United States in 1964. She is an acclaimed writer of poetry and prose. Her poetry, written primarily in Spanish, focuses on women's roles in the home and society. Arriving in the United States during the peak years of the Chicano movement, she began writing and organizing Chicano arts organizations. She was a founding member of Aztlán Cultural (1971) and Centro Chicano de Escritores (Center for Chicano Writers, 1980), two organizations that extol Mexican American culture and art.

Corpi is best known for her series of four poems titled "The Marina Poems," which first appeared in the English translation collection *The Other Voice: Twentieth-Century Women's Poetry in Translation* (1976). Her first solo publication also contains a version of the series. Widely anthologized, these poems re-examine the life of the historical figure known as La MALINCHE, a Mexican Indian woman who translated for Spanish conquistador Hernán Cortés. Corpi's depiction of La Malinche is more positive and individual than most traditional portraits.

Corpi's work is featured (along with that of Elsie Alvarado de Ricord and Concha Michel) in *Fireflight: Three Latin American Poets* (1976). She has also published the poetry volumes *Palabras de mediodía/Noon Words* (1980) and *Delia's Song* (1988).

Corporate enterprise. *See* **Business and corporate enterprise**

Corpus Christi: Widely celebrated in Mexico, both publicly and privately, the Feast of Corpus Christi is a traditional date on the calendar of the Catholic church. Officially, it occurs on the Thursday following Trinity Sunday, in honor of the Eucharist.

One noteworthy festival associated with the holiday is held in Pala, California, about fifty miles north of San Diego. The festival is held on the first Sunday in June as the Corpus Christi Fiesta at the Mission San Antonio de Pala, in a restored building situated on land that is now an Indian reservation. The celebration includes an outdoor religious procession and Mass, games, dances, a Spanish-style pit barbecue, and other secular entertainment. The event can be traced back to the mission's founding in 1816.

Corpus Christi, Texas: County seat of Nueces County. The metropolitan statistical area of Corpus Christi-Nueces-San Patrico-Kieberg had a population of 257,453 according to the 1990 census. Corpus Christi has a harbor on the Gulf Intracoastal Waterway and is connected to the Gulf of Mexico by a deep water channel.

The city is located on Corpus Christi Bay, which was first sighted by Alonzo ÁLVAREZ DE PINEDA in 1519 on the feast of Corpus Christi. The bay area was settled by Spaniards around 1765. Mexican Americans first settled in the area around 1837, and Anglo-Americans in the 1840's. In 1839, an American, Henry Lawrence Kinney, and his partner, William P. Aubrey, established a trading post on the bay, at the mouth of the Nueces River. The trading post went by a variety of names, including the Port of Corpus Christi, Kinney's Trading Post, and Kinney's Rancho at Corpus Christi. Nueces County was formed in 1846, and Corpus Christi became the county seat in 1847.

LATINO POPULATION OF CORPUS CHRISTI, TEXAS, 1990

Total number of Latinos = 181,860; 52% of population

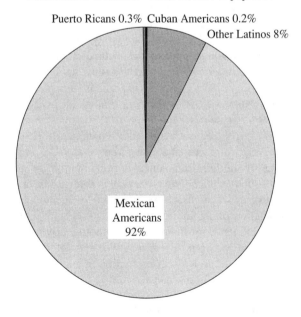

Puerto Ricans 0.3% Cuban Americans 0.2%

Other Latinos 8%

Mexican Americans 92%

Source: Data are from Marlita A. Reddy, ed., *Statistical Record of Hispanic Americans* (Detroit: Gale Research, 1993), Table 110.
Note: Figures represent the population of the Metropolitan Statistical Area as delineated by the U.S. Bureau of the Census. Percentages are rounded to the nearest whole number except for Cuban Americans and Puerto Ricans, for whom rounding is to the nearest 0.1%.

General Zachary Taylor landed in the city in 1845 to prepare for war with Mexico. His United States flag was the first to fly over Texas soil. Kinney, an Army private with the honorary title of colonel, had the channel from Aransas Pass deepened in 1848. Corpus Christi was incorporated as a city in 1852 and recognized as a seaport. The city became a major port in 1926 with the coming of deep water commerce brought about by the digging of the Nueces Ship Channel.

Railroads brought new vigor to Corpus Christi. In 1876, a narrow-gauge line to Laredo was completed, and in 1886 the San Antonio and Aransas Pass Railroad built a line from Gregory across the bay on a trestle to the city.

In 1923, natural gas was discovered in Saxet Field. Oil was discovered in 1939. As a result, Corpus Christi became an oil and natural gas center, with drilling, refining, and manufacturing operations. In addition, the city became a commercial center for several industries, including fishing, cattle, wheat, and tourism.

The first school, established in 1848, was private. A private school for black students was formed in 1877. A special act of the Texas legislature in 1909 formed the Corpus Christi Independent School District. In 1935, Del Mar College was created; Corpus Christi State University was founded in 1973.

The Hill, an old Hispanic area, is the heart of the city's Mexican American community. Ben Garza, a local businessman, was the force behind establishment of the LEAGUE OF UNITED LATIN AMERICAN CITIZENS (LULAC) in 1929. Another national Hispanic political organization, the AMERICAN G.I. FORUM, also was established in the city.

The city's west side is now the predominantly Mexican American sector of the city. Many cultural expressions of the Mexican American community can be seen, such as *panaderías* (bakeries), small cafés, and yard shrines. Latinos compose about 52 percent of the population of the metropolitan statistical area; more than nine-tenths of them, according to the 1990 census, were Mexican Americans. The city of Corpus Christi itself had a larger proportion of Latinos, perhaps as high as 70 percent.

Corridos: The *corrido*, a ballad-like song form, first appeared in Mexican American tradition during the nineteenth century, along the U.S.-Mexico border regions of Texas, New Mexico, and California. As a ballad tradition, the *corrido* can be traced to Spain and the old Spanish Romance form introduced into the Americas by the Spanish conquistadores. The word *corrido* comes from the Spanish verb *correr*, meaning "to run" or "to flow."

In general, a *corrido* is an expression of sentiment, emotion, or political views of the community, expressed in a ballad-like song form. The intent of a *corrido* is not to present the news but to interpret events already known to the community. Traditional *corridos* usually deal with local or regional historical events or people. *Corridos* have been written about love themes, border conflicts, drug smuggling, the immigration experience, the tragedy of losing a friend in the community, and incidents involving heroic figures of the past such as Gregorio Cortez, a South Texas rancher who stood up to the Texas Rangers. *Corridos* also have been composed about international events or personalities such as John F. Kennedy, Ronald Reagan, the U.S. space program, and the 1985 earthquake in Mexico.

Although *corridos* are popular in many regions of the United States, the strongest areas of the Mexican American *corrido* tradition extend from the western coastal states of California, Oregon, and Washington eastward through Arizona, New Mexico, southern Colorado, and Texas to the midwestern states of Michigan, Ohio, Minnesota, Illinois, and Pennsylvania. Although *corridos* first appeared in live, oral form, today recorded *corridos* are frequently heard.

The Corrido in Mexican American Tradition. According to Manuel Peña's study of the Texas Mexican *CONJUNTO* tradition, the duet singing style used in *corridos* began to merge with the instrumental dance music tradition during the 1930's. A more modern Chicano sound was introduced by two popular *corridistas* and recording artists, Tomas Ortiz and Eugenio Obrego, of the group Los Alegres de Teran, based in Monterrey, Mexico. Ortiz and Obrego added lyrics to several instrumental forms, including *corridos*.

The earliest recordings of *corridos* were made during the 1920's. Early recordings were limited by the technology to approximately four minutes per recorded side, thereby eliminating more epic-like genres such as the *bola suriana*, which contained as many as seventy verses. Most Chicano musicians of the day accepted the technical limitations of recording technology, drawn to the social and musical potential of recorded media as a way of exposing their music to larger audiences. *Corridos* on early recordings were sometimes played at faster tempos to meet time constraints; verses and choruses also were sometimes deleted. Time limitations on recordings encouraged the writing and performance of shorter versions of *corridos*, a trend that continued into the 1990's.

The corrido *form, with adaptations, has survived for more than a century.* (James Shaffer)

The Corrido as a Ballad Form. In performance, a *corrido* typically features solo or duet singing accompanied by guitar, guitar with button accordion, a full MARIACHI ensemble, or a *conjunto* of guitar, button accordion, *bajo sexto*, and drums.

The verse form of a *corrido* is typically set in eight-syllable quatrains of four or six lines. Metrically, the *corrido* with eight syllables per text line is considered to be the standard; however, the great flexibility of *corrido* form allows *corridos* to have twenty or more syllables per line. *Corrido* lyrics frequently use formulaic opening or closing patterns (*despedidas*).

Corrido rhyme patterns are usually duple, pairing the first two lines as one set and the next two lines as another. *Corrido* meter typically assumes 3/4, 3/8, 6/8, or 9/8 time, although many *corridos* since the 1950's have been adapted to 2/4 polka beat for dance hall performances. Some *corridos* add a refrain at the end of some verses.

Historically, *corridos* in the oral tradition have reached epic proportion, with *corridos* commonly exceeding twenty or more verses. Since the 1950's, commercially recorded *corridos* have been streamlined to fit the practical requirements of album, tape, or compact disc length, generally resulting in a limit of ten verses.

Corrido melodies are usually very simple and direct, with a melodic range of one octave or less, and accompanied by two or three main chords. *Corrido* melodies exert a strong influence on the rhythmic patterns of the *corrido* text, and the principle of repeated variation in the construction of *corrido* melodies is commonly applied. *Corridistas* regularly substitute one part or link of *corrido* melody for another according to the needs of the text, allowing for continuous re-creation through formulaic recomposition. *Corridistas* of the border *corrido* tradition fitted *corrido* texts to precomposed *corrido* melodies. *Corrido* scholars agree that formulaic reworking of corrido melodies is as common today as it was in the past; however, a definitive corpus of borrowed tunes or tune variants has yet to be identified.

The formulaic reworking of melodies was completed through one or more specific methods. These include regular usage of repeated notes in different phrases to accommodate textual variation, melodic or rhythmic variation, sequential duplication of the musical phrase at different pitch levels within the *corrido*, repetition of a musical phrase, and tune borrowing of a phrase or motif from one *corrido* to another.

Musical and textual features of the recorded *corrido* tradition have maintained important ties to the Mexican American past with regard to musical form, patterns of harmonic movement, and the process of composition. Recorded *corridos*, however, are significantly shorter than *corridos* in the oral tradition. Refrains have become more popular in the recorded *corrido*, accounting for about half the *corridos* in current use. Moreover, the melodies of most refrains are borrowed from the verse form or created by stringing together melodic fragments from different phrases of the *corrido* to create a melody that is new but strongly connected to a pool of known *corrido* melodies. The process of composing a *corrido* moves very quickly when the refrain melody is borrowed from the verse.

—*Clayton M. Shotwell*

SUGGESTED READINGS: • Arteaga, Alfred. "The Chicano Mexican Corrido." *Journal of Ethnic Studies* 13 (Summer, 1985): 75-105. • Dickey, Dan William. *The Kennedy Corridos: A Study of the Ballads of a Mexican American Hero.* Mexican American Monographs 4. Austin: Center for Mexican American Studies, University of Texas at Austin. • Geijerstam, Claes af. *Popular Music in Mexico.* Albuquerque: University of New Mexico Press, 1976. • Loza, Steven. *Barrio Rhythm: Mexican American Music in Los Angeles.* Urbana: University of Illinois Press, 1993. • McDowell, John Holmes. "The Mexican Corrido." *Journal of American Folklore* 85 (1972): 205-220. • Paredes, Americo. *A Texas-Mexican Cancionero: Folksongs of the Lower Border.* Urbana: University of Illinois Press, 1976. • Paredes, Americo. *"With His Pistol in His Hand," a Border Ballad and Its Hero.* Austin: University of Texas Press, 1958. • Robb, John Donald. *Hispanic Folksongs of New Mexico.* Albuquerque: University of New Mexico Press, 1954.

Cortázar, Julio (Aug. 26, 1914, Brussels, Belgium—Feb. 12, 1984, Paris, France): Writer. Cortázar was an extremely prolific and internationally successful writer. He was reared and educated in Argentina but spent much of his adult life in France. Considered one of the world's greatest authors, he is credited with sparking American interest in Latin American literature. A writer of poetry, short stories, and novels, he left an immense body of work before dying of a heart attack. Widely praised for their humor, interplay between realistic and fantastic elements, and social activism, Cortázar's writings are also notable for their experimental styles. Constant experimentation kept Cortázar at the literary forefront.

The novel that brought Cortázar international acclaim and popular success was *Rayuela* (1963), translated into English by renowned translator Gregory Rabassa as *Hopscotch* (1966). Embraced by American readers and critics alike, the novel established Cortázar as a literary genius. Many critics saw *Hopscotch* not only as an outstanding Latin American novel but also as a pivotal text in world literature.

His later works, also translated by Rabassa, include *Libro de Manuel* (1973; *A Manual for Manuel*, 1978), *Alguien que anda por ahi y otros relatos* (1977; *A Change of Light, and Other Stories*, 1980), *Un tal Lucas* (1979; *A Certain Lucas*, 1984), and *Queremos tanto a Glenda* (1980; *We Love Glenda So Much, and Other Tales*, 1983).

Cortés, Ernie (Ernesto Cortés, Jr.; b. 1943, San Antonio, Tex.): Labor organizer. During the last quarter of the twentieth century, Cortés brought his understanding of union organizing and Roman Catholic theology to the service of poor residents of Texas. He was a founder of COMMUNITIES ORGANIZED FOR PUBLIC SERVICE in San Antonio in the 1970's. In 1971, he became a director of the Industrial Areas Foundation, a politically liberal but socially conservative national group connected with and supported by the Catholic church. He supervised INDUSTRIAL AREAS FOUNDATION organizations in San Antonio, Houston, and El Paso, using LIBERATION THEOLOGY to guide the struggles of Mexican Americans and recent immigrants. Known for a combative style of negotiating, Cortés nevertheless insisted that people must be taught to do things for themselves and to work with those in power, and that they must be willing to compromise. He was awarded a John D. and Catherine T. MacArthur Foundation Fellowship in 1990.

Cortés, Hernán (1485, Medellín, Spain—Dec. 2, 1547, Castilleja de la Cuesta [near Seville], Spain): Explorer. Cortés sailed to the New World in 1504. Having studied law in Spain, he settled in Santo Do-

Hernán Cortés. (Library of Congress)

mingo and established himself as a public notary. In 1511, he participated in the settlement of Cuba.

Cortés left Cuba in 1519, sailing to explore, conquer, and settle Mexico in the name of Diego VELÁZQUEZ DE CUÉLLAR, the governor of Cuba. It was always Cortés' intention to keep the conquered areas for himself. Through careful negotiations and cunning, he compelled the Aztec emperor, MOCTEZUMA II, to sign a treaty of vassalage. This peaceful conquest, however, did not last long. Cortés lost his position in Tenochtitlán, the Aztec capital, when he went to confront a Spanish expedition, sent by Velázquez and led by Pánfilo de NARVÁEZ, to arrest him. When Cortés returned to TENOCHTITLÁN, he found an Indian uprising that his troops could not control. He reorganized his troops outside the city, and with the help of reinforcements and Indian allies, he took over the city in 1521 in a bloody struggle. Thousands of Indians died, some as a result of a smallpox epidemic that aided Cortés' efforts.

The Spanish Crown recognized Cortés' claim to Mexico and named him governor and captain general of NEW SPAIN. Cortés explored Honduras and the Pacific coast. He later returned to Spain, where he died in 1547 while planning a return to Mexico.

Cortez, Gregorio (June 22, 1875, Tamaulipas, Mexico—1916, Austin, Tex.): Folk hero. Cortez's family moved to central Texas in 1887. Two years later, Cortez followed one of his older brothers to Karnes County. They worked as farmhands for the area's ranchers until 1900, when they decided to farm on their own and rented some land.

On June 12, 1901, W. T. Morris, the sheriff of Karnes County, attempted to arrest Cortez on a horse-theft charge. Errors made by a translator in the course of their conversation led Cortez to shoot the sheriff. As a result, Cortez embarked on a ten-day, five-hundred-mile journey toward Laredo. He eluded his pursuers, in the process killing a member of the posse pursuing him. Finally, a *VAQUERO* betrayed him to the TEXAS RANGERS. An all-white jury convicted Cortez of murder of the posse member while acquitting him of murder of the sheriff. The governor of Texas pardoned Cortez in 1913. He later fought in the Mexican Revolution.

Cortez's actions earned the respect of Mexicans who lived along the Rio Grande. They admired him for doing what they themselves were unwilling to do. His exploits against the Americans have been immortalized in countless *CORRIDOS* emphasizing the morality of his actions. He defended his rights with a pistol in his hand and then sought to escape. Those were the only possibilities for a Mexican American in Texas.

Cortéz, Ricardo (Jacob Kranze or Krantz; Sept. 19, 1899, Vienna, Austria—Apr. 28, 1977, New York, N.Y.): Actor. Born to a Jewish family of Austrian and Hungarian descent, Cortéz immigrated to the United States as a young man. After working on Wall Street while taking acting classes, he arrived penniless in Hollywood. With his dark good looks, he was considered a potential successor to Rudolph Valentino as a classical Latin lover. He adopted the name Ricardo Cortéz and went on to make dozens of films under the pseudonym. Cortéz appeared with Greta Garbo in *The Torrent* (1926), played Sam Spade opposite Bebe Daniels in *The Maltese Falcon* (1931), appeared opposite Dolores DEL RIO in *Wonder Bar* (1934), and performed with Ann Dvorák in *Masquerade in Mexico* (1945). His other film credits include *Sixty Cents an Hour* (1923), *Pony Express* (1924), *The Sorrows of Satan* (1927), *The Private Life of Helen of Troy* (1927), *Behind Office Doors* (1928), *Ten Cents a Dance* (1931), *Melody of Life* (1932), *The Phantom of Crestwood* (1933), *Special Agent* (1935), *Talk of the Devil* (1936), *Mr. Moto's Last Warning* (1938), *World Premiere* (1940), *I Killed That Man* (1942), *Make Your Own Bed* (1944), *The Locket* (1946), *Blackmail* (1947), and *The Last Hurrah* (1958). In addition, Cortéz also directed several features, including *City Girl* (1938) and *Free, Blonde, and Twenty-one* (1940).

Cortina, Juan (May 16, 1824, Camargo, Tamaulipas, Mexico—1892, Atzcapotzalco, Mexico): Revolutionary. The son of a prominent Mexican landowner, Cortina moved with the rest of his family to his mother's estate around Brownsville, Texas, after his father died in the early 1840's. Although Cortina fought against the United States during the Mexican American War, he did not appear to be concerned with defending Mexican rights. In 1851, he participated in an expedition that sought to separate the Rio Grande Valley from Texas and create the Republic of the Sierra Madre. Eight years later, however, Cortina shot a deputy who had arrested a former Mexican servant of his family. Seeing little possibility of a fair trial, Cortina fled and organized an armed force that occupied Brownsville.

Cortina and his men were the scourge of the Lower Rio Grande Valley between 1859 and 1873. His guerrilla war against the Americans possessed a distinct

Ricardo Cortéz. (AP/Wide World Photos)

ideology. Cortina argued that he had acted on behalf of downtrodden people who were being despoiled of their land for no reason other than their Mexican ancestry.

As U.S. political influence with the Mexican government increased, pressure was brought to eliminate Cortina. He was arrested by the Mexican government on charges of cattle rustling in 1875. He was rearrested a year later and sent to Mexico City under local arrest. He was not allowed to return to the border until 1890, and then only to visit friends and relatives.

Costa Rican Americans: According to consular estimates, there were about 100,000 Costa Ricans in the United States in the early 1990's. Most had emigrated in the 1960's or later. The largest concentrations were in upper New Jersey, New York City, New Orleans, and Los Angeles. The communities are relatively homogeneous in that they are composed primarily of professionals, technicians, and students, along with their families. There were extremely few people of Costa Rican background in Canada.

Located in Central America, between Nicaragua and Panama, Costa Rica has an area of 19,576 square miles and had a population estimated at 3,187,000 in 1992. The bulk of the population, which is chiefly Caucasian and mestizo, lives in the central plateau. There is a sizable black population, chiefly of Jamaican origin, at the Caribbean port of Limón.

Europeans first entered this region after 1520. For the next three hundred years, Costa Rica formed the southern limit of the Spanish viceroyalty at Mexico City. It was briefly part of the Mexican Empire and the Federation of Central America. Independence was declared on September 15, 1821. In the late twentieth century, the country enjoyed a reputation for democratic government and economic stability.

STATISTICAL PROFILE OF COSTA RICAN AMERICANS, 1990

Total population based on sample: 57,223

Percentage foreign-born: 69%

Median age: 29.5 years

Percentage 25+ years old with at least a high school diploma or equivalent: 67%

Occupation (employed persons 16+ years old)

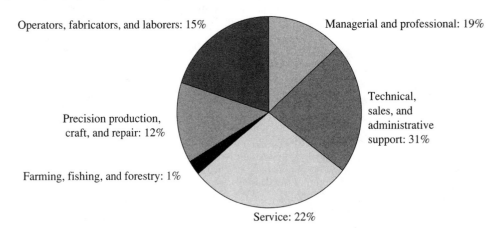

Operators, fabricators, and laborers: 15%

Managerial and professional: 19%

Precision production, craft, and repair: 12%

Technical, sales, and administrative support: 31%

Farming, fishing, and forestry: 1%

Service: 22%

Percentage unemployed: 7.5%

Median household income, 1989: $30,785

Percentage of families in poverty, 1989: 13.4%

Source: Data are from Bureau of the Census, *Census of 1990: Persons of Hispanic Origin in the United States* (Washington, D.C.: Bureau of the Census, 1993), Tables 1, 3, 4, and 5.

Costa Ricans generally are less subject to economic and political pressure to leave their country than are most Central Americans. They consequently immigrate in fewer numbers to both the United States and Canada. U.S. census figures lump Costa Ricans into the "other Central Americans" category because of their small number.

The Costa Rican community in the United States generally maintains close ties with the home country. Public social life is centered on four main holidays: the Feast of the Virgin of the Angels, patron saint of Costa Rica (August 2); Costa Rican Independence Day (September 15); Christmas Eve; and New Year's Eve. On Christmas Eve, Costa Rican families make special TA-MALES. Bands and folklórico dancers characterize the August and September celebrations. The Feast of the Virgin of the Angels typically involves a special Mass, a soccer game, and poetry readings. Most cultural celebrations are held in close consultation with consular personnel.

Costa Ricans also form part of the Chicago-based Central American Civic Society, which elected a Costa Rican as its 1993-1994 queen. Costa Ricans as a group are widely involved in charitable work but eschew political officeholding. With the exception of *Noticias de Costa Rica*, a New York-based monthly, there was no regular Costa Rican press in the United States by the late twentieth century.

Costumbrista: Writer of texts that describe popular regional types. A *costumbrista* writes *cuadros costumbristas*, which describe popular regional or national types and customs. This literary subgenre developed in Spain during the nineteenth century. *Cuadros costumbristas* combine description with social commentary and are considered the predecessors of the modern Latin American short story and journalism. The most influential Spanish *costumbristas* in Latin America were Ramón Mesonero Romanos (1803-1882) and Mariano José de Larra (1809-1837). Inspired by the *cuadro costumbrista*, Peruvian Ricardo Palma (1833-1919) developed the *tradición*, a descriptive narrative that incorporated colloquial language and elements from oral tradition.

Cotera, Martha P. (b. Jan. 17, 1938, Nuevo Casas Grandes, Chihuahua, Mexico): Writer and librarian. Cotera is a professional librarian and writer. Her extensive body of work provides both resource and research materials for Mexican American students and scholars. Most of Cotera's writings are informational or biblio-graphic in nature, but she has also written several scholarly essays about Hispanic women's roles and struggles in the United States. As a feminist scholar, Cotera spans several disciplines in her work, focusing heavily on Chicana and Latina issues.

Cotera grew up in El Paso, Texas. After receiving degrees in English and education, she began a long career as a librarian. Cotera is also a social activist. She and her husband organized a famous student walk-out in CRYSTAL CITY, TEXAS. She later ran for a seat on the state board of education on the ticket of LA RAZA UNIDA PARTY, a political party created in Texas as an alternative to the traditional exclusionary parties. Cotera's works include *The Chicana Feminist* (1977), *Bridging Two Cultures* (1980), *Latina Sourcebook* (1982), *Checklists for Counteracting Race and Sex Bias in Educational Materials* (1982), *Everyone's Guide to Sources on Hispanic Women* (1983), and *Doña Doormat No Está Aquí: Assertion and Communication Techniques for Hispanic Women* (1982).

Cotto-Thorner, Guillermo (b. 1916, Juncos, Puerto Rico): Novelist and clergyman. Cotto-Thorner was a Baptist minister in Wisconsin and New York for five years, and he wrote two works of fiction in Spanish. A professor of literature in his later years, he contributed to literary journals and magazines in both the United States and Latin America. His work appeared in such publications as *Hispania*, *Revista Iberoamericana*, and *La Nueva Democracia*.

With the exception of his publications, little is known about his life. Unlike that of his compatriot evangelist Nicky CRUZ, Cotto-Thorner's religious conversion was neither sensational nor depicted in English-language autobiographical writings. His first full-length prose work was a collection of his sermons titled *Camino de victoria* (1945; victory road). He followed that volume with his best-known work, *Trópico en Manhattan* (1951; Manhattan tropical), a novel published in Puerto Rico. *Trópico en Manhattan* narrates the story of a Puerto Rican migrant family and its struggles to adapt to life in New York City. Cotto-Thorner included a dictionary at the novel's end that translated NUYORICAN slang and English terms into Spanish. Cotto-Thorner published a second book, *Gambeta* (1971), more than twenty years later. The book gets its title from the name of a dance step and an ancient dance.

Coyote: Person who smuggles undocumented immigrants into the United States. During the nineteenth

A farmworker waits for a coyote to pick him up and take him to a job. (Impact Visuals, Philip Decker)

and early twentieth centuries, coyotes operated overtly, arranging for Mexican workers to cross the border and go directly to jobs awaiting them at mines, smelting plants, and fields. Some large, developing United States companies paid these smugglers handsomely because they desperately needed labor in places such as El Paso, Texas; Los Angeles, California; and Chicago, Illinois. Following the Depression, World War II, and the development of restrictionist policies and labor contract regulations, coyotes operated clandestinely and illegally, receiving payment from immigrants as well as from employers for their services.

Crafts. *See* **Folk arts and crafts**

Criminal justice system: Latinos, particularly those living in poverty, have often been treated differently from English-speaking white people by the U.S. law enforcement and justice systems. The United States criminal justice system, controlled primarily by white people of European descent, has often treated members of minority groups unfairly. This is particularly true in the case of Latinos, many of whom have limited proficiency in English and encounter problems communicating with English-speaking police officers and judges.

Historically, Latino migrant workers in the Southwest, most of whom are of Mexican descent, have received the harshest treatment. Reliable figures are difficult to obtain, but it is clear that many of these people, perhaps as many as half, have entered the country illegally. This status gives them less protection from the American legal system. For example, UN-AUTHORIZED WORKERS often are paid less than the minimum wage. Many cases have been reported in which unauthorized (or undocumented) workers have been turned in to immigration authorities when they are about to be paid; they are deported without receiving payment for their work.

As of the early 1990's, approximately twice as many arrests and convictions, proportionately, are made of Latinos than of non-Hispanic white Americans. Both eyewitness reports and studies of police records indicate that Latinos are more likely to be stopped in the street and questioned than are other people, are more likely to be arrested, and are more likely to be convicted if they are arrested.

It is difficult to prove whether prejudice is a large factor in this situation. Not many people will admit to being prejudiced, and some may discriminate without being aware that they are doing so. It has been shown, in simulated court cases, that white, non-Hispanic juries are more likely to convict Hispanic suspects than non-Hispanic suspects, given exactly the same evidence.

In a real courtroom, this is not the only potential problem. Latino defendants more often use public defenders because of the cost of private defense. A public defender is appointed by the court and is paid less than a privately hired lawyer would be. There is thus less incentive to give the best possible defense. In private practice, a lawyer is paid for time in court and will work as long as necessary on behalf of the client. In addition, public defenders often have less time to prepare their cases.

As a result of all these factors, Latinos tend to distrust the criminal justice system in general and English-speaking police officers in particular. Economic factors make crime more likely in Hispanic neighborhoods.

Latinos are more likely than others to be stopped and questioned by the police. (Lou DeMatteis)

The feeling of the police being outsiders, and even enemies of the community, leads to a general distrust of the law, so that criminal behavior is not properly addressed by the authorities. Many crimes are not reported by victims, who do not always trust the police, and witnesses are not always cooperative.

Criollos: Term indicating Spanish heritage. Most commonly, the term is used to describe people of Spanish descent born in the United States. It is used in contrast to MESTIZO, which identifies a person with mixed European and indigenous blood. As descendants of landowning Spaniards, *criollos* traditionally have been among the elite in many Latin American countries. Historically, however, they were not always aligned with the objectives of the Spanish Crown and were involved, along with mestizos and Indians, in revolutionary struggles. In the American Southwest, many of the original landowning families claimed *criollo* origins. For the most part, these families were wealthy and controlled the economies of the region, sometimes using mestizo and Indian labor in a semifeudal, exploitative manner.

Crónica: Satirical opinion column. The *crónica* (chronicle) centers on cultural issues and popular practices. It is intended to promote retention and knowledge of Hispanic culture and prevent Anglicization. The *crónica* first appeared in the Southwest and combined re-creations of legends and stories, taken from old manuscripts and other historiographic sources, with social commentary. These columns were printed by many of the Mexican printers founded in the area during the first half of the nineteenth century. Mexican Adolfo Carrillo (1865-1926) was well known for his ironic depictions of life in early nineteenth century California.

Crusade for Justice: Founded in 1966. Crusade for Justice is a community-based Chicano organization based in Denver, Colorado. It emphasizes involvement of the entire family in the fight against oppression and poverty.

Crusade for Justice was organized by Chicano activist Rodolfo "Corky" GONZÁLES in Denver, Colorado, in April of 1966. The group sprang from his desire to act in the face of urban inequalities and exclusionary Democratic politics as well as his disillusionment with antipoverty programs. In Denver, the group established a school, community center, curio shop, and bookstore. Gonzáles was convinced that Chicanos needed their own schools, where they would not feel threatened or alienated or suffer from the loss of identity usually associated with education within the Anglo system. He believed that these feelings of alienation resulted in part from the Hispanic students' compulsory acceptance of anglicized versions of their names, as when a student named María is called Mary by her teachers, as well as from being punished or humiliated for speaking Spanish. The Crusade's base in Denver comprised approximately thirty working-class families and was directed by an executive board.

Crusade for Justice worked primarily on civil rights activities. It fought against discrimination in schools and against the widespread and numerous cases of police abuse of Hispanic Americans. Crusade for Justice also promoted cultural and alternative educational programs for Hispanics to promote Chicano pride and activism for the good of the community and advocated cultural consciousness and the creation of a society based on humanism rather than on competition.

Protests organized by Crusade for Justice against social injustice in the late 1960's and the 1970's often involved thousands of demonstrators gathered to denounce a particular injustice faced by Chicanos. The organization focused on what it considered to be the core values of the *familia* and the welfare of the collective Hispanic community.

Crusade for Justice played an important role in providing national leadership for Mexican liberal elements throughout the Southwest from 1968 to 1978. Among its landmark contributions to Chicano history are the Poor People's March, the NATIONAL CHICANO MORATORIUM ON VIETNAM of 1970, and its aid in the formation of LA RAZA UNIDA PARTY.

Another important contribution of Crusade for Justice was the sponsorship of Chicano youth conferences in 1969 and 1970. College and university students, faculty, and staff as well as community activists organized under the banner of El MOVIMIENTO ESTUDIANTIL CHICANO DE AZTLÁN (MECHA). Among the problems thwarting the efforts of the group were persistent harassment by law enforcement agencies, who considered its efforts to be a threat to national security. Persecution of members by the government served to create tensions and provoke fissures in the movement. Another source contributing to the waning impact of Crusade for Justice on the Chicano community was the group's own inability to cope with organizational change successfully.

Despite these flaws, the contribution to Chicano history of Crusade for Justice cannot be denied. It aided

Rodolfo "Corky" Gonzáles (right) shown with José Ángel Gutiérrez at the 1972 convention of La Raza Unida Party. (AP/Wide World Photos)

the self-identification process of the CHICANO MOVE-MENT, particularly among young Mexican Americans.

The last volume of the official newsletter of Crusade for Justice, *El Gallo: La Voz de la Justicia*, was published in 1980. The group continued its efforts under the name of its school, Tlataloco, and under the direction of Gonzáles' two daughters.

Cruz, Celia (b. Oct. 21, 1929?, Havana, Cuba): Singer. Cruz is the daughter of Simon Cruz and Catalina Alfonso Cruz. She grew up in a barrio of Havana. She was the second eldest of four children, but ten cousins, nephews, and nieces also lived in the Cruz home.

Cruz developed a love for music as a young child and would sing for the other children in the house. Her aunt encouraged her to listen to music on the radio and escorted her to local ballrooms to listen to live music. Cruz planned to become a teacher, graduating from

República de Mexico public school and studying literature at a teachers' training school. In 1947, she won a talent show, *La Hora de Té*, that aired on the García Serra radio network. Cruz then decided to leave school and pursue a singing career.

She attended the Havana Conservatory of Music, where she studied music theory and piano. In 1950, Cruz joined the popular band La Sonora Matancera. The band toured extensively throughout the Americas for the next ten years. After Fidel Castro came to power in Cuba in 1959, Cruz and the band fled to Mexico. In 1961, they moved to the United States. On July 14, 1962, Cruz married the first trumpeter of the band, Pedro Knight. During the 1960's, she recorded more than thirty albums, becoming known as the "Queen of Salsa" because of her distinctive SALSA music. She was popular in New York City among the Puerto Rican and Dominican communities. In 1978, she was named *Billboard*'s Best Female Vocalist.

Celia Cruz arrives at a 1992 screening of The Mambo Kings, *in which she plays herself.* (AP/Wide World Photos)

Cruz reunited with La Sonora Matancera in 1982 and recorded the album *Feliz Encuentro*. In that same year, she was honored in a concert at New York's Madison Square Garden that drew a crowd of twenty thousand admirers. In 1994, she was inducted into *Billboard*'s Latin Music Hall of Fame.

Cruz, Nicky (b. Aug. 6, 1954, San Francisco, Calif.): Novelist. Cruz is known as an evangelist and social worker. The detailed accounting of his descent into gang violence and his subsequent religious conversion made for best-selling paperbacks. Cruz became an overnight celebrity in the 1970's. He came to represent the power of Christian salvation, appearing on talk shows, befriending politicians as well as church leaders, and opening an outreach program to help runaway children and former gang members.

Born into a family of eighteen, Cruz was sent from the family home in Puerto Rico to find work in the United States. His first book, *Run, Baby, Run* (1968), written with Jaime Buckingham, depicts his life as a young man on the streets of New York City, his involvement in theft, and his struggle with alcoholism. The book's popularity led to a feature film adaptation titled *The Cross and the Switchblade* (1970). Cruz emphasizes the positive changes resulting from his conversion. After bringing media attention to the plight of runaway children, he founded runaway outreach programs. He followed his first book with *The Lonely Now* (1971), a collection of experiences of runaways, and *Satan on the Loose* (1973), his examination of the devil and demonology.

Cruz, Sor Juana Inés de la (Juana de Asbaje y Ramírez de Santillana; November 1648, San Miguel de Nepantla, Mexico—Apr. 17, 1695, Mexico City, Mexico): Writer. Sor Juana was a seventeenth century writer of colonial Spanish America, noteworthy for her lyric poetry and her intellectual genius. She wrote both religious and secular poems, epistolary prose, and religious drama. Her work did not go unnoticed by literary critics, but it took more than three hundred years for her to gain recognition as a major literary figure as well as one of the finest lyric poets of her time.

Sor Juana acquired a remarkable level of education for a woman of her time. Her intellectual accomplishments at the age of sixteen brought her to the attention of the viceroy, the Marquis of Mancera, who brought her into his court. Although she later entered a convent to continue her writing and her intellectual pursuits, the majority of her writings were inspired by secular subjects. She died during an epidemic, leaving behind an impressive and influential body of work.

Her works were gathered and published after her death. They include three collections titled *Inundación castálida* (1689, flood from the muses' springs), *Segundo volumen de las obras de Soror Juana Inés de la Cruz* (1692, second volume of the works of Sister Juana Inés de la Cruz), and *Fama y obras pósthumas de Fénix de México y Dézima Musa* (1700, fame and posthumous works of the Mexican phoenix and tenth muse). These works, along with omitted selections and essays that assess Sor Juana's place in literary history, were edited and unified by Alfonso Méndez Plancarte, whose four volumes of *Obras completas de sor Juana Inés de La Cruz* (the complete works of Sor Juana Inés de la Cruz) were published between 1951 and 1957. *Obras escogidas* (selected works) had been published in 1946. Sor Juana's poem "Primero sueño" (first dream), considered to be her most important single work, is a masterwork of baroque poetry and has been printed several times as a single volume.

Cruz, Victor Hernández (b. Feb. 6, 1949, Aguas Buenas, Puerto Rico): Poet. Cruz moved with his family to the Harlem section of New York at the age of five. While living in New York, he produced several collections of poetry and served as editor of *Umbra* during the 1960's and 1970's. In 1983, he left New York for San Francisco. His poetry has been described as "Puerto Rican soul poetry" and as "Afro-Latin" (his own classification). Cruz has been hailed as one of America's finest young poets and has been among the few Puerto Rican poets to reach a broad U.S. audience.

Crystal City, Texas: County seat of Zavala county. Zavala County, according to the 1990 census, was home to 10,875 Hispanics, who composed 89.4 percent of the county's population. Crystal City itself had a population of 8,263 people.

Crystal City is located slightly more than one hundred miles southwest of San Antonio and is about forty miles from the Mexican border. The city is in an area of Texas that was under disputed ownership until nearly 1900. Texas, the Mexican government, Comanche Indians, and Lipan Indians all laid claim to the area. Adding to the political unrest was the fact that the area furnished hiding places for fugitives. Adding to the problems of Anglo settlers was the climate, with both droughts and floods common. The land was covered by a thick brush of mesquite trees, cactus, and grasses. Disputes concerning grazing rights, water holes, and fences caused tension among the settlers. Because there was no established government, all people had to be prepared to defend themselves.

At first, the area consisted of large ranches, but in 1884 an artesian well was discovered, offering the possibility of farming. Around 1900, large-scale farming began with a profitable crop of Bermuda onions. The owners of the Cross-T ranch, one of the largest in the area, decided to break up the ranch into ten-acre plots to be sold to farmers. The owners also wanted to develop a city. Crystal City was chosen as a name because of the clear artesian water in the area. Widespread advertising brought in people from all over the United States as well as from other countries.

As emphasis shifted from ranching to farming, many changes occurred. Farming required large amounts of labor. Anglos began to look on Mexican people from the area as an excellent source of cheap labor, whereas previously they had attempted to drive Mexicans out.

By 1920, better transportation and packing procedures, along with the addition of spinach as an excellent cash crop, led to a large increase in population in the area. Most of the population increase resulted from

Mexican Americans picking onions in Crystal City, Texas. (AP/Wide World Photos)

Mexican people coming into the area to find work. By 1930, Crystal City's population was predominantly Mexican. Because most farming was done in the cool months, these laborers had to become migrants to find work in the late spring, summer, and early fall. They would return to Crystal City by late fall and considered it as their home.

The Works Progress Administration conducted a study of migrant workers in Crystal City in 1938. This study showed average yearly income to be about $100 per person. World War II brought an increased demand for vegetables, and the city returned to more prosperous conditions. In the middle to late 1940's, Del Monte established a cannery in the area, providing many permanent and seasonal jobs.

By the growing season of 1967-1968, there were 13,320 acres under cultivation, but these represented only thirty-four farms. Mechanization of planting and harvesting on large farms resulted in fewer jobs and a high rate of unemployment. These problems were compounded because use of the artesian well had not been regulated, and its water had been seriously depleted. This led to a decrease in farming activity in the area, which depressed the job market even more. About this time, some of the Mexican American people of the area began to open small shops, helping to stabilize the Mexican American community.

In 1925, a series of small elementary schools was established for Mexican American children, who previously had no schools. Children who were able to continue their schooling after the elementary level attended Anglo schools. In 1938, Crystal City had ten elementary schools: one for Anglos, eight for Mexican Americans, and one for black students. The quality of education was not equal. After the 1954 Supreme Court decision in Brown v. Board of Education, the Anglo school was integrated, and the quality of education was improved in the other schools. Education was badly needed. In 1950, the average Mexican American in the area who was twenty-five years of age or older had less than two years of formal education, and the average family income was less than $2,000 per year. In 1960, a threatened lawsuit by Mexican American parents led to integration of all schools.

Mexican Americans gradually made improvements on the political front. From the beginning, Anglos were politically dominant, and all elected officials were Anglo. By 1960, 74.4 percent of the population of Zavala County was Mexican American. The county seat, Crystal City, was slightly more than 80 percent Mexican American. City government was led by a strong city manager and a weak, unpaid mayor and city council. A few token Mexican Americans were hired. In January of 1963, an all-Latino political party was formed; it soon conducted a very successful poll-tax drive. More than eleven hundred Mexican Americans paid their poll tax and were eligible to vote; only 542 Anglos paid the tax. The Latino party's candidates for city council beat all five of the incumbent Anglos, but the two Latino party candidates for the school board lost. Unfortunately, the elected council members were inexperienced, leading to unrest in the city and loss of the positions in the next election.

After several years of bitterness and political infighting among the city's Latino leaders, La RAZA UNIDA PARTY was formed. By 1974, the party had control of Crystal City and Zavala County. All of its candidates won by large margins.

Cuatro: Small, four-string guitar. Descended from the Spanish *vihuela* and the Portuguese *caraquinho*, the *cuatro* is constructed of native woods and strings traditionally made of gut but now mainly of nylon. The original cuatro has four double courses of strings tuned E, A, D-sharp, and G. At the end of the nineteenth century, a fifth course added the pitch B. Many variations exist. The Venezuelan *cuatro* has four strings usually tuned A, D, F-sharp, and B. The Puerto Rican *cuatro* has a fifth string pitched below the others. *Cuatros* are used in ensembles in Mexico, Jamaica, and Colombia to accompany singing and dancing on secular and religious occasions.

Cuba: The largest Caribbean island, Cuba has an area of 42,827 square miles and extends approximately 745 miles from east to west. It is located about ninety miles south of Florida. The close proximity of Cuba to the United States has intertwined the histories of the two countries, especially in the twentieth century. Since Cuba's revolution in 1959, a U.S. economic embargo and Cold War tensions have isolated the island nation, while an influx of a million Cuban immigrants has changed the face of cities such as Miami, Florida, and diversified the Latino population in the United States.

The Early Colonial Period. The "Pearl of the Antilles," as many Cubans call their country, was claimed for Spain by Christopher Columbus in 1492. At the time, there were about sixty thousand indigenous inhabitants of the island, including Guanahatabeys, Ciboneyes, and Taino. Diego VELÁZQUEZ DE CUÉLLAR began a permanent Spanish settlement in 1511. Diseases and harsh treatment by the Spaniards quickly decimated the native population. The native people were forced to work on large sugar and tobacco plantations under poor living conditions.

Dominican friar Bartolomé DE LAS CASAS was an outspoken critic of such treatment and defended the rights of the native people. His writings influenced Spanish Indian policy in the New World. As the native population declined, the Spaniards began importing African slaves, as early as 1517. They were used for hard labor in the gold mines and later in the expanding sugar industry. Because they were considered valuable, they were better treated than the natives. Nevertheless, some Spanish officials complained about the inadequate food and clothing for the slaves and the use of corporal punishment. The *CIMARRONES*, or runaway slaves who fled to the mountains, were a constant source of concern to the Spaniards. By example, the *cimarrones* encouraged other slaves to escape and revolt.

As early as 1538, black slaves rioted and looted Havana while French privateers attacked from the sea. In 1812, a group of slaves headed by José Antonio Aponte was planning a revolt, but the Spaniards discovered the conspiracy and hanged the slaves involved.

Conflicts with Spain. The Spaniards had built a thriving agricultural economy in Cuba based on sugar, but Spanish rule became increasingly unpopular. José Francisco Lemus was the organizer of the colony's first revolutionary movement, which began in 1821 and collapsed in 1826. In the early 1800's, Simón Bolívar, a South American general known as El Libertador (the liberator) of the Americas, and several Mexican leaders organized an invasion of Cuba and Puerto Rico to free them from Spain. Their plans were dropped when the United States warned it would support Spain.

In 1850, Narciso Lopez, a Venezuelan-born Spanish general, sailed from New Orleans with more than six hundred men to liberate Cuba. He captured the city of Cardenas, Matanzas Province, but was forced to re-

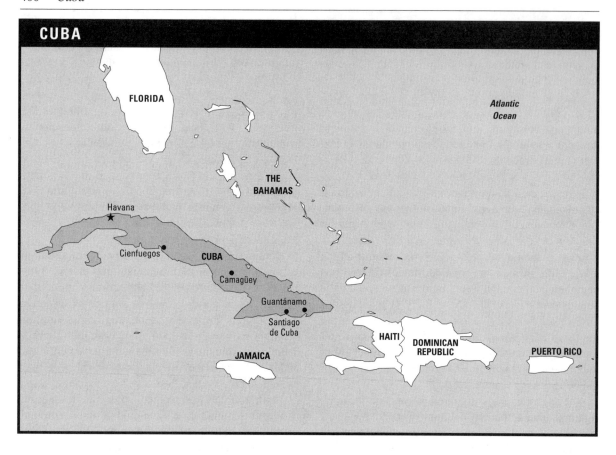

CUBA

FLORIDA

Atlantic
Ocean

THE
BAHAMAS

Havana

Cienfuegos

CUBA

Camagüey

Guantánamo

Santiago
de Cuba

JAMAICA

HAITI

DOMINICAN
REPUBLIC

PUERTO RICO

treat when he found no support from the population against Spanish reinforcements. According to many historians, Lopez wanted Cuba to be annexed by the United States while retaining the institution of slavery. He was executed in 1851 following his second attempt to take Cuba.

Meanwhile, dissatisfaction was growing among Creole plantation owners. They questioned Spanish mercantilistic policies and favored the cheap and unlimited importation of slaves. A new Creole intellectual class became increasingly disillusioned with the possibility of reform within the Spanish Empire. In their view, Spanish rule meant more taxes, ineffective administration, and exclusion of Creoles from responsible positions in government.

The Ten Years' War began on October 10, 1868, when Carlos Manuel de Cespedes, the son of a wealthy plantation owner, issued the historic GRITO DE YARA. He freed his slaves and incorporated them into his army. Cespedes and his followers demanded Cuba's independence and the abolition of slavery. Spain rejected Cespedes' demands, and fighting ensued.

Soon the *mambises*, or Cuban peasant rebels, joined Cespedes and the Dominican military leader Máximo Gómez. Under Gómez, the mulatto General Antonio Maceo, who became one of the most daring fighters of the Cuban army, liberated many plantation slaves and enlisted them in his army.

In more than ten years of fighting, the Cubans were not able to overthrow Spain. They were hampered by internal rivalries, lack of organization, and shortages of supplies and ammunition. After much destruction of the eastern side of the island, the war ended with the signing of the Pact of Zanjon in 1878. This pact provided for the gradual abolition of slavery and the institution of political reforms.

In 1886, slavery was finally abolished in Cuba. It soon became clear, however, that Spain was not going to loosen its hold over Cuba, prompting increasing frustration. José MARTÍ, born in Havana of Spanish parents, was a poet and revolutionary who believed that the only solution for Cuba was independence from Spain. He believed in the distribution of government land and the redistribution of wealth to ensure the economic independence of Cuba's citizens. After spending fifteen years in the United States promoting this cause, Martí led an abortive revolution in 1895. He died soon after taking up arms.

On February 15, 1898, the battleship USS *Maine*, which President William McKinley had sent to Havana to protect Americans in Cuba, exploded mysteriously. The United States blamed Spain for the disaster and sent troops in April for what became known as the SPANISH-AMERICAN WAR. After a victorious blockade by the U.S. Navy, the Spanish army surrendered in August. In the TREATY OF PARIS, Spain gave up all rights to Cuba. Puerto Rico, Guam, and the Philippines also became U.S. territories.

U.S. Control. The United States installed a military government that ruled Cuba from 1898 to 1902. During this time, an important public works program began, and sanitation and health conditions improved. Yellow fever (malaria) was eradicated through mosquito-control programs based on the discovery by Cuban physician Carlos Finlay that yellow fever was carried by mosquitos.

On February 25, 1901, Senator Orville H. Platt introduced an amendment to the Cuban constitution in the U.S. Congress. The PLATT AMENDMENT stipulated that the United States could interfere in Cuban foreign affairs, and it allowed the United States to purchase or lease land in Cuba for naval bases. A naval base was built in Guantánamo Bay.

In 1902, Cuba was declared a republic and Tomás ESTRADA PALMA was elected its first president. A rebellion against Estrada Palma's government while he was running for a second term forced the United States to return its troops to the island. In 1906, a civil-military government was formed, headed by American Charles E. Magoon.

By 1909, the American troops had gone, but newly elected governments did not remedy the problems of the lower classes. In 1912, a group of radical black Cubans formed the Independent Color Association and staged an uprising. After another revolt in 1917, the United States again intervened by sending forces into Cuba.

Gerardo Machado was elected president of Cuba in 1924. Soon recognized as a dictator by the Cuban people, he rigged an election to ensure a new six-year term from 1929 to 1935. Machado's dictatorship provoked the rebellion of university students and faculty. Many innocent people were tortured and killed during this time. In August, 1933, an army revolt forced

Visitors watch the American flag being raised over the Governor's Palace in Cuba in 1899. (Library of Congress)

Machado to resign and leave the country. A month later, Sergeant-Stenographer Fulgencio Batista, united with the students and the military, emerged as a self-appointed chief of the armed forces. A five-man committee headed by Ramón Grau San Martin was appointed to govern Cuba. The United States refused to support this government because it was deemed too extreme and unstable.

The Batista Regime. On January 14, 1934, Army Chief Batista removed Grau San Martin from office. For the next six years, Batista ruled through presidents who served in name only. The United States supported the Batista regime and willingly signed a treaty that canceled the Platt Amendment, leaving the Guantánamo Bay lease intact.

In 1940, Batista was elected president under the new constitution, defeating Grau San Martin. The Cuban constitution allowed a president to serve for only four years, and Grau San Martin regained the post in 1944. Carlos Prío Socarrás won the elections in 1948. In 1952, convinced that he could not win the elections, Batista overthrew Prío's government and again became a dictator.

Batista attracted foreign companies to build businesses in Cuba and established badly needed public works. Corruption flourished, along with the good life for Cuba's elite. Most Cubans, however, continued to live in poverty because of substantial unemployment and inequalities between urban and rural living standards. Another problem was the island's economic dependence on one major buyer-supplier. In the 1950's, about 75 percent of Cuban imports came from the United States, and about 65 percent of Cuba's exports went to the United States.

Castro's Revolution. On July 26, 1953, Fidel CAS-TRO, a young lawyer, tried to start a revolution against Batista. Castro attacked the Moncada Army Barracks in Santiago de Cuba, but he was captured with his followers and was imprisoned. After his release in 1955, Castro went to the United States, and then to Mexico, where he organized the 26th of July movement. Student riots and demonstrations spread throughout Havana. José A. Echeverria, a student leader, met with Castro in Mexico and agreed to support his movement. In December, 1956, Castro's forces, including his brother, Raul, and Argentine physician Che GUE-VARA, landed in Cuba. Most of the rebels were soon killed, but Castro and eleven others escaped to the Sierra Maestra mountains, where they formed a guerrilla band to carry out surprise attacks against Batista's government.

With the support of local peasant groups, Castro's forces began blowing up bridges and railroad tracks in 1957. By 1958, the people had lost confidence in Batista's government, and the rebels were capturing key cities. On January 1, 1959, Batista fled the country. Later many officials and army officers of the Batista regime were tried and executed.

The revolutionaries established a government under Castro and launched fundamental reforms. They broke up large estates into small holdings for landless peasants. They built schools and began an ambitious literacy campaign to reach a population that was then 30 percent illiterate. They made low-income housing and health care more widely available. These moves helped many of the poor, but they alienated the middle and upper classes in Cuba, prompting thousands to leave for the United States and elsewhere. At the same time, the revolutionary changes altered Cuba's relations with the U.S. government and its place in the world.

Relations with the United States. In 1959 and 1960, relations with the United States deteriorated. U.S. president Dwight D. Eisenhower decided to stop buying Cuban sugar after Cuba agreed to exchange sugar for Soviet aid. This prompted Castro to seize American businesses. Because Western European countries, under U.S. pressure, refused to sell arms to Cuba, Castro's government became more hostile toward the United States. In February, 1960, Cuba turned to the Soviet Union for economic and military assistance and signed its first trade agreement with that country.

In January, 1961, the United States ended diplomatic relations with Cuba, following Castro's takeover of all American oil refineries and interests remaining in Cuba. The U.S. trade embargo would continue well into the 1990's, significantly harming Cuba's economy. In 1962, Cuba was suspended from membership in the Organization of American States (OAS). The more isolated Cuba became from its neighbors, the more it turned to the Soviet Union for economic and military assistance.

Although Castro had declared that Cuba's was a socialist revolution, he announced his conversion to Marxism in 1961. He shut down the press, instituted unpopular food rationing, and followed the Soviet model of bureaucratic multiyear plans for the nation. These steps further angered the country's elite and led to continued emigration. Castro's changes also exacerbated tensions with the United States, which feared that Cuba would spread Communism in the region.

The Bay of Pigs. In 1961, the United States planned a covert operation to overthrow Castro. Cuban exiles trained under U.S. officials in Central American camps for an invasion of the island. In April, 1961, they arrived at the BAY OF PIGS on the southern coast of Cuba. U.S. president John F. Kennedy had promised direct military action, but at the last moment, he refused to send military aid. The air support never came, and Castro's army captured most of the exiles. Later, some of the exiles were exchanged for nonmilitary supplies and sent back to the United States.

The CUBAN MISSILE CRISIS occurred the following year. In 1962, Castro asked the Soviet Union for more military aid. He was convinced that the United States was planning another attack. The Russians sent missiles and materials to build launch sites. In October,

A cartoon from the Washington Star *shows Soviet premier Nikita Khrushchev protesting the U.S. blockade of Cuba.* (Library of Congress)

Cuban children have benefited from literacy programs. (Hazel Hankin)

President Kennedy learned that Cuba had missile bases that could launch atomic attacks on the United States. He ordered a naval blockade and demanded that the Russians remove all missile bases from the island. For the next several days, the world feared a nuclear war. The Soviet Union agreed to Kennedy's demands and removed the weapons under U.S. supervision. In return, the United States promised not to attack Cuba.

Relations with Latin America, Africa, and the Caribbean. During the 1960's, Cuba sent military aid to guerrilla groups in Bolivia, Colombia, Peru, and Venezuela in South America and to Guatemala and Nicaragua in Central America. It is believed that Castro made these moves in an effort to expand Marxist-Leninist ideas and Cuban influence in the region. After the killing of Che GUEVARA in Bolivia in 1967 and other major setbacks, Cuba withdrew from Latin America.

Cuba sent troops into at least thirteen African countries in the 1970's. About nineteen thousand combat troops were sent to Angola, and approximately nineteen thousand to Ethiopia in 1979. Cuba's African presence can be explained in several ways. One is the expression of solidarity with the people of the Third World. Others have to do with Cuba's own Afro-Latin culture and social structure, the need to provide combat experience for Cuban troops, and a wish to pressure the United States.

In 1979, revolts took place in Grenada, Suriname and Nicaragua while civil wars in El Salvador and Guatemala intensified. Cuba once again returned to the strategy of the Caribbean, offering military and technical assistance. By June, 1982, 120,000 Cubans had seen military service outside the country, and about thirty thousand doctors, teachers, engineers, and technicians had also gone abroad, according to *The New York Times.* Events in Cuba, such as the 1980 MARIEL BOAT LIFT, combined with the Soviet Union's invasion of Afghanistan and political changes in Central America to thwart Cuba's efforts in the Caribbean.

People and Social Conditions. In 1992, Cuba had a population of almost eleven million, of whom about half were white and of Spanish descent. Most other Cubans were of African descent or mulattoes, persons of mixed black and white ancestry. About two-thirds of the population is not religious, at least in part because of government restrictions on religious practice. Havana, however, maintained relations with the Vatican in Rome.

Cubans are expected to belong to at least one of the government-sponsored political organizations, such as the Communist Party and the Committees for the Defense of the Revolution. Those who do not participate in such organizations may have their loyalty to the revolution questioned.

The literacy campaigns begun in 1961 made significant progress, and the illiteracy rate had shrunk to about 6 percent by the 1990's. There was controversy, however, over the amount of time students spent working in the fields and learning Marxist-Leninist thought.

The Castro government also claimed large gains in public health. Polio and malaria were eliminated by 1963 and 1968, respectively. In 1982, Cuba's infant mortality rate had been reduced to 19.3 deaths per one thousand births.

Cuba's housing shortage has worsened over the years. As a result, fewer Cubans married. For example, the marriage rate decreased by 40 percent between the 1960's and 1978. Married couples often had to share housing with relatives, a situation that may have contributed to the island's declining birth rate and rising number of divorces.

Family structure has also changed in contemporary Cuban society. Before Castro's revolution, children were guided closely by the family, and there were sharp distinctions in the roles of men and women. Today, emphasis is placed on the individual, and gender roles are very similar. Women are encouraged to be part of the labor force, whereas in the past they were limited to the domestic roles of wife and mother.

One of the most controversial aspects of life in Cuba is the rationing system. Originally rationing was meant to ensure that everyone received an equal amount of goods. As it became a permanent part of Cuban life, it has generated resentment about long lines, endless waiting, and inadequate provisions. Everyone has a packet of ration books in which scarce items are listed. For example, during the early 1990's, each member of a family was allotted three-fourths of a pound of meat and one and one-half ounces of coffee per week. Only three cans of milk could be obtained each month, except for children under the age of six and adults over the age of sixty, who were allowed one liter a day. Cars were available only to professionals, such as doctors and government leaders.

Gasoline rationing and cutbacks in public transportation led to crowding on public buses. (Hazel Hankin)

It is difficult to gauge the quality of life in Cuba, in part because of the restrictions on access to information about Cuba and in part because of the mutual suspicion between Cuba and the United States. Clearly, the Castro government has made strides in some areas, while as a whole the economy has continued to suffer. In 1992, Castro blamed the breakup of the Soviet Union for his country's economic woes. One sign of the economic strains faced by Cubans of various classes is their emigration in large numbers since 1959. Most have come to the United States, seeking not only greater political freedom but also greater access to consumer goods.

Early Immigration to the United States. Approximately one million Cubans immigrated to the United States in the twenty-five years following the CUBAN REVOLUTION of 1959. Thomas D. Boswell, in *The Cuban-American Experience* (1983), divided Cuban emigration into seven phases, beginning with the early period from the 1850's to 1959.

The first exodus of Cubans resulted from political upheavals against Spanish rule in the mid-1800's. Several cigar manufacturers moved their businesses from Havana to Key West and Tampa, Florida, as well as to New York City, during the 1860's and 1870's. By 1870, only about five thousand Cuban Americans lived on the U.S. mainland. In the 1930's, exiles left Cuba after the revolution against Gerardo Machado. From 1953 to 1959, others fled the dictatorial Batista regime. The total population of Cubans in the United States in 1950 was 29,295 according to the census. That number reached an estimated forty thousand in 1958, just before Castro took power.

The second phase, or period of the "Golden Exiles," began when Castro's forces overthrew Batista's gov-

ernment in 1959. More than 215,000 Cubans migrated to the United States between 1959 and 1962. Initially, the majority were members of the elite classes who had been involved in the Batista government. After an agrarian reform law was established to eliminate large landholdings, rich landowners began to flee. When rental property in the cities was confiscated, entrepreneurs and the middle class also began leaving the country. By 1960, sixty thousand people had already left Cuba. The sudden rush to depart caused much embarrassment to Castro's government.

Relations between the United States and Cuba were broken after the missile crisis, and legal immigration was suspended until September of 1965. Nevertheless, between 1962 and 1965 about forty-three thousand Cubans left for the United States through other countries such as Mexico and Spain in the third phase. About six thousand prisoners of the Bay of Pigs invasion were also returned to the United States in exchange for medical goods, while another seven thousand escaped by boat and plane.

In 1965, Castro announced that he would allow Cubans who had relatives in the United States to emigrate there. Many Cuban Americans rushed to pick up relatives in small boats at the port of Camarioca on the northern coast of Matanzas, again embarrassing the government. The United States and Cuba then signed a memorandum of understanding, which provided for an airlift from the beach town of Varadero to Miami.

The airlift, consisting of ten flights a week for seven years, became known as the FREEDOM AIRLIFT, Aerial Bridge, and Family Reunification Flights. It transported a total of three to four thousand Cubans each week. An estimated 297,318 persons arrived in the United States during the seven-year airlift, and another 4,993 came by boat from Camarioca. Most of the refugees of the Freedom Airlift who arrived in Miami and Union City/West New York (New Jersey) were professionals from the cities. After many interruptions, Castro decided to stop the airlift in 1973.

Emigration Since the 1970's. The fifth phase of emigration was an interlude from 1973 to 1980 during which only thirty-eight thousand Cubans arrived in the United States. These exiles generally used Mexico or Spain as routes to the United States, just as they had done after the missile crisis. They left the island mainly because of the poor Cuban economy. In 1978, Castro freed thirty-six hundred political prisoners as an act of good will. Because family members were often allowed to leave with them, between ten and fourteen thousand persons emigrated. This wave was more rep-

FACTS AT A GLANCE

Capital: Havana

Area: 42,804 square miles

Population (estimated, 1994): 10,991,000

Percentage living in urban areas: 78

Estimated 1989 Net Material Product (NMP): $18.272 billion

Type of government: socialist republic controlled by Communist Party

Cubans arriving on a Freedom Airlift flight are greeted by relatives in Miami, Florida. (Otto G. Richter Library, University of Miami)

resentative of the Cuban population, including people from small cities, towns, and rural areas. By 1979, Las Villas Province had surpassed Havana as the leading origin for Cubans going to West New York and Miami.

In April, 1980, Cubans were again allowed to leave the country by sea. Castro selected the small port of Mariel, located twenty miles west of Havana, as the point of departure. The MARIEL BOAT LIFT lasted nearly five months (April 21 to September 26, 1980) and involved 124,779 people, or more than 1 percent of Cuba's population, in the sixth phase of Cuban immigration. More would have left if Castro had not closed down emigration in September. As Cubans from the United States came to pick up their relatives, Castro forced them to take with them his "undesirables." These included Cubans with criminal records as well as homosexuals, patients from mental institutions, deaf-mutes, and lepers. Approximately twenty-six thousand of the Mariel refugees had criminal records, but many of them had been jailed for stealing food or trading in the black market rather than violent crimes. Only about 4 percent of the *marielitos*, as they came to be called, were real criminals. These immigrants were

not welcomed in the United States because of the bad publicity given to them by the media. Many suffered at the hands of the authorities and had far more trouble adapting to American life than did previous waves of Cubans.

After September, 1980, Cuban immigration to the United States declined, partly as a result of stricter controls. Cuban exiles continued to leave the island legally or illegally and were routinely granted political asylum. On January 3, 1992, a Cuban pilot confiscated a helicopter in Varadero and flew thirty-three other Cubans to Miami, Florida, where they defected. Cubans continued to arrive by boat daily on the Florida coast.

—José Carmona

SUGGESTED READINGS:

• Bonachea, Ramon L., and Marta San Martin. *The Cuban Insurrection, 1952-1959*. New Brunswick, N.J.: Transaction Books, 1974. Written from the point of view of Cuban insurrectionists. Examines the political and military factors that led to victory in 1959. Maps and photos.

• Boswell, Thomas D., and James R. Curtis. *The Cuban-American Experience: Culture, Images, and*

Emigration from Cuba surged in 1994, when thousands of balseros *(rafters) tried to make their way to the United States.* (Impact Visuals, Steven Fish)

Perspectives. Totowa, N.J.: Rowman & Allanheld, 1983. A discussion of the major social, economic, political, and cultural topics relating to Cuban settlement in the United States. Maps, photos, and illustrations.

• Falk, Pamela S. *Cuban Foreign Policy: Caribbean Tempest*. Lexington, Mass.: Lexington Books, 1986. Concise history of Cuban foreign relations through the periods of Spanish, American, and Soviet dependence.

• Gernand, Renee. *The Cuban-Americans*. New York: Chelsea House, 1988. Examines the history of Cuba and Cuban Americans for juvenile readers. Illustrations.

• Hudson, Rex A. *Castro's America Department: Coordinating Cuba's Support for Marxist-Leninist Violence in the Americas. Washington, D.C.: Cuban American National Foundation, 1988. Describes Cuba's broader political programs.*

• Levine, Barry B., ed. *The New Cuban Presence in the Caribbean*. Boulder, Colo.: Westview Press, 1983. Details the history and nature of Cuba's influence in the Caribbean, Mexico, and Central and South America.

• Oppenheimer, Andres. *Castro's Final Hour*. New York: Simon & Schuster, 1992. History of the Cuban Revolution through the 1980's.

• Suchlicki, Jaime. *Cuba: From Columbus to Castro*. New York: Charles Scribner's Sons, 1974. A concise history of Cuba through the 1970's. Photographs.

Cuba, Joe (José Calderón; b. 1931): Bandleader and conga drummer. Cuba grew up in the Spanish Harlem section of New York City. In 1950, he began his musical career with La Alfarona X. He formed the Joe Cuba Sextet in 1954. The band became popular with its vibraharp sound. "To Be with You" (1962) solidified the group's popularity. The band's piano player, Nick Jimenez, did the arrangements, Cuba played the congas, and Cheo Feliciano and Jimmy Sabater shared vocals.

With the advent of the *bugalú* sound in the 1960's, Cuba changed the sound of the sextet. Recordings such as "El Pito" and "Bang Bang" sold millions of copies. "Bang Bang" was the first *bugalú* song to sell a million copies. In the late 1960's and 1970's, there were various personnel changes in the sextet. In 1984, the original members reunited for a concert in Madison Square Garden that was held to commemorate Feliciano's twenty-five-year career. Cuba will be remembered as one of the leaders of the New York SALSA sound.

Cuban American Foundation (Miami, Fla.): Grassroots lobbying organization. The Cuban American Foundation was founded as the Cuban American Political Action Committee in 1983 and renamed the Cuban American Freedom Coalition in 1987 before taking its current name. It was born of a desire to educate the American public, as well as public policymakers, about the plight of Cubans still living in the nation of Cuba. More important, the organization sought to educate the general population about Cuban Americans.

Americans of Cuban descent and others with an interest in Cuban affairs have joined in this organization. Members engage in grassroots lobbying to promote freedom and democracy in Cuba and around the world. The Cuban American Foundation maintains a speakers' bureau to provide messages that explain the mission of the organization. It also offers educational and research programs about the concerns of the community. The foundation has a computerized database available.

Cuban American Legal Defense and Education Fund (CALDEF): Founded 1980. CALDEF is a nonprofit organization dedicated to securing the civil

CALDEF filed suit on behalf of juveniles held in the refugee camp at Fort McCoy, Wisconsin; the camps were dismantled shortly thereafter. (Impact Visuals, Arvind Garg)

rights and liberties of Cuban Americans. It was established in January of 1980 to aid Cuban American and other Latin American communities of the United States.

CALDEF's principal objectives are equal treatment and opportunities for Cuban Americans and Hispanics in the areas of education, employment, housing, politics, and justice. CALDEF discourages negative stereotyping of Hispanics and actively promotes the education of the general public to the plight of Cuban Americans and Latin Americans. CALDEF also educates Cuban Americans concerning the opportunities provided by local, state, and federal agencies.

CALDEF supports BILINGUAL EDUCATION as a means to obtain equal educational opportunities for Cuban Americans and other Spanish-speaking Americans. It also actively supports women's rights in an effort to aid Hispanic women in overcoming the constraints of societal racism and sexism. CALDEF additionally supports educational programs designed to assist Spanish-speaking people in obtaining job skills necessary to earn a living in the United States.

CALDEF has initiated and won a number of class-action suits concerning ethnic equality. The first among these concerned a group of minors who were subjected to cruel and unusual punishment and denied due process at a refugee camp in Fort McCoy, Wisconsin. The bad publicity from the lawsuit prompted the governor of Wisconsin, Lee Sherman Dreyfus, to appoint a fact-finding commission to investigate the situation of Cuban refugees in the state. The commission, after meeting twice in 1980, found that the allegations concerning the mistreatment of Cuban refugees were true and that juveniles at the camp were being mistreated. The commission recommended that the state accept legal responsibility for Cuban minors who had no relatives in the United States. The federal government agreed to take legal custody of the juveniles without relatives and paid for their placement in state child-care facilities and private homes throughout Wisconsin. The other juveniles were released to relatives in the United States. Shortly thereafter, the three refugee detention camps in the region were dismantled. CALDEF also mediated the cases of several Hispanic women dismissed from their jobs. The women claimed RACISM and sexism on the part of their employers.

The national office of CALDEF is in Fort Wayne, Indiana. In addition to its advocate and educational programs, CALDEF publishes the *Hispanic Newsletter* and holds an annual convention.

Cuban American Literature. *See* **Literature, Cuban American**

Cuban American National Foundation: Nonprofit research organization. Founded in 1981, the Cuban American National Foundation is an independent institution dedicated to producing and disseminating research on the economic, political, and social issues affecting Cubans in the United States and in Cuba. It supports a free, democratic Cuba. The foundation, headquartered in Washington, D.C., advocates Cuban civil rights and attempts to influence public opinion on issues dealing with Cuba and Cubans.

The foundation publishes the periodicals *Boletín Informativo*, *Cuban Update*, and *The Issue Is Cuba*. It maintains a library and a bureau of speakers on issues dealing with Cuban culture, politics, and history. The foundation hosts resident scholars and sponsors media breakfasts, lectures, and symposia. It has a computerized database on the issues pertaining to the foundation's interests.

The foundation is involved in activities to fight bigotry, protect human rights, and promote cultural interests and creative achievement. The foundation's financial support comes primarily from private donors. The foundation has been active in the political and public opinion arenas and maintains a constant lobbying effort on issues related to its philosophical and political views.

Cuban Americans: Cuban Americans were the third largest Latino group in the United States according to the 1990 U.S. census. Many Cuban Americans came to the United States to escape the Communist regime of Fidel CASTRO. Castro initiated a process of revolutionary change that, in its rapidity and pervasiveness, alienated large sectors of the Cuban population. Elite and middle-class Cubans began leaving the island in large numbers in 1959, and their principal destination was the United States. In the thirty years after the Cuban revolution, more than 750,000 Cubans emigrated. By the mid-1990's, more than one million people of Cuban descent lived in the United States.

History. Although most Cuban Americans arrived in the United States after the CUBAN REVOLUTION, the history of the Cuban presence in the United States predates 1959. In the nineteenth century, sizable communities thrived in NEW YORK CITY; NEW ORLEANS, LOUISIANA; and Key West and YBOR CITY, FLORIDA. Cuban hero José MARTÍ organized Cuba's independence movement from New York, which contained one of the

Miami, Florida, recognizes the Cuban contribution to the city's culture. (Martin Hutner)

largest Cuban American communities in the nineteenth century.

Cuban tobacco workers in Ybor City (on the outskirts of Tampa) and Key West were also active in Cuba's struggle for independence. Cuban patriotic societies in Florida raised money for the wars against Spain. Many Cubans, hoping to gain U.S. support for their cause, participated in American politics. Fernando Figueredo of Key West, for example, served in the Florida legislature during the 1885 session. Cuban independence in 1902 ended the first period of Cuban exile politics in the United States but did not end the Cuban presence.

Throughout the first half of the twentieth century, Cubans seeking economic opportunity continued to come to the United States. During that period, Florida did not have the employment opportunities that the Cuban immigrants sought (*see* CUBAN IMMIGRATION). Many were laborers who were attracted to New York City by the high-paying factories and service industries there. Although New York was the destination of choice for many, Miami received many of those seeking refuge from the shifting fortunes of the island's

turbulent politics, largely because of its proximity to Cuba. Two deposed Cuban presidents—Gerardo Machado and Carlos Prío Socarrás—made their homes in Miami.

Meanwhile, the Cuban community in the Tampa area continued to exist. By the early 1990's, the Tampa area had the second-largest Hispanic concentration in Florida. Although Tampa was the site of one of Florida's oldest and most established Hispanic communities, its Hispanic population in the 1990's was only about 8 percent as large as Miami's. Much of the Tampa area's Hispanic population was descended from Cuban immigrants who came to Key West and Tampa during the late 1800's. For example, former Florida governor and Tampa mayor, Robert MARTÍNEZ, is a Cuban American who might be considered representative of those third- and fourth-generation Latinos. Because of long-term acculturation, however, third- and fourth-generation Cuban Americans cannot be said to be representative of a distinctive Hispanic political agenda in the state.

The Cuban Exodus. The prominent role of Cubans in U.S. society began in 1959 with the massive exodus from the island as a result of the Castro revolution. The pattern of Cuban emigration since 1959 reflects primarily the availability of the means to leave Cuba. Despite the severing of diplomatic relations in January, 1961, there was regular commercial air traffic between the United States and Cuba until the CUBAN MISSILE CRISIS of October, 1962. Between 1959 and 1962, about 200,000 persons left Cuba. The missile crisis disrupted diplomatic relations between the two countries, slowing Cuban immigration to a trickle. Persons leaving the island in 1964 and 1965 were forced to do so clandestinely, often in small boats or through third countries, usually Spain or Mexico.

In the fall of 1965, responding to internal pressures for emigration, the Cuban government opened a port and allowed persons from the United States to come to Cuba to pick up relatives who wanted to leave the country. Some five thousand Cubans left from the port of Camarioca before the United States and Cuba halted the boat lift and agreed to an orderly airlift. The FREEDOM AIRLIFT, which started in December, 1965, and lasted until 1973, took 260,500 persons to the United States.

During this period, Congress approved the Cuban Adjustment Act of 1966, which granted Cuban immigrants special status, allowing them to enter the United States without restrictions imposed on people from other countries. The law gave automatic residency to any Cuban who came to the United States, whether a tourist who overstayed or someone who entered without documentation. People fleeing any other country, even other communist countries, were required to submit proof that they were persecuted. For Cubans, escape usually was enough to guarantee permanent resettlement in the United States. No other group benefited from such an exception for so long a time. The act, passed during the height of American-Cuban hostility, endured in large part because of the political clout of Cuban Americans. More than 500,000 Cubans immigrated to the United States under the Cuban Adjustment Act.

Renewed political tensions between the United States and Cuba led to termination of the Freedom Airlift in 1973. The end of the airlift brought about another period of relatively low emigration from Cuba during the mid- to late 1970's. By 1980, however, the pressure for emigration caused a social explosion in Cuba that resulted in the MARIEL BOAT LIFT.

The Mariel drama began when six Cubans in a bus crashed through the gates of the Peruvian embassy in Havana and requested political asylum. The Cuban government announced that those who wished to leave should congregate at the Peruvian embassy, where they would be provided with exit documents. Almost immediately, thousands of people assembled on the embassy grounds. An embarrassed Castro increased the flood of refugees by releasing some criminals and mental health patients.

The crisis in Cuba attracted the attention of Cuban exiles in Miami, who organized a flotilla of about forty fishing boats and small pleasure craft. The flotilla was granted permission by the Cuban government to pick up those wishing to leave at the port of Mariel. From April 21 to September 26, 1980, a "freedom flotilla" referred to as the Mariel boat lift converged at Mariel Harbor to take approximately 125,000 refugees to Florida. At first, the Jimmy Carter Administration announced that anyone leaving Cuba would be welcomed by the United States, but as the full extent of the mass migration became evident, the U.S. government attempted to end the boat lift. On May 14, Carter called for an end to the freedom flotilla, but the influx of immigrants continued.

The end of the boat lift and new restrictions on CUBAN IMMIGRATION imposed by the U.S. government brought about a lull in the exodus during the 1980's. In November, 1987, an agreement between the United States and the Castro government attempted to control the influx of Cubans into the United States. The agreement provided for the immigration of twenty thousand Cubans to the United States each year; in exchange, Cuba agreed to take back some twenty-five hundred Cubans jailed in the United States because of their criminal records. The goals set by both sides were not met: The actual number allowed to enter the United States fell considerably below the projected figure of twenty thousand, and only about four hundred Cubans were deported.

After the 1987 agreements, the United States gave priority to those who qualified for political asylum. Most of the persons who arrived after that date were former political prisoners and their families. Others seeking to leave the island were forced to do so in small boats, risking their lives in the treacherous waters of the Florida Straits. By 1994, about four hundred Cuban rafters a month were reaching Florida. Refugee experts estimated that about the same number lost their lives trying to cross. A much larger group of *BALSEROS*, or rafters, left Cuba in the middle of 1994.

Miami's Cuban Enclave. Most Cuban exiles settled in MIAMI immediately or moved there after first settling elsewhere. Another large Cuban community of about

Cuban pilot Orestes Lorenzo defected in 1991, then tried to get the Castro government to let his family leave the island. (AP/Wide World Photos)

eighty thousand was established in the area around Union City, New Jersey, while smaller communities existed in Chicago and Los Angeles. According to the 1990 census, about half of the more than one million Cubans in the United States lived in the greater Miami area (Dade County). Miami ranked third in the nation, behind only Los Angeles and New York City, in the size of its Hispanic population. Miami had a substantially smaller overall population than either Los Angeles or New York City, and almost all of its Hispanic population settled there after 1960. Miami therefore underwent one of the most dramatic ethnic transformations of any major American city in the twentieth century.

This settlement pattern facilitated the development of a Cuban enclave in Miami. An ethnic enclave is a distinctive social and economic formation characterized by spatial concentration of immigrants who organize various enterprises to serve their own needs as well as those of the general population. The Cuban community in Miami had immigrants with sufficient capital, either brought from Cuba or accumulated in the United States, to create new opportunities for economic growth. An important source of capital was the more than four billion dollars of aid that the U.S. government provided to Cuban exiles. After locating in Miami, the Cuban middle class developed an elaborate network of successful small enterprises rather than relying on the public sector as a primary vehicle for upward mobility. These small and middle-sized enterprises served as a source of employment for ensuing waves of Cuban immigrants.

The proliferation of small businesses, primarily serving Hispanic tastes, was the foundation of Cuban economic and political power in Miami. According to estimates from the early 1990's, Miami had 55,712 Hispanic-owned businesses. Approximately 7,700 of these firms were large enough to have paid workers, and those employed 34,504 people. The Hispanic-owned firms in this enclave generated nearly $3.8 billion in receipts in 1987—about 15 percent of all receipts generated by Hispanic-owned firms in the United States. According to a 1987 government survey, Cuban Americans had the highest business ownership rates among Latino groups, with sixty-three businesses for every thousand Cuban Americans. This rate was more than three times that of Mexican Americans (nineteen per thousand) and nearly six times that of Puerto Ricans (eleven per thousand).

Businesses operated by and catering to Cuban Americans thrive in Miami's Little Havana district. (Martin Hutner)

SIX STATES WITH LARGEST CUBAN AMERICAN POPULATIONS, 1990

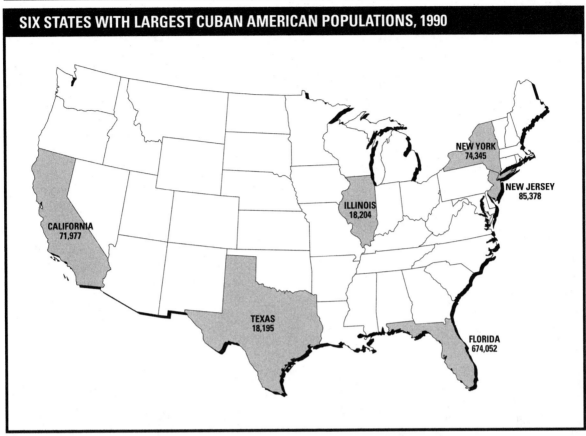

Source: Data are from Marlita A. Reddy, ed., *Statistical Record of Hispanic Americans* (Detroit: Gale Research, 1993), Table 106.

Cuban American Entrepreneurship. The high rate of business ownership among Cuban Americans resulted in part from the selective migration of former business owners and better-educated adults following the Cuban Revolution. Another reason was the heavy concentration of Cuban Americans in the Miami area, which had a booming economy during the 1980's. The large, prosperous ethnic enclave provided Miami's Cuban Americans with a potent small business incubator. They also have been successful in founding larger corporations. With about 5 percent of the country's Hispanic population, Miami had about one-third of the largest Hispanic-owned businesses in the United States. Bacardi Imports of Miami was the nation's most profitable Hispanic-owned business, with total sales in excess of $500 million in 1987. The Cuban presence and the economic success of Cuban Americans also attracted Latin American tourists and capital, resulting in scores of multinational corporations locating their Latin American offices in Miami.

The enclave's strong and diversified entrepreneurial activity was responsible for its most important over-

all feature, that of institutional completeness. Cuban Americans in Miami could, if they wished, live out their lives within the ethnic community. Virtually every product or service was available from a Cuban American source.

The existence of the enclave insulated Cuban Americans from the effects of language-based discrimination. The Cuban enclave became a community in which Spanish-speaking immigrants could settle without fear of being at a serious disadvantage because of a language barrier. The 1990 census showed that Spanish had replaced English in Dade County as the language most often spoken at home. Of those surveyed in 1990, 50 percent said they spoke Spanish at home, compared to 43 percent who spoke English. The proportion of Dade County residents speaking Spanish at home was up from the 1980 census, in which 43 percent of the residents reported speaking a language other than English at home.

The relative prosperity of the Cuban community, and its geographic cohesiveness largely safeguarded Cuban Americans from the prejudice and discrimination that plagued other Latino groups in the United States. Miami, in the view of many Cuban Americans, is largely a Cuban city. The only city in the world in which more Cubans live is Havana. This image of Hispanics making Miami uniquely "theirs" was reflected in surveys that showed that Anglos in Miami perceived as much discrimination as did Latinos, or more.

Cuban American Politics. Cuban Americans not only lived in compact and contiguous neighborhoods but also displayed a remarkable level of political cohesiveness. The anti-Communist ideology of the Miami exile community attracted national and international attention. The clearly articulated goal of much of the Cuban community was the overthrow of Fidel Castro in Cuba and the establishment of a democratic government there. Most Cuban American elected officials and most mainline Cuban American organizations agreed that compromise and dialogue with the Castro regime was impossible.

Voting and poll data of the 1980's and early 1990's reflected a strong Cuban American consensus on the

broad outline of an anti-Castro policy. The centerpiece of this policy was the maintenance of the U.S. economic embargo against the island. Although some exile groups articulated a less restrictive U.S. policy, those groups frequently lacked support within the community. Carlos Alberto Montaner's Cuban Democratic Platform, the Cuban Committee for Democracy, and Luis Gutierrez Menoya's Cambio Cubano had some elite-level support but lacked meaningful grass-roots support.

The Cuban American consensus for a hard-line policy toward Cuba was especially evident in public opinion polls. Polls conducted around 1990 showed that 80 percent of Cuban Americans supported U.S. policy of no diplomatic relations with Castro, 85 percent favored tightening the U.S. trade embargo, and 87 percent supported increasing international economic pressure on Cuba. Many thought the indirect pressure of the embargo did not go far enough. Poll data also showed the militancy of the Cuban exile community, with 60 percent supporting a U.S. invasion of Cuba

A sign in Miami's Little Havana district protests Communist control of Cuba. (Martin Hutner)

STATISTICAL PROFILE OF CUBAN AMERICANS, 1990

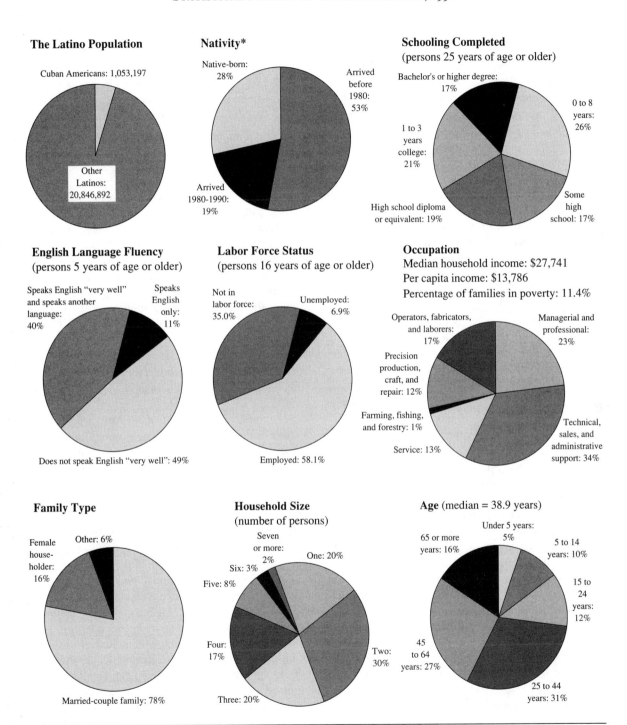

The Latino Population

Cuban Americans: 1,053,197

Other Latinos: 20,846,892

Nativity*

Native-born: 28%

Arrived before 1980: 53%

Arrived 1980-1990: 19%

Schooling Completed
(persons 25 years of age or older)

Bachelor's or higher degree: 17%

0 to 8 years: 26%

1 to 3 years college: 21%

Some high school: 17%

High school diploma or equivalent: 19%

English Language Fluency
(persons 5 years of age or older)

Speaks English "very well" and speaks another language: 40%

Speaks English only: 11%

Does not speak English "very well": 49%

Labor Force Status
(persons 16 years of age or older)

Not in labor force: 35.0%

Unemployed: 6.9%

Employed: 58.1%

Occupation

Median household income: $27,741
Per capita income: $13,786
Percentage of families in poverty: 11.4%

Operators, fabricators, and laborers: 17%

Managerial and professional: 23%

Precision production, craft, and repair: 12%

Farming, fishing, and forestry: 1%

Service: 13%

Technical, sales, and administrative support: 34%

Family Type

Female house-holder: 16%

Other: 6%

Married-couple family: 78%

Household Size
(number of persons)

Seven or more: 2%

One: 20%

Six: 3%

Five: 8%

Four: 17%

Two: 30%

Three: 20%

Age (median = 38.9 years)

Under 5 years: 5%

65 or more years: 16%

5 to 14 years: 10%

15 to 24 years: 12%

45 to 64 years: 27%

25 to 44 years: 31%

Source: Bureau of the Census, *Census of 1990: Persons of Hispanic Origin in the U.S.* (Washington, D.C.: Bureau of the Census, 1993), Tables 1-5.

Note: All figures and percentages are based on a sample, rather than 100 percent, of the Latino population, as done in reports from the Bureau of the Census.

*Of all "foreign-born" Cuban Americans, 50 percent were naturalized.

and 73 percent favoring military raids by exiles against the Castro regime. In direct contradiction to press accounts that spoke of a new moderation among Cuban Americans, the poll numbers were relatively stable over several years. Polls did show that a majority of Cuban Americans favored negotiations with the Castro regime on specific issues such as family visits, telephone communications, and other forms of humanitarian aid. There was also evidence of some willingness to negotiate the political future of Cuba with the Castro regime, but only if negotiations led to a democratic transition on the island, or relinquishment of power by Castro and the Communist Party.

This anti-Communism was underscored by a series of public debates in the Cuban American community over the right of Cubans and non-Cubans alike to dissent from this anti-Castro consensus. In 1992, Americas Watch issued a report condemning the exile community for its lack of tolerance of views that did not conform to the predominant ideology of uncompromising hostility to the Castro regime.

One of the most infamous incidents of intolerance occurred in 1986, when two thousand Latinos, mostly Cuban Americans, attacked two hundred anti-Contra demonstrators at Miami's Torch of Friendship monument. The Cuban Americans pelted the anti-Contra rally with eggs, rocks, and an occasional glass bottle, forcing Miami riot police to bus the smaller group of demonstrators out of the area. The mayor of Miami added to the political tension by referring to "Marxist groups" in the anti-Contra rally.

The anti-Communism issue was not limited to confrontations over substantive foreign policy questions. Symbolic politics and otherwise nonpolitical events frequently became forums for such conflict. Anti-Communist fervor was a regular part of municipal government deliberations, campaigns for local office, and cultural events. Plays by Cuban-born playwright Dolores PRIDA and performances by Latino musical stars such as Denise de Kalafe and Rubén BLADES were canceled in Miami because those individuals visited or performed in Cuba.

The Cuban community's anti-Communism was an important factor in explaining the community's alliance with the Republican Party. The Republican Party, with its reliance on hard-line foreign policy rhetoric, became the natural home of Cuban exiles. Cuban American voting patterns and loyalty to the Republicans were contingent not only on an anti-Castro foreign policy or the enormous popularity of Ronald Reagan. Voting patterns also became more dependent on the Republican Party's ability and willingness to address the other political, social, and economic needs of the Cuban community. Cuban American politics could no longer be understood solely in terms of militant exile politics. A more traditional brand of American ethnic politics emerged. The significance and force of anti-Castro symbolism was still alive, but was combined with more mundane concerns for jobs, domestic social services, and other substantive policy issues.

Cuban Americans were not interested solely in electing staunch anti-Communists. They also expected their elected officials to serve the interests of their community. This tension between the "old" politics of exile and the new ethnic politics created a two-dimensional voting pattern among Cubans. For offices that have symbolic power, such as U.S. president and senator, exile politics continued to be evident. For many state and local offices, ethnic politics and concern with servicing the community became preponderant.

Although this metaphor of a dual political identity within the community is admittedly too clear-cut to apply literally, it helps to explain the fact that Cubans did not vote Republican in all elections. Especially in congressional elections, in which local issues took precedence over foreign policy issues, some Democratic candidates were able to attract Cuban American support.

The rapid growth of Cuban American political power in the United States was extraordinary. In one generation, Cuban Americans elected three congressmen and won nine Florida state house seats, three Florida state senate sats, and the mayorships of Miami, Coral Gables, Hialeah, and other communities in Florida as well as in northern New Jersey. In metropolitan Miami and Dade County as a whole, Hispanics consolidated their status as the core electoral constituency. They also strengthened their local political position after a federal court overturned the country's at-large election system on the basis that it prevented Hispanics and African Americans from electing their preferred candidates.

In state politics, Cuban American Republican legislators from Dade County emerged as an important swing vote on matters ranging from the selection of state legislative leaders to the enactment or defeat of major policies. On the issue of reapportionment, they dramatically modified the Democratic majority's plans for congressional and state legislative district lines. In statewide elections, southern Florida's Hispanic voters demonstrated that in close statewide contests, their bloc voting could alter the outcome.

Cuban Americans are active in the local and state politics of Florida. (Martin Hutner)

The election of three Cuban Americans to the U.S. House of Representatives (two from southern Florida and one from New Jersey), combined with the ongoing lobbying efforts of such groups as the CUBAN AMERI-CAN NATIONAL FOUNDATION and the Valladares Foundation, resulted in an expanded role in Washington, at least with regard to shaping policy toward Cuba. For example, the Cuban American National Foundation won U.S. congressional approval for Radio and TV Martí (*see* RADIO MARTÍ), which broadcast to Cuba, and the Cuban Democracy Act, which tightened U.S. economic sanctions against Cuba.

Cuban Americans emerged as a group whose support was actively courted by a growing number of officeholders from outside the state—from presidential candidates to members of Congress seeking campaign contributions. The community's clout was not only actively asserted at the polls or through lobbying and campaign support, but also was recognized and actively courted. Such voluntary recognition reduced the future costs of exercising influence over the political process.

Impact. The Cuban American community in the United States has been significantly different from other Hispanic groups. Cuban Americans have tended to be wealthier, better-educated, older, and more likely to vote Republican than Mexican Americans and Puerto Ricans. The political and socioeconomic success of the Latino population in Dade County raised an important question for Latino politics: Was the model of political and economic empowerment there unique to conditions in Miami, or could it be replicated by other Latino and minority populations?

The Cuban experience in Miami has been unique. The Cuban political and economic model was shaped by the demographic, political, and socioeconomic status of Cuban immigrants and the geographic conditions of Dade County. The Cuban economic enclave would have been extremely difficult to establish without access to Latin American capital and without the generous aid of the U.S. government. The rapidity and size of the Cuban emigration to the United States, combined with concentration in Dade County, made Cuban Americans politically relevant in a short time.

—*Dario Moreno*

SUGGESTED READINGS:

• Perez, Lisandro. "Cuban Miami." In *Miami Now!: Immigration, Ethnicity, and Social Change*, edited by Guillermo Grenier and Alex Stepick III. Gainesville: University Press of Florida, 1992. Describes the demographics of Cuban immigration to the United States and the establishment of the Cuban enclave.

• Portes, Alejandro, and Robert L. Bach. *Latin Journey: Cuban and Mexican Immigrants in the United States*. Berkeley: University of California Press, 1985. Surveys the establishment of the Cuban enclave in Miami and compares the Mexican and Cuban immigration experiences.

• Portes, Alejandro, and Alex Stepick. *City on the Edge: The Transformation of Miami*. Berkeley: University of California Press, 1993. Analyzes Miami's development as a Cuban American-dominated world city, using a variety of methods including history, survey results, personal interviews, and press accounts.

• Stack, John F., and Christopher L. Warren. "The Reform Tradition and Ethnic Politics: Metropolitan Miami Confronts the 1990s." In *Miami Now!: Immigration, Ethnicity, and Social Change*, edited by Guillermo Grenier and Alex Stepick III. Gainesville:

University Press of Florida, 1992. Describes the political structure of Dade County politics and how three ethnic groups (African Americans, Cuban Americans, and non-Hispanic whites) interact with one another.

Cuban immigration: Thousands of Cubans have moved to the United States since the nineteenth century. The majority came after 1959 as political exiles from Fidel CASTRO's revolution. The Cuban exodus can be divided into several historical stages, reflecting changing relations between Cuba and the United States.

The Prerevolutionary Period. Prior to 1959, a steady stream of Cubans moved to the United States. Large-scale migration began with the Ten Years' War in Cuba (1868-1878), accelerated during the Spanish-American War, and proceeded during the twentieth century. By the early 1900's, Cubans had established immigrant colonies in Key West, Tampa, New York City, and New Orleans, mostly as a result of political and economic turmoil in Cuba. Miami became an important Cuban center during the 1930's after the overthrow of Gerardo Machado's dictatorship (1924-1933). During the 1940's and 1950's, thousands of Cubans migrated to the United States seeking better economic opportunities. By 1959, about forty thousand Cubans lived in the United States; most were either political refugees or labor migrants.

The Golden Exile. The massive exodus of Cuban refugees began with the dismantling of Fulgencio Batista's dictatorship, which lasted from 1952 to 1958. Castro's overthrow of Batista unleashed the first socialist revolution in the Americas and also created thousands of refugees. The first to leave Cuba were military officers, political leaders, government workers, large landowners, and entrepreneurs closely associated with Batista. As the revolution became more radical, disillusioned members of the middle class such as professionals, technicians, managers, and administrators joined the diaspora. The period from 1959 to 1962 has been dubbed the "golden exile" because most of the refugees came from the upper and middle strata of Cuban society. The majority were urban, middle-aged, well-educated, white-collar workers. Many left Cuba for political or religious reasons, fearing persecution by the revolutionary government. About 215,000 Cubans came to the United States during this wave of immigration.

The CUBAN MISSILE CRISIS of October, 1962, interrupted the large-scale migration of Cubans to the United States. Nearly seven thousand Cubans arrived in Florida by boat between 1962 and 1965, in addition to more than fifty thousand who came through other countries such as Spain and Mexico. Commercial transportation between Cuba and the United States was suspended until September, 1965, when the Cuban government opened the port of Camarioca, allowing some five thousand Cubans to leave the country.

The Freedom Airlift. The opening of Camarioca signaled the beginning of a new stage in the Cuban diaspora. Diplomatic negotiations between Washington and Havana created an air bridge that operated between December, 1965, and April, 1973, the so-called FREEDOM AIRLIFT that took approximately 302,000 refugees to the United States. By 1973, the Cuban exodus had become more representative of the island's population in terms of income, occupation, and education. The proportion of professionals and managers

declined; a growing percentage of exiles had working-class backgrounds. The changes in the refugee flow reflected the growing impact of revolutionary programs on wider segments of the Cuban population, such as small-scale vendors and artisans. Thus, Miami's Cuban enclave became primarily a middle- and lower-class community, reproducing the heterogeneous structure of the sending society.

In April, 1973, the FREEDOM AIRLIFT ended, and Cuban migration decreased substantially. Fewer than forty thousand Cubans arrived in the United States between 1973 and 1979, mostly via other countries, including Jamaica and Venezuela. Economic motives became more important than political ones during this phase of the exodus. By the end of the 1970's, material and ideological incentives to emigrate were practically

Thousands of Cubans emigrated in the Freedom Airlift. (Otto G. Richter Library, University of Miami)

inseparable. Cubans increasingly resembled economic migrants from countries such as Mexico or the Dominican Republic, driven abroad by their desire to improve their standards of living.

The Mariel Exodus. The MARIEL BOAT LIFT, a mass emigration of Cubans from Mariel Harbor to Florida, took place between April and September of 1980. The sudden and massive flow of Cubans to the United States resulted in part from the visit of more than 100,000 exiles to Cuba in 1979. The immediate cause of the boat lift was the occupation of the Peruvian embassy in Havana by more than ten thousand Cubans. Contrary to media reports, only about 2 percent of the *marielitos* were common criminals, although about 25 percent had been in Cuban jails for various reasons. (The diminutive term *marielito* itself reflected the public scorn accorded to the new immigrants.)

Altogether, approximately 125,000 Cubans arrived in Key West during the Mariel exodus. Most of the new arrivals were young, single men. Many were black or mulatto; the majority had a working-class background and less than a high-school education. The Mariel exodus deepened the rifts between "old" and "new" Cubans in Miami, where most *marielitos* eventually settled.

Cuban immigration to the United States slowed after 1980 because the U.S. government no longer considered all Cubans to be political refugees. Between 1981 and 1991, about 154,000 Cuban immigrants were admitted to the United States, compared to 264,900 admitted during the 1970's. Most were unskilled laborers and service workers, reflecting the socioeconomic composition of the Cuban population more accurately than before.

Many Cubans were unable to leave their country because of legal and political complications in Cuba and the United States. Thousands of families on both shores still wait to be reunited. In 1985, the Cuban government suspended an agreement to facilitate emigration in protest against RADIO MARTÍ, an anti-Castro station sponsored by the U.S. government. Emigration remained a thorny issue in the relations between the two countries throughout the 1980's.

In 1990, the U.S. census counted 1,043,932 Cubans in the United States, most of whom lived in Florida and New Jersey. Other important Cuban population centers were in New York, California, and Puerto Rico. In the 1990's, the number of Cuban Americans was equal to about 10 percent of Cuba's population. The exodus continued, spurred by growing impoverishment and political repression of the Cuban people.

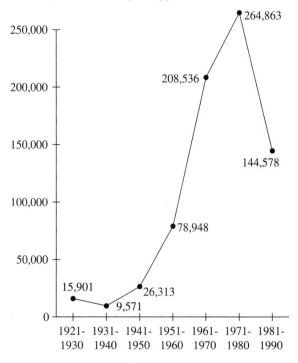

CUBAN IMMIGRATION TO THE UNITED STATES, 1921-1990

Source: Data are from Marlita A. Reddy, ed., *Statistical Record of Hispanic Americans* (Detroit: Gale Research, 1993), Tables 25 and 26.

U.S. Policy. Cuba's socialist revolution seriously challenged U.S. interests in Latin America and the Caribbean. Accordingly, public policy toward Cuban exiles was framed in the context of the Cold War between U.S. capitalism and Soviet communism. The U.S. government classified Cuban immigrants as refugees fleeing ideological or religious persecution in their country of origin. This legal status helped the exiles to adapt and improve economically in the United States and Puerto Rico. Thus, U.S. policy tended to encourage emigration from Cuba in order to destabilize Castro's regime. The concentration of large numbers of refugees in the Miami area became a strategic and symbolic resource in the struggle to overthrow the Cuban government.

The CUBAN REFUGEE PROGRAM, which operated between 1961 and 1981, represented an exceptional case in the immigration policy of an industrialized country. The federal government spent more than two billion dollars to rehabilitate the exiles occupationally, educationally, and linguistically. The program relocated Cubans outside the congested Miami area, provided economic and medical aid, awarded student fellowships, organized English classes, loaned money, and offered technical assistance to regularize the immigrants' legal status in the United States. Even the requirements for the naturalization of Cuban exiles were relaxed. No other immigrant group, with the possible exception of the Vietnamese, has received such massive amounts of aid from the host society.

The Cuban Refugee Program not only supported the exiles' efforts to recover their financial independence, but also promoted their sense of identity as a special group. The federal government favored Cubans over other Latino groups such as Mexicans and Salvadorans. Local authorities and private citizens in Miami reinforced the enthusiastic reception by the federal government during the 1960's. In 1963, Dade County launched the first bilingual program in a U.S. public school, and in 1973 the county declared itself officially bilingual in English and Spanish. The prestigious public image of Cuban Americans remained intact until the Mariel exodus recycled many of the negative stereotypes promoted by the Cuban government. In 1980, Dade County voters approved a measure to prohibit the use of public funds for bilingual activities.

The MARIEL BOAT LIFT transformed the Cuban community abroad. Castro's government coined the term *escoria* (literally "scum") to underline the undesirable elements of the Mariel exodus: petty criminals, mental patients, prostitutes, and other socially undesirable types. Although most of the new immigrants did not fit the stereotype, the U.S. media tended to portray the *marielitos* in a negative light. The sudden influx of thousands of refugees in Miami contributed to housing, employment, crime, and other problems that stigmatized the entire Cuban population in the United States. The Cuban American community had lost its grip on U.S. public opinion and the federal government.

The Mariel boat lift prompted a reevaluation of U.S. policy toward Cuban immigration. After 1980, Cubans arriving in the United States were not automatically considered to be refugees but were classed as "entrants (status pending)," an ambivalent category that placed them in a legal limbo for an indefinite period. This classification did not provide the special benefits accorded to those granted political asylum. To qualify as refugees, Cubans had to prove political persecution in their home country. Only some groups of Cubans, such as former political prisoners, were eligible for refugee status.

In the 1990's, U.S. immigration policy toward Cuba became based less on ideological than on pragmatic grounds. The federal government proved more interested in controlling its southern borders with Latin America and the Caribbean than in attracting new refugees. During the 1980's and 1990's, Washington sought to reduce the Cuban flow because of Cuban immigrants' growing socioeconomic diversity and because Cuba no longer played a key international role in the aftermath of the Cold War against the former Soviet Union. The net effect of U.S. immigration policy toward Cuba in the early 1990's, however, was to stimulate the clandestine flow of Cubans into the United States. This policy proved to be self-contradictory: On one hand, the federal government insisted on closing the border to unauthorized immigration; on the other, it welcomed Cubans with open arms.   —*Jorge Duany*

SUGGESTED READINGS:

• Boswell, Thomas D., and James R. Curtis. *The Cuban-American Experience: Culture, Images, and Perspectives.* Totowa, N.J.: Rowman & Allanheld, 1983. A historical, geographic, and cultural overview of the Cuban community in the United States. Especially valuable for its discussion of language, religion, and politics in Cuban Miami.

• Cobas, José, and Jorge Duany. *Los cubanos en Puerto Rico: Economía étnica e identidad cultural.* Río Piedras: Editorial de la Universidad de Puerto Rico, 1994. A critical analysis of the Cuban community in San Juan, arguing that the exiles have specialized in small-scale commerce and other middleman occupations.

• Esteve, Himilce. *Exilio cubano en Puerto Rico: Su impacto socio-político (1959-1983).* San Juan, Puerto Rico: Raíces, 1984. The first extended treatment of Cubans in San Juan, emphasizing their harmonious integration into Puerto Rican society.

• Jorge, Antonio, Jaime Suchlicki, and Adolfo Leyva de Varona, eds. *Cuban Exiles in Florida: Their Presence and Contributions.* Coral Gables, Fla.: Research Institute for Cuban Studies, University of Miami, 1991. A compilation of recent essays on Cubans in Miami, celebrating their positive impact on American culture and society.

• Masud-Piloto, Félix Roberto. *With Open Arms: Cuban Migration to the United States.* Totowa, N.J.: Rowman & Littlefield, 1988. A historical survey of the Cuban exodus since 1959, emphasizing U.S. immigration policy toward Cuba.

• Pedraza-Bailey, Silvia. *Political and Economic Migrants in America: Cubans and Mexicans.* Austin:

University of Texas Press, 1985. A classic comparison of Cuban and Mexican Americans and the differential impact of immigration policy on their socioeconomic adaptation to the United States.

- Portes, Alejandro, and Robert L. Bach. *Latin Journey: Cuban and Mexican Immigrants in the United States*. Berkeley: University of California Press, 1985. An excellent survey of Cubans and Mexicans who settled in Florida and Texas during the 1970's, contrasting their social, economic, and cultural incorporation.

- Portes, Alejandro, and Alex Stepick. *City on the Edge: The Transformation of Miami*. Berkeley: University of California Press, 1993. A sociological and historical portrait of the Cuban American community and its relations with other ethnic groups.

Cuban Missile Crisis (1962): From October 14 to October 28, 1962, the United States and the Soviet Union were on the brink of war because of the construction of Soviet missile sites in Cuba. This crisis put a halt to all legal transportation and immigration between the United States and Cuba.

On October 14, 1962, U.S. reconnaissance aircraft flew over Cuba, photographing the construction of Soviet medium-range missile bases near San Cristobal. This situation signaled an international crisis that affected already strained relations between Cuba and the United States. President John F. Kennedy and his top advisers decided that the missile bases should not be allowed to remain in Cuba because their proximity presented a risk to national security.

In response to the Soviet military buildup in Cuba, on October 21 the United States set up a limited naval blockade to prevent the shipment of further Soviet military equipment to Cuba. U.S. nuclear forces were placed on high alert. Thousands of militant Cuban exiles living in the United States viewed the crisis as an opportunity for the United States to launch its own missiles into Cuba, then topple Fidel Castro from power. These exiles were still reeling from the failed BAY OF PIGS INVASION, and many felt deserted by the Kennedy Administration. The administration, however, believed that an air strike was a drastic and irrevocable action and that a blockade was less likely to provoke war.

On October 24, U.S. officials learned that Soviet ships had stopped short of the blockade line. Construction of the missile sites continued nevertheless. On October 27, the United States received information that five missile sites in Cuba appeared to be fully operational. Soviet personnel in New York prepared to destroy their diplomatic documents.

The heightened tensions gave way to an announcement on October 28 by Soviet premier Nikita Khrushchev that to prevent escalation to war, work on the missile sites would stop. The missile sites would be dismantled and shipped back to the Soviet Union. The threat of nuclear warfare involving the United States, the Soviet Union, and Cuba was thereby averted.

The missile crisis had a strong impact on Cubans living in the United States and those in Cuba seeking to leave. Legal emigration was halted, forcing an estimated fifty-six thousand Cubans to emigrate illegally between 1962 and 1965. Most of these Cubans made their way to the United States via long and costly routes through Mexico and Spain. Those leaving directly from Cuba were granted immediate entry into the United States because they were considered political refugees. Approximately six thousand Cuban prisoners from the Bay of Pigs invasion and their families were allowed to emigrate legally. These Cubans were exchanged by Cuba for much-needed medical supplies.

Cuban Refugee Program (Feb. 27, 1961—Sept. 30, 1981): The federally funded relief agency, administered by the Florida State Department of Public Welfare, was established in 1961 to help Cuban refugees fleeing Fidel CASTRO's Communist regime. During two decades of operation, it provided $1.4 billion in money, food, medical care, and social services to a total of nearly one million Cuban exiles.

President John F. Kennedy regarded the Cuban refugee plight as one of national responsibility. On January 27, 1961, three months before he sponsored the ill-fated BAY OF PIGS INVASION, Kennedy instructed Secretary of Health, Education, and Welfare (HEW) Abraham Ribicoff to aid the exiles until their repatriation. Ribicoff formulated a comprehensive assistance plan, financed partly from the Mutual Security Contingency Fund appropriated by Congress.

The following month, the Cuban Refugee Center was established in Miami to administer registration, resettlement, and relief activities. *El Refugio* occupied the landmark Freedom Tower from 1961 to 1974. It became Miami's version of Ellis Island, with a staff of 150 medical and administrative personnel. Voluntary agencies, such as the Catholic Relief Services, the Church World Service (Protestant), the United Hebrew Immigrant Aid Society Service, and the nonsectarian International Rescue Committee, helped resettle Cu-

LAUNCH POSITION

MISSILE-READY TENTS

MISSILE ERECTORS

U.S. reconnaissance aircraft photographed Cuban missile bases. (AP/Wide World Photos)

ban exiles throughout the United States and distributed used clothing.

Refugee processing included registration, U.S. Employment Service interviews and classification, a medical examination, a chest X ray, inoculations, a voluntary agency interview for relocation, an American Red Cross personal kit, federal surplus food distribution, and monthly financial assistance, if necessary, of $100 per family and $60 per single case. American nationals repatriated from Cuba also received emergency welfare services.

Refugees with professional and technical skills were retrained for practice in the United States, and HEW provided a loan program for Cuban students in colleges and universities. Bilingual education was created for primary and secondary exile students. In 1965, the U.S. government responded to the chaotic Camarioca boat lift with the FREEDOM AIRLIFT, processing 260,561 refugees, most of them penniless and with no belongings but the clothes they wore, between 1965 and 1973.

In 1975, Ricardo Núñez became the first Cuban American director of *El Refugio*, which had suffered substantial economic and personnel reductions. Núñez presented Congress with statistics showing that since the mid-1960's, between 80 and 90 percent of the registered refugees had been self-supporting, and of the nearly 300,000 resettled, many had returned to Miami. In October, 1978, a five-year phaseout began; the 125,000 exiles of the 1980 MARIEL BOAT LIFT were an exception to the phaseout. When government budget cuts in 1981 abruptly ended the program, 1,200 refugees were left without assistance. Most were women between the ages of fifty-five and sixty-five, many former homemakers who did not speak English and were too young for Social Security benefits but too old to find work. The last *El Refugio* director, Héctor Vilar de Bo, proudly stated that the money invested by the government in the program was paid back in twenty years through taxes paid by successful Cubans.

Cuban Revolution: The Cuban Revolution was a response to sixty years of United States domination. Led by Fidel CASTRO, the revolution attempted to transform Cuba into a self-sufficient, egalitarian, and politically independent society.

The Event. On January 8, 1959, Castro led his ragtag guerrilla army into Havana. A week earlier, Cuban dictator Fulgencio Batista had gone into comfortable exile in the Dominican Republic. For more than two years, Castro's forces had ambushed and harassed Ba-

tista's army into submission. The defeat of the dictatorship and Castro's bold promises of social change signaled the beginning of the Cuban Revolution.

Origins. The Cuban Revolution represented more than the collapse of the old order; it also signified an end to American economic and political domination. The United States had controlled Cuba since 1900. The PLATT AMENDMENT (1902), an American-imposed addition to the first Cuban constitution, gave the United States the right to intervene in Cuban affairs until 1933. The United States also gained perpetual use of the naval base at Guantánamo Bay.

American dominance took on an economic character between 1933 and 1959. During that time, the two nations agreed to various trade arrangements in which the United States would buy most of Cuba's sugar production. In return, Cuba opened its doors to American products. Economically dependent on the United States, Cuba was unable to develop its own industries.

Batista dominated Cuban politics after 1933. A corrupt leader with close ties to American business interests, Batista did little to develop the island. Under his rule, Cuba became a playground for rich Americans who flocked to Havana for its beaches, casinos, and nightclubs. Meanwhile, the quality of life for most Cubans stagnated or worsened. Beset by poverty and unemployment, many Cubans suffered from malnutrition and lived in inadequate housing. The country also had high rates of illiteracy and infant mortality. These conditions angered Cuban intellectuals and students, who began to challenge the old regime.

On July 26, 1953, Castro, then a young lawyer, tried to overthrow Batista by attacking a military garrison in the city of Santiago. Known as the Moncada Barracks Attack, the failed revolt landed Castro in prison. Eventually exiled to Mexico, Castro vowed to return and liberate Cuba. In November, 1956, Castro and a handful of followers sailed home aboard a rickety yacht called the *Granma*. They then began their guerrilla war against the Batista government.

Guerrilla War. Few observers, Cuban or foreign, had given Castro's insurgency any chance of success. After nearly perishing in a storm in the Gulf of Mexico, Castro and fifteen survivors took refuge in the Sierra Maestra in the eastern part of the island. There, they received support and cover among Cuba's poorest peasants. During the early stages of the war, the *fidelistas*, as they came to be known, conducted hit-and-run attacks on isolated military posts. They grew increasingly daring, engaging Batista's army in larger encounters near Cuba's main cities.

Fidel Castro, at right, explains plans for land reform shortly after the revolution. (AP/Wide World Photos)

At the onset of the struggle, the *fidelista* group was one of many anti-Batista organizations active in Cuba. Larger, better-organized movements operated in Havana and Santiago. Over time, however, Batista's repressive measures weakened the urban opposition. At the same time, the *fidelistas* continued to grow in strength, size, and popularity. Toward the end of 1957, Castro's army had grown to three hundred combatants, some of whom were peasants from the Sierra Maestra.

In February, 1957, correspondent Herbert Matthews of *The New York Times* sneaked behind battle lines and interviewed Castro. Matthews' descriptions of the guerrilla war provided the movement with badly needed publicity. Most Cubans and the world were captivated by the romantic mystique of the bearded guerrillas who defied Batista's modern army. Such coverage and an important victory at El Uvero in March, 1957, consolidated Castro's position as the leader of the anti-Batista opposition.

As rebel victories mounted, Batista's army became demoralized and offered meager resistance. By August, 1958, the tide had turned, as the *fidelistas* turned back Batista's last major military offensive. Three months later, Castro launched his own final assault, winning important victories at Las Villas and Santa Clara. By New Year's Eve, 1958, the road to Havana lay open.

Revolutionary Changes. Once in power, CASTRO made good on his promises to reform Cuba. Never forgetting the peasants who helped him during the guerrilla war, Castro moved to ensure that every Cuban had access to the basic necessities of life. Within months of taking power, Castro implemented rent and price controls and raised the salaries of lower-class Cubans. He also provided free medical care, schooling, and nutrition programs. Various studies have shown that most Cubans lived longer and healthier lives after 1970.

Castro financed his social reconstruction of Cuba through socialist economic policies. He expropriated both American- and Cuban-owned businesses, placing their control in the hands of the Cuban state. Castro also initiated a sweeping agrarian reform program that broke up large landed estates, creating peasant cooperatives and larger, state-run collective farms. It was through these state-controlled enterprises that Castro hoped to diversify the Cuban economy and break Cuba's dependence on sugar and U.S. trade.

Not all Cubans approved of the revolution. Having seen Castro as a threat to their own personal interests, many upper- and middle-class Cubans voluntarily left Cuba after 1959. Most emigrated to the United States, where they organized a vocal anti-Castro opposition. The loss of elite elements of Cuban society amounted to a "brain drain," as many lawyers, physicians, scientists, and businesspeople joined the exile community. By 1974, nearly 600,000 Cubans had left their homeland, followed by 150,000 more after the MARIEL BOAT LIFT in 1980.

Obstacles. American hostility represented a major obstacle to the Cuban Revolution. Angered by the confiscation of American interests, the United States attempted to punish Castro through economic and diplomatic isolation. Such animosity pushed Cuba solidly into the Soviet Union's orbit, and the country became Moscow's client state and trading partner. During their long and stormy relationship, Cuba and the United States confronted each other during the BAY OF PIGS INVASION (April, 1961) and the CUBAN MISSILE CRISIS (October, 1962).

The Cuban Revolution reinforced Washington's anti-Communist stand in Latin America. To neutralize Castro's revolutionary fervor, Washington pursued its own "capitalist revolution" by rewarding compliant governments with massive amounts of U.S. assistance. Governments sympathetic to Castro earned Washington's ire and were punished with covert and military intervention. Despite these policies, Washington failed to contain the revolution. During the 1970's and 1980's, the Cuban Revolution projected itself abroad, sending military and humanitarian assistance to developing nations in Africa and Latin America.

Ultimately, it was the collapse of the Soviet Union that blunted the course of Castro's revolution. After 1990, Cubans encountered shortages in foodstuffs, medicines, and hardware. Cuba also remained dependent on sugar production and still imported much of its food. Despite these and other problems, Castro retained much of his popularity. The glamour of the early days had faded, but the Cuban Revolution continued to rumble at a slower, more pragmatic pace.

—*Pablo R. Arreola*

SUGGESTED READINGS: • Benjamin, Medea, Joseph Collins, and Michael Scott. *No Free Lunch: Food and Revolution in Cuba Today.* San Francisco: Institute for Food and Development Policy, 1984. • Lockwood, Lee. *Castro's Cuba, Cuba's Fidel.* Boulder, Colo.: Westview Press, 1990. • Pérez, Louis A., Jr. *Cuba: Between Reform and Revolution.* New York: Oxford University Press, 1988. • Szulc, Tad. *Fidel: A Critical Portrait.* New York: Morrow, 1986. • Wright, Thomas. *Latin America in the Era of the Cuban Revolution.* New York: Praeger, 1991.

The United States sided with Cuba in its war for independence from Spain. (Library of Congress)

Cuban War of Independence (1895-1898): The Cuban rebellion against Spain began on February 24, 1895. The Cuban people struggled for independence without outside support until April 25, 1898, when the United States entered the conflict on their side. Spain and the United States signed an armistice agreement on August 12, 1898, ending the SPANISH-AMERICAN WAR.

From the days of exploration in the sixteenth century, Cuba had been a Spanish possession. Slavery was established on the island. During the nineteenth century, plantation owners in the southern portion of the United States became interested in expanding their cotton plantation system to Cuba. President John Quincy Adams referred to Cuba as a national appendage of the North American continent.

Beginning in 1848, three American Democratic presidents attempted to acquire the island for the United States. Secretary of State William Seward tried to negotiate annexation with Spain's consent. The Ten

Years' War, a struggle for independence beginning in 1868, strained the forbearance of Presidents Ulysses S. Grant and Rutherford B. Hayes. During this rebellion, Spain abolished slavery on the island.

Before the rebellion of 1895, American and European capital flooded onto the island. New methods of farming, particularly in the sugar industry, were brought into Cuba. Americans invested heavily in plantations, railroads, mines, and other businesses. Between 1889 and 1894, the volume of trade between Cuba and the United States increased by 50 percent. The United States became the primary market for Cuban sugar as Europe became self-sufficient in that commodity.

Cuba's prosperity was threatened as European production of sugar beets forced down the price of sugar. The depression of 1893 also contributed to price declines. To protect American sugar growers, the U.S. government imposed a 40 percent tariff on imported sugar, including that from Cuba. Between 1894 and

Xavier Cugat. (AP/Wide World Photos)

1895, the price of sugar on the world market dropped from 8 cents per pound to 2 cents. The Cuban rebellion broke out in the midst of this economic crisis.

American economic interests were endangered by the rebellion, as Cuban rebels attacked American property in an attempt to force American intervention on their side. American business interests renewed their call for annexation of Cuba. Presidents Grover Cleveland and William McKinley tried to mediate the conflict between Spain and Cuba.

There appeared to be no reason for the United States to go to war against Spain. A mysterious explosion aboard the USS *Maine* and the inflammatory press reporting of that event, however, convinced McKinley to declare war.

The TREATY OF PARIS, signed in December, 1898, granted independence to Cuba. American troops left Cuba in 1902, but the PLATT AMENDMENT provided that Cuba could make no agreement that would affect its independence, that the United States could intervene to keep order, and that the United States would be given (by lease or sale) land for naval bases. Cuba remained under a form of U.S. control until 1934.

Cuento: Short story, folktale, or fairy tale. A *cuento* is commonly used to illustrate an argument or effectively communicate a *moraleja*, or moral lesson. The *cuento* is a form of folklore that derives from popular oral tradition and combines mythical sources, actual history, and fantasy. Other cultural forms of expression that incorporate oral tradition include CORRIDOS (or ballads), DÉCIMAS (ten-verse poems), and ROMANCES (narrative fragments). *Cuentos* are used in Chicano activist rhetoric as a strategy for simply stated explanations and persuasion. The oral tradition of the *cuento* is a source of inspiration for Chicano literature.

Cugat, Xavier (Francisco de Asis Javier Cugat Mingall de Bru y Deulofeo; Jan. 1, 1900, Gerona, Spain—Oct. 27, 1990, Barcelona, Spain): Violinist, bandleader, and composer. In 1904, Cugat moved with his family to Cuba. Cugat studied violin, and at the age of twelve he became a violinist with Havana's National Theatre Symphony Orchestra. As a prodigy, he got the opportunity to study in Berlin, Germany, and work with the Berlin Symphony Orchestra. Cugat went to the United States and performed at Carnegie Hall in New York City. Eventually, he moved to Los Angeles and worked as a cartoonist for the *Los Angeles Times*. He also found the time to work as a film producer and as a sound mixer for Charlie Chaplin.

In 1928, Cugat formed his first Latin dance band. During the 1930's, he became a film star. Cugat became the bandleader at New York's Waldorf-Astoria Hotel in 1933; later, he was featured at many hotels and nightclubs as well as on radio stations. Cugat was one of the prominent figures who popularized Latin rhythms in the United States. In 1944, he had a hit song with the original version of "Babalu." With his retirement in 1970, Cugat turned over control of his band to Tito PUENTE. In 1980, he moved back to Spain. He is remembered for popularizing the African-Latin sound as well as for being married to singer Abbé Lane and to guitarist-singer Charo.

Cultural conflict: Clash between individuals or groups belonging to different cultures. Continuous contact with another culture may affect a person's sense of cultural belonging. When entering a new culture, an individual may go through a phase of cultural shock, an adverse reaction to all the new customs experienced. Gradually, the person assimilates or acculturates (*see* ACCULTURATION VERSUS ASSIMILATION).

For a group, the process of cultural adaptation is more complicated. Cohesion among the members of the group may increase resistance to change. This resistance may take the form of open conflict with members of the established community. Conflict can be triggered by the dominance of one cultural group over one or more others. Dominance can include political, economic, and social forms of discrimination.

One of the harshest types of DISCRIMINATION is geographic or other segregation. Latinos historically faced separate facilities for housing and education in the United States. Discriminatory practices are fueled by and result in prejudice, thus forming a vicious cycle of cultural conflict.

The reaction of dominated groups to cultural conflict can be active or passive. They may choose separatism, an active reaction eschewing the structure of the dominant society in order to retain the cultural and other values that have led to discrimination against them. If the attempt to separate is unsuccessful, a pattern of accommodation will take place whereby the members of the dominated group remain within the framework of the dominant society and, out of necessity, accept the conditions they cannot control. They conform to their subordinate position and to the implicit and explicit rules for dealing with the dominating group.

There is always potential conflict in situations of cultural mixing, particularly when one group is at a

In situations of cultural conflict, groups may cling to elements of their culture such as language. (Robert Fried)

clear disadvantage. Members of the disadvantaged group will attempt to change their disadvantaged status to gain cultural advantages. If the cultural conflict is open, the consequences may include protests, terrorism, or other rebellious acts, as evident during the height of the CHICANO MOVEMENT in the 1960's and in expressions of PUERTO RICAN NATIONALISM. If the conflict is repressed, aggression may be turned against the members of another dominated group, such as African Americans, or against members of one's own group, as in cases of domestic violence, because its expression toward the dominating group would be too dangerous.

Cultural democracy: Acceptance of differing cultures. Cultural democracy involves a person's right to identify with his or her own culture in the midst of other cultures. Within a cultural democracy, individuals respect people from other cultures, and the individual is allowed cultural autonomy without a need for assimilation (*see* ACCULTURATION VERSUS ASSIMILATION). This meaning of cultural democracy was introduced in the United States in the 1920's and became particularly important during the Civil Rights movement of the 1960's, when African Americans, Latinos, and others began to more publicly assert ethnic pride and to demand equal rights.

Cultural exchange: Interaction between members of different cultural groups results in diffusion of cultural traits. As a consequence of such cultural exchange, the cultures and people involved will undergo some change. The degree and rate of this change may vary among groups.

During extended periods of colonization or conquest, the dominant group may try to impose its cultural traits by force, leading to resistance and resentment on the part of members of the threatened culture. Cultural domination may occur in ostensibly peaceful endeavors as well. During missionary activity, for ex-

Latino children have adopted American customs such as those surrounding Halloween while introducing new customs to non-Latino children. (David Bacon)

ample, the imposition of cultural beliefs is often less violent but no less influential.

As travel to foreign countries has become common and television has brought the entire world to homes, people have come into indirect contact with more cultures. Cultural exchange therefore may occur more frequently. It may also occur through the expansion of international trade in consumer goods and cultural products such as books and music.

Cultural exchange occurs directly through migration and tourism, as people come into personal contact with other cultures. In the case of tourism, the contact is fleeting. Immigrants, however, must adapt to surrounding cultures by trying to assimilate or by remaining in cultural enclaves among people of similar backgrounds. Even people moving within a country or even a state can experience cultural exchange as they adapt to their new homes.

Cultural exchange resulting from various forms of cultural domination is part of the heritage of virtually all Latino subgroups. Intercultural contact often resulted in adoption of cultural traits on both sides, as when Mexicans and Indians took on the Catholic religion of the missionaries and Anglo settlers adopted words, foods, and architectural styles.

Individuals may resist the influence of another culture in an effort to protect their own cultural identity. This results in an uncomfortable feeling often referred to as culture shock. In severe cases, it is a serious maladjustment. An individual may experience uncertain expectations, confusion caused by new customs, a feeling of being conspicuous and different, and the frustration of not being able to express thoughts in a foreign language. Once the stage of culture shock is passed, cultural exchange often results in a positive experience. It gives people a chance to grow and to adopt what they see as most useful from a wider array of beliefs and customs.

Cultural nationalism: Despite strong assimilationist tendencies within American culture, Latino groups are perceived to be highly culturally nationalist, reinforcing their separate cultures. Some factors that explain this phenomenon include the worldwide rise of nationalism, geographic proximity to Latin American homelands, and the experience of social injustice.

Cultural nationalism takes different forms among the major Latino subgroups. The best-known examples among Mexican Americans were statements and actions of some proponents of the CHICANO MOVEMENT in the 1960's and 1970's, who declared their loyalty to a mythical Chicano homeland of AZTLÁN in the American Southwest. PUERTO RICAN NATIONALISM, favoring independence for the island, has influenced Puerto Rican social and cultural life on the mainland. Many Cuban Americans continue to identify with their homeland, where they hope to return, and take a passionate interest in its politics. Thus, Latinos appear to challenge the notion that the United States is a "MELTING POT" where immigrants shed their original cultures and become culturally "Americanized."

According to Mario Barrera, one important factor in Latino group identity that has persisted for many years, is Latinos' belief that they are in a condition of persistent inequality. The experience of feeling treated unjustly by the majority Anglo population has led many Latinos to find instruments for survival and refuge in the resources provided by their indigenous cultures.

It is not surprising that when the Latino community feels threatened, it develops institutions for survival that tend to reinforce Latino cultural identities. Mutual-aid societies (*MUTUALISTAS*) among Mexican American communities during the nineteenth century served as instruments for both economic and cultural survival. More recently, Mexican Americans have used the symbolic celebrations of Mexican Independence Day (September 16) and of CINCO DE MAYO (May 5) as occasions for cultural and social revival.

When their communities have experienced prejudice and discrimination, Puerto Ricans in the Northeast and the Midwest have responded through institutional development. They have created cultural, civic, and political institutions such as ASPIRA, the Ruiz Belvis and the Pedro Albizu Campos cultural centers in Chicago, and Boricua College and El Museo del Barrio in New York.

Additional factors that have contributed to cultural nationalism among important segments of these communities is the geographical proximity of their lands of origin. Many foreign-born as well as U.S.-born Mexican Americans travel between the Southwest and Mexico. The continuing flow of immigrants across the border likewise reinforces Mexican culture and traditions within Mexican American communities. A similar situation prevails among Puerto Ricans, who move frequently between the mainland and the island.

Cubans also exhibit a strong conservation of their culture despite the rapid assimilation of second- and third-generation Cuban Americans, in part because of the proximity of Cuba to southern Florida, home to the largest concentration of Cuban communities.

Latinos have created their own groups in response to prejudice and discrimination, showing pride in their heritage. (Frances M. Roberts)

A Mexican American teacher introduces students to Mexican food items. (James Shaffer)

Cultural nationalism historically has been a defensive posture for groups that perceive their cultural and social existence to be threatened. As long as Latinos continue to experience subordinate status, they will continue to exhibit high levels of cultural nationalism.

Cultural pluralism: Proponents of cultural pluralism assume that it is beneficial to a society to be composed of a number of different ethnic or cultural groups that maintain their cultural traits while participating in and contributing to mainstream society. The concept of cultural pluralism was introduced by sociologist Horace Kallen in the early 1900's as an alternative to the MELTING POT THEORY, which favored assimilation of immigrants and their cultural traits.

Advocates of cultural pluralism believe that cultural differences benefit society. Diverse groups can contribute to the formation of a healthy, broadly based society, while each of these groups maintains its own cultural distinctiveness and traits, such as language, music, or social customs. Pluralists hold that culturally diverse groups can live in harmony and that mutual understanding rather than assimilation should be the goal (*see* ACCULTURATION VERSUS ASSIMILATION).

In a pluralistic or ethnically diverse society, there is often a dominant culture, frequently the culture of a colonizer. Cultural pluralism may be the result of colonization, with one cultural group entering the geographic territory of another. The presence of diverse groups in a society may be the result of colonization, conquest, or immigration, both voluntary and forced, as in the case of black slaves brought to the Americas. All three patterns are part of the history of the United States, and all have created intergroup tensions that threaten the ideal of cultural pluralism.

In a culturally pluralistic society, assimilation is not a primary goal. Diverse groups are expected to live in mutual understanding and appreciation of one another's cultures. That ideal can be facilitated through education about different subcultures. Study of languages, for example, is a way to familiarize oneself with other cultures, because language is the most immediate instrument of expression of a culture.

Despite the tremendous cultural diversity in the United States, all American groups have structures for certain cultural characteristics and values. These include patterns of work, family life, a system of kinship, foodways, a set of rules for social conduct, religion, forms of material culture, and artistic manifestations. Comparison of these structures for common social systems and practices serves as a bridge for understanding and acceptance among groups in a culturally pluralistic society.

Cultural pluralism is thought to be positive as long as cultural differences do not conflict with the norms of the dominant culture. American history is rife with conflicts between Anglos and Latinos, often centered on language issues, from the border skirmishes of the mid-1800's to the debates on BILINGUAL EDUCATION late in the twentieth century.

Efforts by Latinos to preserve or express their culture often have been met with controversy or hostility, as exemplified by debates concerning declaration of English as an official language and establishment or continuance of Chicano and other ethnic studies departments at colleges and universities. Supporters of the Chicano movement favored a form of CULTURAL NATIONALISM that emphasized Chicano cultural distinctiveness and deemphasized Chicanos' role in a common society. Such tensions between diversity and unity continued to challenge the ideal of cultural pluralism and its modern variant of MULTICULTURALISM.

Cumbia: Folkdance typical of Colombia. The *cumbia* is a courtship dance performed by couples dancing with shuffling steps and hip-rocking motion. Sometimes each female dancer carries a lit candle in her right hand. The *cumbia* can be accompanied by the *conjunto de cumbia*, featuring the *pito* (cane of millet), a transverse clarinet (tube open on both ends, with four holes) of African origin, and single-headed drums. It can also be accompanied by the *conjunto de gaitas*, including *gaitas* (duct flutes), single-headed drums, and a maraca. The music originated as instrumental only, but it has grown to include vocal elements called *coplas* or *cuartetos*.

Curanderismo: The practice of folk medicine or alternative traditional medicine. The *curandero* is a male or female folk health practitioner or spiritualist healer.

Curanderismo, as practiced in Latino communities in the United States, has roots in both Spain and Latin America. It is also closely tied to the medical and health practices of Native Americans. In Spain, there is a long history of traditional folk practitioners, including bone setters, barber-surgeons, *hernistas* (those who reduced hernias), *sacadores de la piedra* (those who remove bladder and kidney stones), midwives, and herbalists.

The Catholic church, the Inquisition, and the *Protomedicato* (the primary medical licensing body in Spain and New Spain) saw to it that only "Old Chris-

Curanderismo *is the use of folk medicine and cures.* (Impact Visuals, Allan Clear)

tians" and those who could demonstrate *limpieza de sangre* (purity of blood as Christians) could be involved in the practice of medicine on any level. Those of Jewish or Arabic background were not allowed to be health practitioners. These same institutions attempted to restrict Aztec native health practices in the New World.

After the New World was colonized by the Spanish, native health practitioners continued to practice secretly. *Curanderismo*, in native forms or in syncretic form, persisted especially among Indians, blacks, and mestizos. It was an essential feature in the survival of traditional culture. It also helped maintain native identity and was an effective mechanism against Spanish acculturation.

The practice of *curanderismo* is said to be one of the most persistent features of Latino culture. It has persisted because it functions within the cultural contexts of Latinos and provides alternatives to mainstream medicine, to which there is not always access.

Curanderos use therapeutic practices that include both supernatural and empirical theories of disease. In curing, they combine herbal and nonherbal remedies

(*see* HERBAL MEDICINE). Empirical (herbal) cures and magical or religious ritual are used to cure both physical and psychological illness. *Curanderos* frequently use what might be called witchcraft (*see* WITCHES AND WITCHCRAFT) and magic in connection with their healing practices. *Curanderos* may also be *SOBADORES* who use massage, rubbing, and manipulation of the body and body parts in their cures.

According to some scholars, *curanderismo* uses elements frequently found in modern psychotherapy. It is said to provide individuals with opportunities to resolve and thereby prevent some disorders. *Curanderas* historically have worked as midwives in Latino communities and have played valuable roles in this practice. Programs have been designed to institutionalize and upgrade the practice of some *curanderas*, particularly midwives, but most have continued in private practice rather than becoming part of a larger system.

This system of traditional medicine has demonstrated its vitality by its accommodation to and adaptation of new features, such as the growing combination of *curanderismo*, Spiritualism, and Spiritism (*see* SPIRITISM AND SPIRITUALISM). It has become an important type of alternate health care along the U.S.-Mexico border.

Curiel, Barbara. *See* **Brinson-Pineda, Barbara**

Cursillo movement: The *cursillo*, a three-day refresher course in Christianity, started in Majorca, Spain, in 1949. It began to spread to other countries in 1953. The first *cursillo* in the United States was held in Waco, Texas, in 1957.

Bishop Juan Herves of Majorca, Spain, in 1949 began what was to become the *cursillo* movement as a means to help Catholics in his diocese renew themselves in the basic truths of their faith. The diocesan council of the young men's branch of Catholic Action, the official organization of the lay apostolate in Spain, gave these three-day-weekend courses to members of Catholic Action groups in Bishop Herves' diocese.

The *cursillo* soon spread throughout Spain, gradually separating from Catholic Action and becoming independent. In 1954, a separate diocesan secretariat for the *cursillos* was established. Over time, the *cursillo* was refined and changed somewhat, but it remained basically the same as those first *cursillos*.

The purpose of the *cursillos* was to make Christian community possible in society through the establishment of permanent friendship groups in work situations and other places. These groups sought to form a movement of apostolic Christians who had a unified vision of how to bring Christian life to every environment. All things in the *cursillo* movement were directed toward this transformation of environments.

The cursillo *movement began in an attempt to help Catholics renew their faith.* (James Shaffer)

The *cursillo* made it possible for the participants (*cursillistas*) to live the fundamentals of Christianity. To encourage one another, weekly meetings, called the *cursillo ultreya*, were held. The ultimate goal of this living Christianity was to form nuclei of Christians, who helped one another discover and achieve their own personal vocations with respect to structuring Christian life and transforming it according to the Gospel.

The *cursillo* movement was brought to the United States in 1957 by two U.S. airmen and a Franciscan priest who had been active *cursillistas* in Spain. In 1960, the *cursillo* movement grew rapidly in the Southwest. Until 1961, *cursillos* were held only in Spanish, but that year the first *cursillo* for English speakers was held, in San Francisco.

By 1965, the *cursillo* movement in the United States had organized on a national basis with a national secretariat and a national *cursillo* office. By 1974, *cursillos* were being given in more than fifty nations on five continents, and it was estimated that more than two million people had participated. By 1981, almost all the 160 Catholic dioceses in the United States had introduced the *cursillo*. The *cursillo* movement joined the National Conference of Catholic Bishops and became a member of the International Catholic Organizations of the Pontifical Council for the Laity in Rome.

D

Dade County, Florida: Dade County encompasses 2,042 square miles at the southern tip of Florida. The area is a hub of Latino community, economic, and cultural life. This has not always been the case. Latinos are fairly recent arrivals in southern Florida. In 1957, they represented only 4 percent of the total population, but by 1985 that proportion had swelled to nearly 44 percent. The city of MIAMI is the main attraction and the focus of life in Dade County. It is also the city where the vast majority of the county's Latinos reside. In 1990, the city was 63 percent Latino.

The most significant period in the Latino history of Dade County began in the early 1960's with the arrival in Miami of thousands of Cuban refugees. This sudden exodus from Cuba occurred in the wake of Fidel Castro's communist revolution in 1959. Most of the early refugees came from the middle and upper strata of Cuban society. Many were well educated professionals who left successful careers at home to escape Castro and Communism. By 1990, one million Cubans had moved to the United States, with 800,000 staying in the Miami area.

Some immigrants faced language barriers, but most of the early arrivals managed to learn English and make a relatively easy entry into the world of business and the professions. In less than two decades, Cuban exiles became an integral part of Miami life. LITTLE HAVANA, part of the city where many of them chose to live, was transformed into a thriving business district and an international tourist attraction, all with a Cuban flair.

Since the 1960's, Miami has opened its doors to thousands of new immigrants. In 1972, fifty thousand Haitians (*see* HAITIAN AMERICANS) fled their island nation, seeking asylum from economic hardship and political oppression. Most settled in Miami, where their numbers continued to grow. In 1985, the number of Puerto Ricans living in the area ranged from fifty thousand to seventy thousand. In the 1990's, the ethnic mix of the area was enriched by new arrivals from Colombia, El Salvador, Nicaragua, and the Bahamas.

In the 1980's, Castro opened the Cuban port of Mariel and allowed unlimited immigration to the United States. As a result of this exodus and the asso-

Cuban Americans have become well established in Dade County. (Martin Hutner)

ciated MARIEL BOAT LIFT of 1980, the Cuban presence in Dade County and the population of Little Havana in particular grew enormously. The *marielitos*, as they came to be known, were substantially different from the first wave of Cubans to arrive in the 1960's. Many were poor, unschooled in English, and bereft of the social and educational advantages that would allow for easy assimilation. Included among them were five thousand criminals Castro permitted to emigrate. These individuals would become a powerful destabilizing influence within the Cuban American community in Miami, where as late as 1994 the difficult process of accommodation and assimilation continued.

Dallas-Fort Worth, Texas: Metropolitan complex with a 1990 population of 3,885,415. Dallas had a population of 1,006,877, about 21 percent of whom were Hispanic. It is the seat of Dallas County and is the second largest city in Texas. Fort Worth, with a population of 447,619, is the seat of Tarrant County. Throughout the metropolitan area as a whole, Latinos composed about 13 percent of the population.

John Neely Bryan became the first settler in Dallas in 1841. J. P. Dumas laid out the town site in 1844, and in 1846 the county was organized. Both were named for George Mifflin Dallas, then vice president of the United States. The city became the permanent county seat in 1850.

Fort Worth lies thirty miles west of Dallas. In 1849, Major Ripley Arnold of the United States Army founded Camp Worth on the Trinity River. That same year, Tarrant County was established, named after General Edward H. Tarrant. The first permanent settler was John Press Farmer, and the first school was started in 1854. In 1856, Fort Worth became the county seat. The first surge in population occurred after the Civil War, as many Confederate Army veterans settled there. The Chisholm Trail went through Fort Worth and brought business to the city, which was the last place before Abilene, Kansas, for cowboys to stock up on supplies and have a good time.

Railroads caused the second population surge. Two major packing companies established plants in Fort Worth in 1902, and it became a major livestock center. After oil was discovered in West Texas, Fort Worth became the gateway to the oil fields. Aviation industries, beginning in World War I, also played a role in increasing the population.

A small number of Mexican Americans moved into Dallas soon after the city was established. With the coming of the railroads in the 1870's, the Mexican

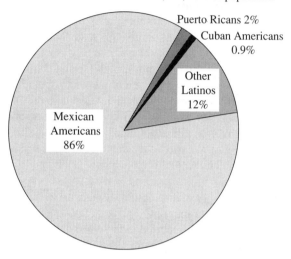

LATINO POPULATION OF DALLAS-FORT WORTH, TEXAS, 1990

Total number of Latinos = 518,917; 13% of population

Puerto Ricans 2%
Cuban Americans 0.9%
Other Latinos 12%
Mexican Americans 86%

Source: Data are from Marlita A. Reddy, ed., *Statistical Record of Hispanic Americans* (Detroit: Gale Research, 1993), Table 110.
Note: Figures represent the population of the Consolidated Metropolitan Statistical Area as delineated by the U.S. Bureau of the Census. Percentages are rounded to the nearest whole number except for Cuban Americans, for whom rounding is to the nearest 0.1%.

American population increased rapidly. The first Spanish-speaking neighborhood developed near the Missouri-Kansas-Texas (MKT) railroad track and McKinney Street. The railroad company provided housing, made from converted railroad cars, for workers and their families. This area became the nucleus of the "Little Mexico" barrio. In 1876, the Texas & Pacific railroad created a stop in Fort Worth. The city became a major shipping point for beef, and Mexican Americans moved into the area to work on the railroad.

The Mexican Revolution beginning in 1910 sent many Mexican Americans into Dallas looking for work. As the number of Mexican Americans in the city increased, they started other areas of settlement, including the Pike Park neighborhood, Cement City at Eagle Ford, and Juares Heights. The western edge of Dallas, including the lowlands of the former floodplains of the Trinity River, became home to Mexican American people in the 1920's. By 1934, Dallas had a Mexican American population of 6,650.

Housing conditions for Mexican Americans generally were poor. On September 15, 1942, a federal housing project, "Little Mexico Village," opened in Dallas. The project's conditions were far better than those in the surrounding community, but there were many more families in need of homes than there were places.

By late in the twentieth century, Mexican Americans were dispersed throughout the area. Dallas had many Latino political officeholders, businesspeople, newspapers, radio stations, and television channels.

Dance, Central and South American: Central and South Americans have a long and varied history of dance, beginning with native or indigenous dances, followed by establishment of multiethnic folk dances. Modern popular sensations have traveled abroad, particularly to the United States.

History. Dance in Central and South America began thousands of years ago. Indigenous peoples such as the Maya in northern Central America and the Incas, who reigned throughout the Andean mountains in South America, developed their own dance customs. At the end of the fifteenth century, Spanish conquistadores began to invade these territories, establishing perma-

nent communities and imposing their traditions upon the native population.

To satisfy labor demands in the conquered territories, the Spanish captured millions of people from western Africa and brought them to the New World to work as slaves in the mines and plantations and to provide domestic service. These three distinct populations—Indian, African, and Spanish—eventually mixed, creating new racial combinations and unique artistic traditions.

In most of Central and South America, the MESTIZO combination of Spanish and indigenous is dominant, and the dances reflect these influences. A sizable black or mulatto population still exists along the Caribbean, Atlantic, and Pacific coastal regions of Central and South America, except in Chile and Argentina. The arts from these areas contain strong and visible contributions from Africa.

During the last half of the twentieth century, a multitude of popular or commercial dance forms came out of Central and South America. Many became so widespread that they are now danced in clubs around the world by Latinos and non-Latinos. The large Central

A traditional Argentine dance costume. (Unicorn Stock Photos, Robert VanKirk)

and South American immigrant communities in the United States have contributed to the perpetuation of both folk and popular dances from Latino homelands.

Folk Dances. In theory, a folk dance is still practiced in its original form by those who have learned it from previous generations of practitioners. Many factors, however, contribute to the constant changes a dance undergoes over time. Around the middle of the twentieth century, national dance troupes emerged throughout Latin America, adapting traditional folk dances for the stage. Many of these troupes have toured internationally, and others have thrived under the direction of Latinos living outside their homelands.

Some of the modifications made by these dance troupes include complex choreographies, elaborate costumes, and artistic innovations. Customs such as weddings and village fiestas have been dramatized. In many cases, a dance troupe's version has completely replaced the original folk dance, and in others, a folk dance has become commercialized. As radio, television, and other technological advances in entertainment have impinged on the social function of commu-

nity dance, many traditional forms have been lost altogether.

The Caribbean Coast. The Caribbean coast spans Central and South America from the tip of the Mexican Yucatán to Venezuela. Most of this region's art forms are characterized by a significant West African presence. The dances of the Garifuna ethnic minority in Belize are particularly notable for their retentions of African traits. Examples are the *punta*, practiced during wakes and festivities, and the *dugu*, a religious dance.

Coastal dances from Panama, Colombia, and Venezuela are more triethnic: They contain elements of Spanish, indigenous, and African movements and choreographies. The CUMBIA, a couple dance done to a fast tropical beat, is one of the best-known dances in Colombia and is an excellent example of this blend of cultures. Panama's national dance, the *tamborito*, and its own version of the *cumbia* exhibit mixed cultural influences. The Venezuelan *tambor*, an improvised couple dance practiced throughout the central coast region, shows less Spanish influence. Caribbean dances

Couples dance the merengue at a club in Brooklyn, New York. (City Lore, Martha Cooper)

are noted for their focus on pelvic movements, which may be subtle. These dances usually differ from Spanish-style dance, which emphasizes an erect body and intricate footwork. The Mexican *zapateo* is one example of a Spanish-style dance.

Central America. Guatemala, El Salvador, Honduras, and Costa Rica have rich MESTIZO and indigenous traditions. The dance of *Los Moros* or *Moros y Cristianos* is practiced in Guatemala and Honduras during the festivities commemorating the clash of Christian and Moorish religions in Spain. The *son*, played on the MARIMBA, is the most popular couple dance in Guatemala. In El Salvador, a popular folk dance is the *carbonero*, which accompanies the song of the same name by Pancho Lara about indigenous coal miners of the Teisalco volcano region. Like Costa Rica's national dance, the *punto Guanacasteco*, the *carbonero* is similar to Mexican folkloric dance in the use of the women's full skirts and couple choreography.

The Andes. The Andean mountains, which run almost the entire length of the western coast of South America, were home to the Inca people for thousands of years. The most widely known dance of Inca origin is the *huayno*. It has been transformed considerably since the Spanish Conquest and is now accompanied by stringed instruments such as the harp, violin, guitar, and CHARANGO. Indigenous ZAMPOÑAS, commonly referred to in English as panpipes, are also representative instruments from the Andean region.

Colombia is the only Andean country in which people do not dance the *huayno*. The best-known Colombian Andean dance is the *bambuco*, which was a result of *mestizaje*, or Spanish-Indian mixing. Another common mestizo dance in this region is the *cueca*, also known as the *zamba* or *zamacueca*. It is a courtship dance, practiced throughout Peru, Bolivia, Chile, Argentina, and neighboring Paraguay. The use of handkerchiefs swung in small circles over the head is a characteristic feature. Although the music of the Andes is now heard all over the world, the dances it accompanies remain almost exclusively within the boundaries of the Andean mountain range.

The Plains (Los Llanos). Plains culture, found in Colombia and Venezuela, is centered on cattle ranching, which dominates most of the region's economy. Spanish customs are most common in music and dance, although indigenous elements are noticeable. The most popular dance of this region is the *joropo*, with its many variations. It is generally danced by a male-female couple, although they do not embrace. The most complex aspect of the dance is the footwork,

based on the Spanish *zapateo*, involving heel stomping and rhythmic accents with different parts of the feet. The accompanying music is played on string instruments (CUATRO, *bandola*, harp) and MARACAS.

The Pacific Coast. In the countries of Colombia, Ecuador, and Peru, African-influenced traditions predominate along the Pacific coast. The *currulao* is the best-known Colombian dance from the region reflecting this African ancestry. Although it is unrelated to the Andean *cueca*, the use of handkerchiefs is similar. Other Colombian dances such as the CONTRADANZA, the mazurka, and the polka show considerable Spanish influence. Peru's *festejo* and Ecuador's BOMBA are also representative of African presence in those countries.

Brazil. Brazil is famous for its African-derived music and dance forms, especially the SAMBA, a commercialized carnival dance form. The samba's most important predecessor is the *lundu*, a dance of Congo-Angolan derivation that is no longer practiced. It was transformed during the colonial era into an elite salon-style dance. African-based religions in Brazil, such as SANTERÍA and Candomblé, have their own dances representing the various deities and their relationships to one another. *Capoeira* is another African-derived dance form, combining martial arts, acrobatics, and intricate partnering. Until the 1970's, *capoeira* was danced exclusively by men.

Popular Dance Forms. Almost all Central and South American popular dance forms were born from folk dances, some of which are still practiced in their original form. In the 1930's, many Latin American countries began to form their own versions of big bands, then popular in the United States and Europe. Band directors arranged their national folk music for Western instruments with additional Latin percussion and sometimes other native instruments. For example, the CUMBIA has been incorporated into modern band or *orquesta* music by musical innovators such as Lucho Bermúdez and Pacho Galán. The *cumbia* soon became an international success, especially in Mexico, where it was incorporated into regional ensembles and has acquired a separate Mexican identity. Throughout the United States, particularly in the Southwest, Mexican and Central American dance clubs feature the *cumbia*. The dance is now almost unrecognizable as the traditional *cumbia* still practiced along Colombia's Atlantic coast.

Throughout the latter half of the twentieth century, musical instruments became electrified, new music and dance forms emerged, and advances in communications allowed once regionally isolated dances to

A couple dances the tango in Buenos Aires, Argentina. (Impact Visuals, Donna DeCesare)

achieve international popularity. Although dances such as the salsa, MERENGUE, *soca*, *soukous*, and others are popular among South and Central Americans, both in Latin America and in the United States, these dances are not of South or Central American origin.

Vallenato. Another folk genre from Colombia is *vallenato*, which has become commercialized and is now the most popular regional music and dance form in Colombia's Atlantic coast region. It contains five rhythms: *paseo*, CUMBIA, *son*, *puya*, and merengue. The step is different for the last two rhythms, which are faster and in a different meter. The dance involves a tight embrace by the partners and no elaboration. *Vallenato* has had some international success but is regarded as a regional art form.

Pindín. In the mid-twentieth century, Panamanian musicians developed a new music and dance form based on folk rhythms such as the *tamborito*. As with the Colombian *vallenato*, *pindín* still remains a folk style even though many groups have added electric instruments and recording companies have marketed the music as a commercial genre. Both the music and the dance are similar to *vallenato*, including the use of the accordion and the dance steps. It is not commonly danced outside of Panama.

Punta Rock. Of Belizian origin, *punta* rock is extremely popular in Honduras and El Salvador as well. In the late 1970's, Pen Cayetano created a contemporary version of his country's *punta* dance that immediately became successful. Although the music has changed dramatically, many of the same dance steps are used for both the folk and popular versions. In the United States, *punta* rock is danced along with other rhythms, such as *soca* and merengue from the Caribbean and Afro-beat rhythms such as *soukous* from Zaire.

Samba. Modern Brazilian SAMBA emerged in the early twentieth century out of the carnival tradition brought to the New World from Europe. Samba schools or *escolas*, individual dance groups that compete against one another in carnival parades, were first created in the late 1920's. Mangueira is cited as the original samba school. The dance involves both scanty and elaborate costumes and a rapid step. Samba is now danced all over the world, not only during Mardi Gras season but whenever the music is played at clubs or festivities. The *escolas* have also taken root among Brazilian immigrants to the United States and others who simply enjoy this highly energetic dance.

Tango. The Argentinean TANGO, born in Buenos Aires, is now the most representative art form of that country and has long been popular around the world. This sensual and elaborate partner dance, now found in salon-style dance clubs and musical productions, is accompanied by a variety of musical ensembles, from a single accordion to a full orchestra.

Lambada. This dance form was created in the 1980's out of Brazilian folk dances from the Northeast region such as the *puladinho*, *deboche*, and *gafieira*. It soon traveled to Europe, where it became an elaborate and virtuosic club dance. Although this altered version of the LAMBADA was met with some resistance when it returned to Brazil in the late 1980's, it was extremely popular for a number of years. Through movie ventures that exploited the partners' tight embrace as erotic, the lambada enjoyed fame all over the world. This fame was short lived, however, and the dance had lost considerable popularity by the mid-1990's.

—Alissa Simon

SUGGESTED READINGS: • Azzi, María Susana. *Antropología del Tango.* Buenos Aires: Ediciones de Olavarria, 1991. • Carvalho Neto, Paulo de. *Antología del Folklore Ecuatoriano.* Quito, Ecuador: Editorial Universitaria, 1970. • Cheville, Lila, and Richard Cheville. *Festivals and Dances of Panama.* Author, 1977. • Garnham, Emilia. *Danzas Folkloricas de Chile.* Santiago, Chile: Ediciones Graficas Nacionales, 1961. • Guillermoprieto, Alma. *Samba.* New York: Alfred A. Knopf, 1990. • Jaramillo de Olarte, Lucia. *Trece Danzas Tradicionales de Colombia.* Bogotá, Colombia: Producciones ATA Fondo Filantropico, 1991. • Manuel, Peter. *Popular Musics of the Non-Western World.* New York: Oxford University Press, 1988. • Manzanares A., Rafael. *La Danza Folklórica Hondureña.* Tegulcigalpa, Honduras: Talleres del Partido Nacional, 1972. • Paredes Candia, Antonio. *La Danza Folklorica en Bolivia.* La Paz, Bolivia: Editorial Gisbert y Cia, 1984. • Ramirez Salazar, J. *Folclor Costarricense.* San José, Costa Rica: Editorial Imprenta Nacional, 1979.

Dance, Mexican American: Mexican American dance has roots in pre-Conquest dance, folk dance, and theatrical dance.

Pre-Conquest Dance. Native tribes and Spanish and African cultures combined to shape Mexican dance. As a general rule, the dances in remote districts in Mexico remain rooted in early tribal culture, while those of the large cities are distinctly Spanish. The native influence itself is a blend of the Olmec, Mayan, Toltec, and Aztec cultures.

Dance was an integral part of Aztec culture. The Aztecs danced for religious purposes, paying tribute to

Ancient dances honored various gods. (James Shaffer)

Macuilxochitl (also known as Xochipilli), god of music and dance, by dedicating houses of song and dance known as *cuicalli* or *cuicacuilli* to him. Aztec theatrical dramatic dances were executed by masked performers who danced in the court of the temple or in the plaza of the community. One such dance honored the god of war. In this dance, dancers surrounded the performer portraying the goddess of love while young male dancers playing birds danced on branches. The climax occurred when warriors emerged from the temple and killed the birds. The goddess then honored those warriors as gods. Other religious dances of the Aztecs emphasized different events, such as the birth of the sun, the harvest, hunting, fishing, combat, victory, marriage, and even death.

The Aztecs also danced for pleasure. All classes of people, from warriors to priests, danced; dancing occurred everywhere, from temples to the streets. The young people of the elite class danced after feasts in the residences of the wealthy. Even the peasants included dancing in their celebrations. Because of the importance of dance, most children attended dancing school.

Unfortunately, because of the SPANISH CONQUEST, many of these ancient dances no longer exist. In regions with natural barriers such as mountains or swamps, however, some dances have survived. Among these is *El Volador*, the dance of the flying pole. The pattern involves dancers climbing a rope ladder attached to a pole. Each dancer takes a turn performing on a small platform placed on top of the thirty-foot pole while the others sit on a wooden framework attached to the pole. When all the dancers are finished, a musician takes the platform and plays while the dancers descend, swinging around the pole from ropes. Four to six dancers usually perform this dance.

The early Spanish friars noticed the importance of dance and drama in the Indian culture and used the arts to promote Christianity. They maintained the elements of outdoor performance, elaborate props, and masks, but replaced pagan gods and festivals with Christian saints and holidays. They allowed the performances of some early pagan dances, but only for entertainment. For example, in 1543, Dominican friars sponsored a theatrical performance of the dance of Hunahpu and Xbalanque in San Juan Chamelco, Guatemala. The dance illustrated the tale of the hero twins, classical Mayan figures who defeated the lords of the underworld.

In the colonial period, the Spaniards and French brought the ballroom dances of the European courts and salons to Mexico. Some Mexican books published in the 1840's and 1850's offered instruction for such dances as the polka, waltz, and schottische. In Mexico, these types of dances were termed *bailes* to distinguish them from the common *danzas* of the native culture.

Folk Dance. Many traditional folk dances are performed in the various states and regions of Mexico. A few cross boundaries and are danced in one form or another throughout the country, such as *El Jarabe*. This dance was so well loved that in 1920 the government proclaimed it the national dance of Mexico. There are two distinct versions of this dance. The native version is associated with food and is performed during wedding feasts. The Spanish version is a dance of courtship. Many variations of this couple dance exist.

One popular variation is JARABE TAPATÍO, commonly known as the Mexican hat dance. In this dance, the man throws his sombrero at his lady's feet. She picks up the hat and puts it on; together they dance the final steps. Another variation is the Jarabe of the Bottle, in which both partners dance toward a bottle placed between them. A coin is placed on top of the bottle; if the dancers knock it off, the dance ends. In the Jarabe of the Knot, a scarf is placed between the partners, who then must tie a knot while the music plays. Many other variations exist based on region, such as *El Jarabe Tlaxcalteca* and *El Jarabe Michoacáno*, named for their respective states.

Another common dance is *Los Huapango*, a courtship dance with many regional variations. The princi-

Mexican folk dancers perform in a 1974 parade commemorating Mexican Independence Day. (AP/Wide World Photos)

pal areas where it is danced are the states of Hidalgo and Veracruz. "Huapango" is the Aztec name for the platform on which the dance is performed. The general pattern is for each man to approach his potential partner and offer her his hat. Each woman then follows her partner to his respective place, and the dance begins. In this dance, the hat is an important form of communication. The hat is also used when a man wishes to switch partners. He signals his interest by placing his hat on the head of the girl's partner.

Los Moros y los Cristianos is a historical dance, inherited from the Spaniards, that traces the conflict between the Moors and the Christians. Generally, the performance consists of four men, with one man representing Santiago or St. James. The dancers perform at each house in the community, receiving gifts from the homeowners. The dancers' last stop is at the home of the chief town authority, where they receive refreshments.

The DANZA DE LOS VIEJITOS, a regional dance native to Pátzaiaro in the state of Michoacán, is primarily performed for humor, but it is also believed to be a totemic dance, performed to scare away the spirits of old age. The performers imitate the movements of old men, usually wearing clay masks with the features of the aged on them, and carrying canes. The dancers generally bend over and move with feeble steps in an exaggerated manner.

La Sandunga, a regional dance native to the Isthmus of Tehuantepec in the state of Oaxaca, is a religious dance usually danced by women. The dancers do not smile, and the body is held erect during the dance to express solemnity. Originally, it was only danced at funerals; later it was introduced at isthmus fiestas which were known as *velas* because of the decorated candles used during the ceremony. *Velas* take place on feast days but also are organized for other special days.

Folk dancers in full costume perform at a public presentation for the Festival of Our Lady of Guadalupe. (Ruben G. Mendoza)

The Rosa Guerrero Ballet Folklórico dances at a Texas festival. (Impact Visuals, Rick Reinhard)

The dance *Los Inditos* parallels European May Day pole dances, featuring a pole around which ribbons are wound. After the dance, a tribute is made to a saint in the form of offerings of beads, eggs, and flowers.

The Mexican Department of Education encouraged the survival of traditional folk dances by including them in the various fiestas and parades, as well as by offering classes in folk dance at public schools and at the University of Mexico.

Dance in the Theater. In the early native cultures, dancers performed for entertainment. The first formal Mexican dance company is believed to have begun in 1790. The company consisted of a family and included the first male dancer in the theater, Gerónimo Marani. Marani joined with José Sabella Morali to choreograph several productions, such as *Los húngaros*, *El baile de Baco y los locos*, and *La conquista de México*.

In the 1800's, performer Andrés Pautret, a student of European dance, choreographed several important dances, including *La niña mal guardada o el novio desesperado* and *Las bodas de Camacho*, based upon the *Wolf of Mancha*. Later, Pautret founded one of the first schools of classical dance in Mexico. His dedication to the dance was such that he did not charge poor students who wished to attend.

Classical dance did not incorporate Mexican themes until 1919, under choreographers Norma Rouskaya and Anna Pavolwa. Rouskaya, in particular, tried to bring Aztec culture to the stage. In the early 1920's, ballets premiered in which primitive music and simple melodies accompanied the dance. In this period, talented classical dance teachers such as Lettie Carroll, Nelsy D'Ambré, and Sergio Unger left their native countries to teach in Mexico. In 1923, Carroll began her teaching career, and it is believed that she was the first to present a futuristic ballet. Nelsy D'Ambré, on the other hand, danced in the Opera of Paris for nine years and spent five years with the ballet of Rodolfo de Maré before going to Mexico, where she taught for nineteen years. Her greatest students were Salvador

Juarez, who danced in *Monte Carlo*, and Lupe Serrano, a prima ballerina who became an international star. Later, D'Ambré left the school to found the official Academy of Dance in the Republic of El Salvador.

In 1931, Mexican natives Nelli and Gloria Campobello founded a school of dance with the goal of breaking away from classical dance in order to establish a distinctly Mexican ballet. That same year, they composed a notable ballet, *30-30*, inspired by the Mexican revolution.

American Ana Sokolov and her disciples, including Ana Mérida, formed The Blue Dove, which spearheaded the Mexican modern dance movement. In 1940, the group first performed in *Entre sombras anda el fuego*, *Antigona*, and *Don Lindo de Almeria*. Another modern dance notable was choreographer Waldeen. She reformed the traditional structure of classical dance by uniting it with modern dance. In 1940, Waldeen premiered *La Coronela*, a dance criticizing the society of revolutionary Porfirio Díaz.

Xavier Francis was another significant performer, choreographer, and teacher of modern dance. He performed in many pieces, including Doris Humphrey's *Pasacalle*. The works that he choreographed included *Imaginerias* and *El muñeco y los hombrecillos*, a piece with musical accompaniment produced solely by the movements of the dancers. During this period, Francis also codirected the New Theater of Dance with Bodyl Genkel. Genkel's own work included *Metamorfosis* (1954), considered technically advanced by critics of the time.

José Arcadio Limón, of Mexican and Yaqui Indian ancestry, was a respected choreographer in both the United States and Mexico. His mentor was Doris Humphrey, who had a profound impact on his work. During 1951, Limón taught dance at the Juilliard School of Music; he later formed his own dance company, the Limón Company. His work included pieces such as *Tonantzintla*, inspired by Mexican art of the Baroque period, and *La Pavana del Moro*, based on William Shakespeare's *Othello*.

Choreographer Guillermo Keys Arenas premiered Jack Offenbach's comic opera *Orfio en Los Infiermos* in 1954. The dancers included Nelli Happee, a student of Nelsy D'Ambré, and the renowned Laura Urdapilleta, who later left Mexico to dance with New York's Ballet Theater. Keys' other works included the modern dance piece *Tienda de sueños*, considered an advance in the Mexican ballet.

Whether in the theater or in remote regions, the pre-Conquest culture has been revived through dance.

For example, in 1951, Ana Mérida choreographed the ballet *Bonampak*, named for one of the temples that survived the Spanish invasion. It brought Mayan culture to the theater by creating a dance based on the pictures of daily life painted on the murals.

In 1954, Felipe Segura, Telésforo Acosta, and Carlos Gaona founded the Ballet of Mexico with the goal of presenting the most significant classical dances. During this time, Segura codirected the Ballet Concierto, a company that featured renowned ballerinas such as Laura Urdapilleta.

Among Mexico's dance companies, Ballet Folklórico de México deserves special mention. The company, under the direction of Silvia Lozano and choreographer Amalia Hernández, debuted in 1960. Hernández's choreography blended traditional Mexican folklore with other dance styles. The company performed traditional and ceremonial dances from the various regions and included Mexican, pre-Hispanic, mestizo, and Native American forms. The company performed at New York's Carnegie Hall in 1990 with a repertoire including *La Gran Tenochtitlán*, based on the legend of the building of Mexico City, and *The Concheros*, which combined primeval symbols with Catholic themes. The company's international acclaim pioneered the proliferation of Mexican folk dance groups in California.

—Dolores Lopez

Suggested Readings:

• Dickins, Guillermina. *Dances of Mexico*. London: Max Parrish, 1954. Illustrated brief account of popular folk dances.

• Mooney, Gertrude. *Mexican Folk Dances for American Schools*. Coral Gables, Fla.: University of Miami Press, 1957. Offers background and description of various folk dances, including regional variations.

• Schwendener, Norma, and Averil Tibbels. *How to Perform the Dances of Old Mexico: A Manual of Their Origins, Legends, Costumes, Steps, Patterns, and Music*. Detroit: Blaine Ethridge, 1975. Details practical information on performance of popular Mexican folk dances.

Dance, Spanish: Spanish dance is a complex art that is commonly subdivided into three major styles: *folklórico* (folk or regional), *escuela bolera* (eighteenth century classic), and FLAMENCO. *Folklórico* encompasses a wide variety of dances from all regions of Spain. *Escuela bolera* is a dance art performed in soft slippers. Although influenced by folkloric dance forms, it approaches ballet in its virtuosity and technical demands. It is accompanied by castanets and or-

A traditional Spanish dancer. (James Shaffer)

chestra. Flamenco, originally a solo dance, is the most popular form of Spanish dance. Flamenco performances often include some *escuela bolera*.

The emotionally charged content of flamenco traditionally requires audience participation through *jaleos* (hand-clapping, shouting, and finger snapping). Characteristic of flamenco dance are the sensuous arm and wrist movements of the female dancers (*bailaoras*) and the complex rhythmic patterns expressed by body movement and *zapateado*, or footwork. Its instrument is the guitar. Throughout its history, flamenco has incorporated elements from different Spanish and Latin American folk dances, such as the *seguidilla* from South Central Spain and the *guajira*, a sixteenth century Cuban dance. Castanets and the use of scarves (as in the RUMBA) are also of extraneous influence.

History. Flamenco is rooted in the blend of cultural traditions of southern Spain (Andalusia). Similar to the Argentine TANGO and the American blues, flamenco is the individual, spontaneous expression of the centuries-old suffering of an oppressed people. It is generally accepted that the Gypsies, originally from India, reached the Iberian Peninsula in the fifteenth century, where they faced discrimination and persecution. Flamenco, which until the eighteenth century remained within Gypsy circles, boasts many influences, among them Greek, Jewish, Arabic, and Indian.

Researchers of flamenco history distinguish five main periods in its development. In the first period (pre-1800), flamenco song and dance were secretive, a cultural manifestation that expressed the inner anguish produced by marginalization. Although occasionally called to perform at non-Gypsy weddings, christenings, or similar celebrations, Gypsy artists remained confined to the Gypsy-quarters (*gitanerías*). Between 1800 and 1850, flamenco became a semipublic art that could be seen in taverns (*tabernas*) frequented by Gypsies. Individual artists became known. In the second half of the nineteenth century, flamenco became a commercialized art. Gypsy and non-Gypsy professionals performed, often in groups, in the *cafés cantantes*, establishments devoted to flamenco dance and song. After 1910, a flamenco form far removed from its roots in the misery of the *gitanerías* became a spectacle in which theatricality overshadowed the original meaning. Since 1950, new interest within Spain and abroad has resurrected some of the original personality of flamenco, both as a popular art form in the *tablaos* (flamenco clubs) and as the subject of study and research.

Spanish Dance in the Americas. Conquest and colonization had a strong impact on the pre-Columbian cultures. The rapid incorporation of the *zapateado* and of certain aspects of seventeenth and eighteenth century courtly dances into pre-Columbian dance forms reflected a unique cultural fusion. Good examples are folkloric dances such as the Argentine *zambra* and the many regional dances of Mexico.

In the United States, flamenco and *escuela bolera* have created a space for the meeting of Spanish, Latino, and Anglo-American cultures, particularly since the 1970's, with the establishment of major U.S. companies and schools. A syllabus and examinations were developed by the Spanish Dance Society USA, located in Washington, D.C., and founded in 1982. The inherent interculturalism of flamenco makes it a captivating art form.

Dancers and Choreographers. One of the first Spanish artists to visit the United States was La Argentina (Antonia Mercé, 1886-1936). Although born in Buenos Aires, Spain was her artistic homeland. Many others followed her, including La Argentinita (Encarnación López, 1900-1945) and Spaniard Vicente Escudero (1885-1980), who attained greater popularity in the United States than in his own country. Among their successors are the Spaniards Antonio Gades, La Tati, and Cristina Hoyos, among many others.

At the close of the twentieth century, New York City was the most important center for Spanish dance in the United States. Artists who have established schools, companies, and management offices there are Gades, José Greco, Nana Lorca, and José Molina. In the Southwest, the Department of Theatre and Dance at the University of New Mexico in Albuquerque has been instrumental in furthering the study and performance of Spanish dance. Beginning in 1987, the annual celebration of Festival Flamenco, under the direction of resident dancer and choreographer Eva Enciñas, assembled some of the greatest talent of the international dance scene. Among the many artists on the West Coast were Teodoro Morca and Rosa Montoya. Mexican dancers Pilar Rioja and Manolo Vargas also have had considerable influence on Spanish dance in the United States.

Two artists who exemplify the multiculturalism of flamenco dance in the United States today are José Greco and María Benítez. Greco, born in Italy in 1918, has been recognized by the Spanish government and Hispanic organizations such as the Hollywood-based NOSOTROS for establishing lasting cultural ties in the Western Hemisphere through Spanish dance. Benítez, daughter of a Chippewa-Oneida mother and a Puerto Rican father, studied flamenco in the United States and in Spain, as did Greco. She founded her company, Estampa Flamenca, in Santa Fe, New Mexico, in 1972.

Trends. The development of Spanish dance from a spontaneous cultural expression with little attention to the audience to an intricate art form for the stage has made flamenco increasingly complex and difficult. Nevertheless, flamenco dance has perhaps stayed closer to its roots than has flamenco music, which during the 1980's explored new modes of expression in its fusion with Latin, North American, and Middle Eastern musical forms. —*Anna Witte*

SUGGESTED READINGS: • Bennahum, Ninotchka. "Flamenco Puro: Art from Anguish." *Dance Magazine* 66 (August, 1992): 38-41. • Gladstone, Valerie, "María Benítez: Fiery Flamenco." *Dance Magazine* 66 (July, 1992): 42-45. • Matteo (Marcellus Vittucci), and Carola Goya. *The Language of Spanish Dance.* Norman: University of Oklahoma Press, 1990. • Thiel-Cramér, Barbara. *Flamenco: The Art of Flamenco, Its History, and Development Until Our Days.* Translated by Sheila Smith. Lidingo, Sweden: Remark, 1991.

Daniels, Bebe (Virginia Daniels; Jan. 14, 1901, Dallas, Tex.—Mar. 16, 1971, London, England): Actress. The daughter of a Scottish theatrical manager and a Spanish actress, Daniels acted in plays as a small child. She made her screen debut at the age of seven in *The Common Enemy* (1910), and at the age of fourteen she began appearing in dozens of short comic films made by Hal Roach. In 1919, Daniels began working for Paramount, playing both comic leading ladies and hardened playgirls and acting opposite such leading men as Rudolph Valentino and Wallace Reid. In 1931, she appeared in the original film adaptation of Dashiell Hammett's *The Maltese Falcon* opposite Ricardo CORTÉZ. Her many other film appearances include *Male and Female* (1919), *Why Change Your Wife?* (1920), *The Affairs of Anatol* (1921), *Pink Gods* (1922), *Unguarded Women* (1924), *Monsieur Beaucaire* (1924), *Campus Flirt* (1926), *She's a Sheik* (1927), *Rio Rita* (1929), *Alias French Gertie* (1930), *Reaching for the Moon* (1930), *Forty-second Street* (1933), and *Counsellor at Law* (1933).

In 1930, Daniels married British actor Ben Lyon and moved to England, where she worked with his family in radio and television. Among the Lyon family features that included Daniels are *Hi Gang* (1941), *Life with the Lyons* (1953), and *The Lyons in Paris* (1955).

Bebe Daniels in a 1934 photo. (AP/Wide World Photos)

Danza: Music and dance form from Puerto Rico. In the *danza*, romantic songs and melodies accompany couples who do a *paseo* (promenade), typified by flirtatious gazes and fluttering fans, followed by a variety of figured steps. Its origin is disputedly attributed to a liaison between the *upa* (Cuban dance) and the CONTRADANZA around the year 1845. The *danza* gained tremendous popularity in Puerto Rico and gave rise to an era of romance and glamour. The *danza* is considered to be the national dance and music of Puerto Rico. The music was selected as the national anthem in 1952.

Danza de los viejitos: Old man's dance indigenous to Michoacán, Mexico. This dance is performed by vigorous young men disguised with masks of old, wrinkled faces, stringy white hair, missing teeth, and crooked canes. A leader shows the steps and movements, and the chorus imitates him. Throughout the dance, the *viejitos* pretend feebleness and decrepitude with their movements. When executing the steps, showing vigorous energy, they create a ludicrous spectacle. The dance, which can last for hours, relies strongly on such steps as the *zapateado* and the *corte* (landing with feet apart as if ready to take a step).

Danzón: Afro-Cuban music and dance form. The original *danzón* pattern of two parts, each with an eight-bar introduction, was established by Miguel Failde (1848-1921). This pattern was later modified by Raimundo Valenzuela (1848-1905), who added a third part, giving the *danzón* a structure with varied feelings and syncopated rhythm. The orchestra and individual instruments took turns, the clarinets usually taking over first, then the violins, introducing a popular tune, with the whole orchestra then resuming. The *danzón* enjoyed its greatest popularity between 1880 and 1940. It influenced other musical and dance forms such as the BOLERO, *CANCIÓN*, *GUARACHA*, and *SON*.

Databases and electronic services: Information on Latinos available in electronic or print form. The most common database products are library catalogs and bibliographic databases, although an increasing number of demographic and full-text items are becoming available. These products can be accessed through a host of private and public information services.

Bibliographic Databases. Research libraries, including major Latino collections, have developed on-line catalogs, simplifying identification of library holdings. Examples of these on-line catalogs are CARL (Arizona State University), LIBROS Online Catalog (University of New Mexico), MELVYL (University of California), NOTIS (City University of New York), SOCRATES (Stanford University), and UTCAT (University of Texas at Austin). Several bibliographic databases are available in a CD-ROM (compact disc) format as well. A major advantage of CD-ROM is that library patrons generally can use it themselves and therefore do not have to pay for the librarian to search for information through a more expensive, online commercial database.

Although several mainstream bibliographic databases include information on Latinos, specialized CD-ROM products exist that focus on Latino topics. As of 1994, the most important of these was the *Chicano Database* (1991), headquartered at the CHICANO STUDIES LIBRARY of the University of California, Berkeley. The *Chicano Database* strives to identify, in one source, all types of material on Chicanos and to provide uniform subject access to this body of literature. Segments of the *Chicano Database* have been published in print format by the Chicano Studies Library Publications Unit as the *Chicano Periodical Index* (six volumes covering 1967-1988), *Arte Chicano* (1985), and the *Chicano Anthology Index* (1990), as well as the *Chicana Studies Index* (1992). The *Chicano Index*, a continuation of the *Chicano Periodical Index*, is a bibliography of books, articles, and chapters from books. The

Chicano Database also contains a sizable collection of books and articles on the Chicano and AIDS, created by the Chicano Studies Research Center at the University of California, Los Angeles (UCLA); the *Spanish Speaking Mental Health Database*, also developed at UCLA; and pre-1982 mainstream journal articles.

Other CD-ROM products focusing on Latinos include *Latin American Studies*, published by the National Information Services Corporation. This product includes the *Hispanic American Periodical Index*, produced at UCLA; the catalog of the Benson Latin American Collection at the University of Texas at Austin; and the *Handbook of Latin American Studies*, produced by the Hispanic Division of the Library of Congress. *Ethnic Newswatch*, published by Softline Information, Inc., provides full text coverage of selected Spanish-language newspapers such as *La Opinión*.

Numeric Databases. Numeric data on Latinos are available from both academic and commercial sources. Some of the most important surveys on Latinos include the Mexican American Study Project, which resulted in the book *The Mexican American People: The Nation's Second Largest Minority* (1970), by Leo Grebler, Joan Moore, and Ralph GUZMÁN; the *Chicano Identity Project*, conducted by Carlos Humberto Arce at the University of Michigan; the HISPANIC HEALTH AND NUTRITION EXAMINATION SURVEY, conducted by the U.S. Department of Health and Human Services; and the *National Latino Political Survey*, conducted by Rodolfo de la Garza at the University of Texas at Austin. In addition, the decennial United States Census and the *Survey of Income and Education* are rich sources of information on Latinos.

Information Utilities. Information utilities have also been established to make accessible a wide variety of Latino electronic resources. Chicano/LatinoNET (CLNET) is an electronic service that brings together Chicano/Latino research as well as linguistic minority and educational research efforts being carried out at the University of California and elsewhere. It seeks to serve as a gateway for faculty, staff, and students engaged in research and curricular efforts in these areas. CLNET is a joint project of the Chicano Studies Research Center at UCLA and the Linguistic Minority Research Institute at the University of California, Santa Barbara. CLNET can be accessed through the Internet, a network of networks linking computers around the world. The specific objectives of CLNET are to provide access to existing electronic information on Latinos on the Internet, to develop an electronic newsletter on Chicano/Latino language and education

Electronic data sources can reduce tremendously the time spent on library research. (James Shaffer)

issues, to develop electronic forums on specific research areas, and to provide access to Latino faculty and graduate students.

Some of the unique resources on CLNET include information on Chicano/Latino-related courses being taught at various institutions; a national directory of Latino researchers and organizations; a library section, which includes electronic library catalogs of collections with strong Latino resources, newsletters, research guides, bibliographies, brochures, and archival inventories; a news center, which includes notices of selected conferences, e-mail gathered from various sources, and information on scholarships, funding agencies, and jobs; a researcher forum, which is arranged by subject discipline and provides access to a wide range of data and information resources and primary literature; a statistical center, which contains selected information on statistical data sets related to Latino research, information on archives containing Latino data sets, and a statistical abstract of Latino

Day laborers typically gather at unofficially designated locations, where contractors hire them for the day's work. (Impact Visuals, Rick Reinhard)

data; the student center, which includes information of general interest to students; and a gateway to other Internet servers. —*Richard Chabrán*

SUGGESTED READINGS: • Castillo-Speed, Lillian. "The Chicano Database and the CD-ROM Experience." In *CD-ROM in the Library: Today and Tomorrow*, edited by Mary Kay Duggan. Boston: G. K. Hall, 1990. • Chabrán, Richard. "Micro-Computers as Research Tools and Community Resources." *Centro* 3, no. 1 (1990-1991): 107-114. • Inter-University Program on Latino Research. *Access to Information and Telecommunication Technology: A Survey of Latino Research Centers—An Exploratory Study*. New York: IUP, 1992. • Rodríguez, Ronald. "Latino Databases." In *Latino Librarianship: A Handbook for Professionals*, edited by Salvador Guereña. Jefferson, N.C.: McFarland, 1990. • Torres, Myriam, and Carlos H. Arce. "Archiving and Disseminating Quantitative Social Research on Chicanos." *Biblio-Politica: Chicano Perspectives on Library Service in the United States*. Berkeley: Chicano Studies Library Publication Unit, University of California, 1984.

Day labor: In the 1980's and 1990's, urban centers of the United States, especially those containing significant minority populations, saw a rise in the phenomenon of day labor. Day labor is employment of workers—often undocumented—on a short-term basis. Immigrants in urban areas frequently gather at central points awaiting employment from contractors, homeowners, and others. Virtually all day labor jobs are manual labor, and most are in construction, landscaping, gardening, and home repair.

The hiring of recent immigrants, both legal and illegal, has been a large factor in the late twentieth century labor force. (*See* UNAUTHORIZED WORKERS.) In Los Angeles, for example, studies in the early 1990's estimated that 81 percent of the work force in the garment industry was of Mexican descent, as was 75 percent of the labor force for the restaurant industry.

Some analysts suggest that the immigrant labor force exists because of willingness of migrant workers to take jobs the majority population does not want. In addition, Mexican immigrants developed an efficient networking system to aid them in obtaining work. This networking system has helped recent immigrants find work quickly and learn the unwritten rules of the informal labor market.

One major study of day labor was conducted in 1983. Based on the testimony of three hundred male illegal aliens apprehended for undocumented status, some of the following conclusions were drawn. Illegal aliens from Canada and Europe earned wages between 20 and 25 percent higher than those of illegal aliens from Latin America. In addition to possible racism on the part of employers, there were other significant reasons for these wage differentials. Canadian and European immigrants generally possessed higher skill levels, more formal schooling, better fluency in English, and job skills more applicable to the U.S. market than did their Latin American counterparts. Wage differentials have also been found to correlate with duration of illegal residency. Those who have been in the United States longer on average had higher wages, higher skill levels, and a higher likelihood of belonging to a union.

In contrast to the sweeping notion of oppressive and unfair employers, the facts gathered in the study showed that hourly wages were significantly related to characteristics of both employers and employees. The study did not uncover a conspiracy against immigrant workers. This is not to deny that exploitation has occurred, particularly for the most recent immigrants. Some employers undoubtedly took advantage of workers' unwillingness to report employer behavior to the authorities.

Day of the Dead. *See* **Día de los Muertos**

Death: Various cultural symbols and practices, as well as aspects of and attitudes toward death, grief, bereavement, funeral practices, rituals, and ceremonies associated with death, have been termed part of the "cult of death" in Latino communities. Some of these cultural elements are a continuation of Spanish, Latin American, and pre-Hispanic traditions involving death.

Issues of death and dying are often colored by Latino religious views, especially conditioned by the teachings of Catholicism and Protestantism. Cultural attitudes toward death and dying are also informed for some Latinos by beliefs in *espiritismo* (*see* SPIRITISM

An ofrenda *for Danny Lozano shows his picture and some of his favorite drinks and foods.* (Diane C. Lyell)

AND SPIRITUALISM), which underscores communication and contact with the dead. Many Latinos believe that the personality continues after death and that the dead need food and care in the same ways as do the living.

Latino funeral ceremonies stress the importance of properly performing death and burial ceremonies. One of these ceremonies is the *velorio*, or wake, which includes the practice of *velar los muertos* (watching over the dead). This ritual takes place in the home of the deceased, from one to three days after death. It involves the ritualistic visit of the deceased's family and friends. The coffin is surrounded by flowers and burning candles, or *capilla ardiente*. Those who come to pay their respects bring food, flowers, or money to help pay the funeral expenses. They usually pray the rosary, if Catholic, and extend the *pesáme*, or traditional condolences, to the family. The *velorio* is part of the Latino *ars moriendi*, or art of dying.

Family interaction is an important part of Latino practices surrounding death. Family members—young and old, adults and children—participate in rituals surrounding death and holidays associated with death, such as El DÍA DE LOS MUERTOS (Day of the Dead). Ceremonies associated with this holiday combine European Christian traditions (All Souls Day, All Saints Day, and grave care) with pre-Hispanic elements that involve elaborate public celebrations at the cemetery as well as celebrations at home altars. These rituals and ceremonies are related to the Catholic concept of communion of saints as well as to beliefs in spiritual regeneration and spiritual covenants between the living and the dead.

Mexicans and Mexican Americans are often perceived as more concerned with death, dying, and death themes than are people of most other cultures. Some have even spoken of an obsession with death. According to some writers, such as Octavio Paz, death for Mexicans has been made into something of a cult. Life and death to many Latinos are not separate and distinct; they are phases in the same cosmic cycle. Death is seen as a natural event and is frequently present in various aspects of Mexican culture such as fiestas, games, and jokes.

Décima: Singing form of Spanish origin. *Décimas* of the fifteenth century have been handed down from generation to generation. Although their authors are unknown, they preserve their original poetic, stylized ten-line verse form. The melody is monotonous, in contrast with the lyrics, which bear important messages about love, hate, fear, religion, history, and grief. The singing style is characterized by the use of the falsetto (voice above its normal range) and the inclusion of nonsensical syllables. *Décimas* typically are accompanied by the CUATRO, guitar, MARACAS, and GÜIRO, and they are sung in all of Latin America.

Declamación: Art of public speech or rhetoric. *Declamación* is a long-standing tradition in Hispanic communities. A persuasive form of communication, public rhetoric developed as a primary strategy for political mobilization in the Chicano protest movement and elsewhere. Leaders such as César CHÁVEZ, Reies López TIJERINA, Rodolfo "Corky" GONZÁLES, and José Ángel Gutiérrez developed rhetorical visions of Chicano heritage and reality that helped mobilize their followers and bring public awareness to their struggles during the 1960's. Chicano activist rhetoric uses clear forceful explanations illustrated by anecdotes and concrete examples in the form of DICHOS (popular sayings or aphorisms) and CUENTOS (stories or folktales).

De Diego, José (Apr. 16, 1868, Aguadilla, Puerto Rico—July 16, 1918, New York, N.Y.): Political leader and writer. De Diego is associated with modernism in Puerto Rican literature, with his works acting as precursors to or initiators of the style. De Diego also symbolizes the ideal of independence for Puerto Rico.

De Diego emerged as the leader of the Unionist Party, which had been founded in 1904 to seek self-government for the island. In 1907, de Diego met with U.S. president Theodore Roosevelt, who was indifferent to any political reform relative to Puerto Rico's status. As a result of that meeting, de Diego began to favor independence, but he never expressed any ill will toward the United States.

De Diego left for Spain following a clash with Luis MUÑOZ RIVERA in 1915, but he returned to Puerto Rico two years later. He then began to campaign for a plebiscite to be held in 1920, with the options of statehood or independence under a United States protectorate (patterned after that of Cuba). In November, 1917, however, de Diego requested that his proposal be tabled, as he did not wish to create any disturbances while the United States fought in World War I. De Diego became ill and died shortly thereafter.

De la Garza, Eligio "Kika" (b. Sept. 22, 1927, Mercedes, Tex.): Public official. De la Garza began representing the Rio Grande Valley area of South Texas in

Eligio de la Garza discusses the North American Free Trade Agreement at a 1993 news conference. (AP/Wide World Photos)

Oscar de la Hoya waves the American and Mexican flags after winning the 1992 Olympic gold medal. (AP/Wide World Photos)

Congress in 1964. After military service during both World War II and the Korean War, de la Garza practiced law, became active in civic affairs, and served in the Texas legislature from 1953 to 1964.

South Texas Hispanics viewed the election of de la Garza to Congress in 1964 as a milestone. Conservative agribusiness concerns consistently supported him. De la Garza assumed the chairmanship of the House Agriculture Committee in 1981, becoming the first Latino to chair a standing subcommittee in the House of Representatives. He is known as a staunch protector of farming interests. De la Garza has also been successful in addressing water and sewerage problems in the small settlements, known as *colonias*, in the Rio Grande Valley.

De la Hoya, Oscar (b. Feb. 4, 1973, Los Angeles, Calif.): Boxer. De la Hoya's rise to prominence from a childhood in which he was surrounded by gangs and drug dealers won him millions of fans. He earned the nickname "Golden Boy" by winning the gold medal in the 132-pound class at the 1992 Summer Olympics, where he was the only U.S. boxer to win a medal. His popularity increased dramatically among Mexican Americans after he waved both U.S. and Mexican flags following his Olympic victory. As an amateur, he compiled an impressive record of 225 wins and only 5 losses, with 153 knockouts.

In November, 1992, de la Hoya moved into the professional ranks by scoring a knockout less than two minutes into his first pro fight. In less than a year, he had built an 11-0 record with 10 knockouts, leading to a fight contract with the Home Box Office cable television service. De la Hoya then stunned his supporters in December, 1993, when he canceled a fight in New York and fired his managers in an attempt to take control of his own career. His first fight under new management came in March, 1994, with a win over Jimmy Bredahl for the World Boxing Organization (WBO) junior lightweight title. In July, 1994, he moved up to the lightweight ranks, capturing the WBO lightweight title with a second-round knockout of Jorge Paez. In May, 1995, he added the International Boxing Federation (IBF) lightweight championship to his collection of titles with a two-round demolition of Rafael Ruelas.

Delano Grape Strike (1965-1970): Historic strike in the struggle to secure the rights of farmworkers. Three thousand Mexican and Filipino farm workers walked off the fields of Delano, California, protesting low wages and indecent working conditions. The farmworkers' organizing campaign took years and was coordinated by César CHÁVEZ, Dolores HUERTA, and the NATIONAL FARM WORKERS ASSOCIATION (NFWA).

Farmworkers had long endured poor wages and some of the worst working conditions in the United States. In 1965, Larry Itliong, a Filipino organizer, and the Agricultural Workers Organizing Committee (AWOC) called a strike against grape growers in Delano, a community in Kern County, California, that relied primarily on grape vineyards for its economic livelihood. In September, 1965, the NFWA, led by Chávez, joined the strike, which included nine ranches and two thousand workers.

The Delano strike was different from typical labor strikes. There was no collective bargaining, discussions of fringe benefits, or negotiation between workers and owners. Delano strikers used tactics resembling those of civil rights demonstrators of the early 1960's. They sponsored marches, folk masses, fasts, and sit-ins. On March 17, 1966, the NFWA began a 250-mile march from Delano to California's state capital, Sacramento (*see* MARCH TO SACRAMENTO). Participants viewed the march, which began on Lent and ended on Easter Sunday, as a pilgrimage. "Penitence, Pilgrimage, and Revolution" was its theme, and the patron saint of Mexico, Our Lady of Guadalupe, was its symbol. "*Viva La Huelga! Viva La Causa!* (Long live the strike! Long live the cause!)" was the rallying cry under a red flag with the union's black eagle emblem and tapestries of Our Lady of Guadalupe. Sixty-seven farmworkers were assigned to the entire march, with others rotating in and out.

Every night, the PLAN DE DELANO was read following opening prayers at rallies. The Plan de Delano was drafted by the farmworkers to state their objectives. It recounted the history of exploitation and described how this movement would create new leaders to represent workers' rights. It also noted that the movement was spreading across the San Joaquin Valley in California to the entire United States.

The first victory came in 1966, when Schenley Corporation, a grower of wine grapes, signed a contract with the striking grape pickers of the NFWA. The NFWA merged with the AWOC to become the United Farm Workers Organizing Committee, winning the right to support field workers in a vote on August 30, 1967. A consumer GRAPE BOYCOTT also proved successful. By 1969 more than 17 million Americans had stopped buying grapes, and two-thirds of the Coachella Valley's grape ranchers went out of business.

Strikers in Delano try to persuade other workers to join them. (AP/Wide World Photos)

The Delano strike influenced farm labor organizing, which became one of the most dynamic union movements in North America in the 1970's. The United Farm Workers Organizing Committee changed its name in 1972 to the UNITED FARM WORKERS and eventually had about 100,000 members and contracts with 80 percent of the grape growers in the San Joaquin Valley. The overall results were improved working conditions and increased wages for farmworkers.

De las Casas, Bartolomé (c. August, 1474, Seville, Spain—July 17, 1566, Madrid, Spain): Spanish missionary and historian. Little is known about de las Casas' early life, although he is believed to have been born in Seville in 1474 and to have served as a soldier in Granada during the religious wars against the Moors in 1497. He is thought to have been a student at the academy associated with the cathedral in Seville.

As an early Spanish missionary, de las Casas traveled to Hispaniola in the West Indies in 1502 in the company of the Spanish governor, Nicolás de Ovando.

Because of his service to the governor, de las Casas received a royal land grant (*encomienda*) and was given responsibility for the Indians who lived on his lands. He began to convert the local Indians to Catholicism and served as a lay teacher. As the first person in the New World to be ordained to the Catholic church, de las Casas is believed to have received holy orders sometime between 1512 and 1513.

Despite his participation in the bloody conquest of the West Indies, de las Casas began to show increased concern regarding the treatment of the Indians by the Spanish soldiers and land owners. Unwilling to keep his Indian converts in slavery, he turned responsibility for the Indians on his lands over to the governor. De las Casas left Hispaniola in 1515 to return to Spain, where he spoke out against the abuses of the *encomienda* system and argued for better treatment of the Indians. With the help of the archbishop of Toledo and other prominent church leaders, de las Casas helped persuade the Spanish crown to draw up the *Plan para la Reformación de las Indias* (plan for the reformation of the Indians). Under the plan, the Crown established the office of Protector of the Indians and gave this post to de las Casas. He was charged with the responsibility of maintaining peace between the warring factions by enforcing the provisions of the plan that would prevent Spanish settlers from harming the Indians.

De las Casas sailed for Hispaniola in 1516 but returned to Spain the following year in order to persuade the Spanish parliament and King Charles V to approve his plan to colonize the Indians by settling them on lands alongside Spanish farmers. After gaining approval for his settlement project, de las Casas returned to the New World, landing in the Gulf of Paria on the coast of present-day Venezuela. Few farmers traveled with him, and the local landowners opposed his project. The colony failed after the Indians attacked the settlement, and de las Casas abandoned his project in 1522.

De las Casas took religious orders with the Dominican fathers in 1523. Withdrawing from the public eye to live a monastic life, he began writing an account of his experiences entitled *Apologética Historia de las Indias*. Although he continued to have a distinguished career in the church, was consecrated as bishop of Chiapas in Guatemala, and returned to the Spanish court during the 1550's to argue on behalf of improved relations in the West Indies, de las Casas earned his greatest fame as a result of the posthumous publication of this masterwork. The book combined a chronicle of his experiences among the Indians and the history of the Spanish presence in the New World with his own interpretation of the religious significance of Spain's unjust actions. De las Casas was convinced that Spanish domination and oppression of the native peoples constituted sinful behavior that would result in dire misfortune and divine punishment. As the first European to draw attention to the injustice of the Spanish colonial system, de las Casas has served as an inspiration to many Latin American independence movements in their struggles against outside control, ranging from Simón Bolívar in the nineteenth century up to the movements for indigenous rule in Guatemala and southern Mexico during the late twentieth century.

Del Castillo, Adelaida (b. 1950, Los Angeles, Calif.): Writer. Castillo is an honored educator and a leading Chicana scholar. An anthropologist by profession, Castillo has focused her research and publications primarily on the status of Hispanic women in society, CHICANAS in particular. Awarded several prestigious research grants and fellowships, she is a prominent lecturer and professor in her field. A Chicana feminist concerned with social equality for Hispanic women, she addresses issues of race and cultural oppression in her work.

Majoring in linguistics as an undergraduate, Castillo moved into social anthropology as a graduate student. Her graduate research, a study examining Mexican women-centered households, led her to do field work near Mexico City that culminated in the book *Negotiated Lives: The Power and Stigma of Women's Domestic Relations in Mexico City* (1981), her dissertation project.

Although she most often publishes scholarly articles, Castillo has extended her expertise to other disciplines. She edited the "La Mujer Latina Series" for Floricanto Press as well as the book *Between Borders: Essays on Mexicana/Chicana History* (1990). She was coeditor, with Magdalena Mora, of *Mexican Women in the United States: Struggles Past and Present* (1980), and she was one of the founders of the feminist journal *Encuento Feminil*.

De León, Patricia: Rancher. Patricia de la Garza married Martín de León in 1795. The couple made their home in Gruillas, Texas. In 1824, the new Mexican government granted Patricia's husband permission to found a colony in Texas. His death in 1833 caused the cancellation of the contract, but the colony was so firmly established that this incident did not affect its prosperity.

Delgado v. Bastrop Independent School District (June 15, 1948): In this case, a federal court in western Texas ruled that the SEGREGATION of Mexican American children in public schools was a violation of the Fourteenth Amendment. Following the Civil War, the state of Texas, like other former members of the Confederacy, passed laws that required the segregation of African Americans from whites. Although these laws never applied to the state's Latinos, local school boards, controlled by Anglos, often required Spanish-speaking children to attend separate schools. This practice of segregation was often justified on the basis of the "separate but equal" doctrine of *Plessy v. Ferguson* (1896), but lawyers noticed that the *Plessy* precedent had dealt with segregation required by statute. Also, it was obvious that the separate schools were usually unequal in their levels of funding.

In 1930, Texas Latinos won a major victory in *Independent School District v. Salvatierra*, in which a state appellate court ruled that school authorities in Del Rio and elsewhere had no authority to segregate Chicano children "merely or solely" because of their ethnic heritage. The school district, however, argued that the children's difficulties with the English language warranted separate schools, and the attorney general of Texas supported this holding, with the result that school districts had a legal excuse to continue segregation. The landmark 1946 California case MÉNDEZ V. WESTMINSTER SCHOOL DISTRICT encouraged the LEAGUE OF UNITED LATIN AMERICAN CITIZENS (LULAC) to challenge the justification of segregation based on special language needs.

In *Delgado v. Bastrop Independent School District*, a federal district court upheld LULAC's position and ruled that the continuing segregation was "arbitrary and discriminatory and in violation of" the FOURTEENTH AMENDMENT. Based on the premise that the Constitution required "social equality" in public education, the court ruled that public schools must be open to all citizens except when segregation was explicitly required by state law. The court told school districts that any separate classes for students with English-language difficulties had to be held on the same campus where other students were taught, thereby denying districts the power to maintain separate Mexican American schools by use of the language-deficiency argument. Following the decision, the Texas Board of Education modified its earlier policy on segregation and instructed local school districts to follow the mandate of the court.

In a related case of 1951, *Gonzales v. Sheely* (96 F. Supp. 1004), the federal district court of Arizona issued a ruling similar to that of *Delgado*. The Arizona court, however, used more expansive language that appeared to condemn all forms of de jure segregation.

After *Delgado*, the public schools of Texas were not allowed explicitly to segregate Latino children from the Anglo majority, but the immediate effect was limited because the decision did not address the question of de facto segregation based on geographical isolation and housing patterns. In addition, the *Delgado* ruling did not consider whether the ruling applied to children of undocumented immigrants.

Del Rio, Dolores (Lolita Dolores Martínez Asunsolo López Negrette; Aug. 3, 1905, Durango, Mexico— Apr. 11, 1983, Newport Beach, Calif.): Actress. The daughter of a bank president who escaped from Pancho Villa's rebels, Del Rio became one of Hollywood's most successful Hispanic actresses. She made her screen debut in *Joanna* (1925) at the age of twenty-one, starred in *The Loves of Carmen* (1927) and *Ra-*

mona (1928), and was among the industry's top ten moneymakers for the 1920's.

Known for her aristocratic grace and beauty, Del Rio played French, Polynesian, and Indian roles as well as Latinas. Already a silent film star, she learned English with the advent of talkies. Her other films include *The Red Dance* (1928), *Girl of the Rio* (1932), *Lancer Spy* (1937), *Journey into Fear* (1942), *María Candelaria* (1943), *Las Abandonadas* (1944), and *The Fugitive* (1947).

Del Rio worked in both Mexican and American films. In the 1950's she was banned from the United States for helping anti-Franco refugees from the Spanish Civil War. She returned to Hollywood in 1960 to play Elvis Presley's mother in *Flaming Star*. During the 1960's and 1970's, she was a guest on numerous television shows and played *The Lady of the Camellias* on stage in Mexico City. Her last role was in the 1978 film *The Children of Sanchez*.

Del Valle, Reginaldo F. (1854, Los Angeles, Calif.— 1938): Diplomat. Shortly after his inauguration in 1913, U.S. president Woodrow Wilson began the practice of sending confidential agents, independent of the diplomatic and consular staff, to report on Mexico. Wilson hoped to influence the course of the 1910 Mexican Revolution. Del Valle was President Wilson's second fact-finding emissary to Mexico.

Del Valle was an attorney and former member of the California state legislature and was one of the few remaining Californios of political prominence. His assignment was to meet with Mexican revolutionary leaders Venustiano Carranza and Emiliano Zapata. Despite his heritage and knowledge of Spanish, del Valle's mission proved to be a disaster. He held a profound disdain for the Mexican masses, had little faith in the workability of democracy in Mexico, and was not sympathetic to the revolutionary leaders. Del Valle also demonstrated extreme carelessness. Although his mission was supposed to be confidential, he granted an interview to a Mexico City newspaper. The U.S. government had no choice but to recall him. Del Valle returned to California and served on numerous government boards and civic committees.

Deportations, expatriations, and repatriations: Deportation is the forced removal from a country of an alien whose presence is presumed unlawful. Expatriation is to leave one's native country and reside in another country, usually on a temporary basis. In some cases, expatriation may refer to a self-imposed exile. Many

Dolores Del Rio in 1960. (AP/Wide World Photos)

The Los Angeles County Charities Department sent more than one thousand dependent Mexicans back to Mexico in 1931 because the county could no longer support them. (AP/Wide World Photos)

Latin American expatriates have been forced to abandon their homelands, often because of political considerations. Repatriation refers to the voluntary return to one's country of origin, allegiance, or citizenship.

Deportations. Among Latin Americans, Mexicans have been the primary focus of U.S. deportation activity. Deportation of Mexicans remained relatively insignificant until the late 1920's. Beginning in the summer of 1928, large numbers of Mexicans in the Rio Grande Valley of Texas came under the scrutiny of the U.S. Bureau of Immigration. The Immigration Service carried out numerous raids throughout the region. Hundreds of Mexicans were rounded up and deported. By late summer, local farmers predicted a labor shortage for the fall harvest. Deportation activity intensified in 1929, and Bureau of Immigration agents sometimes raided homes of Mexican residents without obtaining search warrants.

As the U.S. economy continued to deteriorate in the early 1930's, deportation activity spread from the lower Rio Grande Valley of Texas to other areas of the United States. Mexicans apprehended and detained by the U.S. Bureau of Immigration who refused to "voluntarily" return to Mexico were formally deported. The focus of much of this deportation activity was urban areas, with Los Angeles, California, having a particularly effective deportation campaign.

Urban deportation activity was not limited to the southwestern United States. Large urban centers in the Midwest were also targeted, including Minneapolis-St. Paul, Minnesota; Detroit, Michigan; Chicago, Illinois; and Gary, Indiana. One goal of deportation activity during the 1930's was to create fear among Mexican residents and inspire them to return to Mexico voluntarily. Thousands of Mexicans left the country on their own.

As economic conditions in the United States improved in the early 1940's, deportation of Mexicans abated. During the war years, Mexican labor was urgently needed and deportation all but stopped. In 1954, however, Mexicans throughout the United States faced OPERATION WETBACK. A million Mexicans were deported in the first year of the government program, which continued until 1958.

A major issue related to deportation concerns U.S.-born children, who are U.S citizens by virtue of their birth. Many were deported along with their parents in violation of constitutional rights.

Expatriations. Periodically, internal political and military conflict in various countries has compelled residents to abandon their homes, and the United States has often served as a refuge. During the reign of Porfirio Díaz (1876-1911), for example, thousands of Mexicans were driven into exile in the United States. During the MEXICAN REVOLUTION (1910-1921), the number of expatriates taking up residence in the United States increased significantly. By the end of the revolution, tens of thousands of Mexican expatriates could be found in U.S. border states. Many returned to Mexico

ALIENS DEPORTED, BY REGION OR COUNTRY OF NATIONALITY, 1990

Total aliens deported: 25,228

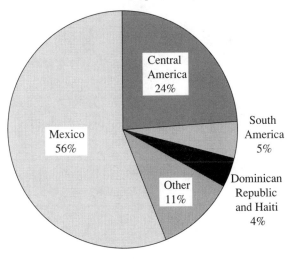

Source: Data are from Marlita A. Reddy, ed., *Statistical Record of Hispanic Americans* (Detroit: Gale Research, 1993), Table 79.

following the cessation of hostilities.

Following the CUBAN REVOLUTION that began in 1959, large numbers of Cubans sought refuge in the United States, especially in South Florida. Cuban expatriates arrived in a series of waves caused by fluctuating emigration policies in Cuba.

Between 1959 and 1962, more than 200,000 displaced Cubans arrived in Miami, Florida. Following a three-year hiatus, about 300,000 Cubans were airlifted from Havana to Miami between 1966 and 1972. Then, during a five-month period in 1980, the MARIEL BOAT LIFT brought another 125,000 Cubans to Miami. Many of these expatriates remained in South Florida.

Civil wars and other conflicts in Central America during the 1970's and 1980's resulted in the departure of thousands of residents from Guatemala, El Salvador, and Nicaragua. These refugees made their way north to the United States or to other Latin American countries to request political asylum. Between 1980 and 1984, as many as 150,000 Guatemalans fled to Mexico to escape the military's campaign of terror. Thousands of Salvadorans and Nicaraguans found sanctuary in the United States.

Repatriations. One of the first repatriation programs was carried out following the Mexican American War. The Mexican government sponsored the return of several thousand Mexicans from Texas. During the remainder of the nineteenth century, Mexicans were periodically repatriated from various locations in the Southwest, often as a response to harassment by Anglo Americans.

Large-scale repatriation did not begin, however, until the twentieth century. During World War I, many Mexicans returned to Mexico, fearing conscription into the U.S. military. As the U.S. economy deteriorated following the war, large numbers of Mexicans were compelled to return to Mexico because jobs were unavailable.

The largest repatriation movement occurred during the Great DEPRESSION, when at least one-half million Mexicans returned to Mexico. This widespread movement peaked in the fall of 1931 but continued through most of the decade. As the Depression drew to a close in the late 1930's, a substantial number of Mexicans were returned to Mexico under the sponsorship of the Mexican government.

About half of the Mexicans who left the United States during the Great Depression departed from Texas. These 250,000 Mexicans and their U.S.-born children came from diverse locations throughout the state. The second largest number of Mexicans to depart

Undocumented immigrants reenter Mexico after a border crossing. (Impact Visuals, Image Latina)

the United States in the 1930's was from California.

Local welfare agencies in major urban centers throughout the Midwest, including Detroit, Michigan; Chicago, Illinois; Gary, Indiana; and Minneapolis-St. Paul, Minnesota, facilitated the repatriation of thousands of Mexicans. Few Mexicans remained in some cities when the Depression ended.

Repatriation activities in Detroit were typical of those in the Midwest. Local welfare workers engaged in coercive tactics to persuade welfare recipients to return. Mexicans who lacked funds to reach the U.S.-Mexico border were provided with free transportation on chartered repatriation trains. The Mexican consulate in Detroit and a local Mexican organization, the League of Mexican Workers and Peasants, assisted in organizing repatriation.

As economic conditions deteriorated during the early 1930's, Mexican workers encountered increased job discrimination. In many areas, workers were required to prove U.S. citizenship in order to retain their jobs. Throughout the country, state and municipal governments enacted measures to restrict public employment to U.S. citizens. Mexican laborers were routinely excluded from federal relief projects. The shortage of employment opportunities encouraged many Mexicans to leave the United States.

Although U.S. welfare agencies were most often responsible for organizing and implementing Mexican repatriation during the 1930's, the Mexican government was usually supportive. Periodically, the Mexican government would announce that large tracts of irrigated land were available. These announcements prompted thousands of Mexicans to repatriate.

In the late 1930's, Mexican government officials traveled throughout the Southwest in an effort to persuade Mexican tenant farmers and sharecroppers to return home. Prospective repatriates were promised free or inexpensive land as well as other material support. Several thousand longtime Mexican residents of South Texas returned to Mexico.

Most Mexican repatriates and deportees who returned to Mexico in the 1930's were destitute on their arrival. Moreover, when they arrived in Mexico they found few employment opportunities. Economic conditions in Mexico were worse than those in the United States in the 1930's.   —*Robert R. McKay*

SUGGESTED READINGS:

• Betten, Neil, and Raymond A. Mohl. "From Discrimination to Repatriation: Mexican Life in Gary, Indiana, During the Great Depression." *Pacific Historical Review* 42 (August, 1973): 370-388. Examines the impact of the Great Depression on Mexican residents of Gary, Indiana.

• Carreras de Velasco, Mercedes. *Los mexicanos que devolvió la crisis, 1929-1932*. Tlatelolco, Mexico: Secretaría de Relaciones Exteriores, 1974. This brief study analyzes the Mexican government's response to massive repatriation during the Great Depression.

• García, Juan Ramon. *Operation Wetback: The Mass Deportation of Mexican Undocumented Workers in 1954*. Westport, Conn.: Greenwood Press, 1980. The definitive study of deportation of Mexicans in the 1950's. Provides useful insights into the various institutions involved in Operation Wetback.

• Hoffman, Abraham. *Unwanted Mexican Americans in the Great Depression: Repatriation Pressures, 1929-1939*. Tucson: University of Arizona Press, 1974. Documents and analyzes Mexican repatriation activity in Los Angeles County during the Great Depression.

• Kiser, George, and David Silverman. "Mexican Repatriation During the Great Depression." *Journal of Mexican American History* 3 (1973): 139-164. Includes two brief case studies about repatriation from Detroit, Michigan, and Los Angeles, California, during the Great Depression. Useful for an understanding of events in the Midwest in the 1930's.

• McKay, R. Reynolds. *Texas Mexican Repatriation During the Great Depression*. Ann Arbor, Mich: University Microfilms, 1983. This Ph.D. dissertation documents Mexican deportation and repatriation activity in Texas and provides basic information on the resettlement of Mexicans following their return to Mexico.

Depression, Great (1929-1939): The Great Depression often is cited as beginning on October 29, 1929, the date of the infamous crash on the New York Stock Exchange. Billions of dollars of wealth were destroyed as investors panicked in a rush to sell their stock shares before prices fell even further. The crash was a symptom of deep fundamental problems in the American economy.

Income distribution became more uneven during the prosperous 1920's. The economy became more dependent on the spending of those with the highest incomes, because those incomes were a larger share of the economy. Business enterprises depended on wealthy investors to fund both new projects and continuing production. Anything that broke the confidence of the upper classes threatened to affect spending and investment, with repercussions throughout the economy.

The Workers Alliance of America staged a sit-in at the city hall in San Antonio, Texas, after being refused a parade permit.
(Institute of Texan Cultures)

Farm incomes had dropped as crop prices fell during the 1920's. Many farmers lost their land because they were unable to repay debts or to pay taxes. Prior to 1925, American farmers had enjoyed high prices that resulted from European demand for food during World War I and the recovery from it. Migrant workers were encouraged to cross the border from Mexico to assist in harvesting the crops that were in such high demand. By 1930, Mexican migrant workers constituted considerable minority populations in California and Texas.

American workers as a group did not gain much benefit from the general prosperity of the 1920's. American industries profited during the war years and afterward, and their high prices contributed to inflation. Despite walkouts and strikes, workers were rarely able to gain wage increases that compensated them for the erosion in purchasing power caused by inflation.

American industry had operated near capacity during World War I and had expanded capacity in response to the demand for products during the war and the rebuilding process in Europe. By the mid-1920's, as demand for products fell, much of the productive capacity was no longer needed. As machines were taken out of use, workers were laid off.

During the Depression years, which witnessed unemployment rates above 20 percent, many Latinos had difficulty finding work. Farms and railroads had long been primary sources of employment, but jobs there disappeared. Many Mexicans and Mexican Americans were fired to create job openings for non-Hispanic white workers. Latino farmers, among others, lost their farms because they could not pay taxes.

A mass exodus to Mexico was encouraged and financially supported by the Mexican and American governments. As many as 400,000 people crossed the border into Mexico during the Depression. Congress debated legislation limiting immigration, but the legislation was defeated, partly as a result of lobbying by agricultural interests that benefited from inexpensive migrant labor.

Latinos who were unable or unwilling to leave the United States during the Depression often found themselves to be the victims of discrimination. Because of the surplus of workers, employers could be choosy about whom they hired. Many job advertisements included the notation "PRX," meaning that only Protestant Christians should apply.

Desegregation. *See* **Segregation, desegregation, and integration**

Desiga, Daniel: Painter. Desiga is one of the few artists to bring a Latino perspective to art produced in the Pacific Northwest region. His individual paintings and public murals draw attention to the labor issues and problems facing Latinos, as well as to the contributions that various ethnic groups have made to development of the Pacific Northwest.

Desiga's *Campesino* (1976), an oil painting of a solitary farmworker bent over a row of seedlings in a vast field, highlights some of Desiga's artistic aims. Because the farmworker is wearing a hat, viewers cannot see his face, perhaps suggesting that he is one of many faceless, nameless Latinos whose labor is essential to the agricultural industry. The style of the painting resembles that used to dignify work and workers in Depression-era public murals in the United States.

Desiga's mural for the Centro de la Raza in Seattle, Washington, presents the darker side of agricultural labor. He pictures a Latino farmworker nailed to a cross on the ground he has cultivated. Desiga's other public murals have incorporated regional symbols with land, water, technologies, and various racial groupings to suggest the physical and natural forces that have shaped the Pacific Northwest.

De Soto, Hernando (c. 1500, either Villanueva de Barcarotta or Jerez de los Caballeros, Extremadura, Spain—May 21, 1542, near modern Ferriday, La.): Explorer. De Soto was an impressive Spanish explorer of the sixteenth century. In 1531, he sailed to Peru with Francisco PIZARRO and participated in the famous conquest of the Inca empire. Sensing problems between Pizarro and his partner, Diego de Almagro, de Soto decided to return to Spain. He had amassed a fortune in gold.

De Soto, however, was not satisfied staying in Spain. In 1537, he obtained a capitulation to conquer Florida and other regions. It was de Soto's hope to find another rich and developed civilization, like those of the Aztecs and the Incas.

De Soto's expedition reached Florida on May 18, 1539. It was an impressive force with more than six hundred men. The party moved inland and crossed the modern states of Georgia, Alabama, and Mississippi. Natives from the regions provided occasional violent resistance.

Around May or June 1541, the party crossed the Mississippi River and traveled west into the modern state of Arkansas. By this time, de Soto's troops had weakened significantly. More than 250 soldiers had

Engraving of Hernando de Soto's burial in the Mississippi River. (Institute of Texan Cultures)

died, and there was no way of obtaining reinforcements. Depressed and beaten, de Soto died near the Mississippi River.

De Soto, Rosana (b. Sept. 2, 1950?, San Jose, Calif.): Actress. De Soto, who attended San Jose State University, has performed in both plays and light opera in Los Angeles and Northern California in addition to her film work. Her film credits include *The In-Laws* (1979), *Serial* (1980), *Cannery Row* (1982), *The Ballad of Gregorio Cortez* (1983), *American Justice* (1985), *About Last Night* (1986), *Family Business* (1989), and *Face of the Enemy* (1990).

In 1987, de Soto had major roles in two important films reflecting on the Latino experience. She portrayed teacher Jaime ESCALANTE's wife in *Stand and Deliver* and played singer Ritchie VALENS' mother in *La Bamba*. On television, de Soto was featured in the 1981 film *Three Hundred Miles for Stephanie* and the 1983 film *Women of San Quentin*. She has also made appearances on numerous television programs.

Detroit, Michigan (founded 1701): Largest city in the state of Michigan (seventh largest in the United States, based on 1990 census figures) and site of the oldest Latino community in Michigan.

Census data indicate that Latinos, specifically Mexican Americans, have resided in Detroit since 1910.

The first Mexican Americans in Detroit began a small, resilient community that later accommodated the influx of other Latino groups. The Midwest's railroad system and the jobs it provided brought the first Mexicans to Detroit, and they settled near the railroad yards.

Between 1910 and 1920, the turmoil of the Mexican Revolution pushed large numbers of Mexicans northward. Increasing numbers settled in southeastern Michigan, providing labor for Detroit's growing industrial base and the local sugar beet farmers.

The onset of World War I forced such Detroit industrialists as Henry Ford to look to Mexico for workers. In late 1920, the *Detroit News* reported that an estimated eight thousand Mexican Americans lived and worked in Detroit. In that year, the government of Mexican president Venustiano Carranza established a consulate in Detroit to protect the interests of Mexican citizens there.

The Latino community fluctuated in size during the 1920's as Latinos, still primarily of Mexican descent, spread throughout a section of Detroit's west side. Farm laborers began to look to the city as a viable alternative to the fields. During this period, the community began to organize groups to promote social and cultural activities.

The Great Depression brought fear and uncertainty, and public sentiment began to oppose the influx of Mexicans and Mexican Americans. Famed Mexican muralist Diego RIVERA, commissioned by industrialist Edsel Ford, in 1932 depicted the automobile industry on the walls of the Detroit Institute of Art in a work titled *Man and Machine*. Rivera temporarily assisted in efforts to "repatriate" Mexicans (*see* DEPORTATIONS, EXPATRIATIONS, AND REPATRIATIONS). Before 1933, according to the Mexican consulate, more than twelve thousand Mexicans left Detroit for Mexico.

The Latino community's recovery paralleled America's economic upsurge during World War II. Prosperity in the postwar era attracted Puerto Ricans and Cubans to Detroit. Bagley Avenue flourished as the center of Latino commercial activity.

Detroit's major freeway system, developed during the 1950's, cut across Bagley Avenue, devastating the business community. Latino families began to join the exodus from Detroit to its suburbs. By 1969, those remaining in the city had organized Latin Americans for Social and Economic Development, a multiservice center; Community Health and Social Services, a bilingual, bicultural health clinic; the Detroit Archdiocese Latin American Secretariat (later the Office of Hispanic Affairs); and the Committee of Concerned Spanish-Speaking Americans, an education organi-

LATINO POPULATION OF DETROIT, MICHIGAN, 1990

Total number of Latinos = 90,947; 2% of population

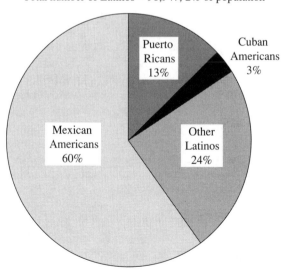

Source: Data are from Marlita A. Reddy, ed., *Statistical Record of Hispanic Americans* (Detroit: Gale Research, 1993), Table 110.

Note: Figures represent the population of the Detroit-Ann Arbor, Michigan, Consolidated Metropolitan Statistical Area as delineated by the U.S. Bureau of the Census.

zation. Latinos became actively involved with New Detroit, Incorporated, one of the nation's first urban coalitions.

The 1990 census indicated that the Latino community of the Detroit-Ann Arbor area, numbering nearly ninety thousand, reflected the cultural diversity of the national Hispanic population. Although Mexican Americans were still the largest group (60 percent), there was a growing number of Central Americans, particularly from El Salvador, Guatemala, Honduras, and Nicaragua. South Americans from Colombia, Peru, and Ecuador, as well as an increasing number of immigrants from the Dominican Republic, were settling in the Detroit metropolitan area.

Devil dance: South American form of religious celebration. Devil dances form an intrinsic component of Latin American religious Carnavals. Devil dancers dressed in elaborate, highly ornate costumes and masks (each of them rich in historical tradition) perform colorful folk songs and dances that reflect traditional native tastes in music and dance, even though some of the instrumentation, musical arrangements, and dance genres show contemporary influence. Devil dancers appear at the Oruro Carnaval in western Bolivia and CARNAVAL festivals taking place at the beginning of Lent in Brazil, the Caribbean region, northern Argentina, and elsewhere in Latin American countries.

Día de la Raza (Oct. 12): El Día de la Raza, or "The Day of the Race," was the name given to Columbus Day in Latin America as part of the Hispanidad movement (or Pan Hispanism) begun at a conference held in Madrid in 1892. Also called La Fiesta de Hispanidad and Discovery Day, the fiesta has become a major celebration in Latin America. It is also observed in the United States, sometimes as part of a broader festival, such as the HISPANIC HERITAGE FESTIVAL in Miami, Florida, which occurs throughout the month of October but includes a Discovery of America Day on or about El Día de la Raza. It is also observed independently, as, for example, in the one-day festival at the Takoma/Langley Community Center in Washington, D.C.

Día de los Muertos (Oct. 31-Nov. 2): El Día de los Muertos, "The Day of the Dead," also known as All Souls Day, is a national holiday in Mexico. Throughout Mexican towns and villages, the spectral figure of death is seen for days before and after the holiday. Bakeries produce *panes de muertos*, "death breads"

El Día de los Muertos is celebrated by festivities and wearing of costumes as well as more somber forms of honoring the dead. (Diane C. Lyell)

shaped in the form of humans or animals. El Día de los Muertos is one of the three religious holidays for which ritual pottery is traditionally made. Special censers and candlesticks made of black, glazed clay, augmented with molded figures of angels, flowers, and birds, are cast and used to honor the dead.

In the United States, the holiday is observed in many Mexican American and other Hispanic communities. Typically, families honor their dead by cleaning and redecorating graves with fresh flowers and other ornaments, but it is also a festive occasion, involving picnics, music, and dancing, often right at the grave sites. November 2 is the actual day of the dead, but the holiday is celebrated for several days beforehand.

Diabetes: Diabetes mellitus is a metabolic disorder in which the pancreas does not adequately secrete or use insulin, causing excessive amounts of sugar in the blood and urine. The disease may cause thirst, hunger, or loss of weight.

According to a 1993 issue of the *American Journal of Epidemiology*, the incidence of non-insulin-dependent diabetes mellitus was 2.5 times higher in Latinos than in non-Hispanic whites. A number of studies have been conducted to determine the reasons for this. A family history of diabetes consistently has been identified as a risk factor. Other identified possible contributors to the prevalence of diabetes in Latinos are lower amounts of education and physical activity, diet, and sociocultural and genetic factors.

The HISPANIC HEALTH AND NUTRITION EXAMINATION SURVEY indicated that the prevalence of diabetes in Latinos between the ages of forty-five and seventy-four was 24 percent for Mexican Americans, 26 percent for Puerto Ricans, and 15 percent for Cuban Americans. The rate of diagnosed and undiagnosed diabetes was 110-120 percent higher among Mexican Americans and Puerto Ricans and about 50-60 percent higher in Cuban Americans than among non-Hispanic whites.

Diabetes is most commonly diagnosed in Latinos in their late forties. The onset of diabetes in childhood is rare among Latinos. The prevalence rate for Latino women is higher than for Latino men.

Diabetes in pregnant women places the fetus at risk for either low birth weight, which reduces neonatal survival, or high birth weight, which sometimes complicates birth and threatens survival at delivery. Diabetic pregnant women are also at risk for kidney problems and high blood pressure.

Diabetes, if left untreated, is considered a progressively debilitating disease. There is evidence that complications of diabetes vary by population and are particularly severe among Mexican Americans. According to the Hispanic Health and Nutrition Examination Survey, diabetes increased the incidence of glaucoma, retinopathy, hypertension, kidney problems, and cataracts, particularly among those who were insulin dependent. Diabetes is a chronic disease, and its long duration has been associated with a risk of loss of limbs, stroke, blindness, and renal failure. Most Latinos on dialysis have insulin-dependent diabetes. The major forms of treatment for the control of diabetes include controlled diet, exercise, and insulin.

According to the Centers for Disease Control Monthly Vital Statistics Report issued in January of 1993, diabetes was among the ten leading causes of death for Latinos aged forty-five to sixty-four in 1990. Diabetes, with a high prevalence among Latinos, is considered a major public health problem for this population. Once acquired, this chronic and debilitating illness increases the risk of complications, especially when medical care is inadequate or compliance with diet and treatment is poor. Almost 15 percent of Latinos with diabetes who completed a clinical examination for the Hispanic Health and Nutrition Examination Survey indicated that their diabetes resulted in inability to perform activities of daily living, housework, or their jobs.

Díaz, Justino (b. Jan. 29, 1940, San Juan, Puerto Rico): Opera singer. Díaz studied at the University of Puerto Rico and the New England Conservatory. He continued his voice training with Frederick Jagel. Díaz first

Justino Díaz dressed for the lead role in Antony and Cleopatra. (AP/Wide World Photos)

appeared with the New England Opera Theater in 1961. After winning the Metropolitan Opera Auditions of the Air, he made his Metropolitan Opera debut as Monterone in the opera *Rigoletto* on October 23, 1963. Díaz went on to make appearances with the American Opera Society as well as at Puerto Rico's Casals Festival and at the Spoleto Festival. In 1966, he sang the part of Escamillo at the prestigious Salzburg Festival.

One of Díaz's most important early career accomplishments was being chosen to sing the role of Antony in the production of *Antony and Cleopatra* at the opening night of Lincoln Center on September 16, 1966. Díaz has performed with many of the world's major opera companies, including the New York City Opera Company. In 1971, he sang in Alberto Ginastera's *Beatrix Cenci* for the inauguration of the opera house at Washington, D.C.'s Kennedy Center. He made his debut at London's Covent Garden in 1976. Díaz has been one of the Metropolitan Opera's leading bass singers, able to perform in a variety of Italian opera roles because of his soothing *basso cantante* voice.

Díaz Valcárcel, Emilio (b. Oct. 16, 1929, Trujillo Alto, Puerto Rico): Novelist. Díaz Valcárcel is an award-winning prose writer. A founding editor of the cultural magazine *Cupey*, he is a professor of Spanish who writes both short stories and novels. Although Díaz Valcárcel has an international reputation and has published works in Spain, Mexico, and his native Puerto Rico, his novel *Figuraciones en el mes de marzo* (1972; *Schemes in the Month of March*, 1979) was his only work translated into English by the early 1990's.

Known for stark realism and frankness, Díaz Valcárcel's prose captures the harshness of modern living for individuals tormented by injustices or misunderstanding. Skillful in the use of modernist techniques, Díaz Valcárcel has been praised for his works' insights into the human psyche.

Díaz Valcárcel was drafted by the United States Army in 1951 to fight in the Korean War. His collection *Proceso en diciembre* (1963) consists of short stories based on his experiences as a Puerto Rican soldier. His other works include a produced play, *Una sola puerta hacia al muerte* (1957); the short-story collections *"El asedio," y otros cuentos* (1958) and *El hombre que trabajó el lunes* (1966); and the novels *Inventario* (1975) and *Harlem todos los días* (1978).

Dichos: Popular sayings, maxims, or aphorisms. *Dichos* are a powerful form for communicating information regarding a common culture and heritage and, therefore, feature prominently in political oratory as well as literature. César CHÁVEZ often used *dichos* as a way of introducing information that educated his listeners to the plight of the agricultural laborer. Many other Chicano activists also use *dichos* as a rhetorical convention to establish a cultural and social bond with their audiences.

Dieciséis de Septiembre: Mexico's independence day At 11 P.M. on the night of September 15, 1810, Miguel HIDALGO Y COSTILLA, the parish priest of Dolores (now Hidalgo Dolores) called for an end to Spanish rule in Mexico. Hidalgo armed mestizos (people of mixed blood) and Indians, then opened the jail and armed the prisoners. The next day, he assembled his troops around the church and declared Mexico's independence with his now famous cry of independence, El GRITO DE DOLORES.

Hidalgo, Ignacio de Allende, and José María Morelos y Pavron led their troops through the town to San Miguel el Grande (now known as San Miguel de Allende) to Guanajuato. There, they conquered five hundred Spaniards. Hidalgo led his troops to victory in other cities during the next several months, but they were defeated at Calderón in January of 1811. Shortly thereafter, Spaniards captured Hidalgo, Allende, and some others. All were executed, and their heads were put on display. Mexico gained its independence in 1821, but the country still celebrates September 16 as its independence day.

Mexico initiates its independence day celebration with the president, governors, and mayors giving the Grito de Dolores on the evening of September 15. September 16 is dominated by military parades in the state capitals and by parades of schoolchildren and other citizens in other cities.

Many cities in the United States, particularly those with large Mexican American populations, celebrate September 16. In San Francisco, California, the celebration is run by the Comité Cívico Patriótico Mexicano (the Mexican Civic and Patriotic Committee). The committee has changed the festivities from a binational nature to a reinforcement of Mexican tradition and nationalism. Celebrations usually include MARIACHI bands, *CHARROS* (Mexican horsemen), folkloric dances, and Mexican songs and music, performed only by persons of Mexican descent.

As in Mexico, Phoenix, Arizona, begins its celebration with the Grito de Dolores. Phoenix's celebration has made more concessions to Anglo culture than has San Francisco's. Both the Mexican and U.S. national

This mural in San Antonio, Texas, commemorates Miguel Hidalgo y Costilla and Mexican independence. (Diane C. Lyell)

anthems are played. Celebrations generally take place on a weekend, regardless of the day of the week on which September 16 falls. Mexican food, costumes, folkloric dances, and mariachi music dominate the festivals.

For the two thousand residents of Mesilla, New Mexico, the September 16 celebration holds dual meaning. It not only recognizes the heritage of most of the citizens but also marks the founding of Mesilla, which occurred at nearly the same time. The celebration starts with a parade that acknowledges traditions from both Mexico and the United States. Spectators can enjoy floats with Aztec warriors as well as cowboys riding horses and twirling lassos. As with September 16 celebrations in other cities, Mexican folkloric dancing with bright, colorful costumes is an important part of the celebration. Mexican food and crafts are sold at booths, and city officials model ethnic fashions for the annual fiesta style show.

Diego, Juan (1474, Mexico—1548, Mexico): Witness to the Virgin Mary. Diego lived during the Conquest period and belonged to the lower but propertied classes of Aztec society. In 1523, he converted to Christianity when Franciscans arrived.

According to contemporary sources, Diego reported seeing the Virgin Mary on December 9, 1531. He immediately informed Bishop Juan de Zumarraga, the highest religious figure in Mexico. Zumarraga did not believe Diego. Diego reported that he saw the Virgin a second time, the next day. This time the bishop requested that Diego bring some sort of proof. Diego

The garment on which the Virgin of Guadalupe appeared hangs in Mexico City's Basilica of Guadalupe. (Ruben G. Mendoza)

reportedly informed the Virgin of this request, and she told him to gather some roses, put them in his gown, and take them to the bishop. Diego obeyed. When he released the roses, an image of the Virgin appeared on his gown.

The bishop now believed Diego and agreed to build a church at the site where he met the Virgin. She was given the name of Virgin of Guadalupe (*see* GUADALUPE, VIRGIN OF). She has become a major symbol of Catholicism in Mexico. Diego lived the rest of his life in a small house by the church.

Di Giorgio Fruit Corporation Strike (1947): In the immediate postwar period, the Di Giorgio Fruit Corporation in Arvin, California, was one of the largest agribusiness concerns in the western United States. Its founder and president, Joseph Di Giorgio, registered $18 million in sales in 1946, and he predicted record profits for 1947. These impressive profits came in part from Di Giorgio's reliance on braceros and even lower-paid undocumented Mexican workers.

In October, 1947, members of Local 218 of the NATIONAL FARM LABOR UNION (NFLU) picketed the company. NFLU demands were straightforward: a ten cent per hour wage increase, seniority rights, and recognition of the union as a intermediary between workers and the company.

Di Giorgio's rejection of these demands hardened the union's stance, and leaders called for a halt to fruit picking. The company immediately began attacking pickets and trucking undocumented workers in to take the place of strikers. Given the conservative, anti-Communist political spirit of the times, many politicians supported Di Giorgio.

Locally, state senator Hugh Burns called for an investigation of the NFLU's possible ties to the Communist Party. When this investigation failed to produce convincing evidence, Di Giorgio tried to extend his influence to the national level. In March, 1948, California congressman Alfred Elliot demanded a federal investigation of the NFLU, based on a document signed by more than a thousand people claiming to be Di Giorgio employees who were opposed to the strike.

A year later, after the strike had been called off, a House subcommittee that included future president Richard Nixon held two days of hearings in Bakersfield. Although these hearings did not yield evidence to indict the union, they did provide Di Giorgio with a way to publicize his newest grievance against labor activists. He had opened a court case against the NFLU and the Hollywood Film Council for libelous suggestions against him in the 1948 film *Poverty in the Land of Plenty*. Di Giorgio not only wanted condemnation of the filmmakers and their NFLU collaborators; he also wished to ban all showings of the film in the United States.

Di Giorgio prevailed on Representative Thomas Werdel to file an independent report in the appendix of the *Congressional Record*. Werdel's document, titled "Agricultural Labor at Di Giorgio Farms, California," concluded that there was no need for legislation to protect agricultural workers through unionization. Although such reports are normally a source of background information, this one became notorious for its open support of Di Giorgio and blatant condemnation not only of the NFLU but also of the presumed grievances of California farmworkers in general.

Dihigo, Martin (May 25, 1905, Matanzas, Cuba— May 22, 1971, Cienfuegos, Cuba): Baseball player. The versatile Dihigo was an extraordinary pitcher whose race kept him out of the American major leagues. Dihigo enjoyed a long career in Latin American baseball and also played in the United States from 1923 to 1936 for such Negro Leagues teams as the Cuban Stars, the New York Cubans, and the Homestead Grays.

In the Negro Leagues, Dihigo performed at all nine positions. As a pitcher with a blazing fastball, he recorded wins in Mexico, Venezuela, the Dominican Republic, and the United States. Also a powerful hitter, Dihigo led the Eastern Colored League in home runs in 1926 and led the American Negro League in hitting in 1929. As a playing manager, Dihigo led the New York Cubans into the Negro National League playoffs in 1935.

Moving to the Mexican leagues in 1937, Dihigo pitched the first professional no-hitter on Mexican soil in September of that year. He also pitched no-hitters in Venezuela and Puerto Rico. A year later, he led the Mexican League with a 0.90 earned run average, an 18-2 record, 184 strikeouts, and a .387 batting average.

Dihigo's popularity made him a national hero. After his baseball career, he went on to become the Cuban minister of sports. In 1977, Dihigo was inducted into the National Baseball Hall of Fame in Cooperstown, New York, making him the only player to have been elected to the Mexican, Cuban, and U.S. halls of fame.

Dime novels and photo novelas: Dime novels, inexpensively printed adventure and romance stories that were popular in the United States from the 1860's to

Photo novelas use photographs of live models, captioned with balloons of dialogue, to tell their stories. (Library of Congress)

the 1930's, often contained damaging negative stereo-types of Mexican characters (*see* STEREOTYPES OF LATINAS; STEREOTYPES OF LATINOS). Photo novelas (*fotonovelas*), romantic and dramatic stories told by photographs with balloon captions, have been success-fully published and sold in Mexico and exported to other Hispanic nations since the 1940's.

Dime Novels. Dime novels appeared in the United States shortly before the onset of the Civil War and were immediately successful. Ranging from twenty-five thousand to thirty-five thousand words in length, the thin books with heavy saffron paper covers earned the nickname "yellow-backed Beadles" because Bea-dle & Company was the best-known dime novel pub-lishing firm. Several novels were printed each month in the Western, romance, ocean adventure, and detec-tive genres. Although most of the Westerns pitted white American heroes against savage Native Ameri-can Indian characters, several of the books published immediately before and during the MEXICAN AMERI-CAN WAR (1846-1848) dealt extensively with Mexican characters.

Norman D. Smith has identified five stereotypes common in the dime novels set in Texas and the sur-rounding areas: the *hidalgo*, an aristocratic Spaniard who was both noble and sad because he lost his fortune and had to marry his daughter to a wealthy man to regain it; the Spanish Venus, a seductive temptress with a fiery temper who tried to lure the hero away from the blond, fair-skinned heroine; the Spanish priest, who used his position in the Catholic church for his own underhanded purposes; the *bandido*, a violent and dishonest man who tried to steal from or murder the hero; and the *peon*, a domestic servant who was either loyal or lazy, depending on his master's person-ality, but who could never rise above his station in life. According to Smith, these stereotypes were popular-ized at a time when tensions between white Americans and Mexicans were already high. They reinforced negative images of Mexicans to the extent that they became widely believed by white Americans. Even when Mexican characters did not specifically fulfill these stereotypical roles, the stories implied that white Americans were superior to their Mexican neighbors and were therefore justified in taking over the borderland between Texas and Mexico that was in dispute during the Mexican American War.

Gradually, the popularity of dime novels began to subside. During the 1920's and 1930's, American publishers rechanneled their efforts into pulp magazines, which were cheaper to produce than dime novels. Rather than a single long self-contained story, these magazines often featured serial stories that continued from week to week. Although Western themes remained prominent in pulp magazines, they did not employ Mexican characters as often as the earlier dime novels did.

Photo Novelas. Although photo novelas began to be widely produced during the 1940's and 1950's, they did not take the place of dime novels in the United States, because photo novelas were not an American phenomenon. Photo novelas were originally a European medium later adapted by Mexican publishers, with continued Italian and Spanish influence. Production of these stories developed into a large industry serving Hispanic nations and the Latino populations in urban areas of the United States and Canada. In addition, photo novela production flourished in Brazil and Argentina during the late 1960's and early 1970's.

The format of photo novelas has remained consistent, with stories told by still photographs of live models with balloon captions. As Cornelia Butler Flora has pointed out, however, the story content of photo novelas has undergone several transformations. From approximately 1950 to 1970, the *fotonovela rosa* (pink photo novela) dominated the market; such books consisted mainly of romance stories of poor but virtuous girls winning the love of wealthy men. The *fotonovela suaves* (soft photo novelas) of the 1970's featured more realistic middle-class plots, with characters working to improve their situations through their own efforts. These stories generally had happy endings, a trend that was reversed when the *fotonovela rojas* (red photo novelas) began to grow in popularity around 1980. These tales were less romantic and more brutal than their earlier counterparts, dealing with disturbing topics such as rape, incest, and prostitution and often ending in death or suicide. Flora hypothesized that these stories appealed to Latino readers because they were viewed as realistic depictions of common problems in the *barriadas* (lower-class neighborhoods) of Mexican and South American cities.

The wide popularity of photo novelas among Latinos resulted in the realization that the medium could be used as an educational tool, both to improve literacy and to distribute information on social and health issues. For example, Flora pointed out that activists working in Ecuador in the 1970's produced photo novelas in an attempt to raise consciousness and promote collective action among the poor. In addition, an organization based at California State University in Los Angeles has produced photo novelas for the city's Mexican American community. —*Amy Sisson*

SUGGESTED READINGS: • Denning, Michael. *Mechanic Accents: Dime Novels and Working-Class Culture in America.* New York: Verso, 1987. • Flora, Cornelia Butler. "The Fotonovela in America." *Studies in Latin American Popular Culture* 1 (1982): 15-26. • Nye, Russel. "The Dime Novel Tradition." In *The Unembarrassed Muse: The Popular Arts in America.* New York: Dial Press, 1970. • Pearson, Edmund. *Dime Novels: Or, Following an Old Trail in Popular Literature.* Port Washington, N.Y.: Kennikat Press, 1968. • Silva, José Luis. "Carlos Vigil on Mexican Comic Books and Photonovels." *Studies in Latin American Popular Culture* 5 (1986): 196-210. • Smith, Norman D. "Mexican Stereotypes on Fictional Battlefields: Or, Dime Novel Romances of the Mexican War." *Journal of Popular Culture* 13 (Spring, 1980): 526-540.

Discovery of the New World: In 1492, after a ten-year siege, the last Moorish stronghold at Granada finally surrendered to the forces of Ferdinand and Isabella, who promoted Catholicism. The end of the religious war on the Iberian Peninsula gave the Spanish Crown new freedom in its spending, as the war was no longer draining the treasury. Spain decided to fund Christopher Columbus, a Genoese sailor, for a highly speculative voyage to the Orient.

What was unusual about this expedition was not that Columbus wanted to sail to the East to trade for spices, silks, and porcelains. Merchants from the Italian city-states had been moving such luxury goods West, following an overland route, for years, and the Portuguese were establishing a virtual monopoly on the sea route around Africa for the same purpose. Columbus' plan differed because he would sail west, across uncharted and potentially dangerous seas. Despite a high-level court committee's warning that Columbus has miscalculated the distance between the East and Europe by as much as 25 percent, the Crown gave Columbus support, including three ships, for his proposed trading expedition.

The Enterprise of the Indies. Before he left, Columbus signed a formal agreement or contract (a *capitu-*

Christopher Columbus landing in America in 1492. (Culver Pictures)

lación) that formalized the details of the expedition and summarized the expectations of both parties. Columbus received financial backing and use of the titles of admiral, viceroy, and governor, as well as the right to call himself "Don," a term denoting noble status. He also was to receive 10 percent of the net proceeds of all products bought, traded, discovered, or obtained on the voyage as well as opportunities to invest his own capital for additional shares in the profits. Columbus' "enterprise of the Indies," as he liked to call his plan, was set up as a trading company with monopoly control over commerce. There was no mention in the contract of rights to settle, hold land, or found communities.

Columbus' Voyages of Discovery. Columbus made four voyages to the area he came to call "another world," never acknowledging that he had not arrived in Asia. To have done so would have meant admitting failure.

His landfall on October 12, 1492, on the island he called "San Salvador," started the exploration and settlement of the Caribbean and eventually of the entire Western Hemisphere. On his first voyage, he founded the settlement of Navidad on the island of Hispaniola. On his second, begun in 1493, he found Navidad in ruins, so he started a new, fortified town, called Isabella, to be the capital of his viceregal domain. This marked the beginning of the settlement of the island by Europeans.

Columbus' last three trips were dedicated to both trading and exploring. Under pressure to bring valuable goods back to Spain, Columbus obtained gold, brasilwood, and Indian slaves. During these trips, Columbus also explored much of the Caribbean, including the islands of Cuba, Jamaica, and the Lesser Antilles.

Because Columbus' strengths, efforts, and interests were directed more toward exploration than administration, discontent and disorder grew in the new Spanish settlements. Complaints and slander, some from well-connected individuals, eventually forced the Crown to replace Columbus as governor.

Columbian Legacies. A lasting legacy of Columbus' voyages is vocabulary. For example, "Indian" came to refer to the inhabitants of the Caribbean. This misnaming was based on Columbus' belief that he had arrived in the East Indies. Likewise, some of the vocabulary of the Taino (native inhabitants of the Bahama Islands, Cuba, Jamaica, Hispaniola, and Puerto Rico), and the concepts or objects these words represented, such as hammock and canoe, were incorporated into Spanish and spread throughout the Western Hemisphere. Another legacy consists of Spanish toponyms (place names), such as Florida, Puerto Rico, and Santo Domingo, that replaced the native names of various locations.

A heritage of miscommunication, misunderstanding, and cultural conflict began almost as soon as Columbus landed. Columbus' diaries of his voyages trace how favorable first impressions of the island inhabitants turned into negative ones. One can understand how Spanish stereotypes of non-Christian peoples influenced what Columbus and other Europeans wrote. For example, the origins of the myth of islanders as cannibals date to his second voyage, when he found bones in Carib huts on the island of Guadeloupe. Not knowing that these bones may have been physical manifestations of the custom of ancestor worship, Columbus interpreted them as the remains of some heathen feast.

Likewise, Spanish reports that Indians pillaged and stole everything they could carry off suggests that the Spanish did not understand the native custom of reciprocity and sharing. They did not realize, at first, that the natives had no concept of private property. Such tales led to the negative stereotypes of some of the inhabitants of the region.

Further Exploration and Colonization. Columbus' search for a new water passage to the East was followed by other voyages of discovery. In the first decade of the sixteenth century, the Crown authorized expeditions under Juan de la Cosa, (who completed the first generalized map of America), Diego de Nicuesa, and Alonso de Hojeda to explore and settle the mainland (Tierra Firme). Hoping to find gold, Vasco Nuñez de Balboa explored Tierra Firme and eventually discovered the Pacific Ocean.

By 1515, Hispaniola, Puerto Rico, and Cuba had been colonized. Puerto Rico had two Spanish towns founded in 1510, and Cuba had seven five years later. By 1521, the Lesser Antilles and Tierra Firme from the Guianas to Central America and Mexico had been ex-

Hernán Cortés leaves Cuba in 1519 as the governor bids him farewell. (Institute of Texan Cultures)

plored. Hernán CORTÉS had invaded and taken TENOCH-TITLÁN, capital of the Aztec empire.

Meanwhile, Juan PONCE DE LEÓN, following his successful governorship and settlement of Puerto Rico, explored the land now called Florida. In 1521, Francisco Gordillo and Pedro Quexos took possession of Chicora, in what is now North Carolina. Ferdinand Magellan led an expedition that circumnavigated the world. Magellan's trip, at its conclusion in 1522, vindicated Columbus by proving that one could reach Asia by sailing west. —*Susan E. Ramírez*

SUGGESTED READINGS: • Columbus, Christopher. *The Diario of Christopher Columbus's First Voyage to America, 1492-93.* Translated by Oliver Dunn and James E. Kelley, Jr. Norman: University of Oklahoma Press, 1989. • Knight, Franklin W. *The Caribbean: The Genesis of a Fragmented Nationalism.* New York: Oxford University Press, 1978. • Lunenfeld, Marvin, ed. *1492: Discovery, Invasion, Encounter.* Lexington, Mass.: D. C. Heath, 1991. • Milanich, Jerald T., and Susan Milbrath, eds. *First Encounters: Spanish Explorations in the Caribbean and the United States, 1492-1570.* Gainesville: University of Florida Press, 1989. • Sauer, Carl O. *The Early Spanish Main.* Berkeley: University of California Press, 1992. • Williams, Eric. *From Columbus to Castro: The History of the Caribbean, 1492-1969.* New York: Vintage Books, 1970.

Discrimination, bigotry, and prejudice against Latinos: According to the 1990 census, Latinos constituted 8.45 percent of the U.S. population. Latinos are a minority group in United States society that faces discrimination and prejudice. Latinos have experienced some forms of discrimination in common; Mexican Americans, Puerto Ricans, and Cuban Americans also have unique histories of prejudice and discrimination.

The number of Latinos is increasing rapidly in a U.S. society in which they experience much prejudice and discrimination. Prejudice is a negative attitude toward an entire group of people and often involves stereotypes, or frequently inaccurate generalizations that attribute characteristics to every person in a group (*see* STEREOTYPES OF LATINAS; STEREOTYPES OF LATINOS). Discrimination is unequal treatment based on group membership. Prejudice and discrimination have affected Latinos in similar ways. Bigotry has also taken unique forms in its effects on the three largest Latino nationalities. This discussion will exclude Canada, because there are few Latinos in Canada. They constituted 0.6 percent of the Canadian labor force as of the early 1990's.

Anti-Latino Prejudice. Regardless of national origin and background, Latinos in the United States are often associated with such false stereotypes as the childlike peasant and the dangerous drug addict. Latinos have in common several interrelated characteristics that make them susceptible to such negative mythical portrayals. First, many speak Spanish. Those who speak English as a second language or do not speak it can be mistakenly labeled as unintelligent in an English-dominant society. Second, Latinos are a highly visible group because of their distinct culture, their pattern of heavy recent immigration, and their residential clustering. A third factor is the cultural contrast that many Latino immigrants present as they enter an urban, postindustrial society. Many Latinos come from agricultural or early industrial societies. Fourth, Latinos may be looked upon unfavorably because they are a predominantly Roman Catholic people in a predominantly Protestant society. Fifth, some Anglos resent the fact that many Latinos are unwilling to give up their distinct cultures and melt into Anglo society. An indication of the strength of this resentment is the fact that as of 1993, nineteen states had declared English as their official language. Sixth, Latinos have an aura of illegality. Many United States citizens overgeneralize from the fact that some Latinos are undocumented, believing that most Latinos are illegal aliens. Seventh, the fact that the Latino POVERTY rate is higher than the United States average leads some people to associate Latinos with welfare dependency and other social problems.

Anti-Latino Discrimination. Discrimination prevents equal opportunity in such realms of life as employment, education, and health care. Statistical comparisons with Anglos show that Latinos in the United States often experience categorical maltreatment despite extensive federal civil rights legislation. Employment statistics for the early 1990's reveal that Latinos, as compared to Anglos, earn lower incomes, have a higher poverty rate, and are more likely to be unemployed. The differences were large. For example, in 1990 26.2 percent of Latinos fell below the federal poverty line, compared to 11.6 percent of all Anglos. The average Latino male's income in 1990 was $14,047, compared to an average of $22,081 for Anglo males. Carefully controlled experiments in several cities comparing Latino and Anglo job seekers have revealed discrimination in hiring. In one such test in 1992, equally credentialed Anglos and Latinos applied for 468 job vacancies in the Washington, D.C., area. The Latinos encountered discrimination 22.4 percent of the time.

Some Latino children are disadvantaged in school by their lesser skills in the English language. (James Shaffer)

Unequal treatment is also apparent in education. Children lacking English language skills are at a disadvantage in the classroom. Legal challenges prompted public schools to provide BILINGUAL EDUCATION in the 1970's, but the 1980's saw a cutback in federal government mandates for bilingual education. Latino children are likely to attend de facto segregated schools with predominantly minority student bodies; this trend increased in the 1970's and 1980's. The effects of unequal education are apparent in the upper grades, as Latinos have a higher high school dropout rate and a lower college completion rate than Anglos. In 1990, 9 percent of Latinos aged twenty-five to thirty-four had completed college, compared to 25.5 percent for Anglos in the same age range.

Health statistics also portray a disadvantaged Latino population. Figures for the early 1990's show that Hispanics have a life expectancy shorter than the United States average. They are also much less likely to have health insurance: One-third of Latinos lacked health insurance or other coverage such as Medicaid, compared to 13 percent of non-Hispanic whites.

Although Latinos suffer from some common forms of prejudice and discrimination, experiences of bigotry have differed depending on nationality. This is seen in the experiences of the three largest Latino nationality groups.

Mexican Americans. Mexican Americans, the largest of the Latino nationalities, have endured two somewhat contradictory stereotypes: the lazy peasant and the violent criminal. Television and films have portrayed Mexicans as ignorant and docile. Derogatory labels such as "greasers" and "chili pickers" imputed uncleanliness and suitability for menial work only. As recently as the 1970's, advertising in the United States featured blatantly stereotyped depictions of a Mexican armed bandit, the "Frito bandito."

Beginning in the early twentieth century, Mexican immigration to the United States was encouraged, discouraged, or denied depending on whether there was a need for cheap labor. United States immigration law vacillated between welcome and rejection. For example, from 1942 to 1964 the BRACERO PROGRAM allowed Mexican aliens to cross the border at harvest time. OPERATION WETBACK (1954-1958) sent back unwanted Mexican laborers. Often the expulsions occurred without due process procedures. Sometimes people who "looked Mexican" were herded into trucks and transported across the border, without regard to

citizenship or family members left behind. Operation Wetback expelled nearly four million people, only 63,525 of whom had formal hearings.

Working conditions and compensation typically are poor for those permitted to stay in the United States. Seasonal agricultural workers are often transported in dangerous open trucks. There have been instances of involuntary servitude in which labor contractors withheld pay and confined workers until the end of the harvest season.

Employment discrimination sometimes takes the form of placement in dead-end jobs. In 1988, more than three hundred agents of the Federal Bureau of Investigation (FBI) successfully sued the FBI for discriminatory placement in undesirable jobs, an assignment known as the "taco circuit." According to U.S. census data, average income for Chicano males in 1990 was $12,527, compared to $22,081 for Anglo males. That same year, 28.4 percent of Chicanos fell

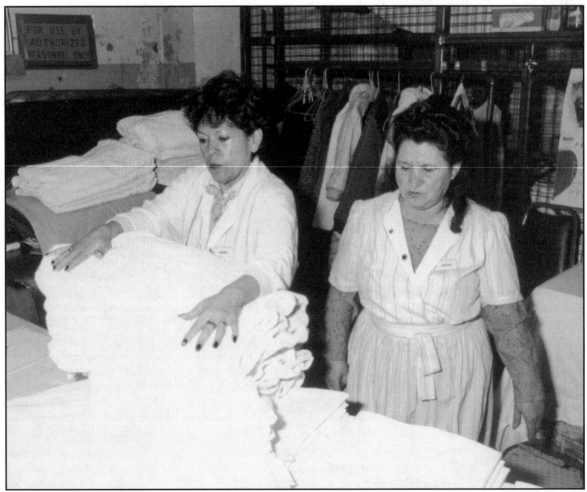

Latinos historically have been shunted into dead-end jobs. (Robert Fried)

EXPERIENCE WITH AND PERCEPTION OF DISCRIMINATION

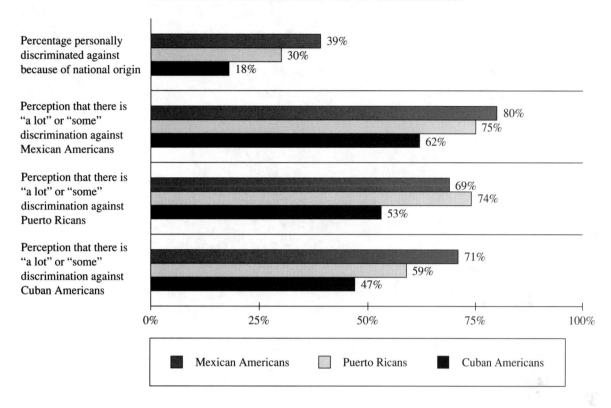

Percentage personally discriminated against because of national origin — 39% / 30% / 18%

Perception that there is "a lot" or "some" discrimination against Mexican Americans — 80% / 75% / 62%

Perception that there is "a lot" or "some" discrimination against Puerto Ricans — 69% / 74% / 53%

Perception that there is "a lot" or "some" discrimination against Cuban Americans — 71% / 59% / 47%

Legend: Mexican Americans / Puerto Ricans / Cuban Americans

Source: Data are from the Latino National Political Survey, which polled a representative sample of 1,546 Mexican Americans, 589 Puerto Ricans, and 682 Cuban Americans in forty metropolitan areas in 1989-1990. See Rodolfo O. de la Garza et al., *Latino Voices: Mexican, Puerto Rican, and Cuban Perspectives on American Politics* (Boulder, Colo.: Westview Press, 1992), Tables 7.5, 7.10, 7.11, and 7.12. Data used are for respondents who are U.S. citizens.

below the POVERTY line, compared to 11.6 percent of Anglos.

Prior to 1960's civil rights legislation, many southwestern states openly segregated Mexican Americans in a manner similar to the Jim Crow segregation of African Americans (*see* SEGREGATION, DESEGREGATION, AND INTEGRATION). Restaurants and hotels denied service, and public parks were closed to Chicanos. Sometimes public swimming pools were open to Mexicans and African Americans one day per week, the day before cleaning or draining. Although housing discrimination was outlawed in 1968, residential segregation of Mexican Americans persisted into the 1990's. In many towns and cities of the Southwest, Chicanos were relegated to separate sections with substandard housing and dirt streets.

Mexican American children attended de jure segregated public schools in some states until a federal court declared the practice unconstitutional in *CISNEROS V.*

CORPUS CHRISTI INDEPENDENT SCHOOL DISTRICT in 1972. Measures of educational achievement show that Mexican American students still were not equally educated by the 1990's, with higher dropout rates and lower scores on achievement tests than Anglo children. College attendance and college graduation rates also remained low for Mexican Americans.

There is a history of violence against Mexican Americans, including lynchings and other mob violence. In 1943, the zoot-suit riots occurred in Los Angeles, California. A mob of white civilians and sailors on leave attacked Mexican American youths. Police and naval authorities did little to stop the violence.

The United States court system has often failed to treat Mexican Americans with justice. The SLEEPY LAGOON CASE occurred in California in the early 1940's. Twenty-four Mexican Americans were tried for killing a man near a gravel pit euphemistically called the Sleepy Lagoon. Seventeen of the defendants

The first wave of Cuban immigration included a large proportion of educated professionals; public opinion about Cuban immigrants changed for the worse upon the arrival of later, less educated immigrants. (James Shaffer)

were found guilty, but the convictions were later overturned on the basis of blatant courtroom bias. Subsequently, the charges were dismissed.

Mexican Americans were not permitted to serve on juries in some areas until 1954. That year, the Supreme Court declared in *HERNÁNDEZ V. TEXAS* that it is a denial of equal protection of the law to exclude persons from jury service because of race or color.

There have been many incidents of improper conduct by law enforcement authorities involving Chicanos. Two important Supreme Court cases concerning the rights of criminal defendants during police interrogation dealt with Mexican Americans: *Escobedo v. Illinois* (1964) and *Miranda v. Arizona* (1966).

Puerto Ricans. Puerto Rico became a United States possession in 1898 as a result of the Spanish-American War. Through the JONES ACT of 1917, Puerto Ricans were granted United States citizenship, which meant that they could migrate freely to the mainland. During World War II and the 1950's, many sought industrial employment in cities of the Northeast. As of the early 1990's, Puerto Ricans were the second largest Latino group on the United States mainland, after Mexican

Americans. They have high unemployment and poverty rates compared to Anglos and compared to other Latino subgroups. Some of their economic difficulties result from the region and timing of their migration. Many Puerto Ricans arrived in the "Rustbelt" Northeast just as manufacturing jobs were beginning to disappear.

A racial mixture of Spanish colonizers, African slaves, and the Taino indigenous people, Puerto Ricans suffer from racial bigotry on the United States mainland. On the island, race is viewed as a "color gradient" of gradual shading along a continuum, rather than there being two or three discrete races. Islanders do not consider race to be as important as social class; Puerto Ricans therefore encounter an unfamiliar and unpleasant racial climate when they come to the United States mainland. Because they tend to be short in stature, Puerto Ricans have experienced employment discrimination resulting from minimum height requirements for some occupations.

Cuban Americans. The third largest Latino group, Cuban Americans, first came to the United States in large numbers as a result of the 1959 Castro communist revolution. They were welcomed and helped financially by the U.S. government. Thousands of middle- and upper-class Cubans brought with them their entrepreneurial skills, their education, and sometimes their wealth. This "displaced bourgeoisie" settled mostly in the Miami, Florida, area and established successful businesses of many kinds. They experienced some discrimination as a result of language difference, but their educational and economic assets helped them to gain acceptance. Throughout the 1960's and 1970's, more Cubans came, and most blended easily into Miami's Cuban community.

In 1980, a different group of Cubans came to the United States in the "freedom flotilla" of the Mariel boat lift. Approximately 125,000 immigrants arrived in this wave, and they were not welcomed. Because some were convicts or mentally ill, a stereotype developed that all were socially undesirable. In fact, of the 125,000, only six hundred had serious mental problems, and many of the convicts had been sentenced for political crimes in Cuba that might not be considered crimes in the United States. After brief periods of confinement, most *marielitos* were judged to be safe and were released, but the highly publicized arrival of the *marielitos* brought an increase in anti-Cuban sentiment.

The Dade County electorate voted in 1980 to reverse an earlier resolution making Dade a bilingual county. Anti-Cuban feeling derives from several sources: Some taxpayers objected to federal funding of the Cuban Refugee Program, some liberals dislike Cubans for their strong opposition to communism, and some African Americans in the Miami area resent economic competition from Cubans.

—Nancy Conn Terjesen

Suggested Readings:

- Bendick, Marc, Charles W. Jackson, Victor A. Reinoso, and Laura E. Hodges. "Discrimination Against Latino Job Applicants: A Controlled Experiment." *Fair Employment Council of Greater Washington, Inc.* (April, 1992): 1-24. This research report details a test of employment discrimination using equally qualified Latinos and Anglos who applied for the same jobs by mail or telephone.
- De la Garza, Rodolfo, et al., eds. *The Mexican American Experience.* Austin: University of Texas Press, 1985. Samples social science research through an anthology of thirty-five scholarly articles, many from *Social Science Quarterly.* Coverage includes language adjustment, health, labor market experiences, and political participation.
- Fitzpatrick, Joseph P. *Puerto Rican Americans.* Englewood Cliffs, N.J.: Prentice Hall, 1971. Contains many tables and figures. Chapters on migration, family, race, religion, education, welfare, and mental illness. Emphasizes the quest for identity and the meaning of migration.
- Mirandé, Alfredo. *The Chicano Experience.* Notre Dame, Ind.: University of Notre Dame Press, 1985. Mirandé, a Chicano sociologist, discusses education, immigration, religion, and family. Contains an analysis of the bandit stereotype, a case study of Chicano-police conflict, a new theoretical perspective, and an extensive bibliography.
- Moore, Joan, and Harry Pachon. *Hispanics in the United States.* Englewood Cliffs, N.J.: Prentice Hall, 1985. Mexicans, Puerto Ricans, and Cubans are jointly discussed in chapters devoted to stereotypes, education, employment, religion, and history. A chapter treats Hispanics in relation to modern state institutions such as schools and the criminal justice system.

Divorce and divorce rates: Since the 1970's, there have been many attempts to compile divorce rate statistics of Mexican Americans, the largest Latino subgroup in the United States. Previously, this information was unavailable in readily accessible form, and data on other Latino subgroups are extremely difficult to obtain. Most attempts to compile the data have aggregated statistics from 1960 and 1970 Census public use samples, seeking comparative approaches by cross-referencing percentiles of African American, non-Hispanic white, and Mexican American divorce rates.

As early as the mid-1950's, a decline of long-term first marriage rates was noticed, coupled with a dramatic increase in divorce rates, which had reached an all-time high. Research sought to discover the precise trends behind the rising rates of marital instability and to ascertain any convergence or divergence of rates among African Americans, non-Hispanic whites, and Mexican Americans.

When comparing different types of marital instability, such as divorce or separation, it was observed that African Americans had the highest rates of marital instability, non-Hispanic whites an intermediate level, and Mexican Americans the lowest level of the three groups. In 1970, the marital dissolution rates of persons between the ages of twenty-five and twenty-nine were 38.7 percent for African Americans, 25.5 percent for non-Hispanic whites, and 17.6 percent for Mexican Americans. Rates converged for younger cohorts, al-

The divorce rate for Mexican Americans is lower than that for other groups. (James Shaffer)

though the ordering among groups remained the same. Marital dissolutions among women between fifteen and nineteen years of age increased between 1960 and 1970 by 24.8 percent for African Americans, 17.4 percent for non-Hispanic whites, and 14.4 percent for Mexican Americans.

Statistics concerning the rates of divorce and remarriage paralleled these trends. Separation rates among these same ethnic groups, however, revealed a different trend. In both 1960 and 1970 records, non-Hispanic whites showed the lowest rates of separation in all age groups, followed by Mexican Americans. African Americans had the highest rate of marital separation. Socioeconomic differences may be one reason that members of minority groups turn more often to separation, relative to divorce, than do non-Hispanic whites.

Researchers have posited several possible reasons for these differing trends. The most significant seem to be demographic, socioeconomic, and cultural. Early age at first marriage unequivocally factored into marital instability among all three ethnic groups. Low socioeconomic status and urban residence also have been shown to be contributing factors.

Culture is believed to be partially responsible for lower divorce rates among Mexican Americans. A cohesive familial unit that embodies traditional beliefs and values has been the norm for Mexican American families. Many Mexican Americans also are members of the Roman Catholic church, which opposes divorce.

Although the Mexican American rate of marital instability has been the lowest of the three groups, it has begun to rise. Some analysts have attributed the rise to widespread Mexican American unemployment and low wages, which inhibit the traditional (male) provider from supporting the family, contributing to marital tension.

Dr. Loco's Rockin' Jalapeño Band: Music group. This band formed in the mid-1980's in the San Francisco Bay Area of California. Its leader is saxophonist Jose "Dr. Loco" Cuellar, a professor and chair of the La Raza Studies department at San Francisco State University. The nine band members, all of Mexican descent, play a diverse mix of rhythm and blues, Tex-Mex, *cumbias*, rock, and salsa. Their repertoire includes original and cover songs, with lyrics that are changed to include CHICANO cultural references. Many of the songs include both English and Spanish. Dr. Loco's popular shows aim to entertain and educate; Cuellar presents brief explanations related to the songs. By the early 1990's, the band had recorded two albums.

Domestic workers: Domestic workers are employed to do paid housework, including housecleaning, laundry, cooking, and child care. Most domestic workers in the United States are women. Since the 1970's, Latinas have constituted the largest category of women entering the occupation. By the 1990's, Latinas had replaced African American women as the majority of private household workers in the United States.

Early History. Following the Mexican American War (1846-1848), the number of women with Spanish surnames engaged in domestic service in the Southwest increased. Anglo employers discriminated in favor of white workers, including European immigrant women, and relegated Mexican women to lower-paying positions within the occupation. Chicanas and Mexican immigrants were more likely to be hired for household cleaning tasks, laundry, and cooking, while European women were hired as nannies. Nevertheless, in many places Chicanas and Mexican women outnumbered white women in the occupation. The "dual wage" practice of paying female Mexican domestic workers less than white women that began in the late nineteenth century continues today, particularly in the case of undocumented Latinas (*see* UNAUTHORIZED WORKERS).

By the beginning of the twentieth century, domestic service had been socially defined as the appropriate wage labor for Mexican women. Job training and adult education courses offered by companies, churches, and welfare programs taught young Latinas domestic skills such as laundry, cooking, sewing, and cleaning. During the 1920's, "AMERICANIZATION" PROGRAMS in the Southwest considered domestic service to be an ideal occupation for Chicana and Mexican immigrant women. Even public school systems tracked Mexican girls into home economics curricula to enable them to acquire the skills needed to work as domestics. Under the NEW DEAL, the WORKS PROGRESS ADMINISTRATION and chapters of the National Youth Administration established household training programs.

Restricting Mexican and Mexican American women's entrance into the factory and office furthered occupational stratification and slowed their movement into higher paying jobs. In 1930, 45 percent of all employed Mexican women were domestics; in some areas of the Southwest, particularly along the border, this percentage was much higher. In Colorado and New Mexico, many Chicanas divided their year between summer work in the fields and domestic service in the winter.

As factory and office jobs became available after World War II, fewer Chicanas born in the United States entered domestic service. Since the 1960's, Mexican immigrant women have dominated the occupation along the border, and by the 1980's significant numbers of Latina immigrants from South and Central American countries other than Mexico were working as private household workers in major cities, including Los Angeles, San Francisco, Washington, D.C., Chicago, New York, and Boston.

Political Issues. A political scandal over household labor brought national attention to Latina maids and nannies in the United States. President Bill Clinton nominated Zoe Baird, a corporate lawyer, as U.S. attorney general. Baird and her Yale law professor husband had hired an undocumented Peruvian woman, Lillian Cordera, as a live-in worker and failed to pay social security or unemployment insurance taxes for her. Opposition to Baird's nomination resulting from her violation of the law eventually led to her withdrawal.

Clinton's next nominee was Kimba M. Wood. Wood had employed an undocumented woman for seven years, but prior to the time that it was illegal for an employer to do so, and she had paid taxes. Clinton and his advisers thought that the distinction between Wood's childcare arrangements and Baird's arrangements would be lost in the public eye, and Wood also withdrew her name. The public debate that ensued revealed the common practice among two-career couples of hiring undocumented Latinas as maids and nannies.

Working Conditions. Private household workers are hired either as live-in or day workers. Live-in workers receive room and board as part of their wages. Traditionally, live-in workers receive Sunday and one after-

The hotel industry relies heavily on Latinas to fill housekeeping positions. (Robert Fried)

noon off. The working conditions of live-in employees are characterized by long hours: They essentially are always on call and have difficulty controlling the length of the workday. They also experience isolation from family and friends.

Job descriptions tend to be extremely broad and frequently include personal services that fall outside housecleaning, such as laundry, childcare, and cooking. The most severe cases of abuse (rape, physical abuse, withholding pay) occur in live-in situations. Live-in domestics are most common among undocumented immigrant women and those applying for residency who are employed by the sponsoring family.

Since the 1940's, the trend in domestic service has been toward day work. Unlike live-in domestics, day workers find it easier to work a set number of hours, usually averaging between six and eight hours a day. Rather than working by the hour, many day workers prefer to negotiate specific tasks to be done and then charge per job. Consequently, day workers are less likely to perform the wide range of personal services frequently expected of live-in workers, such as childcare, laundry, and cooking. Employers hiring workers primarily for housework, rather than childcare, typically employ help one day a week. This practice allows domestic workers to have numerous employers at one time and increases their control over working conditions and salary. The domestic worker can replace lower paying or more exploitative employers with better ones.

Income and Benefits. The average income of domestic workers remained below the federal poverty level into the 1990's. Despite the attention brought by the Zoe Baird case, wages do not usually include social security, health insurance, or other benefits. Immigrants almost universally receive lower wages, are more likely to work in live-in positions, and report higher levels of abuse and exploitation than native-born workers. Employers rarely obey laws regulating employment or pay the minimum wage when hiring immigrant workers. Although average wages for undocumented workers in many positions are well below the minimum wage, domestic workers are paid the least. —*Mary Romero*

SUGGESTED READINGS: • Chang, Grace. "Undocumented Latinas: The New 'Employable Mothers.'" In *Mothering: Ideology, Experience, and Agency*, edited by Evelyn Nakano Glenn, Grace Chang, and Linda Rennie Forcey. New York: Routledge, 1994. • Deutsch, Sarah. *No Separate Refuge: Culture, Class, and Gender on an Anglo-Hispanic Frontier in the American Southwest, 1880-1940*. New York: Oxford University Press, 1987. • Hondagneu-Sotelo, Pierrette. "Regulating the Unregulated?: Domestic Workers' Social Networks." *Social Problems* 41 (February, 1994): 50-64. • Romero, Mary. *Maid in the U.S.A.* New York: Routledge, 1992. • Salzinger, Leslie. "A Maid by Any Other Name: The Transformation of 'Dirty Work' by Central American Immigrants." In *Ethnography Unbound: Power and Resistance in the Modern Metropolis*, edited by Michael Buraway, et al. Berkeley: University of California Press, 1991.

Domingo, Placido (b. Jan. 21, 1941, Madrid, Spain): Opera singer and conductor. Domingo is the son of Placido Domingo and Pepita Embil Domingo, both ZARZUELA singers. Zarzuela is a Spanish operetta form popular in Spanish-speaking countries. In the early 1950's, the Domingo family moved to Mexico City, where Domingo's parents planned to form a zarzuela company. When Domingo was a child, he studied piano and voice at Mexico's National Conservatory of Music, located in Mexico City. He interrupted his music studies briefly and experimented with playing soccer, amateur bullfighting, and doing musical work in clubs for pay. When he returned to his music studies, a vocal coach helped him change his baritone voice upward to the tenor range.

Domingo made his professional operatic debut in 1961 in Monterrey, Mexico, singing the tenor role of Alfred, the hero of *La Traviata*. Domingo sang with Joan Sutherland for the Dallas Civic Opera, also in 1961, and had the privilege of singing with Lily Pons for her farewell performance in Fort Worth, Texas, the next year. He then moved to Israel for a couple of years and sang in a number of multinational opera productions. In 1965, Domingo made his New York City debut with the New York City Opera.

Having earned a reputation as a dynamic opera tenor, Domingo was in demand throughout Europe. In 1968, he made his debut with the New York Metropolitan Opera. By 1979, it was estimated that Domingo had sung in eighty operas, had been involved with the recording of fifty operas, and had appeared in about fourteen hundred performances. In addition to singing opera, he has also sung popular songs, operettas, and zarzuela music. Domingo also began conducting orchestras in 1975.

As one of the most respected and famous contemporary opera tenors in the world, Domingo joined José Carreras and Luciano Pavarotti to sing at the 1990 World Cup soccer event. In 1994, the three great opera

Placido Domingo performs at the 1993 Academy Awards ceremony. (AP/Wide World Photos)

tenors performed together again on the eve of the World Cup soccer event at Dodger Stadium in Los Angeles, California. Domingo was scheduled to assume the artistic directorship of the Washington Opera in 1996.

Dominican Americans: Emigrants (and their descendants) from the Dominican Republic living in the United States.

History. Small Dominican communities were founded in New York City in the early 1960's by families prominent in business and political activities. The immigrants formed social clubs and other voluntary associations that reflected their elitist membership and view of Dominican culture. These groups tended to be politically conservative and geared toward a wider Hispanic audience in the United States. During the early 1960's, Dominicans lacked social institutions such as ethnic churches to assist them in the resettlement process.

As New York's Dominican population increased in the late 1960's and early 1970's, new social and political groups emerged. Many radical and liberal leaders and militants came to the United States to avoid political persecution in the Dominican Republic. The number of Dominican voluntary associations in New York multiplied. Most of these associations were located in upper Manhattan, particularly in Washington Heights, where the majority of the immigrants settled. Community organizations often revolved around the immigrants' place of origin, such as a province, town, or neighborhood in the Dominican Republic. Informal

STATISTICAL PROFILE OF DOMINICAN AMERICANS, 1990

Total population based on sample: 520,151

Percentage foreign-born: 71%

Median age: 27.6 years

Percentage 25+ years old with at least a high school diploma or equivalent: 43%

Occupation (employed persons 16+ years old)

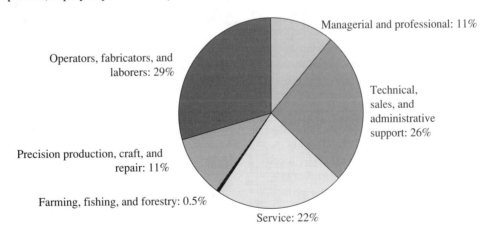

Managerial and professional: 11%

Operators, fabricators, and laborers: 29%

Technical, sales, and administrative support: 26%

Precision production, craft, and repair: 11%

Farming, fishing, and forestry: 0.5%

Service: 22%

Percentage unemployed: 15.6%

Median household income, 1989: $20,006

Percentage of families in poverty, 1989: 33.4%

Source: Data are from Bureau of the Census, *Census of 1990: Persons of Hispanic Origin in the United States* (Washington, D.C.: Bureau of the Census, 1993), Tables 1, 3, 4, and 5.

Note: Percentages for occupations are rounded to the nearest whole number except for farming, fishing, and forestry, for which rounding is to the nearest 0.1%.

Political and social organizations have proliferated among Dominican Americans. (Frances M. Roberts)

networks of kin, friends, and neighbors helped to organize the community. Political ideology, party affiliation, and class interests reinforced ethnic ties.

In the 1970's, the principal political parties of the Dominican Republic were reconstituted in New York. Although conservative groups endured, left-wing exiles organized the community at a grassroots level. Most of these efforts were oriented toward domestic issues in the Dominican Republic, particularly government repression of political dissidents. Self-help associations with various recreational, political, and cultural objectives proliferated.

In the 1980's, Dominican Americans created umbrella organizations, such as Alianza Dominicana, to reduce their isolation and fragmentation. They also initiated a process of political empowerment that culminated in the election of several Dominicans to Manhattan school boards. In 1991, Washington Heights voters chose the first Dominican representative to the New York City Council, former schoolteacher Guillermo Linares.

Demography. Most Dominican Americans reside in New York City, with secondary concentrations in Puerto Rico and New Jersey. The 1990 U.S. census counted approximately 330,000 Dominicans in New York City and 41,000 in Puerto Rico, but these figures did not include a large number of undocumented immigrants. In the early 1990's, an estimated 51,000 Dominicans resided illegally on the U.S. mainland and another 20,000 lived in Puerto Rico. A reasonable estimate would place the total number of Dominicans abroad at 500,000, about 7 percent of the 1990 Dominican population.

The demographic profile of Dominican Americans differs markedly from that of the general U.S. population. First, Dominican Americans tend to be relatively young. In the 1980's, the median age of Dominican immigrants in New York was twenty-two, the lowest of the city's major immigrant groups. Second, the majority of Dominican Americans are women. Third, Dominican immigrants are more likely to be married than are other New Yorkers. Finally, the majority of Dominican Americans are engaged in manual labor, especially as machine operators, unskilled laborers, and service workers. Many work in the garment industry in unstable and poorly paid jobs. Others are taxi drivers, construction workers, and grocery-store attendants.

Settlement Patterns. New York City has the largest Dominican population outside Santo Domingo. Dominicans have clustered in northwest Manhattan, with smaller communities in the South Bronx, the Lower East Side of Manhattan, and the Corona section of Queens. The largest concentration of Dominican immigrants is located in Washington Heights and the adjacent neighborhoods of Inwood and Hamilton Heights. With one-third of New York's Dominicans in 1990, Washington Heights was the hub of Dominican settlement in the United States.

The Dominican community of Washington Heights is largely segregated from non-Hispanic whites and blacks. In 1990, approximately 25 percent of the area's population was Dominican, and another 19 percent was made up of Latinos of other backgrounds, primarily Puerto Rican, Cuban, Ecuadoran, and Salvadoran. Geographic concentration, occupational specialization, and ethnic solidarity have bred an incipient enclave economy, characterized by a thriving network of small businesses catering to immigrant needs. In the 1990's, Dominicans owned nearly twenty thousand businesses in New York, especially BODEGAS (grocery stores), garment sweatshops, restaurants, travel agencies, and taxi agencies. Culturally, Washington Heights has re-created many of the migrants' traditional institutions, such as political parties, labor unions, and ethnic newspapers. Dominican Americans commonly refer to their neighborhood as Quisqueya Heights, Quisqueya being the indigenous name for the island of Hispaniola, shared by Haiti and the Dominican Republic.

The student population in the Washington Heights area is largely Dominican. (Hazel Hankin)

**DOMINICAN IMMIGRATION TO
THE UNITED STATES, 1931-1990**

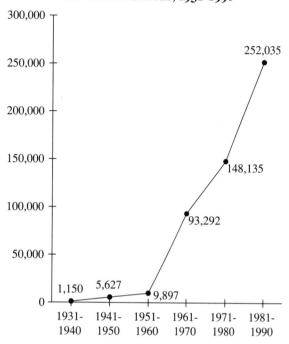

Source: Data are from Marlita A. Reddy, ed., *Statistical Record of Hispanic Americans* (Detroit: Gale Research, 1993), Tables 25 and 26.

Cultural Contributions. Despite their relatively short time in the United States, Dominicans have made important contributions to American society. Their most visible success has been in baseball, the national sport of the Dominican Republic. Their best-known cultural tradition is the MERENGUE, the national music and dance style, which replaced Puerto Rican SALSA in popularity among New York's Latino population. Restaurants and cafeterias offering Dominican food spread throughout upper Manhattan. Dominican Americans proudly celebrate their heritage through colorful community activities, including the Dominican Day parades in Manhattan and the Bronx.

Dominican Americans have begun to penetrate the higher spheres of American culture. Some Dominican immigrants have become bilingual teachers in New York's public school system. In 1992, Dominican American scholars created the Dominican Studies Institute at the City University of New York. A new generation of Dominican American writers has gained wider recognition. These include Julia ALVAREZ, author of the critically acclaimed *How the García Girls*

Lost Their Accent (1991). Most Dominican American culture, however, has not received close study.

—*Jorge Duany*

SUGGESTED READINGS: • Báez Evertsz, Franc, and Frank D'Oleo. *La emigración de dominicanos a Estados Unidos: Determinantes socio-económicos y consecuencias.* Santo Domingo, Dominican Republic: Fundación Friedrich Ebert, 1985. • Del Castillo, José, and Christopher Mitchel, eds. *La inmigración dominicana en los Estados Unidos.* Santo Domingo, Dominican Republic: Universidad APEC, CENAPEC, 1987. • Georges, Eugenia. *The Making of a Transnational Community: Migration, Development, and Cultural Change in the Dominican Republic.* New York: Columbia University Press, 1990. • Georges, Eugenia, et al. *Dominicanos ausentes: Cifras, políticas, condiciones sociales.* Santo Domingo, Dominican Republic: Fundación Friedrich Ebert/Fondo para el Avance de las Ciencias Sociales, 1989. • Grasmuck, Sherri, and Patricia R. Pessar. *Between Two Islands: Dominican International Migration.* Berkeley: University of California Press, 1991.

Dominican Republic: The Dominican Republic, once the Spanish colony of Santo Domingo, shares the island of Hispaniola with the country of Haiti. As European colonization destroyed the island's native people, the Taino, the Spanish replaced them with African slaves. Intermarriage over the centuries produced a people of mixed African and European descent, and a majority of Dominicans are mulatto. Dominican culture and music reflect this mixture of Spanish and African backgrounds. There are also small communities of European Jews, some Japanese farmers, and a Chinese business community.

The population of the Dominican Republic in the early 1990's was approximately 7.3 million. Life expectancy at that time was sixty-two years, and although the birth rate was declining, it remained high, producing an annual rate of population increase of 2.3 percent. Nearly 40 percent of the population was under fifteen years of age. In 1968, the government began trying to decrease population growth rates through family planning.

Rural-to-urban migration significantly increased the population of the country's principal cities. The two largest cities in 1993 were the capital, Santo Domingo (estimated population of 1,900,000), and Santiago de los Caballeros (population 285,000). In the early 1990's, approximately one-quarter of the population lived in a province other than the one in which they were born, and 8 to 15 percent lived abroad. The government actively encouraged emigration to reduce the impact of population growth. Most emigrants went to the United States. New York City has been a major center of immigrants, with 160,000 Dominicans in the 1990's.

In the 1990's, 95 percent of Dominicans professed the Roman Catholic faith, although the Dominican Republic had fewer priests per person than most other Latin American nations. The majority of priests were from other countries, but they were respected by the population. Roman Catholicism was the official religion of the country, but divorce was legal and civil marriages were accepted. Ideally, marriage would be a religious ceremony, but the expense led many to opt for a civil ceremony. In addition, many unions were informal.

The family represented the most important social unit, both in the countryside and in the city. Family loyalty has been so strong that immigrants living in New York City have been reported to send as much as half of their wages back to family members in the Dominican Republic. Family ties were extended through *compadrazo*, godparents who often were chosen for their resources and ability to help.

FACTS AT A GLANCE

Capital: Santo Domingo

Area: 18,816 square miles

Population (estimated, 1994): 7,755,000

Percentage living in urban areas: 58

Estimated 1991 Gross National Product (GNP):
$6.807 billion

Type of government: republic

The rate of literacy reached 74 percent near the end of the twentieth century, but the educational system had mixed results. Primary education was free and compulsory, and secondary and higher education were available. Low pay for teachers and a lack of resources, however, made it difficult to improve the system or encourage more people to remain in school.

The Economy. Approximately 18 percent of the work force was employed in manufacturing in the

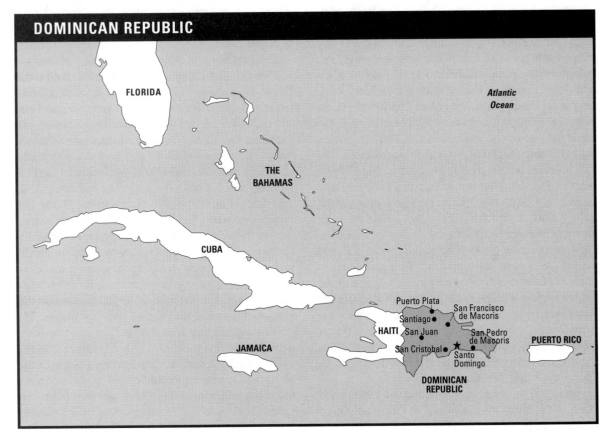

DOMINICAN REPUBLIC

early 1990's, although many were underemployed and the nationwide unemployment rate was 30 percent. Almost half of the work force was engaged in agriculture, which accounted for 25 percent of the country's exports. Many of those in the countryside were engaged in subsistence farming, primarily producing rice and maize. More than half of all rural households owned no land and relied on wage labor for their income. Most farm women contributed to family income by selling vegetables or homemade sweets.

Beginning in the 1970's, natural disasters and United States restrictions on sugar imports led to a decline in the relative importance of agriculture. Tourism replaced agriculture as the leading economic activity, and new hotels were constructed. Business was spurred by one of the most advanced telecommunications systems in Latin America, with fiber-optic cables, digital switches, a satellite earth station, a submarine cable to the U.S. Virgin Islands, and microwave stations. This led to new industries in telemarketing and data entry.

Geography. The Dominican Republic encompasses the western two-thirds of the island of Hispaniola and covers 18,704 square miles. Its northern coast lies along the Atlantic Ocean, while its southern coast overlooks the Caribbean. It is the second largest country in the Caribbean region, after Cuba, and lies 670 miles southwest of Florida. Three mountain ranges run northwest to southeast. The Cordillera Central (Central Range) contains Duarte Peak, the highest mountain in the Caribbean at 10,417 feet. The Central Highlands stand at an elevation of 6,000 feet. The Cibao Valley is one of the nation's most heavily populated areas because of its productive agricultural lands. The mountainous terrain gives the country a mild climate, with an average mean temperature of 77 degrees. The western region is drier, with an average annual rainfall of only thirty inches, while the wetter regions get more than one hundred inches of rain.

Mineral resources include bauxite, iron ore, and nickel. There were still deposits of silver and gold near the end of the twentieth century as well as one of the largest deposits of rock salt in the world. Minerals amounted to nearly 35 percent of the country's exports, but petroleum had to be imported to supply most of the country's electricity. Hydroelectric power was produced from the three principal rivers, the Yaque del Norte, the Yaque del Sur, and the Yuna.

History. The Dominican Republic has called itself the land Columbus loved. Christopher Columbus landed on the large island he called Española on his first voyage to the New World in 1492. Columbus lacked the skills to manage the colonists, who were more interested in obtaining gold than planting crops. In 1499, Spain sent Francisco de Bobadilla to replace Columbus. With twenty-five hundred new colonists, Bobadilla began to establish Spain's first successful settlement in the Americas. From this base in Hispaniola, Spanish explorers set out to conquer Cuba, Jamaica, and Puerto Rico.

By the end of the sixteenth century, Spain's hold on the Caribbean was increasingly challenged by rival European powers. The great English privateer, Sir Francis Drake, captured Santo Domingo in 1586, and returned it only after receiving a ransom. In 1697, the western third of Hispaniola was ceded to the French, who called it Saint-Domingue. That area later became Haiti.

During the seventeenth century, sugar production grew in both French Saint-Domingue and Spanish Santo Domingo. Because nearly all the native islanders had been killed by disease or overwork, African slaves were imported to work the land. By 1800, the European population of Santo Domingo had grown to about forty thousand, while the slave population surpassed sixty thousand. In addition, there were approximately twenty-five thousand free mulattoes, or people of mixed race.

Slave uprisings in Saint-Domingue in 1794 and the 1795 treaty that ceded Santo Domingo to the French linked these two colonies in a way that led to confrontation and hatred for two hundred years. When Toussaint L'Ouverture led his African troops into Santo Domingo in 1801 and freed the slaves, many Spaniards departed. After withdrawing and then establishing the second independent republic in the Americas, the Haitians invaded Santo Domingo unsuccessfully in 1805 and successfully in 1822, incorporating Santo Domingo into Haiti. The Dominicans threw off Haitian rule in 1844, establishing the Dominican Republic. Continuing threats and invasions by Haiti eventually led to the reestablishment of Spain's power and colonial status for Santo Domingo in 1861. By 1864, Spain had withdrawn in the face of armed opposition that Dominicans called the War of the Restoration. The republic reemerged, with the last Spanish troops departing in 1865.

Between 1865 and 1899, two political forces dominated the Dominican Republic, the "Reds" under the leadership of Buenaventura Báez, and the "Blues" led (after 1878) by Ulises Heureaux. Heureaux was ruthless yet effective in providing stability for the develop-

Toussaint L'Ouverture helped abolish slavery in Santo Domingo. (Library of Congress)

Dominican Americans in New York City protest against U.S. intervention in a 1965 revolution in the Dominican Republic. (National Archives)

ment of ports, telegraph lines, and foreign investments. After Heureaux was murdered in 1899, no group controlled the government long enough to provide the economic stability necessary to repay the increasing foreign debt.

By 1904, threats of military intervention by European powers led U.S. president Theodore Roosevelt to issue his Roosevelt Corollary to the MONROE DOCTRINE. Roosevelt stated that the United States would intervene in any state in the region threatened by political or economic chaos in order to stave off European involvement. A 1905 treaty with the Dominican Republic gave the United States authority to intercede in order to settle the claims of European governments. After the outbreak of World War I, and with growing political unrest in the Dominican Republic, President Woodrow Wilson authorized the United States to occupy the Dominican Republic to restore order in 1916.

The occupation by the United States lasted until 1924 and provoked resentment among the Dominicans, even though they recognized that it had accomplished much. Roads and schools were built, debts were paid off, and a new constitution was approved in 1924. A new army was organized and placed under the leadership of Rafael Leónidas Trujillo, who had risen through the ranks of the military constabulary formed by the United States occupation forces. In the 1930 elections, Trujillo used his power over the military to steal the election. He declared himself elected with 95 percent of the votes. Trujillo controlled the Dominican Republic from 1930 until his assassination in 1961. He was one of the most successful, if most ruthless, dictators in Latin America.

Government. A new constitution was promulgated in 1962, and Juan Bosch, a leftist, was elected. His overthrow by a right-wing military coup in 1963 led to a rebellion in early 1965. To restore order and prevent a Communist upheaval, the president of the United States, Lyndon B. Johnson, authorized a military invasion that was later joined by several Latin American countries.

Another constitution was written in 1966. That constitution provided for the election of a president, with broad powers and control over the armed forces, every four years. The president would appoint a cabinet to carry out administration policies. The legislative branch would consist of a bicameral congress, with a Senate of 30 members and a Chamber of Deputies with 120 members. Into the 1990's, there were two major political parties vying for power, the Dominican Revolutionary Party and the Revolutionary Social Christian Party. The constitution also provided for an independent judiciary headed by a Supreme Court.

Joaquín Balaguer was elected president in 1966. He served three terms in office. Antonio Guzmán Fernández, of the opposition Dominican Revolutionary Party, won the 1978 election. Salvador Jorge Blanco, of the same party, won the 1982 election.

Blanco's economic policies, which followed the dictates of the International Monetary Fund for austerity measures, led to increasing opposition. Riots in the spring of 1984 left nearly fifty people dead, and the 1986 election returned Balaguer to power. Balaguer, who had merged his Reformist Party with the Revolutionary Social Christian Party, was reelected in 1990. Although he was criticized for ineffective leadership and advancing years (he was born in 1908 and had become legally blind from glaucoma), he won the 1994 election by claiming that his rival, an Afro-Dominican, was closely tied to Haiti. Many Dominicans still feared another invasion by an overpopulated Haiti; this fear influenced the elections, and Balaguer remained in power.   —*James A. Baer*

SUGGESTED READINGS:

• Fagg, John Edwin. *Cuba, Haiti, and the Dominican Republic.* Englewood Cliffs, N.J.: Prentice Hall, 1965. A general history of the Dominican Republic from its discovery by Columbus until the 1960's. Somewhat dated, because it went to press shortly after the U.S. invasion in 1965.

• Haggerty, Richard A., ed. *Dominican Republic and Haiti: Country Studies.* 2d ed. Washington, D.C.: Federal Research Division, Library of Congress, 1991. Excellent information on government, political parties, history, and recent events.

• Knight, Franklin W., and Colin A. Palmer, eds. *The Modern Caribbean.* Chapel Hill: University of North Carolina Press, 1989. Although not focusing

specifically on the Dominican Republic, this book gives an excellent picture of the entire region, including relations with the United States.

• Mansbach, Richard W., ed. *Dominican Crisis, 1965.* New York: Facts on File, 1971. Detailed account of the political crisis in the Dominican Republic that led to the 1965 invasion by the United States.

• Rogozinski, Jan. *A Brief History of the Caribbean: From the Arawak and the Carib to the Present.* New York: Facts on File, 1992. Up-to-date material on the Dominican Republic, with population figures, economic data, and tables. Good information on pre-Columbian peoples of Hispaniola.

Don Francisco (Mario Kreutzberger; b. 1941, Chile): Television personality. Kreutzberger is the son of Jewish immigrants who fled Germany and settled in Chile. In 1959, he moved to New York to study. He returned to Santiago in 1961 and by the following year was working in Chilean television. He is best known as Don Francisco, the creator and uninhibited host of a weekly television show called *Sábado Gigante* that features games, contests, talent searches, music, celebrity guests, and sober discussion of current topics. For three and a half hours every Saturday morning, Don Francisco leads and entertains an audience estimated in 1992 at forty million viewers worldwide, making *Sábado Gigante* the most popular program on television. Produced in Miami by Univisión, the show is seen in almost every Spanish-speaking nation and has become a required stop for major Latino performers.

In 1991, Don Francisco began hosting another Univisión program titled *Noche de Gigantes,* modeled on a popular Chilean program. Kreutzberger, who travels widely promoting his programs, also owns department stores and a fruit-shipping business in Chile.

D'Rivera, Paquito (b. June 4, 1948, Havana, Cuba): Alto saxophonist. D'Rivera's father played the tenor saxophone and introduced his son to jazz. It was his father who gave D'Rivera his first saxophone lessons. Some of D'Rivera's early influences were Benny Goodman, Charlie Parker, and Paul Desmond.

As a child, D'Rivera listened to jazz records and a radio show by the name of *Willis Conover Jazz Hour,* which was broadcast on the Voice of America. In 1960, D'Rivera went to the conservatory in Havana. At the conservatory, he met Chucho Valdés, who became a major influence on the direction of D'Rivera's career. As a teenager, D'Rivera played in musical theater. He joined the army in 1965 and became a member of the army band.

D'Rivera later joined Orquesta Cubana de Música Moderna. In the early 1970's, he and some other members of that group formed the nucleus for the group Irakere. While touring Europe with Irakere in 1980, D'Rivera defected. At the time of the defection, he was in Spain, but he eventually moved to New York, where eventually he got the opportunity to play with David Amram, Dizzy Gillespie, and McCoy Tyner. He went on to form his own group, which toured extensively. In addition to performing with his own group, D'Rivera has worked as a studio musician. He is one of the leading practitioners of the Latin American bop saxophone sound. Although the alto saxophone is D'Rivera's principal instrument, he also is accomplished on the soprano saxophone, flute, and flugelhorn.

Dropouts and dropout rates: Hispanic students face many academic difficulties and are categorized as at high risk of leaving school. Failure to earn a high school diploma is one of the largest obstacles to Hispanics' full participation in society, and low levels of education negatively affect individual lives as well as the entire community.

The Hispanic student population entering public schools and the number of Hispanic dropouts both are growing rapidly. Every year, in the early 1990's, about 18 percent of Hispanic students dropped out of school. A report from the NATIONAL COUNCIL OF LA RAZA, a Washington-based public policy group, stated that Hispanics were the least educated among the major subpopulations in the United States. By the year 2000, Hispanics were expected to account for 10 percent of the U.S. labor force. Without improvement in their educational level, they could expect to be relegated to low-paying jobs.

Linguistic Factors. Many Hispanic students speak Spanish as a primary language and have limited proficiency in English. This nonstandard linguistic ability is one of the largest obstacles to achieving educational goals. The English immersion model, in which instruction is provided only in English, puts these students at risk for future educational and social problems. Critics of this form of education argue that it is unrealistic to expect students to learn subject matter while simultaneously trying to learn the language in which it is taught. Proponents suggest that the method teaches students English as quickly as possible and motivates them to learn English rather than relying on Spanish.

Emotional Factors. A child's identity and language development are closely interrelated. When Spanish-speaking children arrive at school and find that English is the language of instruction and that it dominates the schooling experience, many feel discouraged and unmotivated. Early school experiences play a large role in future academic difficulties and affect the rate of dropping out.

In addition, teachers' attitudes toward Hispanic students often discourage students from academic endeavors. Teachers and counselors often encourage Hispanic students to go to vocational schools and even to drop out when they are falling behind. This advice is often well-meaning but may be based on false perceptions that the students have no desire to succeed or are incapable of success.

Teachers also tend to make a fundamental attribution error toward Hispanic students. Many teachers believe that Hispanic students' difficulties are a result of the students' personal characteristics rather than being reactions to situational factors. Children internalize these ideas and develop negative self-concepts; low self-concepts often lead them to discontinue their academic efforts and even engage in self-handicapping behaviors.

Hispanic children facing educational difficulties may tune out stimuli that are not personally relevant. Shy, insecure, or introverted individuals who avoid engaging in interactions with their peers and teachers are less likely to learn as quickly as other students who are more actively involved. Hispanic students tend to be less assertive than Anglo children in interactions with adults, including teachers, and therefore receive less classroom attention.

Other Factors. POVERTY is perhaps the single largest obstacle to schoolwork and poses particular problems for Hispanic students. The median income of Hispanic families in 1992 was about $24,000, far below the median Caucasian family income of about $32,000. Hispanic families also had higher rates of poverty than the nationwide average.

Many Hispanic students have conflicting roles. Once they reach high school, they may be pressured to hold jobs to help pay family expenses. In addition, many Hispanic parents do not place a high value on education because they believe that education is not necessary to survive and that it will not improve life circumstances. Many students succumb to these pressures and enter the labor force; some are drawn completely into the world of work and drop out of school.

Pregnancy is another factor that influences Hispanic students to drop out of school. Teenage mothers unable

The strain of holding a job to contribute financially adds to pressures to drop out of school. (James Shaffer)

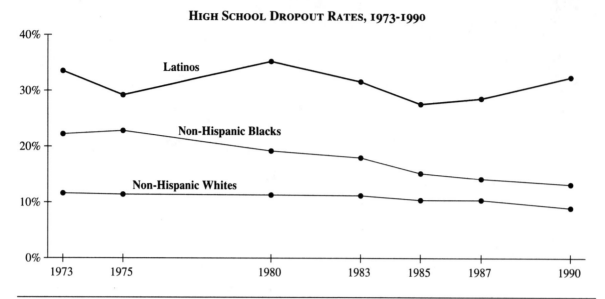

HIGH SCHOOL DROPOUT RATES, 1973-1990

Source: Data are from Bureau of the Census, *Statistical Abstract of the United States: 1992* (Washington, D.C.: Bureau of the Census, 1992), Table 252.

Note: Data are for percentages of "status dropouts," or persons aged 16 to 24 who are not enrolled in high school and have not graduated, regardless of when they were enrolled. In 1987, procedures changed for reporting cases with missing data on school enrollment, so data from 1987 forward are not strictly comparable to data from years before 1987.

to find child care may stay home with their children and away from school, or they may simply believe that they have entered adult family life and therefore have no more need for school. In many cases, teens lack social as well as family support to help them cope with their struggles and crises. The Latino culture may weight their beliefs concerning life choices in favor of rearing a family and away from education.

Solutions. Ways to combat the overall problem of dropping out and the specific causes of it include early intervention programs (focusing on students in elementary and middle grades), bilingual educational programs, and ENGLISH AS A SECOND LANGUAGE (ESL) or English for speakers of other languages (ESOL) instruction. Both ESL and ESOL programs began to be adopted in many public schools in the United States during the 1980's. These programs can provide a bridge into the educational mainstream and help Spanish-speaking students acclimate to school life.

Family and school support and involvement can also help reduce the incidence of dropping out. Providing free or affordable literacy and bilingual programs for Latino parents, developing aggressive programs to teach parents how schools work and how to help their children achieve, employing more bilingual and Latino workers in schools so that the Latino parents feel more welcome and understood, and creating more op-

portunities for parents to volunteer in schools to contribute to multicultural curricula are only some of the approaches that schools and parents can use to keep children in school. —*Angelica C. Fuentes*

SUGGESTED READINGS: • Delgado-Gaitan, Concha, and Henry Trueba. *Crossing Cultural Borders.* New York: Falmer Press, 1991. • Duany, Luis, and Karen Pittman. "Latino Youths at a Crossroads." *The Educational Digest* 56 (January, 1991): 7-11. • Fradd, Sandra H., and Vivian I. Correa. "Hispanic Students at Risk: Do We Abdicate or Advocate?" *Exceptional Children* 56 (October, 1989): 105-110. • Fradd, Sandra H., Richard A. Figueroa, and Vivian I. Correa. "Meeting the Multicultural Needs of Hispanic Students in Special Education." *Exceptional Children* 56 (October, 1989): 102-103. • Kantrowitz, Barbara. "Falling Further Behind." *Newsweek* 188, no. 8 (1991): 60.

Drug trade: Despite attempts at international cooperation between nations and a long, concerted effort by the United States government to curtail smuggling, Latin America has long been a major source of illicit drugs used in the United States.

The abuse of illegal drugs is a growing problem in the United States, especially among urban minority groups. Latinos, who are among the most disadvantaged of all North Americans, are also among the most frequent users of marijuana and cocaine, both of which have their major sources of origin in Latin America.

Because marijuana is illegal in the United States and large crops of the plant are difficult to hide and equally difficult to protect from theft, most of this drug is imported from Latin America, where law enforcement is less efficient. The largest source of marijuana is Mexico, which shares a long land border with the United States that is difficult to patrol effectively.

Efforts to halt the smuggling of marijuana from Mexico have often proved futile, in part because Americans are far from agreement on the relative danger of the drug. In 1975, Mexico, with United States aid, began spraying the highly toxic chemical paraquat on crops of marijuana. This operation was halted in 1979, when the United States withdrew its aid. It appeared that paraquat was causing severe damage to the lungs of Americans who smoked leaves from tainted plants. Congress ruled that this was a health danger not outweighed by any slowing of traffic in the drug.

The other drug imported from Latin America in large quantities is cocaine. As of the 1980's, Colombia produced 80 percent of the world's cocaine. Cocaine exports more than tripled between 1976 and 1986, primarily because of the introduction of crack, a potent and much less expensive form of the drug.

In 1975, the Colombian government "declared war" on the drug cartels, and the United States sent military aid. The Colombian government was unsuccessful in defeating the drug operators, who were among the richest people in the country. Even when dealers were arrested, they generally were soon released. The production of cocaine and its export to the United States continued.

Drug traffic, abuse, and addiction continue to increase. This has had the paradoxical effects of providing billions of dollars in revenue to Latin American drug dealers, but bestowing untold misery on American Latinos, among others. Young children are often used as couriers for cocaine in the barrios of New York, Los Angeles, and Chicago, partly because they are less likely to be punished if caught. Children are born addicted to cocaine because of mothers' use of it during pregnancy. Numerous social programs address these side effects of the drug trade. These programs will remain necessary as long as the "war on drugs" declared in the 1980's must be fought.

Drying out: Detaining and deporting undocumented immigrants, then admitting them into the United States as legal entrants. This term derives from "WETBACK" or *MOJADO* (wet one), pejorative labels for undocumented immigrants to the United States. The reference to wetness comes from the act of crossing the Rio Grande, thereby avoiding the regulated places of entrance along the Mexico/United States border.

Duardo, Richard (b. 1952): Artist. Duardo is a master of the silkscreen medium who helped found the Centro de Arte Publico (center of public art) in Los Angeles, California, in the 1970's. The center attempted to fuse Chicano consciousness with a commercial design and silkscreening business.

Duardo, who has promoted Chicano style and ideas with such well-known silkscreens as *Zoot Suit* (1978) and *Aztlan* (1982), participated in Méchanico Art Center, Self-Help Graphics, and other Los Angeles-based Chicano art collectives before founding the Centro de Arte Publico. A skillful silkscreen designer and technician with a concern for history, he created most of the posters and handled promotions and historical documentation for the center. After the center folded, Duardo established his own business, Aztlan Multiples, to provide interior decorators with fine posters, including those of Chicano artists.

Duardo began creating quality silkscreen posters to promote punk and new wave rock music events. He maintained a print studio and ran his own art gallery, Future Perfect. Duardo also has organized unusual art events. His "Truckload of Art," for example, a semitrailer full of art that functioned as a museum on wheels, made stops in various areas of Los Angeles.

Duran, Roberto (b. June 16, 1951, Panama City, Panama): Boxer. Duran rose from a tough childhood on the streets of Panama City to dominate boxing's lightweight classes during the 1970's. Undefeated until 1971, Duran won the world lightweight title in June, 1972. He successfully defended that title until 1978, when he decided to change weight classes. He knocked out opponents in fight after fight, and his heavy hitting earned him the nickname *Manos de piedra*, or "Hands of Stone."

Moving to the welterweight class, Duran bested Sugar Ray Leonard in June of 1980 for his second title. In a November, 1980, rematch, however, Duran quit in the eighth round, telling the referee "no más, no más" ("no more, no more"). Later, he said that he quit because he was suffering from stomach cramps, but the incident destroyed his aura of invincibility and tarnished his reputation.

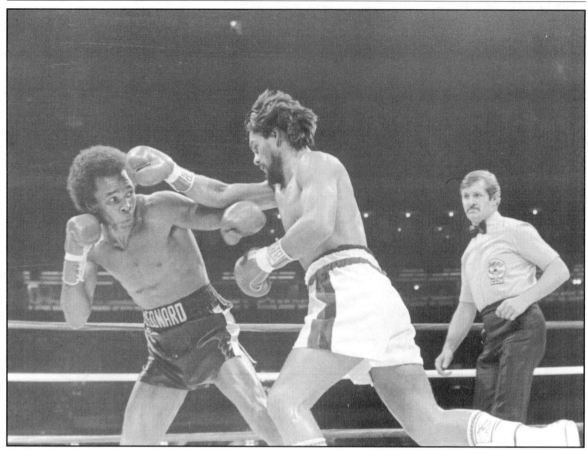

Roberto Duran looks powerful in the first round of his 1980 title defense against Sugar Ray Leonard, but he conceded the fight in the eighth round. (AP/Wide World Photos)

In response, Duran again shifted weight classes, taking the junior middleweight title from Davey Moore in 1983. He captured his fourth championship in February of 1989, defeating Ivan Barkley by decision for the World Boxing Council middleweight title. The victory made him the first Latin fighter to win titles in four weight classes.

In December, 1989, Duran met Sugar Ray Leonard for a third time. Duran lost, but he helped to redeem his reputation by standing toe-to-toe with Leonard for twelve rounds. Still fighting in his forties, Duran spent much of the early 1990's seeking an elusive fifth title.

Durst Ranch affair (Aug. 3, 1913): Conflict over working conditions. The Durst Ranch affair, which resulted in the deaths of a Puerto Rican worker and three other men, brought attention to the conditions faced by migrant workers in California.

The Durst brothers' hop ranch was located near Wheatland, in California's Sacramento Valley. In the summer of 1913, workers familiar with the teachings of the INDUSTRIAL WORKERS OF THE WORLD (IWW) submitted a list of demands to Ralph Durst, one of the ranch owners. The demands included a wage increase and improved living and working conditions.

Durst agreed to some of the demands but refused to grant a wage increase and certain improvements in working conditions. He tried to prevent a strike by removing Richard "Blackie" Ford, who had emerged as the leading organizer. On August 3, 1913, Durst sent a local constable to arrest Ford. The constable did not have a warrant, however, and an angry crowd prevented Ford's arrest.

Durst telephoned authorities in nearby Marysville, reporting that lawless workers had taken control of his ranch. The Yuba County sheriff responded to this exaggerated report by assembling a group of heavily armed deputies and proceeding to the ranch. When the authorities arrived, they found a peaceful crowd of about two thousand men, women, and children singing a union song.

The authorities waded into the crowd, intent on arresting Ford. As the sheriff approached the platform where Ford was standing, he shouted an order to disperse. A shot was fired to add emphasis to the order. The shot touched off a brief but intense battle in which about twenty shots were fired. Yuba County District Attorney Edward Manwell, a deputy sheriff, an English hop picker, and a Puerto Rican worker were killed. The Puerto Rican man had disarmed one lawman and had killed Manwell and the deputy before being killed himself. After the fighting, the authorities fled to Marysville and the hop pickers left the area as quickly as they could. Governor Hiram Johnson sent six companies of the National Guard to the area, but they found the ranch almost abandoned.

Yuba County authorities sought to punish those responsible for the deaths of Manwell and the deputy. On August 7, a coroner's jury instructed county authorities to arrest Ford and other organizers. Detectives hired by Yuba County pursued the Wheatland organizers throughout the West. They arrested dozens of people and used threats, beatings, torture, and bribery to obtain confessions. They used these confessions to implicate Ford and fellow workers Herman Suhr, Walter Bagan, and William Beck in a conspiracy to kill Manwell. Ford and Suhr were convicted and given life sentences; the other men were acquitted.

The pursuit of Ford and the other leaders may have reflected opposition to the IWW more than a genuine desire to find the killers of Manwell and the deputy. The Wheatland riot brought to public attention the demeaning conditions faced by employees of California's industrial farms, many of whom were Latinos. Governor Johnson's investigation of the uprising concluded that inadequate housing and poor sanitary conditions were the real cause of the violence. The investigation resulted in a campaign to improve labor camps throughout California.

E

East Los Angeles: Spanish involvement in what was to become the city of Los Angeles began on September 4, 1781, with the purpose of establishing a far western colonial Spanish outpost. The name Los Angeles was derived from the original appellation El Pueblo de Nuestra Señora la Reina de Los Angeles de Porciúncula. In the mid-1830's, Los Angeles officially was granted city status. California became part of the United States in 1848. That year also marked a mas-

By 1885, the population of Los Angeles was twenty thousand. By the close of the nineteenth century, there was an additional influx of non-Hispanics into California. The need for new houses, roads, and railways created a market for unskilled Mexican laborers.

During the first two decades of the twentieth century, an increase in Los Angeles' Mexican population, as well as the need for cheap land, encouraged eastward movement. The 1910's added to the concentra-

By the mid-1960's, businesses in East Los Angeles reflected the Latino population. (AP/Wide World Photos)

sive influx of settlers, mostly non-Hispanics, after James Marshall discovered gold. More than 100,000 newcomers drastically changed all aspects of this previously minute colonial outpost.

California's population continued to boom in the following decades. The Mexicans' numbers grew, and by the 1860's they made up three-fourths of the entire population. Ten years later BOYLE HEIGHTS was established; its popularity and desirability later was augmented by the arrival of the adjacent Santa Fe Railroad.

tion of Mexicans in East Los Angeles with refugees fleeing from the revolution in Mexico. The population of Los Angeles skyrocketed between 1900 and 1930, from 100,000 to 1,200,000; the population of East Los Angeles was also greatly increased. In the years following, Mexicans moved farther east after the construction of the Civic Center, which dramatically increased housing prices and rents.

By 1941, the Mexican American population in Los Angeles had reached 350,000. As this minority group was growing in numbers, so was the negative media coverage of the Mexican American community. During World War II, the local media, including the *Los Angeles Times*, often stereotyped Mexicans, especially Mexican youth, as drug users and gang members. The SLEEPY LAGOON CASE of 1942 and the zoot-suit riots of 1943 brought about more negative, sensationalized coverage.

Many of the other minority groups in the community of Boyle Heights left to set up communities elsewhere. Among them were Jews, Armenians, and Japanese. By 1950, Boyle Heights and East Los Angeles proper were becoming increasingly Mexican. The 1940's and 1950's also marked an era of nascent political, legal, and social activism among Mexican Americans. The 1947 landmark case of *MÉNDEZ V. WESTMINSTER SCHOOL DISTRICT* demolished de jure educational segregation. In the 1950's, many Mexican Americans migrated to Los Angeles from Texas. During this period, many social service and political organizations were born, including the American G.I. Forum and the Community Service Organization. Many of the Mexican American civil rights groups that flourished in the 1950's and 1960's were overshadowed later by the larger Civil Rights movement, which focused on African Americans.

In East Los Angeles during the late 1960's and early 1970's, continuous Mexican American protest and political activism led to the formation of a Mexican American caucus and La Raza Unida Party. Political activism significantly declined in East Los Angeles in the 1980's. A combination of antiminority sentiments, political disparity, social decay, unemployment, and inflation all contributed to decay and dilapidation in East Los Angeles.

East Los Angeles Community Union, The (TELACU): Community-help organization. TELACU was established in 1968 by Esteban Torres. Formed under the guidance of the United Auto Workers, it became a community development corporation in 1972 and secured federal funding. TELACU's goal is to improve the EAST LOS ANGELES community and bring employment opportunities to the area. The organization has many different departments including housing, community loans, employment, scholarships, senior citizen affairs, immigrant counseling, home loans, and credit. It is one of the largest Latino corporations in the United States. TELACU has been successful in helping Mexican Americans get elected to city government positions.

East Los Angeles riot (1970): In the EAST LOS ANGELES Mexican American community, the year 1970 was marked by tumultuous and eroding relations with local police officials as well as by significant social and political issues that led to various movements and activism. Intolerance of the status quo, coupled with demonstrations and confrontations, resulted in riots, arrests, and deaths.

Late in 1969, an activist group known as CATÓLICOS POR LA RAZA (CPLR) engaged in violent confrontations with Los Angeles police officials. The CPLR demonstrated against the Catholic church, its members angry because the church was funding the construction of a beautiful new church building, St. Basil's, while not relieving the poverty and social injustice inflicted on the Mexican American community, which constituted 60 percent of the church's local support. The result was a violent encounter with law enforcement officials, with protesters arrested and beaten.

The protest continued into 1970. Police struggled for more than two hours to disperse a crowd of about five thousand people on New Year's Day. About one hundred people smashed windows and looted stores. Eleven people were charged with looting and resisting arrest in that incident. A total of twelve CPLR members were convicted of crimes committed during the entire period of disturbance going back into 1969, and five served four-month prison terms.

Violence involving Chicano students erupted at San Fernando Valley State College on May 5. Chicano antiwar demonstrations against supporters of the Cambodia intervention resulted in the fiery destruction of the on-campus Chicano house. The same issue also brought about violently heated confrontations at California College, in Los Angeles.

Another demonstration turned violent on July 4, 1970. This protest took place at the East Los Angeles sheriff's substation, where demonstrators protested the six Chicano deaths at the station within the preceding five months. One protester was shot, and nineteen others were arrested. The protest spread and became so violent that 250 officers were needed to quell it.

The most infamous, as well as the most confrontational, demonstration in East Los Angeles in 1970 was the NATIONAL CHICANO MORATORIUM ON VIETNAM of August 29. The moratorium—supported by numerous Chicano organizations as well as by Congressman Edward R. ROYBAL—was a large antiwar demonstration. More than twenty thousand protesters gathered to listen to speeches, watch folk dances, and have lunch. After several teenagers allegedly stole sandwiches from a nearby liquor store, sheriffs decided to disperse the crowd. Law enforcement officials used tear gas and clubs, and a rebellion ensued that caused more than one million dollars in damage. Police arrested hundreds of demonstrators, and three people died in the violence. Among those killed was Rubén SALAZAR, news director of television station KMEX, who was sitting in a nearby café when a police officer fired a gas canister into the window, hitting Salazar in the head. In the aftermath of the moratorium, Roosevelt High School was bombed as a response to Salazar's murder. Another disturbance, following a parade on September 16, resulted in more than sixty arrests and more than sixty injuries to police officers.

Education and academic achievement: In the United States, education has always been seen as the door to opportunity. Latinos, like other Americans, value education highly, yet for many it has not been the means to achieve the American Dream.

Latino scholars and leaders agree that improving educational attainment is perhaps the primary challenge facing their community. Although Latinos made up 12 percent of the nation's public school population in 1990, they accounted for 29 percent of all high-school dropouts. One-third of all Latinos over the age of twenty-five have less than an elementary school education.

Although there are variations within the Latino population, with Cuban Americans tending to have the most schooling and Mexican Americans the least, all subgroups are less well-educated than the American population at large. Latino students' performance on tests such as the Scholastic Aptitude Test (SAT) and the American College Test (ACT) is consistently below that of non-Hispanic whites and Asian Americans. Only 10 percent of Latinos over twenty-five hold college or graduate degrees, compared to 21 percent of the total American population. Latinos increase their income less than Anglos and African Americans when

There are few Latino teachers to serve as role models. (James Shaffer)

EDUCATIONAL ATTAINMENT OF PERSONS AGED 25 AND OLDER *(percentages of population)*				
Level of Education	Mexican Americans	Puerto Ricans	Cuban Americans	Total U.S. Population
Less than 5 years	16	10	6	2
4 years of high school or more	44	56	64	78
4 years of college or more	5	10	20	21

Source: Data are from U.S. Bureau of the Census, *The Hispanic Population of the United States: March 1990* (Washington, D.C.: Bureau of the Census, 1992).

they earn a college degree. These and other data suggest that education is not working to the full advantage of some Latinos.

Low educational attainment is not surprising given the high proportion of foreign-born, non-English-speaking Latinos and recent waves of immigration. It is, however, cause for alarm, especially in the light of the high growth rate of the Latino population. After a summary of educational statistics on Latinos, this article focuses on three explanations for variations in educational achievement among Mexican Americans, Puerto Ricans, and Cuban Americans: differences in historical immigration patterns, cultural differences, and the failure of schools to adapt to the needs of Latino students.

Educational Opportunity and Attainment. About five million Latinos attended public elementary and secondary schools in 1990. In California, they made up 34 percent of the public school population. School districts such as Los Angeles with large numbers of Latino students are among the few urban districts that grew rather than shrinking or remaining stable after 1970. About 7 percent of Latino children attend private schools, primarily Catholic PAROCHIAL SCHOOLS. Waves of newly arrived, primarily Spanish-speaking immigrant students have put pressures on all schools since the 1960's to accommodate students' needs, but response is often slow, and the education of Latino children suffers.

For example, some students fail to learn either Spanish or English well in BILINGUAL EDUCATION programs. Three-quarters of Latino secondary students are still tracked in nonacademic programs, and about half of Latino juniors and seniors are enrolled below grade level. Only 4 percent of public school teachers are Latinos, thus offering few role models for aspiring students. Latino parents tend to be less involved in their children's schooling than Anglos, either because of their own lack of education or because of their lack of familiarity with the American system.

According to figures from the Bureau of the Census, Latinos are the only American population group whose dropout rate has not improved since the late 1960's. In 1990, about one-third of Latinos between the ages of sixteen and twenty-four had not completed high school, compared to 12 percent of all Americans in that age group. It is important to note, however, that the Latino figures include recent immigrant youth who failed to complete high school in their home countries.

Apart from the high dropout rate, another concern affecting Latino educational opportunity is the increasing educational isolation of Latino schoolchildren. This isolation can occur within schools when children placed in bilingual classes have no contact with other students at the school. It is also common in neighborhoods or school districts with high proportions of Latino and African American students. In 1968, 55 percent of Latino students attended predominantly minority schools. In 1984, the figure was 71 percent, partly because of unprecedented growth in the Latino student population. A 1993 report on the "resegregation" of American schools noted that Latino students in the inner city were particularly vulnerable to the disadvantages of SEGREGATION, such as poor facilities, having been ignored in most desegregation plans since the 1960's.

The Immigration Experience. The circumstances under which Latinos came to be in the United States and the conditions in their homelands are important in determining each subgroup's experience. Some Latino groups came into the United States voluntarily as immigrants, while others became Americans involuntarily when borders were changed.

Although Puerto Ricans can freely enter the U.S. mainland today, they became a part of the United States involuntarily as a result of the Spanish-American War in 1898. They were granted U.S. citizenship (but without representation or voting rights) in 1917. The first heavy flow of Puerto Rican migration to the mainland

ENROLLMENT RATES IN INSTITUTIONS OF HIGHER LEARNING *(persons 18 to 24 years old)*			
Year	Non-Hispanic White	Non-Hispanic Black	Hispanic Origin
1972	27.2%	18.3%	13.4%
1982	28.1%	19.9%	16.8%
1991	36.8%	23.4%	17.8%

Source: Data are from U.S. Bureau of the Census, *Current Population Reports* (Washington, D.C.: Bureau of the Census, May, 1992).

began in the late 1940's with Operation Bootstrap, a failed scheme for industrial development.

Cuba was also acquired as a result of the Spanish-American War. Unlike the Commonwealth of Puerto Rico, it was granted independence in 1902. Most Cubans are in the United States voluntarily, but only because they were pushed from their homeland after 1959 by what they saw as the political and economic threat of Communism.

A large group of Mexican Americans was brought into the United States with their conquered territory as a result of the Mexican American War (1846-1848). Their ancestors, however, had lived on the land since before the Spanish conquest in the 1500's. Despite this ancient heritage, these people are often lumped into an undifferentiated category of "Mexicans" or "Mexican Americans" along with recent immigrants from Mexico. Mexico continues to be the top source of Latin American immigrants to the United States.

Given this variation in the histories of Latino populations, it is not surprising that each subgroup has its own unique experiences with the formal institutions of education. The majority of Mexicans who have immigrated to the United States have been poor and poorly educated. Recent immigrants from rural Mexico and Central America with little or no formal education placed priority on getting a job and aspired for their children to complete high school. By the 1990's, Mexican Americans had become highly urbanized but overrepresented among the poor of the United States.

In contrast, the first refugees from Cuba following the 1959 revolution were businesspeople and professionals who migrated to escape political and economic upheaval. Their most portable forms of wealth were education and skills, although some also brought substantial amounts of financial capital. Their education gave them an advantage in beginning their new lives.

Although Cubans are still the best-educated and most prosperous Latinos, their situation varies with their period of immigration. The first wave of Cuban arrivals were 94 percent white and had an average of fourteen years of education. Subsequent waves were younger, poorer, and contained lower proportions of white persons.

CIRCULAR MIGRATION characterizes the unique relationship between many Puerto Ricans on the island and on the U.S. mainland. By 1970, with the help of inexpensive air travel, one-third of those on the island had immigrated to the mainland to find jobs and to escape economic despair. Some remained, returning to the island only for visits. Others returned to live in Puerto Rico, only to come back to the mainland when there was no work or when savings ran out. Circular migration can have a disruptive effect on young people's education.

Mexican Americans in School. Until at least the first half of the twentieth century, Mexican Americans were viewed by the dominant culture as outsiders, capable only of hard manual work. Educators believed that Mexican and Mexican American children were unequal to Anglo children. The results of culturally biased tests were used to "prove" their case, reinforce their beliefs, and justify school SEGREGATION. Anglos feared that if Mexican Americans became educated, the nation would lose a source of cheap labor for farm and ranch work. At adolescence, if not before, Mexican American children typically were expected to quit school and help contribute to the family income.

In Texas and parts of California before World War II, most Mexican American children attended segregated public elementary schools, and few Mexican Americans were expected to go on to high school. Segregated schools, most often justified by language differences, were developed and maintained by school board regulations, local custom, and segregated housing. Even when Mexican American children did have access to the same schools as Anglos, they were not represented on governing boards or in curriculum decision making. Consequently, education was frequently irrelevant to their needs.

During the 1930's and 1940's, public schools aimed to "Americanize" Mexican American children. School programs incorporated training in vocational and manual arts, English, and health and hygiene, as well as core American values such as cleanliness, thriftiness, and punctuality.

A Changing Environment. The end of World War II led to many social and economic changes in the United States and for Mexican Americans, especially returning veterans. One of the most notable and enduring shifts was Mexican American migration from rural to urban areas, largely because of the job opportunities opening up for all groups in the postwar economy. Their greater visibility in cities and their continuing importance as a source of inexpensive labor led to new concern for the education, language, and literacy needs of Mexican Americans.

In 1946, the First Regional Conference on the Education of Spanish-Speaking People in the Southwest was held in Texas. The conference called for an end to segregated schooling, a relevant curriculum for Mexican Americans, improved teacher preparation, and better school facilities. Such changes have been slow, and some remained unrealized for half a century.

In the 1960's and 1970's, both federal and state governments enacted legislation to support programs for children of limited English-speaking ability and to assist schools with high concentrations of such chil-

dren. These new policies, supported by several court decisions, made at least minimal bilingual education mandatory. Bilingual education and ENGLISH AS A SECOND LANGUAGE (ESL) PROGRAMS, however, have been fraught with controversy and inadequate funding from the start. In the 1990's, there was still little agreement among educators and the public on the content or outcome of such programs.

Cuban Americans and Puerto Ricans in School. Within a year of Fidel Castro's coming to power in 1959, more than forty-seven thousand Cubans moved to Miami to seek exile. The influx of these exiles, most of whom spoke Spanish exclusively, created problems, particularly in the English-language environment of Miami's public schools. The school system moved quickly to implement a bilingual program that became a model for other school districts.

Miami schools had support from several sources, including the federal government. The Dwight D. Ei-

Schools have changed to offer more programs for children with limited skills in use of the English language. (AP/Wide World Photos)

senhower Administration established the Cuban Refugee Emergency Center in Miami to provide health services, training programs for adults, and assistance in the education of Cuban children. From 1961 to 1974, the center provided funds and support services to public schools, some instruction, loans to refugee college students, and English refresher courses for professionals. Among Latino populations, Cubans are unique in having succeeded in building a strong community, or enclave, that sustained their own culture while building a bridge to the larger society.

For Puerto Ricans, there have been even fewer systematic supports than for Cuban Americans or Mexican Americans. A major problem for Puerto Ricans in education has always been a high dropout rate (*see* DROPOUTS AND DROPOUT RATES). This is usually attributed to the language barrier and to students who are educationally delayed. In the 1980's, some predominantly Puerto Rican high schools in New York City had dropout rates as high as 80 percent.

Although the freedom to travel back and forth between Puerto Rico and the U.S. mainland brings economic benefits, it is destructive for those families that are split between the mainland and the island, especially for schoolchildren. Part of the problem is disparities between the Puerto Rican school system and that of the mainland. It was not until the early 1950's that all school-age children in Puerto Rico were enrolled in the first grade. Through the years, there has been controversy over which language to use in Puerto Rican classrooms. The islanders resented English being imposed on them; therefore, Spanish has prevailed in the classroom. This is a disadvantage for children who later enroll in schools on the mainland.

As a result of these disparities and language issues, Puerto Rican children in mainland schools are often labeled "educationally delayed" and set back two or even three grades. Those who are socially mature and streetwise tend to be embarrassed when put in classes with much younger children. This situation results in a high number of dropouts or "push-outs." Meanwhile, Puerto Rican parents who do not speak English and are themselves grappling with a new environment and economic survival find it difficult to advocate for their children with the school. The language barrier has also served as an excuse for the failure of school systems to integrate Puerto Rican schoolchildren with others and with the surrounding community.

In recent decades, some Puerto Rican community leaders have begun to view education as a way out of poverty and inequality. The organization ASPIRA was formed in 1961 to help young Puerto Ricans go to college. ASPIRA, the Puerto Rican Forum, and the Conference on Puerto Rican Education have become the most active organizations in the Puerto Rican community, particularly in New York City. Community leaders have become strong advocates of adding Puerto Rican culture to BILINGUAL EDUCATION, contending that the public schools devalue both the language and the culture of Puerto Rican children.

Cultural Differences. Language and other cultural differences frequently are blamed for causing Latino children to get a slow start in school, fall behind, be mistakenly routed to special education programs, or drop out. Although language is obviously a factor, it alone does not account for low educational achievement. Cubans are more likely than other Latino groups to speak Spanish at home, yet they achieve the highest educational levels.

According to social historian Earl Shorris, Latino children are confronted with cultural barriers at school beginning in first grade. The fault lies not with Latino cultures, in Shorris' view, but with the failure of public schools to meet the needs of Latino schoolchildren. Some schools with predominantly non-Hispanic student populations have been insensitive to Latino students. For example, an Anglo teacher might unintentionally alienate Mexican American students when she teaches the Battle of the Alamo as an unqualified victory. Some evidence suggests that the wall of cultural differences gets thicker and higher for children as they progress in the educational system.

Research by Maria Matute-Bianchi on patterns of school performance found that recently immigrated Mexican young people did better in high school than American-born English-speaking students of Mexican descent. A majority of school dropouts (61 percent) were also found to be born in the United States. These findings were attributed to differences in how students viewed their economic position and opportunities in the United States. The recent immigrants still saw education as an important means of improving their employability and chance for success, whereas the Chicanos tended to be disillusioned about their prospects. Many Latinos believe that with effort, one can achieve anything, but when effort does not work, some students are lost to the school, perhaps even to society. This research is particularly interesting in the light of the common allegation that traditional Mexican values are inconsistent with American educational goals and a prime cause for school failure or dropping out.

Families that support education are instrumental in keeping children in school and ensuring their success. (Marilyn Nolt)

One area of education in which Latino cultural values are often contrasted with those of non-Latinos is parent involvement. Studies consistently have shown that the more parents are involved with their children's schooling through activities such as regular parent-teacher conferences and monitoring of homework, the better the children do in school. The relatively low level of education among Latino parents makes many of them ashamed to interact with teachers or admit their ignorance to their children. Moreover, the widespread veneration of teachers as authority figures in Latin American cultures makes it difficult for some Latino parents to challenge teachers or school administrators, even when they believe their children are being shortchanged. Another aspect of many Latino families is modest expectations for daughters. Many parents are not overly concerned when girls perform poorly in school, especially in science and math, because education in academic subjects is not highly valued for girls.

Higher Education. With inadequate elementary and secondary schooling and a high dropout rate, it is no surprise that Latinos are underrepresented in HIGHER EDUCATION. Latino college enrollment increased only 4 percent during several decades beginning in 1972. There was a 10 percent increase among Anglos and a 5 percent increase among African Americans. Latinos tend to stay in college at the same rate as their more advantaged Anglo counterparts. Institutions in primarily Latino areas are crowded with applicants, bringing the opportunities of a college education to a wider population than ever before. Cuban Americans are a notable success story, with their level of education approaching the national average by the 1990's. Twenty percent of Cuban American youth were completing college, a rate twice that of mainland Puerto Ricans and four times that of Mexican Americans.

There have been some important gains for Latinos in higher education since the late 1960's and the rise of the Chicano movement. College and university AFFIR-

Latino participation in higher education is increasing. (Impact Visuals, Loren Santow)

MATIVE ACTION programs continue actively to recruit Latino students and faculty. A variety of Chicano and Latino student organizations flourish on major college campuses. By the early 1990's, classes in Chicano history or Latino politics had become commonplace at universities, and a dozen colleges offered undergraduate degrees in Chicano, Hispanic, or Latino studies. This has meant a boom in research and publishing on topics of interest to Latinos, including the challenges of education and academic achievement.

Conclusion. It is imperative that the nation's schools find ways to accommodate the needs of Latino children rather than attempting to force learning in an alien environment. The task is formidable but not impossible. There are programs that work.

One predominantly Cuban school in Miami, for example, approaches language learning as a business proposition that gives students a career advantage. All Anglos at Carol Way Elementary School are offered Spanish as a second language, just as Latino students learn English as a second language. Students may continue to study the two languages until they become fluent in both. The school's Cuban American teachers and administrators contend that BILINGUAL EDUCA-

TION is the learning and maintenance of two languages, a skill that is increasingly important in a multicultural society.

Each Latino population has a proud heritage and unique history worth preserving and sharing. The United States is not one people but many people. Schools must meet the challenge of translating the cultural differences of the twentieth century into the cultural strengths of the twenty-first century.

—Joyce E. Williams and Lisa Garza

SUGGESTED READINGS:

• Carrasquillo, Angela L. *Hispanic Children and Youth in the United States.* New York: Garland, 1991. Covers history, culture, and diversity of Latino children with resource material on family life, language, education, health, justice, and other social issues.

• Carter, Thomas P., and Roberto D. Segura. *Mexican Americans in School.* 2d ed. New York: College Entrance Examination Board, 1979. Historical analysis of Mexican Americans and documentation of their experiences in the public schools.

• Feagin, Joe R., and Clairece Booher Feagin. *Racial and Ethnic Relations.* 4th ed. Englewood Cliffs, N.J.: Prentice Hall, 1993. Chapters 9 and 10 trace the history of Latino subgroups and incorporate current research to explain social and economic status.

- Gibson, Margaret, and John Ogbu, eds. *Minority Status and Schooling*. New York: Garland, 1991. Portions deal with the adaptation of immigrant children to American schools.
- MacKey, William F., and Von Nieda Beebe. *Bilingual Schools for a Bicultural Community*. Rowley, Mass.: Newbury House, 1977. Describes the experiences of Cuban immigrants as well as the creation of bilingual education in South Florida.
- Moore, Joan, and Harry Pachon. *Hispanics in the United States*. Englewood Cliffs, N.J.: Prentice Hall, 1985. Historical analysis of the fastest growing minority group in the United States.
- Schaefer, Richard T. *Racial and Ethnic Groups*. 5th ed. New York: Harper Collins College Publishers, 1993. Chapters 9 and 10 offer a historical overview of Hispanic Americans in the United States, including brief discussions of bilingualism, education, poverty, and current trends.
- Shorris, Earl. *Latinos: A Biography of the People*. New York: W. W. Norton, 1992. A descriptive social history of different Latino groups, supplemented with life stories of individuals and families.
- U.S. Bureau of the Census. *The Hispanic Population of the United States: March 1990*. Washington, D.C.: Government Printing Office, 1992. Provides statistics on population characteristics, including educational attainment.

El Monte Berry Strike (1933): Labor disruption. The strike movements of 1928, 1930, and 1934 in the Imperial Valley, as well as the 1933 El Monte Berry Strike, were instances of major organizational resistance. In 1933, no fewer than thirty-seven strikes were carried out in California, including the El Monte strike. All the strikes had the goal of obtaining decent wages.

In the 1930's, El Monte, a small community in the San Gabriel Valley, had an approximate population of sixteen thousand, of which nearly 20 percent was Mexican. Much of El Monte's economic survival was dependent on agriculture. Between six hundred and seven hundred acres of berries (raspberries, youngberries, and blackberries) provided manual laborers with employment at subsistence wages. Wages varied from twenty to forty cents per crate, or nine to twenty cents per hour.

Those who controlled, managed, and hired labor for agriculture were Japanese growers who were members of the Central Japanese Association of Southern California. The farm owners, however, were European Americans. In May, 1933, a mixed group of laborers, non-Hispanic whites, Mexicans, and Japanese sought higher wages by approaching S. Fukami, the secretary of the Central Japanese Association of Southern California. Having failed to achieve positive results, the laborers' group called meetings in Hick's Camp, a Mexican "shacktown" populated by more than one thousand migrant laborers, to organize a strike.

On June 1, five hundred to six hundred workers voted to strike; that day, some fifteen hundred laborers began to picket. On June 2, a multiethnic strike committee was formed. It marshaled support from Hick's Camp, Chino, El Monte, Medina Court, and La Puente. Organizers from the Cannery and Agricultural Workers Industrial Union (CAWIU) backed and controlled the strike. Armando Flores, one of the founders of the CONFEDERACION DE UNIONES DE CAMPESINOS Y OBREROS MEXICANOS (CUCOM), was named as head of the strike committee. Literature printed in Spanish, Japanese, and English was circulated.

On June 4, the growers' representatives met with the strike committee. Swift action on the growers' part was vital, because berries must be picked within two to three days after ripening. The meeting was to no avail, because the growers' offer of fifteen cents an hour or forty cents a crate was drastically lower than the twenty cents an hour or forty-five cents a crate demanded.

On June 7, more than three hundred strikebreakers were brought into the fields. They were encouraged by strikers to join the picket line. The same day, the strikers lost both unity and internal direction when the settlement committee was detained by sheriffs for several hours.

Eight of the CAWIU organizers were arrested and jailed on June 10. By the end of the second week, the strike had spread to Culver City and Santa Monica, where more than five thousand workers participated in a walkout. At the same time, Flores appealed to President Franklin D. Roosevelt to intervene under the Industrial Recovery Act. Flores also appealed to the Mexican government and to former president of Mexico General Plutarco Elias Calles. In the third week of the strike, contributions from Mexico totaled three thousand to four thousand dollars. Calles himself sent $750.

By the fourth week of the strike, three offers advanced by the growers had been declined because they did not meet the laborers' needs. The lack of labor led the growers to offer berries to the public at one cent per box, provided that the buyers did the picking.

On July 6, representatives from the strike committee, the growers, and the State Division of Labor Statistics and Law Enforcement, along with the consuls of Mexico and Japan, reached a settlement that promised a wage of $1.50 for a nine-hour day, or twenty cents per hour when only temporary work was available.

By the time the final agreement was reached, the berry-picking season was all but over. Growers estimated that within two weeks they could no longer employ fifteen hundred members of their former labor force. Approximately half of those unemployed laborers were U.S. citizens, and the others were Mexican nationals. The State Division of Labor Statistics and Law Enforcement determined that unemployment compensation should be sought for the citizens and that the Mexican nationals should be repatriated. Such a division along national lines anticipated later strife among Mexican laborers as well as the formation of unions and other labor organizations according to citizenship status.

El Paso, Texas, and Ciudad Juárez, Mexico: Sister cities and the major point of entry for Mexicans after Tijuana.

Location and Population. El Paso, Texas, is located at the angled corner of Mexico, New Mexico, and Texas. It is the fourth largest city in Texas and the twenty-third largest city in the nation. The southernmost portion of the Rocky Mountains, known in El Paso as the Franklin Mountains, slices El Paso into Eastside, Westside, and Central areas, with Ciudad Juárez, Mexico, directly south across the Rio Grande.

Ciudad Juárez is located in the semidesert in the northern part of the Mexican state of Chihuahua and is Mexico's fifth largest city. The 1990 census showed a population of 591,000 for El Paso; the 1993 population for Ciudad Juárez was 1.1 million.

History. The history of El Paso began in 1581. At that time, Spaniards came through the area to test the missionary and mining possibilities of New Mexico. For centuries, this area had been inhabited by various American Indian groups. In 1598, Juan de OÑATE and his expedition brought European civilization and Spanish rule to El Paso. Oñate called the El Paso area "El Paso del Río del Norte," which means "the crossing of the river to the north."

In 1849, after the Mexican American War, white settlers moved into the area. In 1873, El Paso became an official city.

Ciudad Juárez, Chihuahua, Mexico, was founded in 1659 as Paso Del Norte. In 1888, Mexican president Porfirio Díaz changed its name to Ciudad Juárez in

honor of former President Benito Juárez who, in 1865, took refuge in the city during the French occupation of Mexico.

The TREATY OF GUADALUPE HIDALGO of 1848 set the boundary between the United States and Mexico. This boundary was fixed at the Rio Grande as far north as the thirty-second parallel. The Compromise of 1850 placed El Paso in Texas instead of in New Mexico.

Impact as Border Cities. The central border location of El Paso and Ciudad Juárez has made this area a major point for fast, convenient access to all main markets in the United States. Ciudad Juárez and El Paso have been important border crossings, with many people having experience in binational trade. The MAQUILADORA industry also has contributed to this area's industrial development.

Maquiladoras, or "twin plants" as they are often called, are an example of cooperation to create opportunities for economic growth from which both the United States and Mexico can benefit. These "twin plant" industries paired manufacturing facilities on both sides of the El Paso-Juárez border. Components and parts were manufactured and prepared in the United States and shipped for assembly to Mexico, which had lower labor costs. *Maquiladoras* tended to hire young women and had a high turnover rate, often between 180 and 240 percent per year. The El Paso-Juárez area, in 1990, had the second largest number of *maquiladora* operations, with 293. Tijuana and Baja California had more than 550 such facilities.

Another economic aspect of these border cities is the daily crossing of Mexican workers. Although many borderland residents cross because they have family ties on both sides of the border, many others cross for employment purposes. The benefits and costs of this movement across the border have been debated. In 1990, an estimated 100,000 Mexicans crossed the El Paso-Juárez border on a daily basis, and many thousands more crossed without documents. Many worked as domestic servants in El Paso homes and did not file reports of their wages. One person's pay in El Paso could support a large family in Juárez.

Being sister cities forced El Paso and Ciudad Juárez to share environmental problems. Mexico's environmental standards and enforcement priorities have been lower than in the United States, resulting in problems of atmospheric and groundwater pollution (*see* ENVIRONMENTAL ISSUES). In 1990, several new sources of air pollution along the El Paso-Juárez border were identified: vehicle emissions, in part a result of long delays at border crossings with engines left running;

LATINO POPULATION OF EL PASO, TEXAS, 1990

Total number of Latinos = 411,619; 70% of population

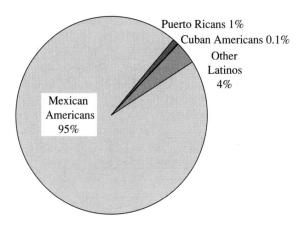

Puerto Ricans 1%
Cuban Americans 0.1%
Other
Latinos
4%

Mexican
Americans
95%

Source: Data are from Marlita A. Reddy, ed., *Statistical Record of Hispanic Americans* (Detroit: Gale Research, 1993), Table 110.

Note: Figures represent the population of the Metropolitan Statistical Area as delineated by the U.S. Bureau of the Census. Percentages are rounded to the nearest whole number except for Cuban Americans, for whom rounding is to the nearest 0.1%.

open burning at dumps; the burning of trash and discarded materials in stoves to warm homes; and industrial smokestack emissions.

El Paso and Ciudad Juárez have shared more than environmental problems. Both cities are reciprocal exporters and importers of various communicable diseases. In 1990, the Texas Department of Health reported that acquired immune deficiency syndrome (AIDS) and other sexually transmitted diseases were exported from the United States to Mexico and that tuberculosis was imported from Mexico. According to the Texas Department of Health, the movement of people back and forth across the border facilitated transmission of diseases. Mexico's immunization programs were not up to U.S. standards. Prenatal care was also a problem in the El Paso-Juárez border area, among both United States residents and nonresident aliens. In 1990, the Texas Department of Health reported that many pregnant Mexican women came to El Paso to deliver American-citizen babies. On the other hand, it was reported that many of El Paso's residents went to Mexico for less expensive medical care.

El Paso and Ciudad Juárez have shared both problems and benefits. As a major border crossing near the end of the twentieth century, El Paso and Ciudad Juárez have intensified the area's bilingual, binational, and bicultural character. —*Maria Isabel Villaseñor*

SUGGESTED READINGS: • Kramer, Mark. "U.S.-Mexican Border: Life on the Line." *National Geographic* 167 (June, 1985): 720-749. • Salinas, Exiquio, Michelle Bensenberg, and Jan Amazeen. *The Colonias Factbook.* Austin: Texas Department of Human Services, 1988. • Texas Department of Health. *Report of the Office of Texas-Mexico Health and Environmental Issues and Interagency Advisory Council.* Austin: Author, 1990. • Tisdale, Penny. *Partnership for Self-Sufficiency: Public/Private Initiatives.* Austin: Texas Department of Human Services, 1989.

El Paso incident (1948): Dispute concerning immigration. As the season for harvesting cotton approached in 1948, Texas growers announced a pay rate for Mexican workers of $2.00 to $2.50 per hundred pounds. The Mexican government insisted on a rate of $3.00. Neither side budged from its position.

In October, growers told local immigration authorities that the crop would rot in the fields unless Mexican workers were hired. American immigration authorities opened the border at El Paso on October 13. During the following five days, more than six thousand undocumented workers crossed into the United States, despite efforts of the Mexican government to stop them. The workers were placed under technical arrest by American officials and were turned over to the United States Employment Service. Texas cotton growers were able to use these workers.

The border closed again on October 18. The Mexican government protested that the action violated an agreement on workers reached by the U.S. and Mexican governments in February, 1948. The American Federation of Labor, the Congress of Industrial Organizations, and the League of United Latin American Citizens also lodged protests. Mexico nullified the February agreement. The U.S. government later expressed regrets to the Mexican government concerning the incident. Cotton, however, had been picked at the growers' rates, and once the crop was in, the undocumented workers returned to Mexico.

El Paso Interreligious Sponsoring Organizations (EPISO): Interdenominational activist group. Of the twenty-eight member congregations in 1994, the majority were Catholic but some were Protestant. Uniting these congregations are traditional Hispanic family values, particularly the central role the home plays in the Hispanic community.

The organization acts as a coalition for political involvement, using the religious affiliation of its members as the main philosophical foundation. The organization is involved in voter registration and lobbying on issues pertaining to infrastructural development in the barrios. This lobbying is carried out at both the local and the state levels.

EPISO projects include bringing potable water to the barrios beyond the suburbs of El Paso, Texas; establishment of low-cost health care in the Hispanic barrios surrounding El Paso; construction of aqueducts and drainage; and general community development. EPISO is also concerned with environmental protection.

EPISO uses a simple method in its work. It targets a particular community, then sends group members house to house, visiting people and gaining vital information about voter registration and family interest in getting involved in community affairs. A local chapter is then organized to oversee the local agenda, with support from the central offices.

Elderly. *See* **Older Latinos**

Elephant Butte Dam: Completed in 1919. The Elephant Butte Dam is located on the Rio Grande in the Mesilla Valley of New Mexico. It is on the southern end of the Elephant Butte Reservoir in Sierra County and north of Truth or Consequences, New Mexico.

The Mesilla Valley area was part of the New Mexico and California territory formally annexed by the United States in 1848 under the TREATY OF GUADALUPE HIDALGO. Agriculture in New Mexico had begun to decline. Colorado farmers drained the Rio Grande for their use between 1850 and 1880. This lowered the water supply in New Mexico and further deteriorated the quality of farming in northern New Mexico.

A rapid increase in livestock farming in the 1870's and 1880's resulted in overgrazing. As this happened, water rights became increasingly important among farmers. The southern reaches of New Mexico had always been dry but had good farmland.

The federal government made efforts to improve agriculture in the Mesilla Valley between 1910 and 1920. These reclamation projects involved leveling and cleaning the land and installing irrigation systems from the Rio Grande to the surrounding farms. The Elephant Butte Dam was constructed north of Las Cruces. Irrigation systems there carried water directly from the reservoir to farms.

The approval of the Mexican government was needed for this project because the Rio Grande formed the border between Mexico and Texas. Felix Martinez, Jr., who was born in Penasco, near Taos, owned *The El Paso Daily News* and played an important part in obtaining permission from the Mexican government for this project. He was later appointed to be the U.S. commissioner general to South America.

The Mesilla Valley became a leading producer of alfalfa, chiles, cotton, and pecans. The irrigation project included approximately eighty-five thousand acres of farmland in the 1990's. Cotton historically has been the largest crop. Celebrities Ted Turner and Jane Fonda owned a large ranch in the area where they raised buffalo commercially.

The Elephant Butte project enabled tremendous growth in agriculture in the area by preventing water runoff to the Gulf and by forming the reservoir. The reservoir and surrounding Elephant Butte State Park were also used for recreation. On the negative side, the increased mechanization brought by the huge farms drove many small farmers out of business. At the same time, there was a huge influx of Mexican laborers who were fleeing the effects of revolution in their own country. With abundant labor available, the average small farmer had trouble competing, even if machines were available. The economies of operating a large farm made small farms impractical. The dam also had the effect of raising the water level of the Rio Grande in the Middle Valley, north of the dam. This caused flooding of some towns and made some farmland marshy.

Elizondo, Hector (b. Dec. 22, 1936, New York, N.Y.): Actor. Son of a Puerto Rican mother and a Basque father, Elizondo studied at the Ballet Arts Company at Carnegie Hall and the Actors Studio in New York. In the 1960's, he starred as a Puerto Rican janitor in the off-Broadway hit *Steambath*, for which he received an Obie Award. His other stage credits include *Drums in the Night*, *Prisoner of Second Avenue*, *The Dance of Death*, *The Great White Hope*, and *The Price*. In 1971, Elizondo made his film debut in *Valdez Is Coming*. He went on to make numerous appearances in Hollywood productions. In 1990, he was nominated for a Golden Globe Award for his supporting role in *Pretty Woman*.

Elizondo, Sergio D. (Sergio Danilo Elizondo Domínguez; b. Apr. 29, 1930, El Fuerte, Mexico): Writer and scholar. Elizondo entered the United States illegally in 1950 and became a citizen three years later. Despite a few interruptions of his college education, Elizondo managed to secure advanced degrees in the field of Romance languages and work as a professor of Span-

Hector Elizondo. (AP/Wide World Photos)

ish for most of his professional life. Elizondo's interests range from Spanish and Mexican American literature to sociology to creative writing. He has published poetry, short stories, and novels.

Elizondo is considered to be one of the strongest proponents of Chicano CULTURAL NATIONALISM. His first volume of poetry, *Perros y antiperros: Una épica chicana* (1972; dogs and antidogs: a Chicano epic), is a stinging indictment of European American oppression of Mexican Americans. His later works are less militant but strongly extol Chicano culture and ideology. Elizondo finds more satisfaction writing in Spanish than in English, and he actively promotes other Spanish-language writers of the United States through his literary scholarship.

Elizondo's other works include a book of poems, *Libro para batos y chavalas chicanas* (1977; a book for Chicano guys and girls); the short-story collection *Rosa, la flauta* (1980; Rose, the flute); and the novels *Muerte en una estrella* (1984; death on a star) and *Suruma* (1990).

Emigrant Agency Law (1929): A Texas state law designed to discourage recruiters from other states from luring farm laborers away from their jobs in Texas. Mexican and Mexican American laborers in Texas were being recruited to work for sugar beet companies in neighboring states during the 1920's. Under the provisions of this law, employment agencies were required to pay a license fee and an occupational tax, post a bond, and obtain an employment license before they could recruit such laborers. A county tax also was assessed against recruiters. None of these measures was completely effective in staving off the drain of Latino workers from Texas.

Empanadas: Filled turnovers made with wheat, plantain, or starchy-root dough. *Empanadas* originated in Spain, where their dough is made from wheat flour and is filled with a savory or sweet filling. In Spain, they often are baked in a dish as a pie. In Mexico, *empanadas* usually are made of wheat dough that is cut into circles, filled with either savory or sweet filling, and folded over. In northern Mexico, sweet *empanadas* sometimes are called *coyotas*. In the Caribbean and Central America, *empanadas* may have either a wheat dough or a dough made from cooked, mashed plantains or starchy root vegetables such as MANIOC. Most *empanadas* in Latin America are baked on a sheet, but some in Central America are griddle-fried. *Empanadas* are eaten primarily as snacks.

Empresario land grants: In 1825, the Mexican government offered large tracts of land to entrepreneurs who settled colonists in Texas. This offer led to increased United States migration there and conflict with Mexicans that culminated in Texas' independence from Mexico.

In the early nineteenth century, Spanish officials saw the westward-expanding United States as both a threat to northern New Spain (Mexico) and a potential source of colonists to develop the ill-defined region of Texas. In February, 1819, the ADAMS-ONÍS TREATY established the border between Texas and the Louisiana Territory. By removing confusion as to which lands belonged to each nation, the accord enabled settlers and land speculators to approach the appropriate government and request land grants. In 1821, Moses Austin, an American speculator, trader, and mine operator in Missouri, secured a large grant from Spain to settle three hundred non-Hispanic families in Texas. Spain hoped to develop Texas economically with immigrants who would become loyal subjects, thereby blocking attempts by the United States to seize Texas.

When Austin died, his son Stephen used the grant to establish a colony in 1822 on the Gulf of Mexico near the lower Brazos River. At about that time, Mexico asserted its independence from Spain, thereby raising questions as to the legal position of the colony. Austin went to Mexico City, where he managed to secure reconfirmation of the original grant. Under the new federal constitution of 1824, the Mexican legislature enacted a colonization law on August 18, 1824. It permitted immigrants to settle on unoccupied lands more than twenty leagues from a foreign border and ten leagues from the coast. The law of 1824 further stipulated that individual Mexican states should adopt appropriate provisions to regulate colonization.

On March 24, 1825, the state of Coahuila-Texas enacted a policy that became known as the *empresario* system. The *empresario* (entrepreneur or speculator) became a government agent with authority to establish a colony and settle it with a stipulated number of immigrants within six years. In compensation for paying the expenses of the settlers, the *empresario* received five leagues of land (a little more than twenty-two thousand acres) for each one hundred families who settled there. The settlers also received land of their own. Individual families might immigrate and petition for lands, but most found it easier to rely on an *empresario*.

Settlers were subject to Mexican law, which outlawed slavery and required that all colonists be Catho-

Harry McArdle's painting Settlement of Austin's Colony *(1885).* (Institute of Texan Cultures)

lics. Coahuila-Texas made little attempt to enforce either of these restrictions, however, and as news of Austin's success spread, other speculators stepped forward. Between 1824 and 1834, the government authorized thirty-one *empresario* contracts for Texas. Roughly half failed to settle any colonists, but largely as a result of the *empresarios'* efforts, the population of Texas grew from 3,334 in 1821 to more than 25,000 in 1830. By then, U.S. settlers accounted for two-thirds of the population, with Mexicans a declining minority. Most immigrants were proslavery, Protestant Southerners.

The *empresario* grants failed to protect Mexican interests, but they populated Texas and led to its development. Friction developed between Mexicans and the unassimilated American colonists, leading the latter to declare Texas independent on March 2, 1836. Victory in the ensuing war gave the American colonists control of Texas, to the detriment of its Mexican citizens.

Enchilada: Mexican casserole dish of filled tortillas. Enchiladas are made throughout Mexico and have great variety in their fillings. Enchiladas are corn tortillas dipped in a chile sauce, then fried very briefly. Each TORTILLA is rolled around a filling and placed in a casserole. The enchiladas then are topped with sauce or cheese and briefly broiled. Fillings can include meat, cheese, BEANS, vegetables, and eggs. In parts of Central America, especially Costa Rica, an enchilada is a flaky pastry with savory filling.

Encomienda system: Grants to Spanish settlers. This system, established during the early colonial period of Spanish America, assigned a certain number of Indians to a Spanish settler. The Indians owed the Spaniard labor or payment in products or money; the Spaniard was obligated to civilize and Christianize these Indians.

Background. When the Spanish arrived in the New World in 1492, they brought with them practices and values developed over centuries. Having retaken their homeland from Muslim invaders, they were accustomed to placing conquered people under obligation in a form of feudalism whereby the conquered people owed the victorious rulers such things as taxes and labor service.

Establishment in the Caribbean. When the Spaniards entered the New World, first in the Caribbean islands, Christopher Columbus rewarded his companions by assigning favored Spaniards a certain number of Indians. These Indians were not slaves but were obligated to provide labor services to the Spaniards. To protect the Indians from abuse and ensure a regular labor supply, the Spanish Crown reluctantly agreed to the creation of this system, called *encomienda*. The Crown's hesitancy sprang from the teachings of such men as Bartolomé DE LAS CASAS, who warned that God would hold the king responsible for the care of a conquered people, as well as from an unwillingness to create feudal lords in the New World.

The physically fragile Caribbean Indians died rapidly under European dominance, despite protective legislation. The amount and kind of work required took its toll, as did diseases introduced by the Europeans. Because the indigenous people had not developed immunity, the diseases caused virtual extinction. The *encomienda*, intended to adjust the Spaniards and Indians to their mutual relationship based on Spanish domination, never developed fully in the Caribbean islands.

Establishment on the Mainland. When Hernán CORTÉS led the Spaniards into Mexico in 1519, he faced the challenges created by Spaniards and Indians occupying the same territory. The Indians of central Mexico, however, were involved in settled agriculture and cottage industry. They were accustomed to delivering regular payments and work to their overlords. Cortés viewed the *encomienda* as the best means of rewarding his companions. The Spanish rulers, although reluctant, were persuaded to endorse the *encomienda*'s necessity. The *encomienda* took root in Mexico, then later in Peru and various outlying areas.

The fully developed *encomienda* was designed to accommodate Spaniards and Indians to joint habitation. The Indians, considered to be subdued subjects of the Crown, owed loyalty and taxes (tribute) to the monarch or to the men of Cortés, who had taken substantial risks and made tremendous sacrifices to establish Spanish rule. Because of the geographical remoteness of the Spanish king, the desire to reward victorious Spaniards, and the perception that Indians were barbarians who must be civilized and supervised, Cortés assigned the favored Spaniards a certain number of Indians as an *encomienda*. The award did not include a land grant. The Indians remained on their own land but were required to pay the Spaniard (called an *encomendero*) a certain amount of goods (for example, cotton, wood, cacao, or corn) or a set amount of labor. Because the Spaniards believed God had given Spain the New World and required certain things in return, the *encomendero* was required to teach the Indians how to live as "civilized" people and bring in a cleric to Christianize them.

Hernán Cortés used the encomienda *as a means of rewarding those who assisted in his conquest.* (Institute of Texan Cultures)

Development and Decline. The *encomienda* seemed, to the Spaniards, to be a realistic arrangement. The Indians of central Mexico, accustomed to paying tribute to the Aztecs, did not find the system unusual. Indians who had been required to supply the Aztecs with human sacrifices might gladly have provided labor or products instead. Spaniards used Indian labor in private enterprises or exchanged products for cash. With such a stake in the colony, the *encomenderos* served as militiamen, guarding against possible Indian uprisings.

Abuses abounded, but in consideration of the dismal experiences in the Caribbean, the Spaniards accepted more readily the Crown's attempts to protect the *encomienda* Indians. Although initially opposing laws limiting how an *encomienda* could be passed on as an inheritance, the *encomenderos* gradually bowed to these, as well as to decrees that tribute could no longer be in the form of labor and that Indians could not be used as carriers. Eventually, courts were established to hear Indian suits against *encomenderos*.

The *encomienda* prospered particularly in central Mexico and in Peru, the regions of densest Indian population. In sparsely populated areas with semi-sedentary Indians, the *encomienda* never became a major feature of the Spanish colonial world. Although it reached briefly into New Mexico with the early Spanish settlements around Santa Fe, its effectiveness was restricted and short-lived.

Even in central Mexico, the *encomienda* thrived as a vital institution for scarcely fifty years. Only about five hundred Spaniards received *encomiendas* there; a large majority of Spaniards were not *encomenderos* but wanted access to Indian labor. They successfully opposed the spread and survival of the system. They were joined by some clerics and others who opposed the system on humanitarian grounds. The Spanish Crown still distrusted the *encomienda*. In addition, in the late sixteenth century, terrible plagues of epidemic diseases such as smallpox swept across Mexico and Peru. With no natural immunities, Indians died in droves, and many *encomiendas* vanished as a result of this tragic natural process. Before 1600, the *encomienda* had ceased to be an important economic, social, or political system.

Conclusion. The *encomienda* illustrates the difficulties of two different cultures attempting to occupy the same land when one is a conqueror. Because the Spaniards never questioned their own culture's superiority, they did not involve the Indians in the negotiations that led to the *encomienda*'s establishment. Although many Spaniards struggled to restrict or prohibit the *enco-mienda*, this struggle took place entirely on Spanish terms.

The *encomienda*, by thrusting Spanish and Indian cultures into intimate association, became one part of the process by which Indians and Spaniards merged to form the base of the Latino civilization. In this process, vital elements of the Indian and Spanish people joined to form a new and different culture, one made stronger by having drawn the best from the two separate worlds. —*John Robinson*

SUGGESTED READINGS: • Burkholder, Mark A., and Lyman L. Johnson. *Colonial Latin America.* New York: Oxford University Press, 1994. • Gibson, Charles. *The Aztecs Under Spanish Rule.* Stanford, Calif.: Stanford University Press, 1964. • Hanke, Lewis. *The Spanish Struggle for Justice in the Conquest of America.* Philadelphia: University of Pennsylvania Press, 1949. • Simpson, Lesley Byrd. *The Encomienda in New Spain.* Rev. ed. Berkeley: University of California Press, 1982. • Villamarin, Juan A., and Judith E. Villamarin. *Indian Labor in Mainland Colonial Spanish America.* Newark: University of Delaware Press, 1975.

Enganchista: Labor contractor. Synonyms include *enganchador*, CONTRATISTA, and COYOTE. The term comes from the Spanish word *enganchar*, meaning to hook, enlist, or attract a person. Labor contractors, usually Mexican or Mexican American, operated on both sides of the U.S.-Mexico border arranging to provide workers for U.S. farms, railroads, and other enterprises. The term ENGANCHISTA refers in particular to recruiters of farm labor. The labor contractor often provided workers to a grower for a flat fee or acted as supervisor in the harvest. In this latter case, the *enganchista* and the grower agreed upon a task rate or wage rate that the *enganchados* (contracted workers) were to be paid. The contractor then received a percentage of the total wages or simply paid workers a lower rate than the one agreed upon so as to earn a profit.

English as a Second Language (ESL) programs: Classes that teach English to children or adults who speak another language. As the largest language minority in the United States, Spanish speakers have been the primary users of ESL programs. The development of ESL and BILINGUAL EDUCATION programs since the 1970's has helped improve the socioeconomic status of Latinos.

History. Native Americans were probably the first people to be taught English as a second language in the United States, centuries before any formal programs

Students might use word processing and educational software to increase proficiency in English. (Impact Visuals, Mark Ludak)

were in place. Their teachers were missionaries and colonists who believed that acquisition of English would have a civilizing influence on the natives. Non-English-speaking European immigrants faced various problems in colonial America and the early republic but were generally allowed to teach their children in other languages without state interference. Notable exceptions to this tolerance in the nineteenth century were government schools, in which Indian and Mexican American children were punished if they did not speak English. The spread of compulsory education and the dramatic increase in immigration in the late nineteenth and early twentieth century led to greater stress on schools as an agent of assimilation and Americanization.

Teaching ESL as a field of study in the United States dates to World War II, when linguists developed the so-called "Army method." This later became known as the audiolingual approach, the aural-oral method, the mim-mem method, and sometimes the ESL method. This approach became popular during the 1950's and 1960's, when the United States became preoccupied with upgrading education to compete with the Soviet Union. The Civil Rights and Chicano movements, meanwhile, were raising public awareness of the needs of language minorities.

Two important government decisions in the 1960's and 1970's set ESL programs in motion throughout the United States. The BILINGUAL EDUCATION ACT of 1968, an amendment to the Elementary and Secondary Education Act of 1965, provided the first federal funds for bilingual education. The landmark Supreme Court case *LAU V. NICHOLS* (1974) had an even greater impact on bilingual education. A Chinese parent took the San Francisco school board to court, claiming that the district's lack of a program to meet the linguistic needs of non-English-speaking children violated Title VII of the CIVIL RIGHTS ACT OF 1964 and the equal protection clause of the FOURTEENTH AMENDMENT to the Constitution. The Court ruled unanimously in favor of Lau, and Lau Centers around the country, serving under the Department of Education, became responsible for developing appropriate programs to implement the decision. The "Lau remedies" state that an ESL component is an integral part of a bilingual education program. These developments, combined with federal

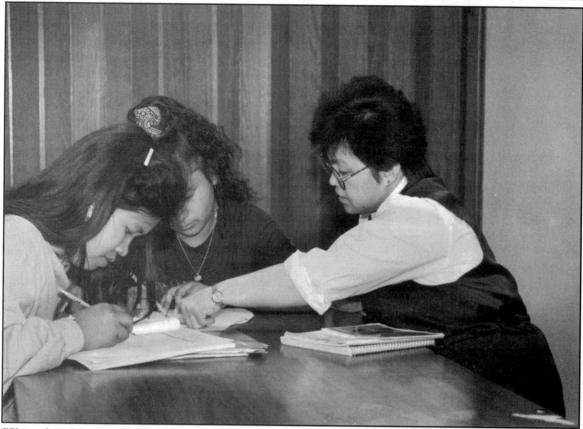

ESL teachers in some programs take students aside for small-group instruction; the students need not have the same primary language. (James Shaffer)

funding and increased immigration, caused ESL programs to mushroom in the 1970's and 1980's.

ESL and Bilingual Education. By definition, TESOL (teaching English to speakers of other languages) involves bilingual education. Scholars observe that all bilingual education programs need an English-teaching component, and ESL programs that ignore the students' native language are doomed to failure. Maintaining the mother tongue has never been discouraged by specialists in the field of English as a second language.

BILINGUAL EDUCATION programs in the United States take various forms. Some use bilingual teachers who divide the day between the teaching of the native language and general subjects in the native language, and the teaching of English. Other programs hire a native English teacher with an aide who is a native speaker of the children's first language. Canadian bilingual programs separate the languages by teacher, using a native speaker of English and a native speaker of French. (Few Canadian ESL programs directly address the needs of speakers of Spanish.) Finally, some programs keep a monolingual English teacher but have

visits from an ESL-trained teacher, who works individually with limited English-proficient (LEP) students in "pull-out" classes.

Methodology. The audiolingual method of teaching ESL was the first approach developed by American linguists after World War II. Although it was used for many years, this method was often discredited in the late twentieth century in favor of other approaches. Methods that became popular in the United States include community counseling-learning, notional-functional syllabus, rapid acquisition, the silent way, suggestopedia, total physical response, and English immersion.

In community counseling-learning or community language learning, students sit in a circle and learn by means of audiotapes. The teacher serves only as a counselor or resource person. The notional-functional syllabus was developed in Europe and emphasizes communicative competence. Rapid acquisition stresses a natural sequence in language learning, with students mastering listening comprehension before being allowed to speak. The silent way emphasizes that the responsibility of learning lies within the student. The teacher uses a color-coded wall chart for pronunciation and speaks each new word only once. Suggestopedia is an oral listening and speaking approach with an emphasis on vocabulary acquisition. Total physical response also stresses listening comprehension and is reinforced by physical action; students listen to commands and then carry them out. In English immersion, limited English students are taught completely in English but are separated from other students who are fluent in English. As each of these methods has its advantages and disadvantages, teachers or school systems must decide which method is appropriate for their students.

Program Availability and Usage. Adult ESL classes attract tens of thousands of Latinos who wish to improve their job prospects, immigration status, and communication skills. Because immigration law requires that English proficiency be demonstrated by all applicants for legal permanent residency, immigrants seek English classes. In 1986, forty thousand people were turned away from ESL classes offered by the Los Angeles Unified School District. In New York, thousands are on waiting lists.

In addition, ESL components are found within most public school bilingual programs at the elementary and secondary levels. Although many of these ESL programs are found within large cities, smaller programs such as ESL for Native Americans function throughout the country. Total Department of Health, Education, and Welfare expenditures on bilingual education and/or ESL projects for fiscal year 1980 amounted to nearly $150 million.

ESL programs benefit a variety of linguistic and cultural minorities. Latinos, however, make greater use of ESL programs than any other minority group. Studies suggest that Latinos are acquiring English at the same rate or faster than members of other immigrant groups. Calvin Veltman has found that among Spanish speakers, the shift to English dominance may take only two generations, rather than the three generations shown by other immigrant groups in the past. Veltman also found that seven out of ten children of Hispanic immigrants in 1988 were English speakers, and bilingual education had had no measurable impact on slowing the rate of English acquisition.

As the public debate on BILINGUALISM continued in the 1990's, the funding and nature of ESL programs remained controversial. Such programs, however, have allowed many Latino and other immigrants to improve their socioeconomic position in American society. —*José Carmona*

SUGGESTED READINGS: • Alatis, James E. "Linguistics and TESOL: A History of the ESL Profession in the U.S." In *The Adult Basic Education TESOL Handbook*, edited by D. E. Bartley. New York: Collier Macmillan International, 1979. • Cartagena, Juan. "English Only in the 1980's: A Product of Myths, Phobias, and Bias." In *ESL in America: Myths and Possibilities*, edited by Sarah Benesch. Portsmouth, N.H.: Boynton/Cook, 1991. • Lambert, W. "Psychological Approaches to the Study of Language." In *Teaching English as a Second Language: A Book of Readings*, edited by Harold B. Allen. New York: McGraw-Hill, 1965. • Paulston, Christina Bratt. *English as a Second Language*. Washington, D.C.: National Education Association, 1980. • Robinett, B. W. *Teaching English to Speakers of Other Languages: Substance and Technique*. Minneapolis: University of Minnesota Press, 1978.

English language acquisition: Latino subgroups have differed in their success in acquiring ENGLISH AS A SECOND LANGUAGE (ESL). Many personal and social factors affect second-language acquisition. Current teaching trends include authentic communication and a positive recognition of the cultures of all learners. Citizenship requirements involve a basic knowledge of English for most applicants.

Motivation for Acquisition of English. According to the 1990 U.S. census, 90 percent of the total population of the United States spoke English at home. Latinos constituted the largest minority group in the country, and Spanish was the second most important language in the United States. The majority of Spanish speakers surveyed reported no difficulty in speaking English.

As a general rule, first-generation immigrants continue to speak Spanish and learn some English. Second and third generations usually learn English as a first language and may or may not learn to speak Spanish fluently. In general, those eighteen years of age and older are more likely to use Spanish than are children. Proportionally, more Latino adults speak Spanish at home and are not able to speak English well or at all.

Puerto Ricans and Mexican Americans have often experienced high rates of school failure and less proficiency in use of English than have members of other Latino groups. A long history as politically, economically, and linguistically marginalized minorities in the United States is thought to contribute to this relative lack of proficiency, although other cultural and individual factors may be involved.

Some Latinos live in Spanish-speaking enclaves where acquisition of English is not necessary. (Martin Hutner)

Cuban Americans, excluding those who arrived in the United States during the 1980 MARIEL BOAT LIFT, became known for their industriousness and determination. As a group, they have achieved higher levels of English acquisition and economic success than other Latino subgroups.

Central American immigrants have tended to learn English at a fast pace. Their ability to adjust and adapt to the U.S. school environment appears to be greater than that of Mexican and Puerto Rican immigrants. Some successful Central American students were among those sent out of war-torn countries with their families' life savings. A sense of responsibility or guilt may have created a unique motivation to achieve within this group.

Among newly arrived Latino immigrants who are members of groups without long histories as minorities in the United States, there is a common strong belief that they can and will succeed in acquiring English. The challenges of learning English and adapting to the school environment are viewed as only temporary problems.

Many Latino immigrants found work, at least initially, in agricultural and service occupations that require little or no English. Cubans, as an exception, often settled in urban areas where their access to the labor market was more dependent on their ability to speak English, although in some areas, particularly in Florida, a Cuban immigrant could easily conduct routine business entirely in Spanish.

As individuals and family members of any Latino group learn sufficient English, they gain greater access to the labor market and become upwardly mobile. The barrios in the cities of the United States, however, are always refilling with new immigrants who do not speak English. This situation may give the mistaken impression that Latino immigrants never acquire English.

The Equality of Languages. There is evidence of language bias or prejudice in many countries of the world, including the United States, even though linguistically all languages could be considered to be equal. Languages are the product of the creative human mind. Languages of minority groups, however, are often the victim of language bias. When some individuals experience an atmosphere of language bias, they may feel psychologically defeated and inhibited from succeeding in the society.

Second Language Acquisition. People have a natural ability to learn the primary language of their culture of upbringing. All human beings, regardless of culture, social class, intelligence, or environmental factors, are able to do this as children if they have sufficient interaction with others.

Learning to speak a second language, however, is a different and more difficult process. As one begins to learn a second language, the mind invents incorrect forms of language in an attempt to try to figure out how the new language works. Sentences and pronunciations become more accurate as the individual hears language that can be understood. Given enough exposure to comprehensible language, these "in-between languages" become more like the language being acquired. This is an entirely natural process. The formal, written form of the language, however, has to be taught.

Both social and cultural factors affect the eventual success of language learners. People are more likely to learn a language quickly if they feel a personal desire to gain access to the second culture; have a need to learn the language for a particular reason, such as employment; and have repeated opportunities for exposure to the language as well as positive social interaction with native speakers. Motivation, attitude, aptitude, cognitive style (for example, whether an individual learns better through listening or seeing), and personality (such as introverted or extroverted) all may affect the eventual level of language proficiency attained.

Most young children, particularly between the ages of five and eleven, who learn English as a second language in U.S. schools eventually are able to speak English without any trace of an accent. They may, however, not do well in school during these early years because of the dual burden of learning the new language and simultaneously learning to read and develop other important grade-level concepts. Bilingual instruction can often facilitate their progress.

Older children and young adults can achieve nativelike fluency over time but often retain an accent. Some young adult Latinos who have lived in the United States for several years or longer have made significant adjustments to the new culture and language.

Even if they do not yet speak or write fluent English themselves, they quickly learn current slang and can manage everyday communication. These youths sometimes, however, express hostility toward the newer Latino immigrants who cannot speak English as well as they do, perhaps as part of the adjustment process.

Given the opportunity, even adults can learn to speak, read, and write English fluently as a second language. They are likely, however, to retain the accent of their first language. Scientists believe that this is a result of biological changes that coincide with puberty.

Time Needed for Acquisition. Other factors being equal, learning conversational English during school age in the United States usually takes about two years. Learning the academic language necessary for successful completion of high school in the United States, however, is estimated to take from five to seven years. If individuals are not literate in their first language, a longer learning period can be expected. If students are made to feel ashamed of their first language or culture, second-language learning may also be delayed.

Trends in Language Teaching. Before World War II, individuals who did not speak English were required to "sink or swim" in the mainstream classrooms of the

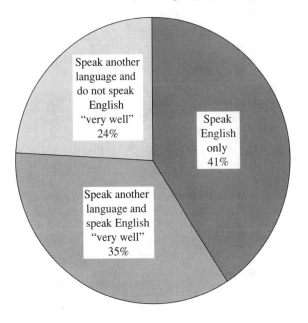

ENGLISH-SPEAKING ABILITY AMONG LATINO CHILDREN, AGES 5-17, 1990

Speak another language and do not speak English "very well" 24%

Speak English only 41%

Speak another language and speak English "very well" 35%

Source: Data are from Bureau of the Census, *Persons of Hispanic Origin in the United States: Census of 1990* (Washington, D.C.: Bureau of the Census, 1993), Tables 1 and 3.

United States. This "submersion" approach was not successful in equipping students with either language or academic skills. In 1974, the Supreme Court decided in *Lau v. Nichols* that this approach was unconstitutional. Thereafter, instruction either in the language of the learner (where numbers justified it) or in English as a second language was required.

New models and approaches for second-language programs in the schools had to be developed to meet this new mandate. Some schools patterned their new programs after those of Canada's French "immersion" schools. The first language was used in the early grades while children learned to read and acquire other important concepts. A limited amount of time each day was spent introducing children to English. English was phased in gradually. By the fifth or sixth grade, instruction was entirely in English. One goal of these programs was to enable learners to retain and develop their first language while becoming bilingual in English.

Methods of Teaching English. In the early days of language teaching, learners translated passages from one language to another in what was known as the grammar-translation method. After World War II, methods were borrowed from techniques used by the U.S. military. These methods were teacher-centered, involved an emphasis on grammatical form, and required students to laboriously repeat and practice sentence patterns. This method was not successful for many learners. The learners could repeat the sentences but could not carry on a conversation with a native speaker. As a result of these problems, during the 1960's and 1970's, a major change took place in the teaching of English as a second language.

Students learning English can acquire skills by participating in classes conducted solely in English. (James Shaffer)

The new approach was more practical. Classes were more learner-centered and thematically organized. Instead of only grammar, learners practiced social conversation, such as how to apologize and how to get information. Free, interactive practice was an important aspect of this approach, which capitalized on the learner's natural desire to communicate with others. The newer curriculum also sought to validate other cultures' contributions by designing a multicultural environment within the schools. Most bilingual teachers and teachers of English as a second language used a combination of methods and approaches.

"Sheltered" classes taught math, science, and social studies primarily in English, with use of the first language allowed when necessary. This approach was thought to assist learners in acquiring English while learning other subjects. Newcomers' centers, a public school arrangement to accommodate newly arrived immigrants, were effective as a transitional program. These centers emphasized intensive language instruction, bilingual support, and partnerships with families. Combined with programs in English as a second language, these centers allowed newly arrived immigrants to enter regular programs within a year or two of their arrival. —*Peggy J. Anderson*

SUGGESTED READINGS:

- Carrasquillo, Angela. *Latino Children and Youth in the United States.* New York: Garland, 1991. Discusses the characteristics, status, and future of Latino youth in the United States. Also discusses health, labor force participation, education, and criminal justice status.
- Freeman, Yvonne, and David Freeman. *Whole Language for Second Language Learners.* Portsmouth, N.H.: Heinemann, 1992. Describes a whole-language approach to second-language learning and teaching.
- Gann, L. H., and Peter J. Duignan. *The Hispanics in the United States: A History.* Boulder, Colo.: Westview Press, 1986. Describes the results of a large survey covering the history, politics, and culture of all major Latino groups in the United States. The authors describe immigrants' experiences in adapting to American life.
- Hispanic Policy Development Project. *The Hispanic Almanac.* New York: Author, 1984. Provides statistics and facts about social, economic, and language-use factors of Latinos in the United States as well as detailed profiles of the top twenty Latino markets (cities).
- Moore, Joan, and Harry Pachon. *Hispanics in the United States.* Englewood Cliffs, N.J.: Prentice Hall, 1985. Analyzes important factors in the history of Latinos, focusing attention on recent developments in Latino education.
- Suarez-Orozco, Marcelo M. "Towards a Psychosocial Understanding of Hispanic Adaptation to American Schooling." In *Success or Failure?*, edited by Henry T. Trueba. Boston: Heinle & Heinle, 1987. Examines the differences in school failure among Latino subgroups.

English-only controversy: Movements to establish English as the official language of the United States, possibly through attempts to amend the U.S. Constitution, sparked controversy within the Latino community and the U.S. population as a whole. In the early 1980's, a movement known as "official English" by supporters and "English only" by opponents began gaining popular support in the United States. In several state legislatures and through the election process, supporters introduced statutes, amendments, and other bills aimed at proclaiming English as the official language of such states. Proponents hoped eventually to garner enough support through state initiatives to call for an amendment to the United States Constitution proclaiming English as the official language of government and public business. The movement proceeded into the mid-1990's without resolution.

History. The first major event of the movement that attracted widespread attention occurred in 1980 in Dade County, Florida, the same county that, in 1963, had instituted the first contemporary BILINGUAL EDUCATION program in a U.S. public school. In 1980, Dade County voters passed a bill prohibiting public funds from being used for languages other than English or for promoting any culture other than that of the United States. This bill banned Spanish language from use in such items as fire safety information pamphlets, marriage ceremonies, and public transportation signs.

In 1980, Senator S. I. Hayakawa (R-California) introduced for the first time an amendment to the U.S. Constitution that would proclaim English as the official language of the United States. His bill also would have prohibited federal and state governments from requiring the use of any other language. Although the resolution did not advance in the Senate, it set the tone for what would become a series of bills introduced in the U.S. Congress during the 1980's and early 1990's.

Organizations Supporting the Movement. Another major event in the "official English" movement was the founding in 1983 of the organization U.S. English, headquartered in Washington, D.C. Primary founders

S. I. Hayakawa was president of San Francisco State University until 1972, when he stepped down to pursue academic interests. (AP/Wide World Photos)

were Senator Hayakawa and John Tanton, an ophthalmologist from Michigan. Tanton had earlier founded the Federation for American Immigration Reform and had been a board member of Zero Population Growth. By the late 1980's, U.S. English claimed a dues-paying membership of more than 300,000 nationally, with an annual budget of $7 million. By 1994, the group claimed a membership of 550,000. U.S. English described itself in its newsletter *U.S. English Update* as both an educational and a lobbying organization.

In 1986, two smaller organizations similar to U.S. English were formed. English First was headquartered in Springfield, Virginia, and the American Ethnic Coalition was headquartered in Bryan, Texas. U.S. English continued to lead "official English" efforts.

Legislative Efforts. In 1984, Indiana, Kentucky, and Tennessee adopted statutes declaring English as their official language. In the same year, the United States Senate Subcommittee on the Constitution held hearings on Resolution 167, an English language amendment proposal introduced the previous year jointly by Senator Walter Huddleston (D-Kentucky) and Senator Steve Symms (R-Idaho). Congress did not act on the proposed amendment, but the hearings reflected the widening of "official English" efforts.

Also in 1984, voters in California approved a ballot initiative requiring voting materials to be prepared in English only, giving rise to the term "English only" by which opponents would increasingly characterize the issue. This initiative, however, could not supersede the federal Voting Rights Act reauthorization legislation of 1975, which provided for bilingual ballots in areas where a single language-minority group accounted for at least 5 percent of voters.

The year 1986 marked a dramatic acceleration in the controversy and a sharper delineation between opposing positions, especially with the introduction in California of Proposition 63, which came to be known as the "English Only" initiative. It marked the maturation of the issue as a political movement and established U.S. English as a powerful, well-financed lobby. Supporters spent between $800,000 and $900,000 to put the proposition on the ballot. Proposition 63 became the first state measure regarding use of the English language to be passed by ballot initiative instead of through state legislatures. It succeeded by a margin of 73 percent to 27 percent. The initiative proclaimed it was intended to preserve, protect, and strengthen the English language; declared English as the official language of California; and authorized state residents or anyone conducting business in the state to sue to enforce the amendment.

Momentum for such measures continued in 1987; they were considered in thirty-seven state legislatures and passed in five (Arkansas, Mississippi, North Carolina, North Dakota, and South Carolina). Linda CHÁVEZ, former staff director of the U.S. Commission on Civil Rights and director of public liaison in the White House under President Ronald Reagan, was hired to head U.S. English.

Opposition to Official English. The English Plus Information Clearinghouse (EPIC), headquartered in Washington, D.C., was formed in 1987 as a coalition of organizations involved with education and civil rights issues, many concerning ethnic minorities. EPIC was aimed at promoting English supplemented by other languages, providing limited-English speakers with the opportunity to gain English proficiency in addition to learning other subjects. It also promoted the idea of monolingual English speakers gaining proficiency in additional languages. Such organizations as the American Civil Liberties Union, American Jewish Committee, MEXICAN AMERICAN LEGAL DEFENSE AND EDUCATION FUND, and National Council of Teachers of English supported English Plus in its efforts to promote bilingual or multilingual proficiency and to encourage the positive viewing of ethnic differences.

Efforts opposing "official English" saw further success in 1988, when the California case of *Gutierrez v. Municipal Court* struck down "English only" rules in the workplace and the Ninth U.S. Circuit Court of Appeals declared Proposition 63 to be "primarily symbolic." Also in 1988, the House Subcommittee on Civil and Constitutional Rights held hearings on five proposed Constitutional amendments regarding use of English but did not advance any for full congressional hearings. Voters in three states, however, approved state constitutional amendments proclaiming English as their official language. Arizona's measure passed with 51 percent approval, Colorado's with 61 percent, and Florida's with 84 percent.

The campaign in Arizona provided a benchmark for gauging the strength and the volatility of the issue. U.S. English contributed more than $160,000 to support the Arizona proposition, while opponents received less than $3,000. The proposition nevertheless passed by only a narrow margin.

In 1988, the press obtained an internal memorandum, perceived by many to be anti-immigrant and anti-Latino, written by Tanton. Disclosure of the memorandum caused resignations by Tanton and Chávez. Newsman Walter Cronkite resigned from the U.S. English advisory board.

In 1989, difficulties for U.S. English continued as the New Mexico legislature endorsed the concept of "English plus" rather than "English only." The same year, Washington and Oregon passed "English plus" legislation. In the 1990 court case of *Yniguez v. Mofford*, Arizona's 1988 amendment was struck down as unconstitutional by the courts, which held that the requirement that the "State and all political subdivisions of [Arizona] shall act in English and in no other language" violated free speech guarantees under the First Amendment to the Constitution. During the same year, however, Alabama voters passed an "official English" bill with 89 percent approval. By 1994, according to the U.S. English organization, nineteen states had designated English as their official language; the earliest was Louisiana in 1811, and the most recent was Alabama in 1990. The nineteen states included Hawaii, which in 1978 declared English and Hawaiian as its official languages.

The various proposed bills were either open-ended or proscriptive. The open-ended laws were brief, proclaiming English as the official language and providing legislative bodies with the authority to enforce them. For example, the Florida state constitutional amendment passed by voters in 1988 read: "(a) English is the official language of the State of Florida. (b) The Legislature shall have the power to enforce this section [of the Constitution] by appropriate legis-

An "official English" amendment could have prevented Spanish-language identification of this public library branch in Miami, Florida. (Martin Hutner)

lation." Proscriptive versions were lengthier and characterized by ordinances promoting English and forbidding use of other languages for governmental business. For example, the Arizona ballot initiative passed in 1988 had four sections. It declared English as the official language; required the preservation, protection, and enhancement of English; prohibited the state from requiring any other language; and allowed the amendment's enforcement. Each section had various subsections governing the amendment's applications, exceptions, or means of enforcement.

Proposed Constitutional Amendments. State campaigns to which "official English" supporters devoted their efforts during the 1980's were intended to aid the larger cause of promoting an amendment to the U.S. Constitution designating English as the official language of the United States. The process that all amendments must follow is set forth in Article V of the Constitution. Two-thirds of the members of the U.S. House of Representatives and the Senate, or two-thirds of the states, must call for an amendment. After that, three-fourths of the state legislatures or three-fourths

of state constitutional conventions must ratify the proposed amendment for it to become law.

Sixteen "official English" amendments, in addition to statutes and resolutions, were proposed to the U.S. Congress between 1981 and 1990. In 1993, four bills were introduced in Congress, each addressing a different aspect of the issue. For example, House Resolution 123 declared English as the official language of government business. House Resolution 2859 sought to amend the Immigration and Nationality Act so that public ceremonies for admission of new citizens would be conducted solely in English.

The various "official English" amendments to the U.S. Constitution proposed from 1980 through 1993 contained several common features. First, they sought to declare English as the official language of the United States. Second, they sought to prohibit any law from requiring any language other than English to be used for most government functions. Third, most of the amendments would have allowed languages other than English to be used for educational purposes and selected areas of official government business, such as public safety. Fourth, most amendments would have given the U.S. Congress and the states authority to pass legislation implementing the amendment.

Effects of the Controversy. The "official English" or "English only" movement is understood by both supporters and opponents as an attempt to eliminate bilingual education programs for public school children for whom English is a second language. In 1986, for example, following passage of California's Proposition 63, supporters targeted bilingual education as the first battlefield resulting from the amendment's passage. Opponents saw this as a threat to students from historically Spanish-speaking groups. Elimination of BILINGUAL EDUCATION programs would also have affected numerous Asian American students, such as speakers of Chinese, Vietnamese, and Korean. American Indians who maintained indigenous languages also would be affected. The federal BILINGUAL EDUCATION ACT, effective in 1968, had funded bilingual programs to develop educational materials in various American Indian languages to help American Indians maintain cultural identity. The "English only" movement was also seen as having threatening implications for American Sign Language (ASL) for the training of deaf persons, because ASL could be viewed as an independent language separate from English.

The English-only controversy was particularly significant for Latinos in the United States. Their historical bond to the Spanish language dates to the early 1500's, when Spaniards began colonization efforts throughout the Americas and the Caribbean region. Attempts to diminish the use and importance of Spanish, through force of law, are often considered to be threats to the cultural integrity of Latinos and to the education of Latino children. *—Luis A. Torres*

SUGGESTED READINGS:

• Adams, Karen L., and Daniel T. Brink, eds. *Perspectives on Official English: The Campaign for English as the Official Language of the USA*. New York: Mouton de Gruyter, 1990. Provides articles on "official language" questions internationally. Reviews successful state campaigns, language-minority rights, and legal perspectives on the issue.

• Baron, Dennis. *The English-Only Question*. New Haven, Conn.: Yale University Press, 1990. Surveys language issues in American politics back to the colonial period. Discusses educational implications, constitutional questions, and the symbolic importance of language.

• Crawford, James, ed. *Language Loyalties: A Source Book on the Official English Controversy*. Chi-

cago: University of Chicago Press, 1992. A major anthology of articles about the issue. Covers the history of U.S. language policy, education, minority communities, and international perspectives.

• Daniels, Harvey A., ed. *Not Only English: Affirming America's Multilingual Heritage*. Urbana, Ill.: National Council of Teachers of English, 1990. A collection of articles covering the "official English" movement's origins, dangers of the movement, arguments against language restrictions, and proposed responses to the movement.

• Fishman, Joshua, ed. *The Question of an Official Language: Language Rights and the English Language Amendment*. New York: Mouton de Gruyter, 1986. A useful introductory article by David F. Marshall covers various state amendments, their histories, and their consequences. Subsequent articles provide comments on Marshall's article.

Enriquez, Gaspar (b. July 18, 1942, El Paso, Tex.): Artist. Enriquez is a diverse and prolific artist who weaves Hispanic themes and cultural sensibilities into his prints, sculptures, jewelry, crafts, and mixed-media pieces. After studying printmaking and jewelry at the University of Texas at El Paso, Enriquez earned a master's degree at New Mexico State University, where he specialized in metalsmithing.

Many of Enriquez's sculptural forms are derived from the niches and altars that traditionally adorn Hispanic homes and establish a spiritual center for families. Enriquez's *La Familia IX* (1985), for example, is a mixed-media altar with small doors adorned with and opening to family photos. Other similar works incorporate family photos with crosses and metal sculptures of Southwestern plants.

Enriquez's work has been exhibited at various museums and universities in New Mexico and California, and it continues to be marketed from galleries and studios in Texas. In 1970, he began working as an art instructor in the public schools of El Paso, Texas, and at El Paso Community College. Through this work, he has helped sustain a unique Latino perspective on the arts for subsequent generations of students.

Enriquez, Rene (b. Nov. 25, 1933, San Francisco, Calif.): Actor. The son of a prominent businessman and politician, Enriquez made his film and stage debuts in 1960, performing in New York in Tennessee Williams' play *Camino Real* and on the big screen in *Girl in the Night*. He built his career on portrayals of political and authority figures, including Nicaraguan president

Rene Enriquez appeared in the television series Hill Street Blues. (AP/Wide World Photos)

Anastasio Somoza in the 1983 film *Under Fire* and Lieutenant Ray Calletano in the 1980's television series *Hill Street Blues*. His numerous film appearances include *Bananas* (1971), *Harry and Tonto* (1974), *Night Moves* (1975), *The Evil That Men Do* (1984), and *Bulletproof* (1985). In 1985, he was nominated for an Emmy Award for his performance in *Imagen*.

Enriquez is founder and president of the National Hispanic Arts Endowment. In 1984, he joined the board of directors of the Screen Actors Guild. His honors in the Latino community include the LULAC Theatre Award and the Golden Eagle Award from Nosotros.

Environmental issues: Latin America and the border region of the United States face severe environmental problems including water pollution, pesticides, air pollution, and losses in the rain forest. The area within fifty miles or so of the U.S.-Mexico border is called the BORDER REGION. The major environmental problems of this area are water and air pollution.

Water Pollution. Water pollution in the border region stems from several related sources. Many homes have no running water, no sewer system, and access only to contaminated water. The problem of water pollution is most severe at the ends of the border, near the Gulf of Mexico and the Pacific Ocean.

Many people living in the border region live in rural neighborhoods in houses that they have built themselves. These neighborhoods are called COLONIAS. In the United States, people generally buy the land for their homes, although a few are squatters. In Mexico, homes are more often built without permission on land that is owned by someone else. Because housing is built without authorization, running water, sewer systems, and electricity do not exist in these homes.

Water for these homes is brought from relatives who have water hookups or is pulled from irrigation ditches, pumped from individual wells, or supplied by inadequate public systems. These sources of water are almost always contaminated by sewage and bacteria. The contamination comes from the lack of sewer systems. Homes in the *colonias* get rid of their sewage in septic tanks, open pits, or outhouses. Septic tanks are large covered pits that filter waste material into solids and liquids. The liquids from all these methods are

This boy plays next to a sewage-filled ditch in Rancho de los Diabolos, a migrant worker settlement in Southern California that by 1993 still did not have plumbing or electricity in individual homes. (Impact Visuals, Michelle Gienow)

filtered by sinking further into the ground. If the liquids filter far enough, they can reach underground water that is used for drinking, bathing, and cooking. The liquids can still be contaminated when they reach the underground water.

Water that is contaminated with sewage causes many preventable diseases including dysentery, tuberculosis, typhoid, and hepatitis. Wastewater from the *colonias* usually flows into rivers from which people downstream get their water. This leads to spreading of disease.

Pesticides. Water pollution also comes from agricultural pesticides used to kill insects, bacteria, and fungi that harm plants. When pesticides are spread or sprayed on the ground, some pesticide is absorbed by the ground, and some runs off when it rains. The pesticides in the rainwater eventually reach a river, lake, or ocean. After the pesticide reaches a body of water, it kills plants and fish that live in and around the water. The effects of pesticides do not end there. Animals that hunt fish can die because the pesticides tend to concentrate in their blood and fatty tissue, building higher levels than were found in the food they ate.

People also are affected by pesticides, through direct contact or contact with contaminated water, or from eating contaminated plants and animals. Incorrect usage of pesticides is high among farmworkers in the border region who cannot understand verbal instructions from their bosses or cannot read instructions printed in English, either because they do not know English or because they cannot read. Coming in contact with even a small amount of pesticide can cause long-term damage in the form of cancer, birth defects, and mutations.

Industrial Waste. Another form of water pollution is industrial waste. Businesses dump chemicals into streams and rivers. Oil spills also put chemicals into the water system. These chemicals, like pesticides, can also cause illness and birth defects. Besides causing human and animal damage, the chemicals in polluted rivers can actually catch fire and burn. Such fires as well as explosions can occur in sewer tunnels where toxic gases have accumulated.

Texas produces more hazardous waste materials than any other state, and California is in the top ten producers. Hazardous wastes pose disposal problems.

The United Farm Workers picketed against the harms of pesticides, but their use persisted. (Impact Visuals, Les Stone)

Hazardous wastes have been buried in barrels that have rusted and cracked, allowing the materials inside to leak into the ground and the water underground. Hazardous materials also have been taken to regular landfills and treated like ordinary trash. Illegal dumping of hazardous chemicals is another large problem. Studies in the 1980's and 1990's showed as much as 80 percent of all hazardous materials being stored or dumped unsafely and illegally in the United States. Producers of such materials may wish to avoid the costs associated with legal forms of disposal and therefore dump waste illegally.

Air Pollution. Air pollution can be as simple as pesticides sprayed from airplanes or automobile emissions. Cars, buses, and trucks produce the greatest amounts of air pollutants, contributing to smog. Mexico City, Mexico, has some of the world's highest smog levels. Air pollution is concentrated there because mountains completely encircle the city, preventing pollution from dissipating. Other Latin American cities that have severe air pollution problems include São Paulo and Rio de Janeiro in Brazil. Industries also contribute to air pollution. For example, pollution from lead smelters has caused problems in Mexico.

A unique air pollution problem affecting Latin America is smoke from large-scale burning of the rain forest. Peasants of the area burn the rain forest to increase the amount of farmland or rangeland.

Deforestation relates to other pollution problems. Tree roots help slow rain runoff, and when runoff increases, soil more readily accompanies the water. This soil erosion is especially dramatic in the former rain forests. For all the life a rain forest supports, the soil it stands on is actually very thin. When a rain forest is burned and then farmed, the soil will only grow several seasons of crops before the nutrients in the soil are gone. Farmers then burn more of the rain forest, repeating the cycle.

Fighting Pollution. At the first Earth Summit in Rio de Janeiro, Brazil, in June of 1992, the leaders of the world met to increase awareness about the problems of the rain forest as well as other ecological problems including water pollution, pesticide poisoning, hazardous materials, and air pollution. The world leaders signed treaties protecting forests of the world and biodiversity.

Mexico, Canada, and the United States signed the NORTH AMERICAN FREE TRADE AGREEMENT (NAFTA) in 1992, with provisions effective on January 1, 1994. Most Mexicans expected American companies to continue building Mexican plants to take advantage of less strict environmental laws in Mexico. Although Mexico does have environmental laws to cover air and water pollution, hazardous waste, and pesticides, many such laws were put in place to respond to NAFTA and the influx of American companies. Mexico thus has a history of lax environmental standards. To help combat and prevent environmental problems, the United States and Mexico have written joint environmental plans. One plan focuses on the problems of the border region. The United States has also engaged in training Mexican environmental workers.   —*Elise M. Bright*

SUGGESTED READINGS:

• Betts, Dianne C., and Daniel J. Slottje. *Crisis on the Rio Grande: Poverty, Unemployment, and Economic Development on the Texas-Mexico Border.* Boulder, Colo.: Westview Press, 1994. A detailed description of the unique problems facing the border region.

• Cunningham, William P. *Understanding Our Environment: An Introduction.* Dubuque, Iowa: Wm. C. Brown, 1994. A textbook for general environmental data, problems, and solutions.

• Miller, G. Tyler, Jr. *Environmental Science: An Introduction.* 2d ed. Belmont, Calif.: Wadsworth, 1988. An undergraduate textbook covering major environmental problems.

• Miller, G. Tyler, Jr. *Resource Conservation and Management.* Belmont, Calif.: Wadsworth, 1989. An introduction to management issues such as rain forest destruction.

• U.S. Environmental Protection Agency, and Mexico, Secretaria de Desarrollo Urbano y Ecologia. *Integrated Environmental Plan for the Mexican-U.S. Border Area (First Stage, 1992-1994).* Washington, D.C.: United States Environmental Protection Agency, 1992. A comprehensive plan regarding environmental problems and solutions, produced by the U.S. and Mexican environmental agencies.

• Von Rumker, Rosmarie. *Production, Distribution, Use, and Environmental Impact Potential of Selected Pesticides.* Washington, D.C.: Environmental Protection Agency, 1975. An EPA report regarding various aspects of pesticide use.

• World Resources Institute. *World Resources 1994-1995.* New York: Oxford University Press, 1994. A United Nations document describing the state of the world in 1994.

Epazote: Mexican herb with both culinary and medicinal uses. *Epazote* is a species of *Chenopodium*, a genus of weedy plants, and grows throughout its native

Mexico and adjacent areas. Its leaves have a pungent, almost rank, taste and are used in all of Mexico except the northern and west-central parts. *Epazote* is especially important as a seasoning for beans, and it is widely used in QUESADILLAS, certain MOLES, and some tomato and tomatillo SALSAS. The same plant also is used in herbal curing, but the *epazote* sold for this purpose consists primarily of hard stems and generally is unsuitable for cooking. In Yucatán, the herb is called *apazote*.

Epidemics and indigenous populations: As Europeans explored and conquered the Americas, they inadvertently introduced diseases that caused a biological catastrophe among the indigenous peoples, annihilating millions of them. Prior to 1492, the American continents existed in virtual biological isolation from the Old World. When the Europeans invaded, they carried with them pathogens previously unknown in the Western Hemisphere. The diseases included smallpox, measles, chicken pox, malaria, influenza, typhus, yellow fever, hemorrhagic dysentery, and perhaps bubonic plague. Because of their isolation, the Amerindians had evolved no genetic immunities to these diseases. The horrific effect of European diseases on the Amerindian population exceeded that of the Black Death in Europe.

The first great epidemic began in December, 1518, when smallpox erupted in Santo Domingo. Between one-third and one-half of the natives died during the initial outbreak, although it had little effect upon the Spanish on the island. It rapidly spread to Puerto Rico and other parts of the Caribbean, with similar consequences. An infected black slave in the Pánfilo de NARVÁEZ expedition, which had been sent to arrest Hernán CORTÉS at Veracruz in 1520, carried smallpox into Mexico. Cortés took Narváez's men, including the slave, back to TENOCHTITLÁN, the Aztec capital. Although the Aztecs drove the Spaniards out of the city, a smallpox epidemic devastated the capital and weakened it for Cortés' eventual triumph the following year. Meanwhile, the disease spread into Central America and southward into the Andes. There it apparently killed the ruler Huayna Capac in the 1520's, touching off a dynastic struggle and civil war that contributed to the Spanish conquest of the Incas.

Demographers conclude that between 1520 and 1600, Mexico suffered fourteen epidemics of these

The arrival of Europeans in the Americas brought diseases that were previously unknown in the area. (Institute of Texan Cultures)

diseases and Peru seventeen, with appalling human costs. Although there is no consensus among scholars as to the size of the Amerindian population in 1492, it may have numbered more than fifty million. Mortality from the new diseases in the tropical regions was especially high, and the Indians of the Caribbean virtually died out. In central Mexico, where there were perhaps fourteen million inhabitants when the Spaniards arrived, the population dropped precipitously. By 1622, it reached its nadir of 750,000. The central Andes followed a similar course, dropping from eleven million to a little more than half a million in the early eighteenth century. Brazil and North America witnessed equivalent catastrophes.

Other consequences followed. Epidemic diseases undoubtedly traumatized those Indians who survived and called into question the efficacy of Indian medicines and religions. Colonial economies suffered labor shortages, remedied in part by enslaving black Africans for work in the Americas. Had their populations remained large, indigenous cultures probably would have been more resilient, but the high Amerindian mortality facilitated the spread of European culture and Christianity. Perhaps Latino culture would reflect an even greater Indian influence had epidemic disease not proved so devastating in the Americas after the arrival of the Europeans.

Equal Educational Opportunity Act (1974): Law regarding BILINGUAL EDUCATION. Through this act, Congress made bilingual education available to Latino youngsters in order to ensure equal access to good public education. Equal facilities and the provision of English-language teachers were deemed insufficient to meet the educational needs of the growing Spanish-speaking school-age population in the United States. The public began to accept the idea that bilingual teaching could be a solution in improving Spanish-speaking children's skills in reading, writing, and speaking English. The intent of this legislation was later interpreted to require schools to meet the needs of other nonnative English speakers. The act changed official policy from a 1968 act, which stated that languages other than English were to be used primarily for helping students in the transition to use of English.

Equal Employment Opportunity Act (1972): Federal labor legislation. Congress, by passing this law, enabled the Equal Employment Opportunity Commission (EEOC) to file suit on behalf of plaintiffs who had experienced job discrimination. As part of President Lyndon B. Johnson's GREAT SOCIETY PROGRAMS, the EEOC had been established as the result of provisions of the CIVIL RIGHTS ACT OF 1964. That act prevented job discrimination and discriminatory practices in employment on the basis of race or gender. Complaints regarding job discrimination and failure to comply with the act were to be brought before the EEOC, which was to be given authority to monitor and enforce the provisions of the act through mediation between employees and employers. Guidelines established by the EEOC particularly affected hiring practices in federal agencies and those companies that received federal funding or provided goods and services directly to the federal government.

Although the EEOC was intended to correct the inequities that faced minority employees and job seekers, it had little clout until the Equal Employment Opportunity Act of 1972 gave it the power to file suit against those who violated equal employment standards. After passage of this act, the EEOC filed class-action suits on behalf of large groups of workers who had been discriminated against. Nevertheless, the act had little immediate effect on the Latino community, because many Latinos were employed in agricultural jobs that were not affected by EEOC guidelines. Many Latinos who had lost their jobs as harvesting and planting became more mechanized were forced to seek low-paying, nonunion jobs as unskilled workers. That job sector also was barely affected by the new guidelines. As AFFIRMATIVE ACTION guidelines were more vigorously enforced by the EEOC in the 1980's, more Latinos began to benefit from the act. When the EEOC turned its attention to preparing suits on behalf of individual claimants in the 1980's, many Latinos and other minorities criticized this change, arguing that fewer individuals who had experienced discrimination would be willing or economically secure enough to accuse their employers in court.

Equal opportunity programs: Programs intended to increase the job opportunities of minority group members. Through the CIVIL RIGHTS ACT OF 1964, discrimination on the basis of race, national origin, sex, or religion became illegal. The act also created the Equal Employment Opportunity Commission, a federal agency designed to ensure that the civil rights law was enforced. Interpretations of the law, however, changed in many ways following its passage.

The original idea of the Civil Rights Act was to prevent discrimination at all levels of American life, but discrimination in hiring can be difficult to prove.

Equal opportunity programs attempt to move more Latinos into high-level positions by opening doors to advancement. (Robert Fried)

Latino unions and leaders fight for equal rights in the workplace. (David Bacon)

Members of ethnic minorities on average have less education than do white, English-speaking Americans and therefore are less qualified for many jobs. This problem is particularly acute among Latinos, who as a group are among the least educated people in the United States and who often do not have a thorough command of the English language.

Beginning with the administration of President Richard Nixon (1969-1974), AFFIRMATIVE ACTION programs were developed and private enterprises were encouraged to bring more minority members and women into the work force. In 1971, the federal government sent out a new set of guidelines that insisted on "equal utility" of women and minorities in any company that had more than five employees. Most large companies and almost all government agencies put such plans into effect. Such programs, however, created new problems.

The biggest problem has been an outcry of "reverse discrimination" when members of minority groups or women are favored over white men with equal, or even better, qualifications. Numerical hiring quotas and pressure to balance work forces often created such situations.

Equal opportunity programs do not guarantee equal opportunities in all areas. Lack of qualifications still keeps people out of some jobs. Immigrants from Mexico and Central America often lack the education and language skills required for most nonagricultural work. Many become migrant farmworkers, working for low pay without hope of advancement or training in other skills.

Equal opportunity programs have prevented discrimination at the lower levels of employment, but social problems remain. Some large Latino families are stuck in a cycle of poverty. A household with many children in some cases can receive a higher income from government assistance if the father is absent than if he is present and working at a minimum-wage job. This situation does not allow positive role modeling for employment. Children in Latino families are sometimes not well prepared for school because their parents are not well educated. If Spanish is spoken at home, children may have difficulty taking advantage of instruction offered primarily in English. They therefore will have less success in school and be less qualified for employment. A further social problem is the resentment, sometimes referred to as "white back-

Vice President George Bush visits Jaime Escalante's classroom in 1988. (AP/Wide World Photos)

lash," felt by some white Americans against beneficiaries of equal opportunity programs. The programs can add to the very prejudice that they were enacted to curtail.

The impact of equal opportunity programs is difficult to determine. They have made it easier for minority group members to find employment. On the other hand, the programs have been difficult to enforce, and the government has been far from efficient. A 1987 congressional report revealed that 80 percent of complaints brought to the Equal Employment Opportunity Commission were not investigated thoroughly.

Escalante, Jaime (b. Dec. 31, 1930, La Paz, Bolivia): Educator. Escalante's work in teaching mathematics was dramatized in the 1987 feature film *Stand and Deliver*. Later, he hosted a television series titled *Futures: Exploring the Role of Mathematics in the Working World* for the Public Broadcasting System. The ARCO Foundation established a $25,000 grant to

honor him and his work, and in 1990 Escalante received the Jefferson Award from the American Institute for Public Service.

Escalante earned a degree at San Andreas University in La Paz and studied at Pasadena City College in California before earning his B.S. in mathematics from California State University, Los Angeles. He taught mathematics and physics at several high schools in Bolivia before joining the staff of Garfield High School in East Los Angeles. He taught at Garfield from 1974 to 1991, when he moved to Hiram Johnson High School as a calculus teacher. At Garfield, Escalante developed an innovative program to teach mathematics. The film based on his work showed how he helped a group of inner-city students pass an advanced-placement test in calculus.

Escalona, Beatriz (Aug. 20, 1903, San Antonio, Tex.— 1980): Actress. Reared by her widowed mother, Escalona began working in the box offices of San Antonio theaters at the age of thirteen. She married José Areu, of the well-established theatrical Areu family, and became a member of its troupe, making her stage debut in 1920. Soon thereafter, she rearranged the letters of her surname (changing one "a" to an "o") and took on a nickname, rising to fame as La Chata Noloesca. She toured the Southwest with the Areus and by the mid-1920's was beginning to eclipse the troupe in popularity.

Escalona was an agile comic actress with wonderful charm and charisma on stage. Her persona, La Chata, was a fast-talking street character in a maid's or child's costume. By 1930, she had her own company, Attrac-ciones Noloesca, in Los Angeles. The company relocated to San Antonio in 1936. With the Depression taking its toll on San Antonio theater, Escalona took her brand of Mexican vaudeville on the road in 1938, traveling to Tampa, Miami, Chicago, and New York, as well as to Cuba. She later became an influential theater manager on New York's Hispanic circuit. Escalona's daughter, Belia Areu, also went on to become a stage star.

Escobar, Sixto (Mar. 23, 1913, Barceloneta, Puerto Rico—Nov. 17, 1979, Barceloneta, Puerto Rico): Boxer. After entering the Puerto Rican fighting circuits

Sixto Escobar in 1935. (AP/Wide World Photos)

in 1933, Escobar went to the United States in 1934. That year, he won the National Boxing Association bantamweight title against Baby Casanova and became the first Puerto Rican world champion. Escobar would keep the title for a year before losing it, then quickly regaining it three months later.

Escobar extended his honors to include the world bantamweight title with a 1936 win over Tony Marino. He lost that title in 1937 and regained it a year later. Weight problems forced Escobar to vacate his title in 1939; he fought his last fight in December of 1940 before serving in World War II. His career included twenty-one knockouts in sixty-four bouts. A Puerto Rican national hero, Escobar has a stadium named for him in San Juan.

ESL. *See* **English as a Second Language (ESL) programs**

Española, La (Hispaniola): Island in the Caribbean, the first colony of the New World. In 1492, Christopher Columbus' voyages took him to the island now known as Hispaniola. He gave it the name of La Española. Despite many difficulties, within twenty years the island was a colony with towns, villages, and several seaports. Nobles from Spain as well as soldiers and merchants had settled on it. La Española became the center of Spanish activities in the New World. Expeditions departed from it to explore the rest of the Caribbean. Eventually it lost its importance as new and wealthier colonies, such as New Spain, developed on the mainland.

Esparza, Moctezuma Díaz (b. Mar. 12, 1949, Los Angeles, Calif.): Filmmaker. Esparza, a longtime activist in Chicano issues, is the cofounder of Esparza/Katz Productions and a leading producer of films that deal with Hispanic people, themes, and lifestyles. He was coproducer of *Alambrista!* (1977) and *The Milagro Beanfield War* (1988), producer of *Only Once in a Lifetime* (1978) and *Radioactive Dreams* (1986), and director of *The Ballad of Gregorio Cortez* (1983). *Agueda Martínez*, a 1978 documentary on the elderly of northern New Mexico, earned for Esparza an Academy Award nomination as coproducer.

Espinosa, Aurelio Macedonio, Sr. (Sept. 12, 1880, Carnero, Colombia—Sept. 4, 1958, Stanford, Calif.): Folklorist and educator. A prolific scholar, Espinosa produced more than thirty textbooks and a dozen scholarly monographs in addition to more than a hun-

dred articles in scholarly journals. His studies of the "tar baby" were pioneering works in scholarship on folktale origins. The Spanish government honored his scholarship and leadership in Spanish and folklore studies with the Order of Isabel la Católica in 1922. Spain awarded him the Grand Cross of the Order of Alfonso el Sabio in 1950. Among his best-known works are *Cuentos populares españoles* (1946-1947) and *Romancero de Nuevo Méjico* (1953).

In 1902, Espinosa earned his bachelor's degree in Spanish from the University of Colorado, where he obtained his M.A. two years later. While pursuing his education, he taught Spanish at the University of Chicago (1908-1909) and at the University of New Mexico (1902-1910). He received his Ph.D. from the University of Chicago in 1909 and was immediately appointed as assistant professor at Stanford University on the basis of his doctoral thesis. He remained at Stanford for the rest of his teaching career, acting as chair of the department of romance languages and literature from 1932 to 1947. He directed more than fifty master's theses and twelve doctoral dissertations and was active in founding the American Association of Teachers of Spanish. He was the first editor of that group's journal, *Hispania*, from 1918 to 1926. In 1928, he was elected president of the association. He also served as editor of the *Journal of American Folklore* (1914-1946) and associate editor of *Western Folklore* (1947-1953). Espinosa was president of the American Folk-Lore Society from 1923 to 1924.

Espinosa, Paul (b. Aug. 8, 1950, Alamosa, Calif.): Filmmaker and television producer. Espinosa received his B.A. in anthropology from Brown University and his Ph.D. from Stanford University, where he specialized in the cultural analysis of television. He has had a long and fruitful affiliation with KPBS-TV in San Diego, where he created and directed the Office of Chicano Affairs and has been executive producer for public affairs. A founding member of the California Chicano News Media Association in San Diego, Espinosa specializes in Latino and U.S.-Mexican border topics. His major production credits include *The Trail North* (1983), which re-creates an ancestral journey north from Mexico; *Ballad of an Unsung Hero* (1984); *The Lemon Grove Incident* (1986), about the nation's first successful legal challenge to school segregation; *Uneasy Neighbors* (1990); *The New Tijuana* (1990); *Los Mineros: American Experience* (1991); *1492 Revisited* (1992); and *The Hunt for Pancho Villa: American Experience* (1993). Espinosa received an Emmy

Award in 1988 for *In the Shadow of the Law*, a documentary profiling four families living illegally in the United States.

Espiritista: Believer in the existence of spiritual entities and the possibility of establishing direct communication with them. The *espiritista* believes in the existence of a spiritual world that wishes to establish contact with the corporeal world. Direct communication with the entities inhabiting the spiritual plane is achieved through an intermediary called the medium. *Espiritismo*, or Spiritualism, is practiced throughout Latin America and the Caribbean as well as by Mexican Americans. For many communities, the focus of this spiritual practice is the *centro espiritista*, or spiritual center. Spiritualists believe that the communication established with the spiritual plane usually involves family members, friends, or personal concerns.

Esquivel, Laura (b. 1950, Mexico City, Mexico): Novelist and screenwriter. Esquivel is a former schoolteacher whose first novel, *Como agua para chocolate* (1989; *Like Water for Chocolate*, 1992), became an international best-seller and a critically acclaimed Mexican film. Esquivel's novel of the de la Garza family, set against the backdrop of the Mexican Revolution (1910-1921), mixes romance, Magical Realism, and cooking recipes. The novel sold well in the United States in both its original Spanish and in the English translation.

Like Water for Chocolate was made into a feature film in 1989, with a screenplay by Esquivel and direction by Esquivel's husband, Alfonso Arau. Their collaborative effort won eleven Mexican Academy of Motion Pictures Ariel Awards and became an international success. The film also became the highest grossing foreign film shown in the United States.

A shop in Brooklyn, New York, selling objects related to espiritismo. (City Lore, Martha Cooper)

Like Water for Chocolate *brought fame to writer Laura Esquivel.* (AP/Wide World Photos)

Esquivel worked as a teacher until marrying Mexican director Alfonso Arau. In 1985 they collaborated for the first time, Esquivel writing the screenplay for and Arau directing the hit Mexican film *Chido One*. Esquivel has also scripted a children's feature, *Little Ocean Star* (1984).

Estefan, Gloria (b. Sept. 1, 1957, Havana, Cuba): Singer and songwriter. Estefan's father, José Manuel Fajardo, was a security officer for Cuban president Fulgencio Batista when Fidel CASTRO took control of the country and made himself head of state in 1959. The Fajardo family was forced to leave Cuba and seek refuge in the United States. They settled in Miami, where Fajardo continued the struggle against Castro. In 1961, he participated in the unsuccessful BAY OF PIGS INVASION of Cuba. After being imprisoned in Cuba, he returned to the United States.

As a child, Estefan liked to write poetry and listen to music. She took classical guitar lessons but was drawn to more popular forms of music. Her father was diagnosed with multiple sclerosis, and the burden of caring for him fell on Estefan and her mother. During the day, while her mother was working, Estefan cared for her younger sister as well as her father. Singing became an outlet, a way of coping with her father's illness and adjusting to life in Miami.

As a teenager, Estefan began singing publicly for family and friends. In 1975, she auditioned for the band the Miami Latin Boys. She met the percussionist and leader of the band, Emilio Estefan, who was impressed with her singing and asked her to become the band's vocalist. She was able to sing only on the weekends while she attended the University of Miami. She was married to Emilio Estefan on September 1, 1978.

The band, later renamed the MIAMI SOUND MACHINE, became popular with local audiences. In the early 1980's, the Miami Sound Machine recorded a number of Spanish-language albums that became popular in Spanish-speaking countries. In 1984, the group released its first English-language album, *Eyes of Innocence*. The mixture of Latin rhythms and more mainstream musical elements caught on with the American audience. With the release of such songs as "Conga," "Bad Boys," and "Words Get in the Way," the Miami Sound Machine became one of the most successful bands of the mid-1980's.

With the help of her husband's managerial skills, Estefan focused on becoming a solo performer. In 1990, she was involved in a serious accident necessitating spinal surgery and several months of physical

Gloria and Emilio Estefan. (Otto G. Richter Library, University of Miami)

therapy before she could perform again. Estefan was as popular as ever in the early 1990's. In 1993, she released a Spanish-language album titled *Mi Tierra*. She continued to balance her Cuban traditional music with American popular music to create an authentically passionate sound all her own.

Esteves, Sandra María (b. May 10, 1948, New York, N.Y.): Novelist and poet. Esteves is a Puerto Rican poet and artist who was born and reared in New York City. Esteves is one of the few women to emerge with significant artistic reputations from New York City's Puerto Rican cultural re-awakening of the 1970's. Traveling in both Puerto Rican literary and artistic circles, Esteves established herself as a leading figure of her cultural group. She was part of "El Grupo" (the group), an artists' collective that used art as a form of social activism.

For a short while, Esteves lived in Puerto Rico, where her sense of ethnic pride was heightened. Upon returning to the United States, she began writing poetry and became a social activist. As a child, Esteves mediated between the English-speaking dominant society and her Spanish-speaking household. Her work reflects the strains and successes of bicultural living. Although bilingual, Esteves writes and publishes in

English, giving her a wider potential audience than some of her contemporaries. Her work also focuses on two other main issues: identity and gender constraints.

Her volumes of poetry include *Yerba Buena* (1980), which was selected as the best small-press publication of 1981; *Tropical Rains: A Bilingual Downpour* (1984); and *Bluestown Mockingbird Mambo* (1990).

Estrada, Leobardo (b. May 6, 1945, El Paso, Tex.): Demographer. Estrada's areas of expertise include ethnic and racial demographic trends, particularly those of the Latino population. He was one of eight researchers selected to advise Secretary of Commerce Robert Mosbacher on adjustment of the 1990 census to reflect undercounting of Latinos. Estrada also drew the redistricting plan accepted by the court in *GARZA V. COUNTY OF LOS ANGELES, CALIFORNIA BOARD OF SUPERVISORS*. In that case, the county was ordered to redraw district boundaries to create a district in which election of a Latino board member was likely if votes were cast according to racial and ethnic identification. Estrada's was one of several competing redistricting maps. Estrada has also worked on redistricting for various school boards and cities, along with helping to develop the plan proposed by the MEXICAN AMERICAN LEGAL DEFENSE AND EDUCATION FUND (MALDEF) for redefining congressional districts following the 1990 census.

Estrada has served in numerous consulting roles, including work with the SOUTHWEST VOTER REGISTRATION AND EDUCATION PROJECT, the state of California, and various public and private research institutes. He was a member of the Christopher Commission, which investigated the Los Angeles Police Department following the 1991 beating of Rodney King. Acquittal of the police officers who beat King touched off rioting in Los Angeles in 1992.

Estrada joined the faculty of the University of California, Los Angeles, in 1977. Prior to that, he held academic positions at the University of North Texas, the University of Texas at El Paso, and the University of Michigan at Ann Arbor. He received his B.A. (1966) from Baylor University and his M.S. (1968) and Ph.D. (1970) from Florida State University. He has published widely on demographic issues.

Estrada Palma, Tomás (July 9, 1835, near Bayamo, Cuba—Nov. 14, 1908, Oriente Province, Cuba): Political leader. Estrada Palma fought for Cuban independence during the Ten Years' War (1868-1878) and headed the Cuban government-in-exile that was estab-

lished in New York, New York, after that conflict. Unlike his compatriot José MARTÍ, who perceived the United States negatively, Estrada Palma favored annexation. He was fluent in English and was a naturalized U.S. citizen.

The U.S. government saw Estrada Palma as an ideal candidate to become the first elected president of Cuba in 1902. He was very popular at the beginning of his presidency, but he could not stand up to the domestic political factions. His first term as president witnessed the expansion of U.S. economic interests in Cuba.

Estrada Palma rigged the 1905 presidential elections to obtain a second term. When the opposition rebelled, Estrada Palma called for U.S. intervention under the PLATT AMENDMENT and resigned his post. He left the island in September, 1906.

Estrada Palma's presidency set the tone of Cuban politics and economics for the next fifty years. These patterns contributed to the rise of Fidel CASTRO and the 1959 CUBAN REVOLUTION.

Ethnic identity: Ethnic identity is a synthesis of language, geographic origins, religion, shared traditions, values, symbols, literature, folklore, music, food preferences, and race. Ethnic identity is strongly connected to a belief in cultural distinctiveness. People come to believe that they are different from other individuals and groups and are perceived by other individuals and groups as being different.

Ethnicity is also a social phenomenon. Ethnic identity can be formed from one's relationship to the economic and political institutions of a society and is often manifested through residential and occupational concentration. The meaning of ethnic identity is not fixed: It is constantly emerging and undergoing reformulation.

Terminology. A variety of labels, such as Hispanics, CHICANOS, and LATINOS, are used in everyday conversation to describe Spanish-speaking people. The English-language term "HISPANIC" has been used to identify persons of Mexican, Puerto Rican, Dominican, Cuban, and Central and South American background. The term stems from the word "Hispania," the ancient Roman name for Spain. The terms "Hispanic" and "Latino" refer to people who trace their ancestry to the Iberian Peninsula.

Chicanos are people of Mexican origin or descent. "Chicano" is a politically charged word, according to sociologist Alfredo Mirandé. He points out that the term "Hispanic" denies the Indian heritage of Chicanos while emphasizing their Spanish or European heri-

Flags displayed at a New York City parade show Cuban American spectators' ethnic identification. (Richard B. Levine)

tage. The term "Chicano" includes the indio/mestizo roots of Mexican people. Use of the term expanded significantly in the 1960's.

"Hispanic" and "Latino" are collective labels used to describe Spanish-speaking people. Sociologist Felix Padilla proposes that Latino ethnicity emerges from the combination of shared cultural (language) and structural (institutional inequality) similarities among Spanish-speaking people. The term "Latino" implies a collective ethnic group identity versus a more narrow ethnic identity based solely on country of origin. Latino ethnic identity assumes an identification with a language group, and Latino ethnic mobilization represents the result of interaction among Spanish-speaking groups.

Sociologist Edward Murguia indicates that one of the major differences between the terms "Latino" and "Hispanic" is that the former term incorporates persons from Portugal and Brazil; the latter term excludes them. (It should be noted that Murguia's definitions are not universally agreed upon.) Neither term identifies a connection with African heritage. "Latino" emphasizes cultural pluralism, while "Hispanic" emphasizes assimilation. The concept of "Hispanic" implies more accommodation concerning economic integration into mainstream society, while "Latino" emphasizes maintaining cultural and ethnic distinctiveness from mainstream Anglo society. The term "Latino" is used more frequently in California and on the East Coast of the United States, while "Hispanic" is more prevalent in the Southwest.

Measuring Ethnic Identity. Data from the 1980 U.S. census reveal that 14.6 million persons identified themselves as being of Hispanic origin. Self-identified Hispanics represented 6.4 percent of the United States population in 1980. Persons of Mexican, Puerto Rican, Cuban, and Central and South American origin constituted approximately 86 percent of that Hispanic population. By 1990, the Hispanic population had grown to 9.0 percent of the U.S. population. Chicanos constituted 60 percent of Hispanics, Puerto Ricans 12 percent, and Cubans 5 percent. The Bureau of the Census projected that by 2010, 14 percent of the U.S. population would be Hispanic, increasing to approximately 23 percent in 2050. It was estimated by the bureau that Hispanics would surpass African Americans as the nation's largest ethnic minority group in the year 2010.

Racial Group, Ethnic Group, and Minority Group. These terms are often used to categorize Hispanics/Latinos. Sociologist Joe R. Feagin defines a racial group as "a social group that persons inside or outside the group have decided is important to single out as inferior or superior, typically on the basis of real or alleged physical characteristics subjectively selected." Physical characteristics include such traits as skin color, hair and eye color, and hair texture. Hispanics/Latinos are not a racial group; they are black, white, and Amerindian. Most Hispanics are white, although larger percentages of Puerto Ricans and Cubans are racially mixed.

Feagin defines an ethnic group as "a group socially distinguished or set apart, by others or by itself, primarily on the basis of cultural or nationality characteristics." Hispanics/Latinos are an ethnic group. As discussed earlier, "Hispanic" and "Latino" are collective labels used to describe Spanish-speaking people from a variety of national origins and cultural backgrounds.

A subordinate group is one distinguished by physical or cultural traits; its members typically are socially disadvantaged as a result of unequal treatment through prejudice and discrimination by the dominant or majority group. The majority group has more power in the society. Minority groups and ethnic groups are not variants of one another, although some ethnic groups are considered to be minority groups. Cuban Americans are seldom identified as a minority group in the United States, but Mexican Americans and Puerto Ricans are frequently identified as minority groups.

Similarities and Differences Among Latinos. Significant socioeconomic diversity exists among the three major Hispanic groups. When compared to CUBAN AMERICANS, MEXICAN AMERICANS and PUERTO RICANS have fewer years of schooling. Of the three groups, Cuban Americans have the highest incomes, followed by Mexican Americans and Puerto Ricans. Next to Native Americans, Puerto Ricans are the poorest minority group in the United States. Puerto Ricans have the highest level of English language proficiency of the three groups. Cuban immigrants are less proficient in use of the English language but are better off economically. Among those born outside the United States, self-employment is higher among Cuban Americans than among Mexican Americans and Puerto Ricans living in the United States. Rates of self-employment are similar for Cuban Americans and Mexican Americans born in the United States, while U.S.-born Puerto Ricans are rarely self-employed. Cubans have experienced higher levels of cultural assimilation than have Mexicans and Puerto Ricans as a result of their socioeconomic success and position in the middle class. Foreign-born Hispanics retain their Spanish-speaking

Factory workers of the 1930's identify with their heritage using a parade float. (Security Pacific Collection, Los Angeles Public Library)

abilities at a much higher rate than do Hispanics born in the United States. Among those born in the United States, persons of Mexican and Puerto Rican background have a higher Spanish-language retention rate than those of Cuban background.

The two most disadvantaged groups, Mexican Americans and Puerto Ricans, identify themselves as members of an ethnic group at higher rates than do Cuban Americans. Research by sociologists Candace Nelson and Marta Tienda indicates that ethnic identity is created by the relationship of a national-origin group to the system of production, in particular labor market conditions. This relationship is influenced and shaped by the time of immigration, how each group was received, and the race of those immigrating.

Pan-Ethnic Identity Versus National Identity. Spanish-speaking people may choose to identify themselves under the rubric of the pan-ethnic labels "Hispanic" and "Latino" rather than on the basis of their ancestral country of origin. The most important advantage of doing so, according to sociologists Murguia and Padilla, is group size. The larger the ethnic population, the more political strength it has. A second advantage is that national-origin groups face similar sociopolitical and socioeconomic issues. Political alliances can promote the shared agenda of these groups. A third advantage is that a pan-ethnic identity can incorporate immigrants from Central and South America. These people are often neglected because of their small numbers. Allying themselves with the three larger groups gives them a voice and representation.

There are some advantages as well for retaining a national identity. First, there might be important political issues that affect only one group. For example, Murguia indicates that Mexican Americans are much more concerned about immigration legislation than are Puerto Ricans. Puerto Ricans are citizens of the United States and are less worried about this particular issue. Second, there are cultural differences between groups. Third, the groups are geographically quite diverse.

Mexican Americans are concentrated primarily in the southwestern United States, Puerto Ricans in the northeast, and Cuban Americans in the southeast.

—*William L. Smith*

SUGGESTED READINGS:

• Abalos, David T. *Latinos in the United States: The Sacred and the Political*. Notre Dame, Ind.: University of Notre Dame Press, 1986. Discusses models (traditional, assimilationist, the fragmented, and the transforming) for explaining everyday life of Latinos.

• Barrera, Mario. *Beyond Aztlan: Ethnic Autonomy in Comparative Perspective*. Notre Dame, Ind.: University of Notre Dame Press, 1990. Presents a history of the development of Chicano ethnic goals and argues that the struggle for cultural survival is being lost as a result of the effects of assimilation.

• Bean, Frank D., and Marta Tienda. *The Hispanic Population of the United States*. New York: Russell Sage Foundation, 1987. This volume is one of a series describing and analyzing major changes and trends in the United States based on the wealth of information provided by the 1980 census and other national data. Highly recommended. One of the most important resources for social science literature on Hispanics/Latinos.

• Blea, Irene I. *Toward a Chicano Social Science*. New York: Praeger, 1988. Presents an overview of Mexican Americans in the United States by examining their culture, values, social institutions, and relationships with Anglo society.

• Boswell, Thomas D., and James R. Curtis. *The Cuban-American Experience: Culture, Images, and Perspectives*. Totowa, N.J.: Rowman & Allanheld, 1983. Examines the major social, economic, political, and geographical issues affecting Cuban Americans.

• Chávez, Linda. *Out of the Barrio: Toward a New Politics of Hispanic Assimilation*. New York: Basic Books, 1991. Tells the story of the progress and achievement of Hispanics in the United States. The author encourages Hispanics to adopt a new politics of assimilation.

• Feagin, Joe R., and Clairece Booher Feagin. *Racial and Ethnic Relations*. 4th ed. Englewood Cliffs, N.J.: Prentice Hall, 1992. An important source for literature on racial and ethnic groups. See chapter 9 (Mexican Americans) and chapter 10 (Puerto Ricans and Cubans).

• Keefe, Susan E., and Amado M. Padilla. *Chicano Ethnicity*. Albuquerque: University of New Mexico Press, 1987. The authors create a multidimensional model of ethnicity that incorporates change and continuity, integration and pluralism. Their findings do not support the acculturation-assimilation model.

• Mirandé, Alfredo. *The Chicano Experience: An Alternative Perspective*. Notre Dame, Ind.: University of Notre Dame Press, 1985. Mirandé argues that the acculturation-assimilation model is inappropriate for Chicanos. He offers fourteen components of an emerging perspective on Chicano sociology.

• Padilla, Felix M. *Latino Ethnic Consciousness: The Case of Mexican Americans and Puerto Ricans in Chicago*. Notre Dame, Ind.: University of Notre Dame Press, 1985. Discusses the development of a collective Hispanic/Latino ethnic identity. A Latino ethnic identity is created out of the social interaction of at least two Spanish-speaking groups. Probably the single best reference on Latino ethnic identity.

Evangelicalism: Usually applied to groups of Protestants, Evangelicalism refers to people's perception of themselves as preservers of belief in the authority of the Bible and in other traditional Christian teachings and lifestyles that are being abandoned by modern churches (*see* PROTESTANTISM).

General Features. Most Evangelicals speak of being "born again" and believe in the virgin birth, deity, and imminent return of Jesus Christ. Most Evangelicals also believe that society ought to be ruled by biblical principles. Evangelicals usually distinguish themselves from groups such as the Jehovah's Witnesses, the Mormons, and the Seventh-day Adventists, which are perceived to be unorthodox in some central teachings. Conservative strains of Evangelicalism (for example, fundamentalism) may be strongly anti-Catholic. The foremost representatives of American Evangelicals have included Charles Colson, Jerry Falwell, Billy Graham, Carl F. Henry, and Pat Robertson.

Among Hispanics. Evangelicalism gained much ground among Hispanics in the late twentieth century. Pollster George Gallup, who uses the "born-again" experience as a litmus test to identify Evangelicals, estimates that 6 percent of American Evangelicals are Hispanics and that Evangelicals constitute the vast majority of the 18 percent of Hispanics who are Protestants. In some surveys, 19.4 percent of Cuban Americans have been reported to consider themselves "born-again," along with 35.7 percent of Puerto Ricans and 29.0 percent of Mexican Americans, even though the proportion of self-professed Hispanic Protestants can be much less. This disparity indicates that the "born-again" criterion must be used with great caution in identifying Hispanic Evangelicals.

These Salvadoran Americans attending an Evangelical wedding service wear their white veils even when not at religious observances. (Impact Visuals, Donna DeCesare)

One of the major strains of Evangelicalism among Hispanics is Pentecostalism, which stresses that the miracles and other supernatural phenomena (for example, speaking in tongues, faith healing, and Holy Spirit baptism) depicted in early Christianity are still achievable and should be actively cultivated. In New York City, Pentecostal Puerto Ricans reportedly outnumber all other Protestant Puerto Ricans combined. Many Puerto Rican Pentecostal churches, particularly the Assembly of Christian Churches, are independent of any larger Anglo denomination.

The educational achievement of Evangelicals resembles that of Protestant Hispanics (average of 11.3 years). Many Evangelical denominations consider the training of Hispanic ministers to be very important in their efforts to evangelize Hispanics. The graduate-level School of Theology of the Church of God (Cleveland, Tennessee) has produced more than one hundred graduates since 1979. In one fourteen-year period, 43 percent of the Hispanic graduates in the Church of God School of Theology were Puerto Rican, 18 percent were Mexican, and 9 percent were Guatemalan.

Several important Evangelical publishing houses cater to Latinos. Editorial Evangélica, affiliated with the Church of God, publishes a magazine for the Latino segment of the denomination. Editorial Caribe, based in Miami, publishes books in Spanish for Latino Evangelicals living in the United States and Latin America. Life Publishing (Assemblies of God) in Miami is perhaps the largest publisher of Spanish religious materials in North America.

Most well-known televangelists (for example, Pat Robertson and Jerry Falwell) are Evangelicals, and such preachers have a small but loyal Hispanic audience. Morris Cerullo, a televangelist based in San Diego, specifically targets Latin Americans. Most Hispanic televangelists operate at local levels in such cities as Phoenix, Los Angeles, and Boston.

Notable Hispanic Evangelicals include Reies López Tijerina, a Pentecostal minister famous for his battle to regain ancestral Mexican lands lost to the United States in 1848. Maria Atkinson (d. 1963), a Mexican American from Douglas, Arizona, founded a number of Pentecostal missions in Arizona and is the founder of the Church of God (Cleveland, Tennessee) in Mexico, one of the largest Pentecostal denominations in

Activist Reies López Tijerina is one of the more noted Latino Evangelicals. (AP/Wide World Photos)

that country. Nicky Cruz, the Puerto Rican author of a celebrated autobiography (*Run, Baby, Run*, 1968), has achieved much recognition even among Anglo Evangelicals.

Reasons for Conversion. The reasons for conversion to Evangelicalism, and to Pentecostalism in particular, are as complex as the reasons for conversion to Protestantism. Although some sociologists have suggested that conversion to Pentecostalism may be linked to social maladjustments, Vivian Garrison has concluded that Hispanic Pentecostals are no more socially or economically maladjusted than are members of more traditional churches. Pentecostal Evangelicalism can also be seen as an alternative health-care system. Its emphasis on immediate healing attracts those who have little access to proper health care or who are dissatisfied with conventional medicine. Many Catholic converts (for example, Maria Atkinson) to Pentecostalism specifically cite health problems as an initial motive for joining or visiting Pentecostal churches.

Problems and the Future. Many of the problems and trends among Hispanic Evangelicals are similar to those of Hispanic Protestants. Yet Hispanic Evangelicals are not monolithic. Although some Hispanic Evangelicals remain staunchly anti-Catholic, others form political coalitions with Catholics with whom they share unifying features (for example, a growing number of Pentecostal Catholics and ecumenical Protestant Pentecostals). Some Hispanic Evangelicals object to the ordination of women, but other strains (particularly Pentecostalism) have a long tradition of female ministers.

Anglo Evangelical groups have attempted to build coalitions with Hispanic Evangelicals in order to advance political agendas on such issues as abortion, sex education, and creationism in schools. In contrast to earlier years, much of the growth among Hispanic Evangelicals in the United States in the 1980's and 1990's came from immigrants who have converted in Latin America. In some surveys, for example, 25 percent of Hondurans who immigrate to the United States are non-Catholic, and the majority of those are probably Evangelical. In general, the study of Hispanic Evangelicals is one of the most promising endeavors in sociology, anthropology, and religious studies.

—*Hector Ignacio Avalos*

Suggested Readings: • Avalos, Hector. "Who Is Morris Cerullo?" *Free Inquiry* 14 (Winter, 1993): 7. • Calderon, Wilfredo. "Educación." *El Evangelio* 48 (April, 1993): 18-21. • Gallup, George, and Jim Castelli. *The People's Religion: American Faith in the Nineties.* New York: Macmillan, 1989. • Garrison, Vivian. "Sectarianism and Psychological Adjustment: A Controlled Comparison of Puerto Rican Pentecostals and Catholics." In *Religious Movements in Contemporary America*, edited by Irving I. Zaretsky and Mark P. Leone. Princeton, N.J.: Princeton University Press, 1974. • Gonzalez, Roberto O., and Michael La Velle. *The Hispanic Catholic in the United States: A Socio-Cultural and Religious Profile.* New York: Northeast Catholic Pastoral Center for Hispanics, 1985. • Greeley, Andrew. "Defection Among Hispanics." *America* 159 (July 30, 1988): 61-62. • Montoya, Alex D. *Hispanic Ministry in North America.* Grand Rapids, Mich.: Ministry Resources Library, 1987. • Sandoval, Moises. *On the Move: A History of the Hispanic Church in the United States.* Maryknoll, N.Y.: Orbis Books, 1990.

Evelina Lopez Antonetty Puerto Rican Research Collection (New York, N.Y.): This collection is part of the Centro de Estudios Puertorriqueños at Hunter College, City University, New York. The Centro Library and its archives are the preeminent collection related to Puerto Ricans in the United States. The library's mission is to document Puerto Rican history comprehensively and to make available the cultural and intellectual production of Puerto Ricans in Puerto Rico and in the United States. The library houses a rich diversity of materials on Puerto Rican history, migration, culture, the arts, education, and language. The library has collected and microfilmed many of the major Puerto Rican newspapers on the mainland. The library has an archival program to identify, collect, preserve, and make available primary sources that relate to the history of the Puerto Rican community in the United States. The archives include the papers of Puerto Rican activist Jesús Colón and primary documents on Pedro Albizu Campos. In addition, the archives house the records of the Puerto Rican Legal Defense and Education Fund, a civil rights organization. The library has published several important bibliographic guides on Puerto Ricans in the United States and has contributed to major exhibitions and documentaries.

Extended voluntary departure: Immigration term. The Immigration and Naturalization Service (INS) began the extended voluntary departure policy in the early 1950's just prior to the initiation of Operation Wetback in 1954. The INS presented a new policy toward undocumented immigrants that involved helping them achieve legal status. These friendly overtures encouraged many immigrants to register their names in this new program. Undocumented people signed papers agreeing to leave the United States at some point but were given permisos, or permits, to stay and work in the country. Once Operation Wetback got under way in 1954, the INS sent out letters to those who had been given permisos, telling them to come in to the INS office. Subsequently, many were given "baggage letters" informing them that they and their families had thirty days to pack their bags and leave the country.

F

Fábregas, Virginia (1870, Yautepec, Mexico—Nov. 18, 1950, New York, N.Y.): Actor and manager. The daughter of a Mexican mother and Spanish father, Fábregas earned her teaching credential in 1890 and taught at a school for deaf mutes. Theatrical managers became interested in her after she gave a monologue at a charity show, and she made her stage debut on April 30, 1892. She made her first of six tours to Spain in 1904, and hers was one of the first Mexican troupes to visit the United States, touring through El Paso as early as 1899.

Fábregas became a leading theatrical manager in Los Angeles during the 1920's and 1930's. She was known for her productions of Mexican and European dramatic works, in which she generally starred, and for her encouragement of local Mexican American playwrights. A leading company of the period, her troupe played many Los Angeles theaters and toured as far as Guam, Spain, Argentina, and the Philippines.

Fábregas retired to Mexico City in 1933 and continued staging plays at the Teatro Fábregas, built for her by her husband. In the late 1930's, she returned to Hollywood to star in Spanish-language features. In 1945, she was decorated with the Mexican Medal of Civic Merit. Fábregas' son, Manuel Sánchez Navarro, became a successful film actor.

Fages, Doña Eulalia (Eulalia de Callis;?, Spain—?, Spain): Wife of a California governor. Doña Eulalia Fages was the wife of Pedro Fages, a Spanish governor of Alta California. Eulalia joined her husband there in 1782, during his second term as governor. Eulalia Fages was a generous woman who possessed both a fiery temper and great love for her husband. Her generosity was shown in many cases. The most famous of these was her 1882 trip to Monterey, her husband's capital city. Noting poverty and nakedness all around her, Eulalia reportedly gave away most of her clothing. Once resident in Monterey, she continued to perform charitable works.

Eulalia's fiery nature was shown in late 1784. She decided to return to Spain, but her husband did not agree with her decision. She banished him from their home for three months. In 1785, convinced that he was philandering during this banishment, she vowed to divorce him. Eventually reconciled with her husband, who was innocent of infidelity, Eulalia schemed and pestered Fages until he agreed to return to Spain. After their return to Spain, she disappeared from recorded history.

Fair Employment Practices Committee: Government agency. This committee was established by President Franklin D. Roosevelt in 1941 to protect workers from discrimination in private companies that held government contracts. President Roosevelt appointed Carlos E. Castañeda to the committee as a special assistant with expertise on the concerns of Mexican Americans. The committee had the power to investigate charges of discrimination and to take measures to eliminate any discrimination that was discovered. The committee was dissolved after World War II, but some states created similar agencies. In 1964, the United States Congress created the Equal Employment Opportunity Commission, modeled after the Fair Employment Practices Committee.

Fair Labor Standards Act (1938): Law establishing a minimum wage. Congress established a minimum wage of twenty-five cents per hour through this act. Although it did little to improve the collective bargaining power of minority workers, the law particularly affected the employment standards faced by low-skilled and migrant workers, many of whom were Latinos.

Fajita: Beef skirt steak, usually broiled, then finished in a hot pan with lime juice. In Texas and northern Mexico, a fajita is the flavorful skirt steak of beef; the usual synonym in the rest of Mexico is *arrachera*. To make this cut tender, it usually is broiled (preferably over mesquite), then dumped into a hot, dry pan and splashed with lime juice for the final cooking. The result usually is cut into strips (the word "fajita" means "little belt") and used as a filling for tacos or other ANTOJITOS. Fajitas were discovered by the rest of the United States in the 1980's, and they are widely available in American restaurants, usually served with sautéed onions.

Falcon, Angelo (b. Bayamón, Puerto Rico): Political activist and researcher. Falcon was graduated by Columbia College and the State University of New York at Albany, which named him the 1991 Distinguished Alumnus of the Department of Political Science. He founded the INSTITUTE FOR PUERTO RICAN POLICY and served as its president. The institute, based in New York City, is a nonpartisan, nonprofit center focusing on issues of interest to Puerto Ricans and members of other Latino communities. The institute's mission is to educate the public and policymakers about Puerto Ricans and their interests, to measure the responsiveness of policymakers and other officials to the needs of Puerto Ricans, and to promote civic participation among Puerto Ricans.

Falcon also served as one of the principal investigators in the LATINO NATIONAL POLITICAL SURVEY, the largest social science examination of politics and trends among Latinos ever conducted in the United States. He has analyzed the impact of the Latino vote in local, state, and national elections in New York City.

Falero, Emilio (b. 1947, Sagua la Grande, Cuba): Painter. Falero has distinguished himself with finely detailed figurative paintings that have the look of Renaissance works. Falero's interest in art was sparked by an exhibit of colonial and modern paintings he saw in Cuba when he was fourteen years old. He learned much about painting by watching a Spanish priest in his hometown paint methodically for an hour each day. The priest's orderly painting style impressed him. In 1962, when Falero was only fifteen, he left Cuba for Miami, Florida, where he lived in a refugee camp for children.

Because he was familiar with the abstract art he saw on visits to museums in Miami, Falero's first works were abstract. Gradually he adopted a figurative style. In Barry College and later in Miami-Dade Community College in Florida, he studied painting, ceramics, and sculpture. He was exposed to and experimented with various styles of painting. Eventually, he achieved a unity of different styles.

Falero's best-known paintings feature the expressive faces of young women involved in tasks of daily life. Included in these works are *The Music Lesson* (1983) and *The Lace Maker* (1979), which depicts a girl absorbed in her handicraft.

FALN. *See* **Fuerzas Armadas de Liberación Nacional**

Family life: There is considerable agreement that the family unit transmits its own culture and socializes children into the family organization, community, and society. In the same way that there is no uniform mainstream American or African American family, there is no "Latino family" in the United States. Instead, there is a variety of Latino family structures and organizations. Family types are closely associated with such factors as time of entry and length of residency in the United States, regions of residence, socioeconomic and educational status, level of assimilation, age, and marital status.

Defining Family. The definition of "family" varies across societies and ethnic groups. In some societies, family units consist of parents and offspring, whether biological or adopted. In others, the family is extended to include blood relatives (grandparents, aunts, uncles, and cousins), godparents, and fictive kin (unrelated individuals who have been adopted informally as family members). The value placed on family and individual family members varies as well. In some societies, a competitive model of child rearing emphasizes individual members and their personal success. Other societies use the cooperative model, in which each member is taught to work toward fulfilling the needs and desires of the entire family.

Traditionally, Latino families have been of extended forms, including relatives in addition to the nuclear family of parents and children. Educational opportunities, changes in socioeconomic status, and geographic mobility have contributed to the growing trend toward nuclear families and single-parent households. For example, many nuclear families and individuals left extended families and migrated alone to the United States. Families residing in the United States, pressured by economic conditions, began allowing family members to leave home in search of better jobs. As evidence of this trend, the 1990 census indicated that 23.8 percent of Latino households were headed by single women and 6.8 percent by single men.

Differences Among Latinos. To understand family life among Latinos, differences and commonalities among Latino subgroups should be examined. A label such as "Latino" implies that an ethnic group is homogeneous. That is, Latinos are assumed to share historical background, culture, migration experiences, and family values. Although Latino families are united by several specific cultural values, their attitudes and perspectives toward the United States vary based on whether they entered American society voluntarily or involuntarily.

Migration and Absorption Experiences. Many families moved to the United States more or less voluntarily, for socioeconomic or political reasons. They may have suffered prejudice and discrimination in the United States, but many of them saw the chance for a better life than was possible in their homeland.

Latino families tend to take extended forms, with members of several generations maintaining close contact. (James Shaffer)

In contrast, many Mexican American, Native American, and African American families can be classified as castelike minorities. They have been incorporated into the fabric of American society involuntarily and permanently through slavery, conquest, and colonization. Historically, these minority groups have been relegated to low status in the United States. The fact that they were victims of conquest of various sorts cast a shroud of inferiority on them. Even members of these groups who arrived in the United States long after the period of conquest and official domination have been unable to escape stereotyping and prejudices. These different migration and absorption experiences have contributed to diverse Latino family behaviors, attitudes, and perspectives toward U.S. society.

Mexican American Families. Mexican Americans have had a unique historical experience on the North American continent. They are not necessarily new-comers to the geographic area of the United States; their Indian ancestors are believed to have occupied the Americas beginning in 30,000 B.C.E. The Mexican people are the product of the combination of Native American and European (predominantly Spanish) peoples. They are the MESTIZO people, a blend of races and cultures fused to form a new Mexican culture.

Mexicans retained certain aspects of Indian and Spanish family life as they adapted to the conquest of the Spaniards, freedom from Spain, conquest by the United States, and harsh economic realities in the United States that tested the resilience of Mexican American families. Mexican and Mexican American family life reflects many of the family values of Native American ancestors, such as a strong emphasis on family, kinship, and neighborhood relationships. Traditionally, married children remained close to their parents' home, maintained close ties with the family unit, and actively participated in rearing the children of their siblings. Grandparents were the ultimate authority in the extended family and were respected profoundly. Children commonly were reared jointly by the parents, older siblings, relatives, and villagers. Children were treated with respect and taught to have reverence for their elders.

The Spanish converted many of the natives to Catholicism. The Indians began baptizing their children and giving them godparents (PADRINOS), who were responsible for child-rearing duties in the absence of the parents. COMPADRAZGO (coparenthood) established social ties with people outside the blood-related family and incorporated them into the extended family.

In pre-Hispanic societies such as the Mayan, women represented fertility and were a vital pillar of the social structure. Native religions associated women with the elements of fire, warmth, earth, and darkness. Men were associated with air, water, and rain. Males and females were seen as divine twins, separate entities but part of a whole.

The Spanish reigned for three centuries in what is now Mexico, the southwestern United States, Central America north of Panama, the West Indies, and the Philippines. During this time, elements of their culture such as language, surnames, and Catholicism became integral parts of Mexican culture.

The Spanish saw that women were a vital part of the family and community structure of the native people. Spanish culture venerated the male as a strong protector. This value entered Mexican societies and evolved into MACHISMO.

U.S. Influences. Many Mexicans were separated from their extended families as a result of Texas' independence from Mexico (1836) and the MEXICAN AMERICAN WAR (1846-1848). In an attempt to colonize the Southwest, the Mexican government had allowed settlers from the United States into Texas and other regions of the Southwest. In 1836, these settlers and a few Mexicans declared their independence from Mexico, dividing the Mexican people geographically, but not culturally.

In 1846, the United States declared war on Mexico. By the TREATY OF GUADALUPE HIDALGO, which ended the war, the United States acquired about half of Mexico's territory. The Rio Grande became the official border dividing the two countries. An estimated seventy-five thousand Mexicans were given the choice of leaving their land to move to what remained of Mexican territory or staying on their land and becoming U.S. citizens. Most chose to stay, further separating the Mexi-

can people geographically. Those caught on the U.S. side of the border were able to maintain their unique heritage and culture and maintain close ties with their extended families in Mexico.

As a whole, families of Mexican heritage have remained united by strong historical, cultural, and family ties, but they differ in terms of their migratory experiences. Families on the north side of the Rio Grande at the end of the Mexican American War were, in a sense, involuntarily woven into the fabric of American society. In contrast, some Mexican families residing on the south side of the border, pressured by harsh economic and political conditions in Mexico, voluntarily migrated into the United States.

Discriminatory treatment of Mexicans who remained in the United States after 1848 has been documented. Traditional sociologists and historians such as Rodolfo ACUÑA argue that Mexican American family life was nearly destroyed as a result of the atrocities committed by U.S. soldiers and the U.S. government. Mexicans were lynched, land was stolen from Mexicans, and Mexican women were raped. These negative experiences were revisited through storytelling and documentation across generations. As a result, the past was transmitted to the children and ingrained in the culture.

The Twentieth Century. For many twentieth century Mexican immigrants and their families, life in the United States has been better than the life they had in their homeland. Although they recognize prejudice and discrimination, they have contended that as newcomers they have no choice but to tolerate it. Some researchers have found that, unlike castelike minorities brought into the United States by conquest, first-generation Mexican immigrant families may not have had time to internalize the effects of their negative experiences in the United States. As a result, the effects of discrimination have not become part of their culture.

Mexican American families, particularly first-generation immigrants, have adopted attitudes and behaviors that help them overcome cultural, language, and other barriers in pursuing a better life in the United States. They perceive educational credentials to be important for social advancement. Educating children is perceived as an investment for the entire family.

Unlike Mexican American children from long-established families, children of more recent immigrants have been taught not only to accept school rules of behavior but also to ignore discrimination or mistreatment because of the fear of being deported or

Mexican American families have adopted many of the characteristics of mainstream Anglo families. (James Shaffer)

labeled as rebellious. Well into the twentieth century, the fear of deportation was based in reality even for people with valid residency or citizenship status. The U.S. government in several cases rounded up people who "looked Mexican" and transported them across the Mexican border.

Puerto Rican Families. Puerto Rican individuals and families generally have come to the United States for employment opportunities. Puerto Ricans migrated to New York in large numbers during the early part of the twentieth century. Puerto Rico had become a U.S. territory following the SPANISH-AMERICAN WAR (1898), but it was not until 1917 that Puerto Ricans were granted U.S. citizenship and were permitted to migrate between Puerto Rico and the United States without restrictions. Citizenship status, low-priced air transportation between Puerto Rico and New York City, and family ties between the island and the mainland encouraged large-scale migration of Puerto Ricans to the continental United States. Puerto Ricans usually migrated as families; in some cases, the father moved first and then brought the family when he had established a home and a job.

In Puerto Rican families, both parents have the same status in some aspects of family life. Establishing a family is an important goal and is taken as a serious responsibility. Family membership includes being part of an extended family as well as part of the nuclear family. The extended families include several generations of blood relatives and close friends.

In both nuclear and extended families, children are loved and cherished, and protecting children is a top priority. Children are taught to respect their parents and other adults. Independence is curtailed, and adherence to parental and family demands is encouraged.

For some Puerto Rican families, mobility and the search for economic security have resulted in severance of the extended family relationships. In the 1990's, nuclear families living in the United States appeared to rely less on extended families did than their island counterparts. One possible explanation is that mainland Puerto Ricans were becoming more economically secure and adopting a family organization pattern closer to the nuclear lifestyle common in the United States.

Puerto Rican extended families often live in a single house or in the same neighborhood. Relatives are visited frequently, and strong support exchanges are maintained, keeping any nuclear family from isolating itself. The stereotyped belief that Puerto Rican extended families live together is exaggerated, at least for mainland families. One study found that in the United States, only one-fifth of Puerto Rican extended families shared housing, primarily in response to economic conditions.

Gender Roles. Puerto Rican women traditionally have been reared to provide love and affection, not punishment. They have been expected to be submissive, passive, and selfless, and to devote their lives to the maintenance of a good home and family. Men have been reared to be respectful and submissive to adults during their childhood years but were expected to be active, restless, daring, and more independent than females. As adults, they have been expected to adopt beliefs in MACHISMO and *MARIANISMO*, dictating male and female roles. Parents were more likely to forgive males than females for disobedience.

Males have been expected to be the sole providers for the home and their wives. Traditionally, spouses shared few activities. Traditional Puerto Rican marriages, dominated by the husband, have tended to be stable.

Changes in Family Life Structures. Two important changes in family structure are worth noting. First, the number of Puerto Rican female-headed households in the United States increased in the late twentieth century. This was true of other Latino groups as well. Women were expected to be nurturing and loving as well as being disciplinarians in the family. This change in parenting role, along with the burden of dealing with other household matters, resulted in many women experiencing stress-related health problems.

Second, studies of middle- to lower-middle-income Puerto Rican families on the mainland have found that Puerto Rican fathers of the late twentieth century did not fit the stereotype of being distant, avoiding intimacy, and being uninvolved with nurturing of young children. Although mothers were still the primary caregivers, Puerto Rican fathers were found to spend a considerable amount of time as caregivers, with their daughters as well as with their sons.

Cuban American Families. The Cuban presence in the United States is more recent than that of Mexican Americans and Puerto Ricans. Although Cuban communities in Florida and New York existed as early as the 1870's, the largest numbers of Cuban immigrants arrived in the United States shortly after the 1959 revolution led by Fidel CASTRO and during the 1980's. Initially, Cubans migrated to the United States for political reasons, because they did not share the political or philosophical views of the socialist revolution. Later, thousands fled Cuba because of economic hardships.

Puerto Rican women traditionally have been socialized to play certain roles in the family, but those roles are changing. (Hazel Hankin)

Typical of many Cuban American extended families, members of the Hector Diaz family in Miami arrived at different times: the nuclear family in 1967, after five years in Chicago; then Hector's sister-in-law early in 1970; and finally his grandmother three months later. (Library of Congress)

Most Cubans who left before and during the CUBAN REVOLUTION were from the middle and upper classes. Many brought substantial financial resources and skills. They were familiar with the business world of the United States and immediately established their own businesses.

Cuban families that came to the United States immediately after the revolution were mostly middle-class professionals and technicians, along with smaller numbers of skilled and semiskilled workers. This group, although of slightly lower socioeconomic status on average, also assimilated quickly.

In contrast, Cubans who entered the United States in the 1980's, particularly those who were part of the MARIEL BOAT LIFT of 1980, were mostly dark skinned, had lived under the socialist government, and were less skilled on average. Their transition into U.S. society was not as successful as that of earlier Cuban migrants.

Cuban American family life has received little attention from researchers. Most studies have focused on the similarities to and differences from members of other Latino subgroups in regard to education, economic conditions, migration, and success in the United States.

Cuban Americans have family structures and values similar to those of Mexican American, Puerto Rican, and Central and South American families. Extended families are common, and individuals are expected to establish and maintain a family. Children are considered a lifelong investment and are taught the value of respecting parents and other elders. Education is at the center of family life, because it means advancement and better economic opportunities.

Cubans also have a strong tradition of extended families. Although mobility from the island to the mainland has resulted in the severing of the extended family in many cases, a significant number of Cuban American families have maintained close ties with extended families on the island.

Gender Roles. Cuban women, like many other Latinas, traditionally have been reared to provide love and affection, not punishment, and to be submissive and devote their lives to the maintenance of the home. Men have been reared to protect the family, be the financial providers, and take the dominant role in the family.

Cuban Americans have undergone changes in the traditional gender roles after living in the United States for an extended period of time. For example, husbands in general have become comfortable with assuming part of the responsibility of childcare, and more women work outside the home. Some of these changes are the result of economic factors.

Central and South American Families. In the last quarter of the twentieth century, many families and individuals made their way into the United States from Central and South America. Many migrants left political or economic upheaval in their home countries. Others migrated in search of a better life for their families. Among these immigrants were many educated urban professionals, but the majority, particularly from Central America, were poor peasants and laborers with little or no formal education.

More than half of these immigrants were women, many of whom left their children behind to be cared for by relatives. Others were adolescents and young adults who came to find jobs to help support families in their homeland. Some immigrants came in complete nuclear families.

Many Central and South American immigrants of the 1980's and 1990's became employed as domestic, construction, and maintenance workers. They began forming multinational Latino communities, making it easier for relatives and friends to come to the United States. Latino communities became well established, so that most newcomers had at least one relative or friend living in the United States.

Central and South American families, like other Latino families, tended to gravitate toward communities populated by people from their home country. Members of the extended family living in the United States served as buffers between newly arrived immigrants and U.S. society, teaching the newcomers standards of behavior and methods of assimilating. Children were often the first to learn American ways, because they attended school and established friendships more quickly than did adults. As they learned the culture, traditions, values, and mores of the new country, they transmitted this knowledge to their families.

Central and South American families have migrated to the United States voluntarily. They tend to embrace American culture but not necessarily substitute it for their own. The dominant society has been respected because it offers better opportunities than are available in the homeland. As a result, people of Central and South American background have tended to become subordinate to the dominant, non-Hispanic white

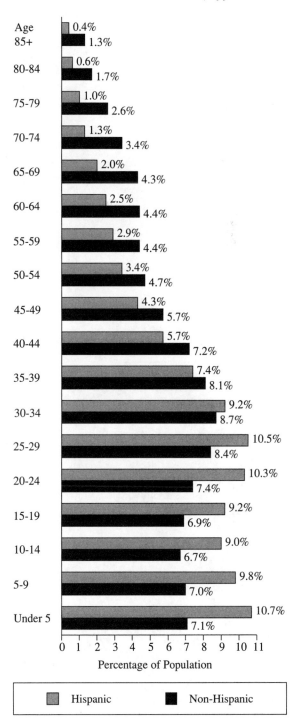

AGE OF THE POPULATION, 1990

Age	Hispanic	Non-Hispanic
Age 85+	0.4%	1.3%
80-84	0.6%	1.7%
75-79	1.0%	2.6%
70-74	1.3%	3.4%
65-69	2.0%	4.3%
60-64	2.5%	4.4%
55-59	2.9%	4.4%
50-54	3.4%	4.7%
45-49	4.3%	5.7%
40-44	5.7%	7.2%
35-39	7.4%	8.1%
30-34	9.2%	8.7%
25-29	10.5%	8.4%
20-24	10.3%	7.4%
15-19	9.2%	6.9%
10-14	9.0%	6.7%
5-9	9.8%	7.0%
Under 5	10.7%	7.1%

Percentage of Population

■ Hispanic   ■ Non-Hispanic

Source: Bureau of the Census, *1990 Census of Population and Housing* (Current Population Report Series P-20, No. 465) (Washington, D.C.: Bureau of the Census, 1991), p. 7.

A Salvadoran man and his child attend a 1994 rally in Washington, D.C., to support granting temporary protected status and permanent residency to immigrants. (Impact Visuals, Rick Reinhard)

group and have endured incidents of prejudice and discrimination because they believe they are "guests" in the country.

Parents have placed a strong emphasis on education for their children as a means of breaking the cycle of poverty established in their country of origin. Educated children with good jobs can also help support their parents who become unable to work.

Family Size and Fertility Rates. Between 1970 and 1990, the U.S. Latino population doubled, growing from about eleven million in 1970 to about twenty-two million in 1990, about 9 percent of the U.S. population. Projections from the early 1990's indicated that by the year 2050, Latinos would constitute 21 percent of the nation's population, making them the largest minority group in the country.

The high growth rates in the Latino population are the result of immigration and fertility factors. According to researchers, immigrants will continue coming to the United States to escape violence, political oppression, poor economic conditions, and unemployment in their native countries.

Latinos have experienced and will continue to experience high fertility rates. Data from the Bureau of the Census reported that 39 percent of all Latinos in the United States in 1988 were under the age of nineteen, a higher proportion than for other racial and ethnic groups. This large cohort both indicates that Latino families tend to have relatively large numbers of children and portends population growth in the future as these children grow up to have children of their own.

Historically, Latino families have tended to be larger then those of the general population in the United States. In 1992, for example, the average number of persons per Latino family was 3.8, compared to 3.1 for non-Latino families. One reason for the larger family size is the greater tendency to belong to the Roman Catholic church, which encourages large families and discourages birth control. Research has found that Latinas tend to bear more children, at younger ages, than other women in the United States. Latino families are twice as likely as other U.S. families to include three or more children.   *—Luz E. Gonzalez*

SUGGESTED READINGS:

• Abalos, David T. *The Latino Family and the Politics of Transformation.* Westport, Conn.: Praeger, 1993. Examines Latino family structures from the perspective of a theory of transformation. Discusses how life in American society can be in conflict with traditional roles of individual family members.

• Acuña, Rodolfo. *Occupied America: A History of Chicanos.* 3d ed. New York: Harper & Row, 1988. Traces the history of Mexican Americans in the United States, beginning with the American invasion of Mexico in the mid-1830's. Special attention is given to the nature of the relationship between Anglos and Chicanos over time.

• Ambert, Alba N., and Maria D. Alvarez, eds. *Puerto Rican Children on the Mainland: Interdisciplinary Perspectives.* New York: Garland, 1992. Twelve scholarly essays from various disciplines that refute negative myths that have emerged as a result of deficit models used to study Puerto Ricans.

• McLemore, S. Dale. *Racial and Ethnic Relations in America.* 3d ed. Boston: Allyn and Bacon, 1991. The author suggests that in order to understand intergroup relations, the sociological analysis of intergroup processes and the history of racial and ethnic groups in the United States need to be examined.

• Ready, Timothy. *Latino Immigrant Youth: Passages from Adolescence to Adulthood.* New York: Garland, 1991. Highlights a longitudinal study that maps the lives of one group of Latino immigrants who attended a Washington, D.C., high school during the 1980's. Illustrates how despite financial, cultural, linguistic, and political obstacles, these students made good use of social networks and succeeded in the United States.

Family life—Spanish borderlands: The Spanish borderlands, as the term most commonly is used, refers to the northern frontier of the viceroyalty of NEW SPAIN. There were three major enclaves—California, New Mexico, and Texas—of Spanish colonial settlement within the region absorbed into the United States from Mexico. Most of the region had Spanish colonial origins. Dynamic cultural fusion defined family life in the Spanish borderlands for about three hundred years before the independence of Mexico in 1821.

Colonial Motives. Although religion was a major motivating factor behind Spanish colonization in Central and North America, it was Spanish foreign policy that directly led to the first borderland colonization efforts. Spain's King Philip II rejected the advice of his father, Charles V, to be cautious with European politics; Charles V's experience as Holy Roman Emperor had drained Spanish resources. Philip II brought Portugal into the Spanish Empire in 1580 and engaged in various European wars. The failed Spanish Armada invasion of England in 1588 was followed by English raids against Spanish shipping. The fleet system em-

Juan de Oñate leads a band of soldiers, missionaries, and colonists into the borderlands. (Institute of Texan Cultures)

ployed as a defense seemed to prompt the English to expand their scope of operation.

As English pirates threatened the Manila trade in the Pacific Ocean, the desirability of Spanish ports along the California coast became apparent. In 1595, Sebastián Vizcaíno received Spanish governmental authority to colonize California, although true colonization of upper California was based on religion and the Franciscan MISSION SYSTEM. Juan de OÑATE gained the contract to colonize New Mexico in 1595 and led colonists north in 1598. Colonization efforts in Texas occurred in response to religious motives and French threats in the early eighteenth century.

Oñate traveled a new route to New Mexico in 1598 as he led 130 soldiers, some of their families, a band of Franciscan missionaries, Indian allies, and seven thousand stock animals to that area. The historian of the expedition recorded the celebration of Holy Week as the Oñate expedition encamped at El Paso del Norte. The play of "los moros y los cristos" was enacted on horseback as the governor indulged in penitent self-flagellation. With the introduction of the penitente

celebration, cultural adaptation and family life on the New Mexican frontier began.

Oñate held the titles of captain-general and *adelantado* (provincial governor), enabling him to give thirty-five *encomiendas* to his followers. This type of land grant had been designed to encourage immigration to the Western Hemisphere, but Spanish abuse of the system had led to new systems, though old practices remained.

Spaniards initially lived in Indian pueblos. The Spanish village of Santa Fe was constructed in 1609. Spanish colonists were driven out of New Mexico by the successful insurrection led by Pueblo Indian medicine man Popé in 1680 (*see* POPÉ'S REVOLT). They returned with the conquest of the region by Diego de Vargas Zapata Luján y Ponce de León in the early 1690's. De Vargas reestablished Spanish colonial life in New Mexico. The Pueblo insurrection led to a closer relationship with plains and nomadic Indians.

The Colonial System. The Spanish imperial system, with its many alterations over time, shaped Spanish cultural and familial life in the borderlands in unique regional ways. Although basic Spanish colonial precepts remained constant, the nature of cultural adaptation was dependent upon native people as well as the environment. For example, one basic precept that affected Spanish colonial life was that Spaniards wished to incorporate natives into the system as Christians and taxpayers, not to eliminate them.

Other Spanish colonial traits such as Spanish regionalism, cultivated during the country's centuries-long war against the Moors, were continued. Colonists in the three major areas of California, Texas, and New Mexico lived in unique ways, though their lives had common traits. Although missions and presidios (forts) were common to the three regions, the nature of those institutions differed in the three areas.

The Spanish colonial system attempted to ensure dependence of the colonists on their mother country through the allocation of monopolies and the prohibition of certain types of production. Spain wanted to ensure religious purity and political fealty through controlling immigration as well as economics. These considerations helped shape daily life in the borderlands. Spanish institutions such as the Holy Office of the Inquisition, however, evolved in the borderlands in ways different from in other regions.

The Spanish colonial system was founded on a class system. As a result of contacts in New Mexico, a new ethnic class evolved. The *genízaro* was usually a nomadic Indian assimilated into Spanish culture. The caste system favored Spaniards (*peninsulares*) over CRIOLLOS (Spaniards born in New Spain), MESTIZOS, and Indians. Regional variations of the caste system evolved throughout the empire, but the basic concept of Spaniard as superior to Indian shaped daily life in the empire.

Economic status also was a factor. Throughout the borderlands region, the wealthier one became, the more "Spanish" one became. In California, economic classes became more apparent as a HACIENDA SYSTEM of ranching developed alongside self-sufficient missions.

Spain introduced citrus fruits as well as cows, horses, sheep, pigs, and other livestock to the region. The colonists also brought weaving and silver-working skills. In California, Spanish missions attempted to become self-sufficient while relying upon the presidio to capture, as "heretics," Indians who fled from them.

In New Mexico, Spanish settlements were often built adjacent to Indian pueblos. Acculturation of Indians caused the creation of unique communities for

Missions shaped the lives of many colonists by imposing a social order. (Security Pacific Bank Collection, Los Angeles Public Library)

genízaros. The sheep-raising industry in New Mexico prospered sufficiently to allow exports to be sent south.

In Texas, a presidio/mission combination brought Spanish colonists into contact with Indian neophyte converts. The system of forts and churches in Texas was also designed for defense against both hostile Indian tribes and the French.

The Spanish Crown reformed the political structure and created *provincias internas* for the northern region in 1776. These Spanish villages often exercised self-government through a *cabildo* (council). The communities were often constructed in a classic plaza style with distinct barrios. Family life on the frontier thus included self-government.

Community and Family Structure. Spanish villages were usually organized in a plaza plan with a central park. Various neighborhoods were often reserved for distinct social classes. Homes made of adobe were more common than those built from wood, which often was plastered with adobe. The Spanish added straw, windows, and doors to the adobe construction of the pueblos. Wealthy residents often constructed home chapels within their estates.

The nuclear family was embedded in an extended family relationship. Grandparents, uncles, aunts, and cousins were cultivated into an extended family system that provided support on the frontier. It was common for orphaned children to be taken in, just as it was common for a child to be given to grandparents, to be reared by them and to comfort them in their later years. *Genízaros* became common in Spanish homes, and many of these Indians were accepted as family members.

The COMPADRAZGO system of ritualized extended families also greatly influenced colonial society. A child's parents and godparents became *compadres*, or joint parents, in much the same manner as the parents of newlyweds developed that relationship. PADRINOS and *madrinas* became more than godparents or a wedding entourage: They became family.

This interdependence among generations and among families helped to create regional affinity. As the Spanish government most often awarded community, rather than individual, land grants, interdependence became more than a unique familial system. The family protected the individual and expected appropriate behavior in return.

Spanish and Indian heritages combined so strongly that it became almost impossible to separate them. Nearly all New Mexicans became Roman Catholic, but nearby Indian pueblos also influenced the practices of Spanish colonists. A folk Catholicism thus evolved. Ancient Indian herbal lore, for example, combined with Spanish beliefs to produce a folk medicine system with a *curandera* (medicinal healer) as center.

Probably because of the Indian influence and matrilineal clan concept, New Mexican women were more liberated than their counterparts to the south. Although the ideal male fulfilled his agrarian role responsibilities such as providing food, shelter, and discipline within the family, the matriarch established religious responsibilities, engendered respect, cultivated values, and often served as a mediator between children and their father. The family usually encouraged a sibling subsystem that was based on age and gender. The eldest son was granted special privileges and responsibility for younger children, while girls were expected to devote their energies to household chores. Age and sex discrimination played an important role in Spanish colonial society. When guests were present, meals were often segregated.

Surrounded by hostile Indians and separated from the interior villages of El Paso del Norte and Chihuahua by a vast desert, New Mexicans adapted to their environment. Every settler was also a soldier. A caravan usually traveled north along the Camino Real from Chihuahua into New Mexico once a year, but New Mexicans remained starved for manufactured goods until the opening of the eastern border for trade in 1821. Annual trade fairs were organized throughout the region, allowing greater trade between the Indians and the Spaniards.

The paucity of priests led to the development of lay religious groups such as Los Hermanos Penitentes. This folk Catholic group included a unique church as well as officers to ensure the well-being of the community. During Holy Week, penitent services were observed. Each community had its own crucifixion commemoration. The requirements of the religious communities were often more stringent than local law, as members were required to perform good and charitable acts as well as to treat their neighbors well, under threat of expulsion. Religious rules also regulated marriage, with anyone of the community allowed to speak out against a marriage of people who were perceived to be too closely related.

The fusion of Indian with Spanish beliefs as well as the impact of an abrasive frontier can be seen in New Mexican art forms such as santo sculptures. Religious lessons were altered for their audience. The story of Jonah and the whale, for example, became "el capitan y el cíbolo" for New Mexico's children, who could imagine a buffalo of a size able to swallow a ship but not a fish of that size, as they were familiar only with those from New Mexican streams.

Entertainment. Entertainment and sport reflected the nature of the people. Anglo-Americans observed that the Mexicans danced from the cradle to the grave. The democratizing effect of the frontier can be observed through an egalitarian dance, the *cuña*, in which one danced with whichever partner one matched. Such pairings resulted in a poor Indian dancing with the governor's wife on one occasion noted by an Anglo-American observer.

Music in the region was made up of divergent elements with a Mexican cultural core but with historical origins in Renaissance Spain. CORRIDOS told historical tales, while the ALABADO combined religious and secular music, just as the PENITENTES joined lay and religious persons.

New Mexicans became adept at horsemanship and played a game called *correr el gallo*. A rooster would be buried to its neck, and a number of *caballeros* would compete to secure its feathers through a melee that favored the best horseman. Californians, on the other hand and in response to their environment, became adept at bearbaiting.

The key to understanding Spanish colonial life in the borderlands is the isolation of the people. The pueblo life of Indians shaped the lives of Spanish colonists in New Mexico much as the mission and presidio systems shaped colonial life in California and Texas.
—*David A. Sandoval*

SUGGESTED READINGS:

• Chávez, Angelico. *My Penitente Land: Reflections on Spanish New Mexico.* Albuquerque: University of New Mexico Press, 1974. A combination of scholarly and personal observations concerning the culture and history of New Mexico.

• Hurtado, Albert L. *Indian Survival on the California Frontier.* New Haven, Conn.: Yale University Press, 1988. An excellent analysis of the impact of Spanish colonization on California Indians.

• John, Elizabeth A. H. *Storms Brewed in Other Men's Worlds: The Confrontation of Indians, Spanish, and French in the Southwest, 1540-1795.* College Station: Texas A&M Press, 1975. A comprehensive and detailed analysis of reaction to Indian societies, with a special focus on Texas, New Mexico, and Chihuahua.

Horsemanship was both a practical skill and a source of entertainment. (University Libraries, Arizona State University, Tempe)

- Jones, Oakah L., Jr. *Los Paisanos: Spanish Settlers on the Northern Frontier of New Spain.* Norman: University of Oklahoma Press, 1979. A cultural history of New Mexican settlements, with emphasis on cultural adaptation.
- Nostrand, Richard L. *The Hispano Homeland.* Norman: University of Oklahoma Press, 1992. Addresses elements of cultural-geographic dynamic fusion from Oñate to the American period.
- Spicer, Edward H. *Cycles of Conquest: The Impact of Spain, Mexico, and the United States on the Indians of the Southwest, 1533-1960.* Tucson: University of Arizona Press, 1962. A comprehensive analysis and comparison of foreign impact on Indian societies.
- Weber, David J. *The Spanish Frontier in North America.* New Haven, Conn.: Yale University Press, 1992. The Spanish borderlands are placed in the context of the entire Spanish empire in North America.

Family names: In Spanish, an individual's full name, *el nombre completo*, consists of a first name and possibly a middle name, followed by the person's father's first surname, then the mother's first surname (her maiden name). Whereas most people in the United States use only one surname, the Spanish naming system attaches two surnames to each person. For example, in English, a person's full name may be "John Paul Jones," consisting of a first name, a middle name, and one surname; this person's family name would be "Jones." In Latin America, a person's full name may be "Maria Isabel Baca Mares," consisting not only of first and middle names but also of two surnames—both parents' first surnames. Thus, this person's family name would be "Baca Mares." Because names are "personal items" that people carry with them and that express self-identity, Latin Americans consider their names incomplete if they are missing one of the two surnames—even if they are single, married, divorced or widowed. Two surnames are essential. In fact, in Latin American countries, formal legislation requires citizens to have two surnames (*apellidos*).

Apellidos have no gender, unlike given names, or *nombres*. First and middle names typically carry an "o" or "a" ending to indicate male or female names. For example, the name "Patricia" refers to a woman; the name "Ricardo" refers to a man. Surnames, on the other hand, do not generally carry these endings, and if they do, they are not a reference to gender.

Other endings to surnames, however, may reveal information about the names' historical origin and function. Spanish surnames belong to one of three types: patronymics, appellations, and toponymics. "Patronymic" literally means "the son of," and patronymic surnames are identified by the endings of "az," "ez," "iz," "oz," and "uz." An example of a patronymic in Spanish would be "Fernández," meaning "the son of Fernando"—as "Johnson" in English would literally mean "the son of John."

Appellations can describe an outstanding personal quality of an individual. Examples of such surnames are Delgado, which means "thin," and Caballero, which means "gentleman." Color names are also used as surnames in Spanish and can be part of a family name. "Blanco" ("white") and "Moreno" ("dark") are examples.

The third category of surnames is toponymics. These refer to a physical location or place of origin of the family. These surnames are preceded by one of the following prefixes: "de," "de la," "de los," and "del." These prefixes in Spanish mean "belonging to" or "from." Examples of toponymics are "De la Fuente" (meaning "of the fountain") and "Del Valle" (meaning "of the valley").

The combination of surnames changes from parents to children. In addition, a woman's full name changes upon marriage, but a man's full name remains the same even if he marries. Consider the following example. A hypothetical nuclear family consists of a father, mother, one daughter, and two sons. If the father's full name is Guillermo Adrian Villaseñor Cisneros, his name remains the same when he marries Maria Isabel Baca Mares. Her name becomes Maria Isabel Baca de Villaseñor, dropping her second surname and adding her husband's first surname. The preposition "de," in this case, indicates that she "belongs to" the family of the man she marries. Guillermo and Maria have a daughter and two sons. Even though they have children of both genders, all three children take on the family name of Villaseñor Baca, their father's first surname and their mother's first surname. The sons will carry on this family name whether they remain single or marry, but the daughter will drop her mother's first surname, Baca, upon marrying. Thus, family names give considerable information about kinship relations in Latin America.

Fandango: Andalusian and Castilian song and dance form. Descending from popular Moorish folk tunes, the *fandango* is in triple time, accompanied by guitar, with castanets or tambourine providing percussion. The *fandango* includes lively sung couplets. Local variants of the fandango are the *malagueña* (Malaga) and *granadina* (Granada). It originated in the early eighteenth century as a dance performed by muleteers at roadside inns and street masquerades. Danced by men, it becomes a contest of skill and virtuosity; danced by couples, it displays vigorous *braceo* (carriage of the arms). The fandango was incorporated into various dance forms, including the ballet. By the late

eighteenth century, the aristocracy admitted it and the guitar into their drawing rooms.

Farah Strike (1972-1974): Labor stoppage. In the second half of the twentieth century, many clothing manufacturers moved to the Southwest to take advantage of cheaper prevailing wages and the relative

Picketers at the Farah plant in El Paso, Texas, in 1972. (AP/Wide World Photos)

Members of the FLOC at a rally for the American Federation of Labor-Congress of Industrial Organizations. (Jim West)

weakness of unions in the region. Farah Manufacturing made men's slacks at plants in El Paso, Texas. Most of that plant's employees were Mexican Americans. Many workers there showed an interest in joining the Amalgamated Clothing Workers of America, but the company vowed to defeat unionization.

A major strike began in 1972, crippling Farah's operations and resulting in the arrest of more than one thousand strikers. Farah's use of dogs against the strikers was widely publicized, and a national boycott of Farah products won widespread support. The backing of Catholic church leaders for the strikers was also important. Farah put up strong opposition to the strike but capitulated in 1974, after massive financial losses and adverse rulings by the National Labor Relations Board.

During the strike, Cecilia Espinoza brought suit against Farah. Espinoza asserted that her civil rights had been violated when Farah refused to hire her because of her Mexican citizenship. The case helped focus the anger of Mexican Americans against Farah, but the U.S. Supreme Court ruled in *Espinoza v. Farah Manufacturing* (1973) that discrimination by employers on the basis of alienage was permissible under the Civil Rights Act of 1964.

Farm Labor Organizing Committee (FLOC): Labor organization. The FLOC was founded by Baldemar VELAZQUEZ in 1967. This organization attempted to improve the lives and working conditions of farmworkers in Ohio. Farmworkers in the Midwest often earned less than the minimum wage and were subjected to miserable working conditions. The FLOC negotiated numerous contracts with Ohio's growers to increase farmworkers' wages and improve their living situation. When the contracts expired, growers refused to renegotiate on the grounds that canneries did not pay enough for farm produce to allow payment of higher wages. FLOC representatives viewed the canneries as part of the farmworker problem. Various nationwide boycotts on canneries helped the FLOC to negotiate with cannery companies, but neither growers nor canneries have made a significant commitment to improve the work and living situation of farmworkers.

Farolito: Small fire used in Mexico and the American Southwest in the celebration of the days before Christmas. *Las POSADAS*, the ritual re-creation of the search of Mary and Joseph for a place to stay at the time of the birth of Jesus, has been common in Mexico since colonial times. Often, small bonfires were set along the way to serve as guides for the procession. In the 1820's, paper bags became available in many areas, and the bonfires were replaced with candles inside paper bags, which were folded over at the top and weighted with sand. These candle-bags became known as *farolitos* (little beacons), *iluminarias* (illuminators), or *luminarias*. Many modern Mexican and Mexican-American families place *farolitos* along their driveways in the days preceding Christmas.

Favela, Ricardo (b. 1944): Artist and community organizer. A former student of muralists and Sacramento State College art teachers Esteban Villa and José MON-TOYA, Favela is best known for his contributions to Chicano art in California.

In 1968, Favela dropped out of college to join Villa, Montoya, and Juanishi Orozco in organizing the Rebel Chicano Art Front, later dubbed the Royal Chicano Air Force (RCAF). The purpose of the group was to bring political action and artistic expression together in the Chicano community. By recruiting students and barrio residents, hosting art shows and installations that celebrated their roots, and creating a forum for education and political action, Favela and the other RCAF organizers sought to retrieve Chicano history and culture.

Favela's silkscreened poster *Huelga!* (strike!), which depicts RCAF members dressed as pilots organizing a supermarket strike in support of labor organizer César CHÁVEZ and California farmworkers, is typical of his politically charged art. Other silkscreened posters that Favela produced throughout the 1970's mixed his own graphic designs with Latino poems and literature at a time when the publishing industry usually rejected Chicano manuscripts.

Federación Libre de los Trabajadores (FLT): Labor organization. This federation was organized in Puerto Rico at the end of the nineteenth century and affiliated with the American Federation of Labor (AFL) in 1901. This affiliation was unusual in that the AFL usually excluded Hispanic workers, but in this case it feared that Puerto Rican labor organizations might become too powerful if not absorbed. The FLT's first major strike was conducted in 1905 and 1906 against sugarcane growers. The FLT later concentrated its efforts on political concerns.

Feliciano, José Monserrate (b. Sept. 10, 1945, Lares, Puerto Rico): Singer, guitarist, and songwriter. Feliciano is the son of José Feliciano and Hortencia Gar-

cia Feliciano. His father worked as a farmer and a longshoreman. Feliciano was one of twelve children, and he was born blind.

When Feliciano was still a child, his family moved to the United States, settling in the SPANISH HARLEM section of New York City. Feliciano learned to play the guitar and the accordion. He dropped out of high school and began playing guitar in Greenwich Village clubs in the early 1960's. In 1964, Feliciano signed a recording contract with RCA Records and released his first album, *The Voice and Guitar of José Feliciano*. The album was popular in both Central and South America.

Feliciano reached the English-speaking audiences of the United States and England with his version of the Doors' song "Light My Fire" (1968). The single sold more than a million copies. "Light My Fire" was included on *Feliciano!* (1968), his first gold album. He won Grammy Awards for "Light My Fire" as Best New Artist and Best Contemporary Pop Vocal Performance. His popularity led to his performance of "The Star-Spangled Banner" at the fifth game of the 1968 World Series.

José Feliciano's music reaches both Spanish- and English-speaking audiences. (AP/Wide World Photos)

Mexican film star María Félix had a limited career in the U.S. film industry. (AP/Wide World Photos)

During the 1970's, Feliciano's concerts routinely sold out. In 1973, *Guitar Player* magazine named him Best Folk Guitarist. The Spanish-language albums he recorded during the 1980's were popular around the world; and in 1983, 1986, 1989, and 1990, Feliciano won Grammy Awards for Best Latin Pop Performance. At the first annual Latin Music Expo in 1991, he was presented with a lifetime achievement award. His East Harlem high school changed its name to the José Feliciano Performing Arts School.

Félix, María (María de Los Angeles Félix Guereña; b. Apr. 8, 1914, Alamos, Sonora, Mexico): Actress. Félix was born in a small village in the Sonoran desert. When still young, she moved with her family to Guadalajara, where she became a carnival queen. She married Enrique Alvarez, a makeup salesman from an established family, and had a son. She abandoned her marriage and family to seek her fortune in Mexico City.

Discovered in the street by Fernando Palacios, Félix went on to become the queen of Mexican films during the 1940's, 1950's, and 1960's. She made her debut in 1942 in *El peñon de las animas* (1942), and her following two films, *María Eugenia* (1942) and *Doña Bárbara* (1943), firmly established her career. Other Mexican film credits include *La mujer sin alma* (1943), *El monje blanco* (1945), *La noche del Sábado* (1950), *La pasión desnuda* (1953), *Miércoles de Ceniza* (1958), and *La cucaracha* (1958). Félix had a limited career in Hollywood in such films as *The Devil Is a Woman* (1952) and *French Can-Can* (1955). Known for her strong personality, Félix ultimately refused to work in Hollywood when producers would not meet her conditions.

Feminism and the women's movement: Some Latinas, believing that they were situated in value systems and social structures that oppressed them as women, contributed to, and developed ideas about, feminism and the women's movement, hoping that these movements could address their needs. (*See* LATINAS, HISTORY AND ISSUES OF.)

Background. The women's movement developed in earnest in the 1960's. It encompassed a wide range of other movements, two of which were women's rights and women's liberation. The women's rights movement included demanding the rights to vote, to make reproductive choices, and to have health care and childcare. In general, the women's rights movement called for the recognition of institutional equality between men and women. The women's liberation movement was understood to require more than the institutional recognition of equality. It called into question the very institutions, the church and government, for example, that implicitly dictated women's roles in society.

Feminism can be distinguished from women's rights movements because not all women who called for institutional equality considered themselves to be feminists. On the other hand, women who were committed to the rejection of women's traditional roles in society tended to see feminism as a philosophy that was compatible with their agenda. Feminism, in this context, refers to an explanation of society from a woman's perspective. This perspective criticized the organization of society in terms of male power and privilege, or what is called the patriarchy. Feminism can also be considered to be a set of ideas that asserts women's perspective as a different and valid way of looking at the world.

Suffragist and Workers' Movements. Histories of early women's movements outline at least two precursors to the movements of the 1960's. One movement, composed primarily of middle-class women, had a history of struggling for equality in the political process, the hallmark of which is the struggle for voting rights. Another movement, composed primarily of working-class and poor women, had a history of struggling for women's rights as workers and as a group that did not have equal access to economic and social resources.

In the United States and Canada, the suffragist movement included primarily non-Hispanic women. A few Latinas, primarily women of Mexican and Puerto Rican descent, participated in the mainstream suffragist movement. There was also a tradition of Puerto Rican women struggling for suffrage on the island of Puerto Rico.

Latinas also have organized consistently as women in a working class that sought access to social and economic resources. These movements were organized primarily on the basis of a socioeconomic class affiliation. During workers' movements of the 1920's and 1930's, women's movements that were feminist, or that called for women's liberation in terms of a separation from men, rarely emerged.

Civil Rights and Women's Liberation. During the 1960's, many Latinas—most notably Chicanas and Puerto Rican women—participated in various social protest movements, including those opposing the Vietnam War and promoting civil rights and the rights of Chicanos, Puerto Ricans, Native Americans, and Afri-

Latinas' activism focused on workplace issues. (David Bacon)

can Americans (*see* CIVIL RIGHTS MOVEMENTS). At the height of these movements, female activists began to critique the patriarchal value systems and structures of the organizations in which they participated. They noted not only that women rarely held visible leadership roles but also that women's needs, such as health care and childcare, were neglected in organizational and movement platforms. Many Latinas began to believe that their rights were denied them not only as members of minority groups but also as women in a patriarchal society.

Increasingly, participation in the mainstream women's movement attracted Latinas, despite the fact that some activists viewed feminism and the women's movement as part of the oppressive social structure being challenged. Nevertheless, activist Latinas insisted that their participation in a women's movement or their embrace of feminism did not preclude a commitment to their Latino group movement.

Emergence of Latina Feminism. Latinas were involved in mainstream feminist and women's movements, but participation in these movements became,

by the mid-1970's, increasingly difficult. Latinas began to vocalize their experience of the racism of the women's movements, evidenced by attitudes and agendas that overlooked the specific needs of Latinas. Many Latinas were members of the working class, which caused tensions in their relations with mainstream women's movements, which were often composed of middle-class women whose concerns differed from those of Latinas. Mainstream feminism and women's liberation, while suggesting desirable goals for Latinas, did not take full account of the social changes that Latinas sought, changes that directly related to the needs of Latinas as members of minority groups and as members of particular socioeconomic classes.

In response to the lack of attention to issues relevant to Latinas in both their minority group movements and in mainstream women's movements and feminism, Latinas formed their own feminist and women's movements. Latina feminist and women's movements not only insist upon the right of women of their minority groups to be free from patriarchal value systems and the regulation of women's roles but also contest inequality among races and socioeconomic classes.

—*Dionne Espinoza*

SUGGESTED READINGS: • Acosta-Belén, Edna, ed. *The Puerto Rican Woman.* New York: Praeger, 1979. • Anzaldúa, Gloria, ed. *Making Face, Making Soul-Haciendo Caras.* San Francisco: Aunt Lute Books, 1990. • Cotera, Marta. "Feminism: The Chicano and Anglo Versions." In *Twice a Minority: Mexican American Women*, edited by Margarita B. Melville. St. Louis, Mo.: C. V. Mosby, 1980. • Garcia, Alma M. "The Development of Chicana Feminist Discourse, 1970-1980." *Gender & Society* 3 (June, 1989): 217-238. • Moraga, Cherríe, and Gloria Anzaldúa, eds. *This Bridge Called My Back: Writings by Radical Women of Color.* 2d ed. New York: Kitchen Table, Women of Color Press, 1983. • Nieto-Gomez, Anna. "La Feminista." *Encuentro Femenil* 1, no. 2 (1974): 34-47. • Vasquez, Enriqueta, "The Mexican American Woman." In *Sisterhood Is Powerful*, compiled by Robin Morgan. New York: Random House, 1970.

Fender, Freddy (Baldemar Garza Huerta; b. June 4, 1937, San Benito, Tex.): Singer. Fender's parents, Serapio Huerta and Margarita Garza Huerta, were migrant workers. In 1954, Fender joined the United

Freddy Fender joined the Texas Tornados after a solo career. (AP/Wide World Photos)

States Marines. After his stint in the Marines, he began playing in Texas honky tonks. He continued to play these small venues between 1956 and 1959. He married Evangalina Muniz on August 10, 1957. In 1959, he had his first hit single, "Wasted Days and Wasted Nights." His rockabilly style prompted some music analysts to call him the "Mexican Elvis."

Fender's promising career was sidetracked by his arrest for possession of marijuana in Baton Rouge, Louisiana. From 1960 to 1963, he was in Angola State Prison. After his release, Fender attempted to revive his singing career by playing clubs in New Orleans. In the early 1970's, he switched from rockabilly to country music.

Fender had a hit single, the bilingual "Before the Next Teardrop Falls," in 1975. During the late 1970's, he had a number of successful singles, including a remake of "Wasted Days and Wasted Nights," "Secret Love," "You'll Lose a Good Thing," "Vaya Con Dios," and "Walking Piece of Heaven." He continued to record country-flavored music throughout the 1980's. In 1988, he acted in Robert Redford's *The Milagro Beanfield War*. In 1989, Fender, Doug Sahm, Flaco JIMÉNEZ, and Augie Meyers formed the TEXAS TORNADOS. The group released its first album, *Texas Tornados*, in 1990. During the early 1990's, the band toured the United States.

Fernández, Agustín (b. 1928, Havana, Cuba): Painter. Fernández is famous for paintings that convey a feeling of menace by contrasting erotic images with precisely rendered metallic objects. Once a classmate of Cuban revolutionary Fidel CASTRO, Fernández traveled and studied extensively in Paris, France, and Madrid, Spain, before settling in New York City. Paintings and drawings from various stages of his career reflect international art trends. Some of his paintings emulate the French cubists' tendency to reduce images into geometric forms; others convey the eerie, dreamlike quality of paintings by Spanish surrealists. Beginning in the 1960's, however, Fernández's work focused almost entirely on erotica.

Images of eyes, sexual organs, and fleshlike textures dominate Fernández's paintings. Razor blades, spikes, hoods, and leather and metallic restraints often frame the sensual images, as they do in his oil painting, *Leather Belt* (1979). Critics have suggested that this contrast between hard and soft textures represents the terrors of the Spanish Inquisition, the clash between conquerors and their victims, or the struggle of the human spirit amid the harsh political realities of the modern world.

Fernandez, Carole Fragoza (b. July 1, 1941, New York, N.Y.): Novelist. Fernandez was born to Puerto Rican parents Victoria Diaz and Ralph Fragoza. She attended Brentwood High School in New York and was graduated from the City College of New York in 1963. In 1988, she completed a master's degree in English at the State University of New York at Stony Brook.

After her marriage, Fernandez taught Spanish and English in the public schools on Long Island, New York. When she left full-time teaching in 1975, Fernandez continued to provide tutorial services in both English and Spanish. After moving to Santurce, Puerto Rico, in 1978, she did graduate work in English at the University of Puerto Rico at Rio Piedras while continuing to tutor students in Spanish and English. In 1983, she moved back to Bay Shore, Long Island, where she was active in civic affairs. In 1991, her first novel, *Sleep of the Innocents*, was published. The novel concerns a young woman in an unnamed country (suggestive of Guatemala) whose life is shattered by military violence.

Fernández, Joseph A. (b. 1935, New York, N.Y.): Educational administrator. Fernández was a high school teacher and superintendent of Florida's Dade County School System (1987-1989) before becoming chancellor of the New York City Public Schools. He has also served on the advisory board of the National Institute for Hispanic Leadership and on the national advisory literacy council of SER-Jobs for Progress, Inc. In 1991, he was chair of the National Urban Education Task Force for the Council of Great City Schools.

Fernández's work has earned him numerous awards. These include Dade County Administrator of the Year (1979); Cuban Teacher in Exile, Award of Honor (1987); a National Puerto Rican Coalition Life Achievement Award (1990); the School Administrator of the Year Award from the National Caucus of Hispanic School Board Members (1991); and the Award for Education from the Hispanic Heritage Awards Committee (1991).

Fernández, Manuel José "Manny" (b. July 3, 1946, Oakland, Calif.): Football player. Recruited from the University of Utah in 1968, Fernández was a dominant force on the Miami Dolphins defense. During the 1972-1973 season, Fernández, as part of the famed "No-Name Defense," played a key role in the Dolphins' 17-0 season and Super Bowl victory. That year,

Joseph Fernández. (AP/Wide World Photos)

Manny Fernández had an outstanding career as a defensive player for the Miami Dolphins. (AP/Wide World Photos)

Fernández won the prestigious Johnny Unitas Award. He received five American Football Conference Second Team selections and was nominated for the Pro Bowl; he also was named to the United Press International All-Time Super Bowl All-Star Team.

After retiring in 1977, Fernández went on to a successful career in the mortgage and title business. He also served as the chairman of the board of directors for the NFL Alumni Association.

Fernández, Ricardo (b. Dec. 11, 1940, Santurce, Puerto Rico): Educator and administrator. A scholar of desegregation and education, Fernández has published several books, including the coauthored *Reducing the Risk: Schools as Communities of Support* (1989). His professional interests lie in the field of bilingual and multicultural education. He was chosen as president of the board of directors of Multicultural Education Training and Advocacy, Inc., in 1987 and served as president of the National Association for Bilingual Education from 1980 to 1981. In addition, he began serving on the board of directors of the PUERTO RICAN LEGAL DEFENSE AND EDUCATION FUND in 1981.

Fernández holds a B.A. (1962) and M.A. (1965) from Marquette University and an M.A. (1967) and Ph.D. (1970) from Princeton University. He began his teaching career at Marquette University as an assistant professor, in 1968. He moved to the faculty of the University of Wisconsin-Milwaukee in 1970 as an assistant professor, rising to the rank of professor. In 1990, he became president of the Herbert H. Lehman College of the City University of New York.

Fernández, Roberto (b. Sept. 24, 1951, Sagua la Grande, Cuba): Writer and academician. Fernández was born into a family of professionals who left Cuba in 1961 and settled in Florida. Reared in a family of talented musicians and composers, Fernández chose literature as his mode of artistic expression. His formal education culminated in his earning a Ph.D. in linguistics from Florida State University in 1978.

By the early 1990's, Fernández had published two collections of short stories: *Cuentos sin rumbos* (1975; directionless tales) and *El jardín de la luna* (1976; the garden of the moon). His first novel, *La vida es un special. 75* (1981), received critical acclaim. *La montaña rusa* (1985, the rollercoaster) and *Raining Backwards* (1988) followed. Fernández's main concern is with the life of Cuban exiles in Miami, a group whom he sees as a vanishing culture. Along with his brother, social historian Jose Fernández, he has published a bibliography of Cuban literature written in the United States.

Fernández, Royes (July 15, 1929, New Orleans, La.—Mar. 3, 1980, New York, N.Y.): Dancer. Fernández began his study of ballet at the age of eight with Lelia Haller and went on to work with Vincenzo Celli and Alexandra Danilova. He made his professional debut in 1946 with Colonel W. de Basil's Original Ballet Russe and over the next two and a half decades danced with a variety of companies, including the Borovansky Ballet, the San Francisco Ballet, and the London Festival Ballet. Fernández was a principal dancer with the American Ballet Theatre, performing with the company from 1950 to 1953 and again from 1957 through 1972. Among his most notable performances were such classical pieces as *Swan Lake*, *Giselle*, *La Sylphide*, and *Les Sylphides* and contemporary ballets including *Lilac Garden*, *Etudes*, and *Theme Variations*.

During his performance career, Fernández was partnered with many of the world's leading ballerinas, among them Alicia Markova, Margot Fonteyn, Maria Tallchief, Lupe Serrano, and Carla Fracci. A technically exceptional artist, he was admired for his elegance, lyricism, theatricality, and smooth charm. During the 1970's, Fernández taught dance at the State University of New York at Purchase and at the Ballet Theater School. He died of cancer in 1980 at the age of fifty.

Fernandez, Rudy (b. 1948, Trinidad, Colo.): Artist. In the tradition of Hispanic RETABLOS, Fernandez's relief paintings and sculptures combine regional and ethnic images with universal and personal symbols.

Fernandez's mixed-media works enclose paint, canvas, three-dimensional wooden forms, tooled pieces of tin, and even neon tubing. A heart is his signature symbol, and knives appear repeatedly in his art.

Fernandez's father worked for a drilling and mineral exploration company, so the family moved frequently throughout Arizona, New Mexico, Colorado, and Utah. This experience cultivated a strong affection for the Southwest in Fernandez, who later incorporated Southwestern animals and plants, such as cacti, roosters, and magpies, into his art.

After graduation from high school, Fernandez traveled with a rock-and-roll band and worked as a driller to earn money for college. He earned a bachelor's degree in painting in 1974 from the University of Colorado and a master's degree in sculpture in 1976 from Washington State University.

Tony Fernandez after making a double play in the 1993 World Series. (AP/Wide World Photos)

In 1978, Fernandez began working for an art gallery and exhibiting his work. In 1981, he was awarded a Visual Arts Fellowship in Painting from the Arizona Commission on Arts. In the late 1980's, his work was featured in a traveling art show, Hispanic Art in the United States.

Fernandez, Tony (Octavio Antonio Fernandez y Castro; b. Aug. 6, 1962, San Pedro de Macoris, Dominican Republic): Baseball player. Switch-hitting shortstop Fernandez, one of many outstanding major league players from the town of San Pedro de Macoris, signed with the Toronto Blue Jays organization in 1979. After four minor league seasons, he made his major league debut with Toronto in 1983. A graceful and exceptionally mobile defensive player, Fernandez also proved to be a solid hitter. In 1986, he had 213 hits, the highest total by a major league shortstop in the twentieth century. That season, he also set an American League record by playing in 163 games at shortstop and won the first of four consecutive Gold Glove Awards.

In 1986, 1987, and 1989, Fernandez was named to the American League All-Star Team. In 1990, he led the American League with 17 triples. Traded after the 1990 season, he spent two seasons in the National League with the San Diego Padres, earning a National League All-Star selection in 1992. He played briefly with the New York Mets in 1993 before a midseason trade sent him back to Toronto, where he helped the Blue Jays win the World Series title.

Ferre, Luis A. (b. Feb. 17, 1904, Ponce, Puerto Rico): Governor of Puerto Rico. Ferre was born in Ponce to a family headed by an industrialist. He was educated at the Massachusetts Institute of Technology, earning his master of science degree in 1925.

Ferre was a strong advocate for statehood and ran unsuccessfully for governor three times on the Statehood Republican Party ticket. In 1965, he was appointed to the U.S.-Puerto Rico Commission on the Status of Puerto Rico. Ferre organized the United Statehooders Association, which became the New Pro-

Luis Ferre discusses the issue of statehood for Puerto Rico during a 1969 speech at the National Press Club. (AP/Wide World Photos)

Mayor Maurice Ferre speaks at a meeting of the Miami city commissioners. (AP/Wide World Photos)

gressive Party in 1967. He was elected to serve as governor one year later, ending almost thirty years of domination by the PARTIDO POPULAR DEMOCRÁTICO.

Ferre, Maurice Antonio (b. June 23, 1935, Ponce, Puerto Rico): Mayor of MIAMI, Florida. Ferre completed his undergraduate studies at the University of Miami in 1957. He began his political career by serving in the Florida House of Representatives in 1966. Ferre was a city commissioner in Miami from 1967 to 1970. Three years later, he became mayor of Miami, a position he held until 1985.

Ferre has been very active nationally, both in Democratic Party politics and in civic organizations. In 1976, he served as National Hispanic Co-Chairman for Jimmy Carter's presidential campaign. Ferre was also an early member of the NATIONAL ASSOCIATION OF LATINO ELECTED AND APPOINTED OFFICIALS. He has also been active in the U.S. Conference of Democratic Mayors, the Hispanic Council on Foreign Affairs, and the Pan American Development Foundation. Ferre served on various advisory boards and committees during the Carter Administration.

Ferré, Rosario (b. July 28, 1942, Ponce, Puerto Rico): Writer and publisher. Ferré was born into a distinguished family. Her father, a financier and public figure, was once governor of Puerto Rico. From childhood, she read avidly from her library of fairy tales, an experience that would later influence her writing. After attending Dana Hall and Manhattanville College, she earned a master's degree in Spanish literature at the University of Puerto Rico and a Ph.D. in comparative literature from the University of Maryland.

In the 1970's, Ferré founded a literary magazine of new Puerto Rican literature, *Zona de carga y descarga*. Her work explores the marginal position of women within a culture dominated by men. Three of her well-known works are *Papeles de Pandora* (1976; *The Youngest Doll*, 1991), *La caja de cristal* (1978; the glass box), and *Maldito amor* (1986; *Sweet Diamond Dust*, 1988). Ferré has also embraced the cause of Puerto Rican independence.

Ferrer, Fernando (b. Apr. 30, 1950, Bronx, N.Y.): Public official. Ferrer was born into a family headed by a bookkeeper. He attended school in the South Bronx and majored in political science at New York University. After his graduate studies in public administration at New York University and Baruch College, Ferrer joined the state assembly staff. He also worked

for a state commission on rental housing. In 1979, Ferrer became the director of housing for the Bronx Borough President's Office. He also served as coordinator of the Bronx Arson Task Force.

Ferrer was elected to the city council in 1982. Four years later, he rose to the chairmanship of the health committee. Ferrer was the youngest city council committee chairman and oversaw hearings that exposed serious problems in the city's hospital system. He was appointed as Bronx borough president to fill a vacancy in 1987. Ferrer was elected to the post the following November, then reelected in 1989 and 1993. Throughout his political career he has been an active leader of the Puerto Rican community.

Ferrer, José Vicente (José Vicente Ferrer de Otero y Cintron; Jan. 8, 1912, Santurce, Puerto Rico—Jan. 26, 1992, Coral Gables, Fla.): Actor, director, and producer. Ferrer received his A.B. degree from Princeton University in 1933. His theatrical career, spanning half a century, included roles in hundreds of stage plays and films. He debuted on Broadway in 1935 in *A Slight Case of Murder* and became known for such performances as Iago opposite Paul Robeson in *Othello* (1943), the title role in *Cyrano de Bergerac* (1946), and Don Quijote in *Man of La Mancha* (1966). He made his film debut in 1948 as the Dauphin in *Joan of Arc* (1948). Ferrer was the first Latino to receive an Academy Award, for the film version of *Cyrano de Bergerac* (1950), and he was nominated for an Academy Award for his portrayal of French artist Henri de Toulouse-Lautrec in *Moulin Rouge* two years later. His other notable films include *The Caine Mutiny* (1953), *I Accuse* (1957), *Lawrence of Arabia* (1962), *The Greatest Story Ever Told* (1965), *Ship of Fools* (1965), *Enter Laughing* (1967), *The Voyage of the Damned* (1976), *A Midsummer Night's Sex Comedy* (1982), *To Be or Not to Be* (1983), *The Evil That Men Do* (1984), and *Dune* (1984). In 1981, Ferrer was elected to the Theatre Hall of Fame.

Festival of the Flowers (El Paso, Tex.): Annual festival held on Labor Day weekend. La Fiesta de las Flores, sponsored by the El Paso Chamber of Commerce, is held in Washington Park in El Paso. It is a carnival festival, including traditional and folk music, dances, games, arts and crafts, and costumes. More than half the performers in the fiesta traditionally have been Mexican or Mexican American.

Fiesta de los Remedios (Sept. 8): Cultural celebration. The Virgin de Los Remedios, or Our Lady of the

Remedies, is a crude, foot-tall wooden carving of the Virgin Mary and the Christ child that was brought to Mexico by one of Hernán CORTÉS' followers in the sixteenth century. As opposed to the Virgin of GUADALUPE, the Patroness of New Spain, Our Lady of the Remedies was favored by the Spanish invaders, who gave her the title of La Conquistadora. During the Mexican struggle for independence, her image was used on the battle banners of the Royalists, while the rebels used the figure of the Virgin of Guadalupe on their banners.

In Mexico, the fiesta of the Virgin of Los Remedios is second in importance only to that of the Virgin of Guadalupe, and in the village of San Bartolo, where its sanctuary is located, the fiesta is celebrated for a week, starting September 1 and ending on September 8, the main day. It commences with *mañanitas* (birthday songs sung at dawn), church services, and fireworks, also including music, dancing, and vendors selling food, folk crafts, and holy relics. Many Mexican festivals in the United States are held in mid-September in celebration of Mexican independence (September 16), overshadowing the slightly earlier fiesta or, in the case of longer fiestas, such as the FIESTAS PATRIAS in Houston, Texas, incorporating or subsuming it in the festivities.

Fiesta de San Juan: Commemorative celebration. San Juan Bautista, or St. John the Baptist, is celebrated as the patron saint of Puerto Rico, both on the island Commonwealth of Puerto Rico and in the United States, primarily by *puertorriqueños*. One celebration is the three-day Celebración San Juan, held at the Newport Beach Resort in Sunny Isles, Florida, near Miami. It features Puerto Rican MERENGUE music, traditional foods, folk arts and crafts, costumes, and dances.

San Juan Bautista also is celebrated as part of the somewhat earlier Puerto Rican Fiestas Patronales in Chicago, Illinois, sponsored by Puerto Rican Parade Committee of Chicago. The Puerto Rican Fiestas Patronales is held annually, during the second week of June, in Humboldt Park. Although it is attended by diverse Hispanic Americans and features traditional Hispanic music, food, folk dances, costumes, and arts and crafts, its performers are exclusively *puertorriqueños*. The celebration attracts about 400,000 people each year.

Fiesta de San Juan de los Lagos (Feb. 2): Commemorative event. In San Juan de los Lagos, Jalisco, Mexico, a *feria* (combination fair and fiesta) occurs annually on February 2 in honor of the Virgin of Candlemas, or the Purification, a small figurine made of vegetable paste that is said to have miraculous powers. The figurine is kept in San Juan de los Lagos in a shrine that dates back to 1732. The celebration originally lasted two weeks and became one of Mexico's most famous, drawing pilgrims and curious visitors from all over the country. It also served as a market fair for the sale of fine horses, mules, and burros, a feature unusual for a fiesta. The date is also celebrated in other Mexican and Mexican American Communities.

Fiesta of Our Lady of Guadalupe (mid-December, starting on or around December 10): Religious event. A fiesta in Tortugas, Mexico, and near Las Cruces, New Mexico, celebrating the three-day visitation in 1531 of the Virgin of Guadalupe (*see* GUADALUPE, VIRGIN OF) to a Mexican Indian, Juan Diego, has been part of a Hispanic-Indian tradition for centuries. Held in Tortugas Village, in the Mesilla Valley, and at Tortugas Mountain, adjacent to Las Cruces, New Mexico, the fiesta draws pilgrims who testify to their Catholic faith in a religious procession up the mountain, bearing candles and roses, representing the items found by Diego as a sign from the Virgin. Mixed with various religious ceremonies, including the Mass in both English and Spanish, the fiesta features some cultural events, including Hispanic and native Indian dances and a traditional dinner.

The fiesta, which in Las Cruces has had its current form for more than a hundred years, is also celebrated by Mexicans and Mexican Americans elsewhere in the United States. Other smaller sites include Garden City, Kansas, and the Centro Guadalupano in Pauma Valley, California.

Our Lady of Guadalupe is also honored at other times of the year, frequently within a generic celebration honoring the ethnic heritage and culture of Hispanic Americans. For example, at the Tucson Festival in Tucson, Arizona, held in late March or early April, following Easter Sunday, a large statue of the Virgin of Guadalupe is illuminated with fireworks on a hill near the Mission of SAN XAVIER DEL BAC, following a candlelight procession of celebrants who sing both Indian chants and Spanish hymns.

Fiestas patrias: Patriotic festivals, celebrated with parades and festivities. There are various *fiestas patrias* throughout Latin America, usually commemorating independence from a colonial overlord. Mexico, for ex-

Our Lady of Guadalupe is celebrated at various times of the year but primarily in December. (Ruben G. Mendoza)

ample, celebrates the well-known CINCO DE MAYO (commemorating the Battle of Puebla), as well as Constitution Day, Benito Juárez's birthday, Independence Day (September 16, shared with Central American countries receiving their independence from Spain at the same time), and the anniversary of the MEXICAN REVOLUTION. These holidays often are celebrated by picnics, PACHANGAS (parties), and other activities.

Figueroa Cordero, Andrés (1923, Puerto Rico—1979, Puerto Rico): Puerto Rican nationalist. Figueroa Cordero was a member of the Puerto Rican Nationalist Party, which has consistently worked toward the goal of independence for Puerto Rico. He established himself in New York City, where he came into contact with others who shared his vision and followed the ideology of Pedro ALBIZU CAMPOS.

On March 1, 1954, Figueroa Cordero joined with Lolita LEBRÓN SOTO, Rafael CANCEL MIRANDA, and Irving Flores in an armed attack on the U.S. House of Representatives. Five congressmen were injured. The four attackers were captured immediately. Figueroa Cordero was sentenced to serve twenty-five to seventy-five years in prison and was sent to Springfield, Missouri. President Jimmy Carter pardoned him and the other nationalists in 1979. Figueroa Cordero died of cancer in Puerto Rico shortly after his release.

Figueroa family: The Figueroa family occupies a prominent place in Puerto Rican music history. The family name has been associated with music for more than one hundred years, since Jesús Figueroa Iriarte (1878-1971) wrote musical arrangements for dance bands and concert halls. Jesús established himself as an arranger and was sought by the leading composers Morel Campos, Manuel Gregorio Tavárez, José Mislán, José Ignacio Quintón, and José Enrique Pedreira. In 1903, he married Carmen Sanabia Ellinger (1882-1954). She was an outstanding woman who, amid economic crisis and a prejudiced society, established herself as an accomplished pianist and one of the most talented music educators on the island.

Their children included violinist José "Pepito" (b. 1905), composer and pianist Narciso (b. 1906), pianist and teacher Leonor (1908-1945), violinist and orchestra conductor Jaime "Kachiro" (b. 1910), pianist and instructor Carmelina (1911-1994), piano teacher Angelina (b. 1914), violist and conductor Guillermo (b. 1916), and cellist Rafael (b. 1917). A third generation of musical Figueroas has continued the musical tradition of the family. They include violinists Gui-

llermo, Jr. (first violinist of the internationally acclaimed musical group Orpheus), talented violinist Narciso, award-winning piano educator Ivonne, and virtuoso cellist Rafael.

Child prodigy Pepito began his violin lessons with his parents and later with Cincinnati Conservatory professor Henri Ern, with whom he traveled on tour through Cuba and Mexico. He entered the Real Conservatorio de Madrid in 1923 and won the prestigious Sarasate award two years later. His impressive musical career took him to the most famous concert halls in the world. Pepito was also an excellent administrator and pedagogue. He retired as first violinist of the Puerto Rico Symphony Orchestra in the late 1980's.

Narciso distinguished himself as an excellent concert pianist in Europe and as a teacher in the Conservatorio de Música de Puerto Rico (beginning in 1960). He studied piano and music theory with his mother, then at the Real Conservatorio de Madrid in 1924 and in Paris with Alfred Cortot. Narciso is an important composer of *danzas* who also wrote the ballet piano suite *Estampas del San Juan que yo amo* and a piano concerto premiered by the Orquesta Sinfónica de Puerto Rico. Narciso played the piano at the premiere.

The Quinteto Figueroa was established in the 1940's, consisting of brothers Pepito, Kachiro, Narciso, Rafael, and Guillermo. In 1968, the group was honored with the title of Official Quintet of the Commonwealth of Puerto Rico. The group performed on some of the most prestigious musical stages of Europe, the United States, and South America, and in the 1974 Festival Casals in San Juan. The original Figueroa Quintet members acted as ambassadors of Puerto Rican music around the world for more than forty years. The third generation of Figueroas promises to carry the family's musical tradition into the twenty-first century.

Filipinos: Filipino immigrants to North America brought a Spanish-tinged culture. They experienced bigotry and discrimination, but World War II and labor unions brought some relief. Reforms of U.S. (1965) and Canadian (1967) immigration law led to a surge of Filipino immigrants.

Spanish Influences. Although located in Southeast Asia, the Philippines has a history of Spanish impact. Spanish influence began with the arrival of Ferdinand Magellan in 1521. In 1542, López de Villalobos named the islands "Las Filipinas" in honor of Spain's Prince Philip. Settlers and friars soon arrived.

For 350 years, the islands were a Spanish colony. The Philippines became a United States possession in

This group of Filipino immigrants, some of them nurses and doctors, arrived in New York in 1953. (Filipino American National Historical Society)

1898, a commonwealth in 1935, and an independent nation in 1946. Spanish influence continues in that most Filipinos have Spanish surnames and 80 percent belong to the Roman Catholic religion. The Spanish language is spoken by a minority, along with two hundred native dialects. Tagalog has been the official language since 1946. Because Tagalog has no "f" sounds, Filipino is sometimes spelled "Pilipino."

U.S. Involvement. In 1898, the TREATY OF PARIS ending the SPANISH-AMERICAN WAR ceded the Philippines to the United States. As long as the islands remained a territory, Filipinos were designated as United States nationals and could easily migrate to the United States. Filipino men were recruited for menial jobs, especially when immigration restrictions made people of other nationalities, such as Chinese, Japanese, and Mexicans, unavailable. Agricultural labor recruitment for Hawaiian plantations began in the early 1900's. Beginning in the 1920's, large numbers of Filipinos were enticed to California to take jobs as farmworkers.

Discrimination and Prejudice. Only occupations low on the pay scale were available to Filipino immigrants. In addition to agricultural work, they took service jobs in restaurants, hotels, and hospitals. Many became houseboys and drivers. Some took seasonal jobs in Alaska's fish-processing plants. Many lived in areas nicknamed "Little Manila." Such districts were often crowded and unsanitary. An all-male subculture developed around poolhalls and taxi-dance halls.

Filipino Americans were often denied service in restaurants, hotels, and barber shops, and even on occasion were prevented from entering amusement parks. Discrimination heightened during the 1930's as a result of job scarcity. Race riots were directed against Filipinos in California in 1929 and 1930.

Some states passed laws prohibiting land ownership by Filipinos and intermarriage of Filipinos with people of other backgrounds. Because of the antimiscegenation laws and the unavailability of women of Filipino background, many men remained single for life. In

A Filipino American settlement in Barataria Bay, Louisiana. (Filipino American National Historical Society)

1934, the Tydings-McDuffie Act converted the Philippines into a commonwealth, effective in 1935, with an effect on Filipino immigration status. Filipinos were designated as aliens, and the act set an immigration quota of only fifty Filipinos per year.

Several inaccurate stereotypes of Filipinos were commonly held in the United States. Filipinos were viewed as flashy, ignorant, and diseased. They were characterized as violent criminals or cannibalistic headhunters. A stereotype of Filipinos as "red hot lovers" developed because most migrants were young male bachelors. A condescending positive stereotype pictured the Filipino as a polite "little brown brother" whose short stature suited him for stoop labor. Early immigrants thought of themselves not as Filipinos but as members of ethnic subgroups such as Tagalogs or Visayans. Bigotry drove the previously separated ethnic subgroups into a more unified Filipino identity.

World War II. The war brought some benefits to Filipinos. The islands were a major ally of the United States in the war in the Pacific, where Filipino and U.S. troops fought side by side to retake the islands from the Japanese. Many Filipinos joined the United

States armed forces; completion of active service entitled them to United States citizenship. Many Filipinos purchased farms from Japanese Americans facing wartime internment.

Labor Union Involvement. Filipino Americans sought membership in existing labor unions in the 1930's. Mainstream unions, fearing economic competition, were not receptive to Filipino membership and even lobbied to deter Filipino immigration. Filipinos formed independent unions and conducted strikes.

While César CHÁVEZ was organizing Mexican American farmworkers in the 1960's, Filipino Larry Itliong was unionizing Filipino farm laborers in the Agricultural Workers Organizing Committee. Chávez agreed to assist the Filipino grape workers in California's Delano area as they planned a strike. The two organizations merged in August of 1966 to form the United Farm Workers Organizing Committee.

Immigration Since 1965. Filipino immigration to the United States surged following passage of the IMMIGRATION AND NATIONALITY ACT OF 1965, which eliminated national quotas. Often the new immigrants were highly educated, but state licensing rules prevented many of them from practicing their professions in the United States. Immigrants after 1965 usually came in families and were more likely to be female than male.

Filipino Americans numbered 1,407,000 in 1990. They constituted the second-largest Asian American population, exceeded only by Chinese Americans. The 1990 census reported that 52 percent of Filipino Americans lived in California and that three other states jointly held 13 percent: Illinois, New York, and New Jersey.

Canada liberalized its immigration policy in 1967, allowing an increase in Asian immigrants. Most of the 157,000 Filipinos living in Canada in 1990 arrived following the 1967 change. Political instability and limited economic opportunities in the islands encouraged emigration.

Filipinos in Hawaii. In the early 1900's, many Filipinos were recruited to work on pineapple and sugar plantations in Hawaii. Heavy migration to Hawaii continued throughout most of the twentieth century. In 1990, about 12 percent of Filipino Americans lived in Hawaii. They experienced less racial bigotry there than on the U.S. mainland, although their socioeconomic status was lower than that of white Hawaiians and Hawaiians of Japanese descent.

—*Nancy Conn Terjesen*

Suggested Readings: • Cordova, Fred. *Filipinos: Forgotten Asian Americans.* Dubuque, Iowa: Kendall/Hunt, 1983. • Kim, Hyung-chan, and Cynthia Mejia, eds. *The Filipinos in America 1898-1974: A Chronology and Fact Book.* Dobbs Ferry, N.Y.: Oceana, 1976. • Kitano, Harry H. L., and Roger Daniels. *Asian-Americans: Emerging Minorities.* Englewood Cliffs, N.J.: Prentice Hall, 1988. • Meister, Dick, and Anne Loftis. *A Long Time Coming: The Struggle to Unionize America's Farm Workers.* New York: Macmillan, 1977. • Pido, Antonio J. *The Pilipinos in America.* New York: Center for Migration Studies, 1986. • Takaji, Ronald. *Strangers from a Different Shore: A History of Asian Americans.* Boston: Little, Brown, 1989.

Filmmaking and filmmakers: Hispanic actors and actresses have been involved in filmmaking since the first silent movies. When Latinos learned to work on the other side of the camera, control of the images projected became possible.

By the 1930's, Filipino Americans were active in the union movement. (Filipino American National Historical Society)

Ramón Novarro was an early Latino film star. (AP/Wide World Photos)

Silent Era. Theatrical melodrama was a familiar form of entertainment in which the audience related to a simple good-and-evil plot by enthusiastically cheering the obvious hero and hissing the villain (recognizably dressed in black). Audiences were provided psychological catharsis and unrealistic but comforting moral clarity.

Into this market came silent movies, which in some ways marked a golden time for Latino actors in Hollywood. Not only were voices and accents irrelevant, but "foreigners" were in demand. Foreign names created interest, and foreign faces dominated the screen. Nevertheless, the 1910's and 1920's were a time in which racial stereotypes were at their worst.

Latino stars such as Dolores DEL RÍO, Lupe Valdez, Ramón NOVARRO, Gilbert ROLAND, and Antonio MORENO lit up the screen as heroes and heroines in this era. Unfortunately, many Latinos were offered only stereotypical "bad guy" roles. From the filmmaker's perspective, formula casting allowed audiences to recognize villains.

In early films, the word "GREASER" was commonly used to refer to Mexicans. The Mexican government initiated protest, and U.S. president Woodrow Wilson officially intervened. Some producers responded and began to feature Native American villains, who also were easily recognizable. After World War I, "greaser" films were revived. The Mexican government again protested and banned all films produced by an offending studio. Hollywood complied by changing the nationality but not the recognizability. Filmmakers had found a financially successful vehicle—a villain audiences loved to hate—and were not going to give up the character.

The 1930's. "Talkies" and the Great Depression brought a new genre: Hollywood social problem films. In depicting minorities, including Chicanos, Mexicans, and other Latinos, Hollywood formulas produced some noteworthy if flawed films. *Bordertown* (1934), starring Paul Muni in brownface and Bette Davis as a lunatic, created a more psychologically complex character in Johnny Ramirez. The strong but evil Hispanic lobbyist in *Washington Masquerade* (1932) is revealed to be running the country secretly.

In films such as *Border G-Man* (1938), *Durango Valley Raiders* (1938), and *Rose of the Rancho* (1936), the emphasis changed from hero as conqueror of "greasers" to hero as good Samaritan defending Mexican rights. Typically the white hero tramped like a tourist through the exotic Latino community, rescuing good, defenseless Mexicans from bad Mexicans. Classic American cowboys such as Hopalong Cassidy, Gene Autry, the Lone Ranger, Roy Rogers, and Tex Ritter strutted this theme in films such as *In Old Mexico* (1938), *Song of Gringo* (1936), and *South of the Border* (1939). In the 1930's, terms such as "GRINGO" and "greaser" were used unabashedly in film titles.

The 1940's. Another facet of motion pictures matured in the 1940's: animation. The advent of World War II underlined the need for the Americas to pull together. Studio head Walt Disney was asked to tour Latin America in support of the GOOD NEIGHBOR POLICY. Two films featuring Donald Duck, *Saludos Amigos* (1943) and *The Three Caballeros* (1945), were the result.

The latter film featured el pato Pascual, a Latino Donald Duck; José Carioca, a Brazilian parrot; and Panchito, a sombrero-wearing, pistol-packing rooster. Panchito was likable, fun, and assertive. He showed his pals José and Donald Duck some of the wonders of Mexico: piñata parties, *jarochos* (dances), POSADAS (Christmas pageants), and other celebrations of Mexican and South American folklore. Finally, Latin America had been given a benign, positive image. Represented by Donald, José, and Panchito, the United States, Brazil, and Mexico were three pals—each equal. Audiences were enchanted.

The 1950's. *The Lawless* (1949) and *Salt of the Earth* (1954) were the most daring of all the Hispanic social problem films. Each of these independently produced films exposed the deplorable working and living conditions of the Latino community, and each linked racism to social authority.

The Lawless deserves recognition for its artistry, its transcendence of the genre, and its psychological depth. Both Latino and Hispanic characters are realistically varied in their attitudes and behaviors.

Salt of the Earth is one of the best works on Latino subjects and a significant feminist film. It has been described as the first feature film made in the United States of, by, and for labor. Attacked in its time by eccentric tycoon Howard Hughes, the American Legion, and others, it went on to become a classic on university campuses.

"Message" biographies were closely related to social problem films. The masterpiece of this genre was *Viva Zapata* (1952). Scripted by John STEINBECK, this film about the MEXICAN REVOLUTION is not only about power and rebellion but also concerns insidious corruption and the ease with which a social movement can be diverted from its original purpose.

The 1960's. The Civil Rights movement and the liberalization of social values had their impact on filmmaking. Films became graphic in depictions of sex and violence. "Bad-guy" characters became more horrifying, and the "good" bad guy emerged. In *The Good, the Bad, and the Ugly* (1966), both whites and Mexicans are morally evil, and the good is characterized by skills such as a quick draw.

In relative contrast to this amoral Western, *The Wild Bunch* (1969) fused a sense of moral purpose and interethnic camaraderie with its harsh violence and explicit sex. Set against the background of the Mexican Revolution, this film in its own way manifested a declining social code and an increasing awareness of minority rights.

In the 1960's the film industry began to make an effort to hire directors, camera operators, and other production people of Latino origin. This paved the way for independent Latino films of the future.

The 1970's. Hollywood rediscovered the importance of ethnicity with regard to plot as well as box office appeal in the 1970's. Jobs for hot-blooded, "Latin

Actor Edward James Olmos, at left, consults teacher Jaime Escalante during the filming of Stand and Deliver, *which was based on Escalante's classroom experiences.* (AP/Wide World Photos)

lover" types shrank, however, as all actors and actresses began to portray increased sexuality.

Gang films became a popular genre, although the majority of them were damaging to racial relations. *Boulevard Nights* (1979), with its all-Latino cast, was one of Hollywood's better Chicano-focused films.

Latin American revolutions were a common topic of screwball films in the 1970's. Woody Allen's *Bananas* (1971) embraced every imaginable South American stereotype, only to turn them inside out while also making fun of revered white institutions and people.

The 1980's and Beyond. This period brought exhilaration for Latinos in the film industry. They learned film and television in junior roles and worked as principals in the development and execution of independent films such as *Sequin, Alhambrista!* and *Once in a Lifetime.* Latino directors, producers, and writers entered the mainstream as well, bringing Hollywood production values to the creation of strong Latino images.

La Bamba (1987), written and directed by Luis VALDEZ, encapsulated the career of teenage rock star Ritchie VALENS, who had been killed in a plane crash in 1959. The film was a significant crossover success: Latinos, teenagers of all backgrounds, critics, and former fans of Valens found much to praise and enjoy in this film biography of a sensitive artist who was able to see, feel, and communicate beyond cultural differences.

Producer and actor Edward James OLMOS gained forty pounds to play Jaime ESCALANTE, a high school teacher in East Los Angeles, who motivated his unruly students, in *Stand and Deliver* (1988). Olmos earned a nomination for an Academy Award for his work in this critical and popular success. The film was directed by Ramon Menendez and costarred Lou Diamond Phillips, Rosana DE SOTO, and Andy Garcia.

Latino themes and actors ranged across a broad spectrum. Beautifully filmed, *The Milagro Beanfield War* (1988) portrayed lovable Hispanic characters of humor and integrity. Its unique treatment of death was memorable and sensitive. Cheech MARIN and Tommy Chong, on the other hand, portrayed drug-using, antiestablishment comic characters in films made with little purpose or meaning beyond cheap laughs.

With knowledge of Hollywood production values, more behind-the-scenes employment, and a wealth of talent, Latinos in Hollywood continue to evolve artistically and commercially.   —*L. J. Sullivan*

SUGGESTED READINGS: • Keller, Gary D., ed. *Chicano Cinema: Research, Reviews, and Resources.*

Binghamton, N.Y.: Bilingual Review Press, 1985. • Miller, Randall M., ed. *The Kaleidoscopic Lens: How Hollywood Views Ethnic Groups.* Englewood Cliffs, N.J.: Jerome S. Ozer, 1980. • Pettit, Arthur G. *Images of the Mexican-American in Fiction and Film.* College Station: Texas A&M University Press, 1980. • Richard, Alfred C., Jr. *Contemporary Hollywood's Negative Hispanic Image: An Interpretive Filmography, 1956-1993.* Westport, Conn.: Greenwood Press, 1994. • Roffman, Peter, and Jim Purdy. *The Hollywood Social Problem Film: Madness, Despair, and Politics from the Depression to the Fifties.* Bloomington: Indiana University Press, 1981. • Woll, Allen L. *The Latin Image in American Film.* Los Angeles: UCLA Latin American Center Publications, University of California, 1977.

Fitzpatrick, Joseph (b. Feb. 22, 1913, Bayonne, N.J.): Sociologist. Fitzpatrick's research focuses on Puerto Ricans on the U.S. mainland. Among his publications is *Puerto Rican Americans: The Meaning of Migration to the Mainland* (1971). He has also written on delinquent behavior and families. Fitzpatrick has served as vice president of the Puerto Rican Family Institute and on the board of directors of the PUERTO RICAN LEGAL DEFENSE AND EDUCATION FUND.

Fitzpatrick, a Roman Catholic priest, earned his bachelor's degree from Woodstock College (1936), his M.A. from Fordham University (1941), and his Ph.D. from Harvard University (1949). He was director of Xavier Labor School from 1938 to 1940. He began his university teaching career in 1949 at Fordham as an associate professor, rising to the rank of professor in 1965. He served as chair of the department of sociology and anthropology from 1960 to 1965. He has also worked as a summer lecturer at the Catholic University of Puerto Rico (1957-1972).

Flamenco: High-spirited style of music and dance. Elaborate scale patterns, full chords, arpeggios, and complex rhythms strummed passionately on the guitar characterize flamenco music, while rapid whirls, finger snapping, hand clapping, and heel taps or *zapateado* characterize flamenco dance. Based on the *cante hondo* or deep, tragic song of old Spain, flamenco can be classified as *cante grande* (*hondo* type) and *cante chico*, (popular and commercial). Flamenco is performed by a *cuadro flamenco* or *tablao*, a group of singers, dancers with castanets, and guitarists who sit on a platform, each of them taking turns as soloists while others perform the accompaniment.

The Most Reverend Patricio Flores and the Most Reverend Robert Sánchez arrive in Miami, Florida, following expulsion from Ecuador in 1976 for allegedly subversive activities. (AP/Wide World Photos)

Flan: Caramel-coated custard widely eaten as a dessert in Latin America. Flan is a custard dessert adopted intact from Spanish cooking. Usually a thin layer of caramel is made in a pan before the eggs, cream, vanilla, and sugar for the custard are added. After baking and chilling, the flan is unmolded with its caramel coating. Eaten throughout Latin America, flan is one of the most common Mexican desserts.

Flauta: Northern Mexican snack. *Flautas*, consisting of a corn TORTILLA rolled up with filling and fried, are a specialty of northern Mexico and the adjacent United States. They were largely unknown elsewhere until the 1980's. Each *flauta* is made from one or two corn tortillas, spread with a filling then rolled into a tight tube. After being pinned with a toothpick, the *flauta* is fried and served with or without SALSA. The usual filling is shredded meat, although a thin slice of meat sometimes is used. Very similar to *flautas* are *taquitos*, prepared identically except with thinner tortillas.

Flores, Juan (b. Sept. 27, 1943, Alexandria, Va.): Scholar. Flores has established a reputation as a distinguished researcher of Puerto Rican and Latin American topics. He received his bachelor's degree in German from Queens College in 1964; he completed his master's work in 1966 and received his Ph.D. in 1968 from Yale University. Following completion of his formal education, he joined the faculty of Stanford University as an assistant professor of German. In 1975, he turned his efforts to Puerto Rican studies, serving as research director and consultant for the Center for Puerto Rican Studies at Hunter College.

For two years, Flores was associate professor of sociology at Queens College. He then joined the graduate sociology faculty of the Graduate Center of City University of New York. In addition to teaching, Flores has distinguished himself as a researcher, winning the prestigious international Casa de las Americas prize for *The Insular Vision: Pedreira's Interpretation of Puerto Rican Culture* (1978) and the American Book Award for his introduction to and edition of Jesús COLÓN's *A Puerto Rican in New York* (1984).

Flores, Patricio Fernández (b. July 20, 1929, Ganado, Tex.): Catholic archbishop. One of nine children who grew up as part of a family of migrant farmworkers, Flores worked as a cotton picker around Houston and other parts of Texas. His early education was haphazard, and he dropped out of high school during his sophomore year. Eventually he returned to complete his high school education and went on to attend St. Mary's Seminary in Houston. After being ordained to the priesthood in 1956, Flores served for some fourteen years as a parish priest in the Houston diocese. In 1970, he was appointed as a titular bishop. On May 5 of that year, Flores was appointed by the pope to serve as auxiliary bishop of San Antonio, Texas. In 1978, he was consecrated as bishop of the El Paso diocese. After the death of his good friend and sponsor, Archbishop Francis Furey, Flores was named to succeed Furey as archbishop of San Antonio in 1979.

An activist on behalf of civil rights for Mexican Americans, Flores has used his influence to support a number of causes and has long been a supporter of improved conditions for migrant workers. He chaired the Texas Advisory Committee of the U.S. Civil Rights Commission and served as national chairman of PADRES ASOCIADOS POR DERECHOS RELIGIOSOS, EDUCATIVOS, Y SOCIALES, an organization of Mexican American priests. In 1972, Flores helped Father Virgil Elizondo establish the MEXICAN AMERICAN CULTURAL CENTER to train residents of San Antonio's Mexican barrio to become problem-solving leaders and religious social activists. Flores also helped found COMMUNITIES ORGANIZED FOR PUBLIC SERVICE in 1974.

Flores, Tom (b. Mar. 21, 1937, Fresno, Calif.): Football player and coach. The son of Mexican American farmworkers, Flores played college football at Pacific University before beginning his professional career with the Calgary Stampeders of the Canadian Football League in 1958. In 1959, he played briefly for the Washington Redskins of the National Football League. In 1960, he came into his own as the starting quarterback for the Oakland Raiders of the American Football League (AFL). He led the AFL in passing percentage in 1960 and earned All-Star status in 1966; on December 22, 1963, he threw six touchdown passes in a single game. He also played for the Buffalo Bills and Kansas City Chiefs before retiring as a player after the 1969 season.

Flores began coaching in 1971 as an assistant for the Bills. A year later, he returned to the Raiders as an assistant to head coach John Madden, whom he replaced in 1979. In his second season, he led the Raiders to an 11-5 record and a Super Bowl victory over the Philadelphia Eagles. In 1982, after the franchise moved to Los Angeles, Flores was named the United Press International American Football Conference Coach of the Year. The following season, Flores di-

Tom Flores became head coach of the Seattle Seahawks in 1992. (AP/Wide World Photos)

rected the Raiders to a 38-9 Super Bowl rout of the Washington Redskins. After an unsuccessful 1987 season, Flores took front-office jobs with the Raiders and Seattle Seahawks. In 1992, he returned to the sidelines as Seattle's head coach.

Flores Magón, Ricardo (Sept. 16, 1873, San Antonio Eloxochitlán, Oaxaca, Mexico—Nov. 21, 1922, Fort Leavenworth, Kans.): Revolutionary. In 1900, Flores Magón and his two brothers, Enrique and Jesús, founded *Regeneración*, a newspaper that attacked the rule of Porfirio Díaz in Mexico. Flores Magón fled to the United States after being released from jail in 1903. In St. Louis, Missouri, Flores Magón reinstated *Regeneración* and formed the anarchist Mexican Liberal Party, which called for Díaz's overthrow, political and labor reform, and agrarian justice.

Flores Magón planned three abortive raids to Mexico from the United States. On one expedition, he captured and briefly held the city of Tijuana. These attacks and Flores Magón's virulent editorials led federal and state authorities, as well as private detectives, to harass him for the next eight years. In 1918, he was sentenced to twenty years in federal prison for violating United States neutrality acts. After the United States approved his return to Mexico in 1922, he mysteriously died in his cell, perhaps the victim of murder.

Flores Magón's activities helped fuel the 1910 revolution that liberated Mexico from Díaz's rule. In addition, many of his proposals for social justice were implemented in the 1917 Mexican constitution.

Flores Salinas, Juan (1835—Feb. 14, 1857, Los Angeles, Calif.): Guerrilla. In 1856, Flores Salinas escaped from San Quentin Prison, where he was serving a term for horse theft. He assembled more than fifty Mexican Americans into what has been called the largest bandit gang ever seen in California.

Some men joined his band to avenge personal slights. The War of the Reform that had recently broken out in Mexico may have inspired others to become outlaws as a means of redressing grievances. All of Flores' followers sought to strike out against the American regime.

Operating out of San Juan Capistrano, Flores shot a German rancher who denied aid to his men, who then broke into three shops in the town. The American community of Los Angeles interpreted these events as a political rebellion in the making. Immediately, prominent American leaders (and Californios as well) organized a vigilante committee, declared martial law, and surrounded the barrio where the band reportedly had been hiding. Flores and fifty-two of his men were captured in February, 1857, and he was hung immediately.

Flores' activities helped generate heroic legends symbolizing the daily struggles of Mexican Americans. The fact that several Californios helped the Americans track down the bandits illustrates the split within the Mexican American community.